D1433471

ARTHUR MILTON

Last of the
Double Internationals

ARTHUR MILTON

Last of the
Double Internationals

'There'll Never be
Another'

Mike Vockins

SPORTS
BOOKS

Published in Great Britain by
SportsBooks Limited
1 Evelyn Court
Malvern Road
Cheltenham
GL50 2JR

© Mike Vockins 2011
First Published May 2011

ROTHERHAM LIBRARY SERVICE	
B53005722	
Bertrams	16/01/2012
AN	£18.99
WAT	920 MIL

All rights reserved. No part of this publication may be produced or transmitted in any form or by any means, including photocopying and recording, without written permission of the publisher. Such written permission must also be obtained before any part of the publication is stored in any retrieval system of any nature.

Cover designed by Alan Hunns.

A catalogue record for this book is available from the British Library.

ISBN 9781907524 03 5

Printed and bound in England by TJ International.

For Joan,
Robert, David and Richard

and for Arthur's countless fans and
admirers for whom his name and his memory
bring a ready smile to their lips and in their hearts

and, not least, for the '… light lean chap with
buttercup hair … looking like everyone's kid brother …'

Contents

Foreword

IT WAS A dreadful shock to hear that Arthur Milton had died at 79 in the springtime of 2007. Yet how apt and telling, I thought, for good Arthur to die in the last week of April, the very calendar quintessence of the traditional changeover of the sporting seasons – the week he would have bid adieu to the raucous wintry fever-pitch of Highbury and its stately marble halls, sling his football boots into his London landlady's cupboard and whistle expectantly to himself all the way across to Paddington and the train back to Temple Meads, home, and the mellow warm westerlies of another pastoral Gloucestershire summer.

Arthur Milton embodied that timeless ritual of the seasons. We shall never – ever – see his like, for Arthur was the very last of an exceptional line: only a dozen men have ever played for England at both football and cricket – Lyttelton, Gunn, Gay, Foster, Fry, Sharp, Makepeace, Hardinge, Ducat, Arnold, Watson and – finally and forever, and the last to go – Milton himself. It was an exceptional line; and Milton was an exceptional man.

Gentle Arthur was one of the giants of my boyhood. A giant he remained even when childhood's callow, eyes-wide worship grew into warm man-to-man friendship.

Is it just my generation? There was a lasting and valorous chivalry in the craft-versed cigarette card heroes of our youth. They taught us urchins pride – and boy, oh boy, what pride we had in them. I recall vividly still the wondrous flush of it three-score years ago when, out of the blue, our favourite smiling young god of a natural cricketer was suddenly picked on the wing for England at Wembley (Stan Matthews dropped, Tom Finney injured, wow! third in line!), and the same sort of local pride too, much later, when the England team came calling again, this time in the summer and, of course, Arthur answered the call with a chanceless debut century in the Headingley Test to seal the whole deal for history.

The small-print logs all Milton's breathless 90-minute winter heroics and, to be sure, all his timeless long days of summer runs down to the last decimal point – as well as his fabled bag of catches, too: why, only seven men in the whole of cricket history held more catches – but to us behind the ropes all those years ago, with our pound of plums and our autograph-books, it was Arthur's congenially boyish one-of-us enjoyment and constancy which most appealed; that and the jaunty, feel-good zest of his inborn talent and authentic artistry and, of course, his friendly, foppish mop of 'buttercup' hair.

Someone said that everyone was 11 in 1948. Well, everyone romantic, that is – which I most certainly was on both counts. The year saw the London Olympic Games, and the launching of that cultural sporting base-touching signpost *Sports Report* – on the BBC radio still on Saturday teatimes. It was the year of what many continue to reckon was Wembley's most sumptuously appealing FA Cup final ever (Manchester United 4 Blackpool 2); 1948 was the year Bradman's 'Immortals' ruthlessly laid waste all England and its cricket shires.

And 1948 in late August was the first time us urchins in the north of the county came down from the hills to witness a one-off school holiday fixture (Gloucestershire against the Combined Services) at the genial, grimy old Gloucester Wagon Works ground in which two brand new fresh-faced heroes blazed a trail into our consciousness for ever – when Tom Graveney scored his first 100 for Gloucester in a beguiling buddies' century stand in collaboration with (as the GCCC Yearbook called him) Clement Milton (58 not out) ... the former lanky, languid, elegant, princely;

the latter shorter, more athletic, matier, more carefree and certainly more smiling. As Arthur remembered in his reverie not long before he died:

'I played because I loved it. It was born in me to play. I didn't make much money, but I was very happy always. They were, simply, wonderful days, wonderful days in the sun. They were days that were never long enough.'

In collaboration far, far later than that wondrous day at Gloucester, Arthur was also to choose his partner with skill and sound judgement. His amanuensis here is another generous and rounded man, a cricketing man of achievement, too, and one without whose jollying and encouragement the too-modest subject would never have agreed to produce this book. It is solely thanks to Mike Vockins that you have in your hands, lucky reader, an enchanting and rewarding biography.

Arthur was the wise innocent personified, the stupendous all-rounder whose deeds together with his chivalry and generosity added a shining lustre to the trade of professional sport.

Having finished with his football after blazing across the sky for all too short a time Milton played another 20 seasons of cricket. Then he became a postman – up daily at dead of night and across the Downs at Clifton on his regulation GPO boneshaker bike:

'Sun up, dawn chorus, all alone, truly wonderful … Best of all the winter mornings, snow or heavy frost, eerie silence, whiteness all around, not a footprint, not a tyre-tread and sometimes a great huge bulbous moon … utter perfection.'

For some earlier happy summers the happy postman coached the dark-blue scholars of Oxford University's 1st XI. Sometime captain was Vic Marks, Test player and now a distinguished journalist, who remembers fondly what an inspired choice Arthur had been – 'not least because he could finish the *Daily Telegraph* crossword each morning before any of us' – and star batsman and classicist John Claughton (now equally distinguished Chief Master of KES Birmingham) recalls the done-it-all all-knowing coach's modesty by, as you'd expect, nicely paraphrasing Ovid: *Ars Arthur est celare artem* ('Art's art is to conceal his art').

From his Arsenal digs in north London, like all *Boys' Own* heroes should, Arthur had married the landlady's beautiful daughter. It was a blissful marriage. Happy families. Once the Post Office had insisted on him acknowledging their official retirement age, Arthur bagged the same district, sorted out every local newsagent and continued his dawn watch for another couple of decades. In 2002, in front of a packed house, harmonious choirs, Latin quotations, and the full purple-gowned works, Bristol University gave Milton an honorary MA. That morning he'd delivered the newspapers to the Common Room. How many other universities anywhere in the world have given an MA to their paperboy?

Oh, happy man. Oh, happy days.

Frank Keating
2011

Chapter 1

Up on the Downs

SETTING OUT ON his early-morning round across the Clifton Downs in Bristol, the paperboy could barely see over the Sunday papers piled high on the front pannier of his trusty red bike.

'Paperboy' might be something of a misnomer. In truth, this paperboy was fast approaching his biblical three-score years and ten.

No matter. He was fit, and loved keeping active. He loved the Downs. He relished the fresh air and the outdoor life. He valued being able to serve others. His paper round allowed him to embrace all of these.

As the clear morning air filled his lungs and heightened his gratitude for all the good things life offered, did he often wonder what stories the papers were telling? More intriguingly, did he wonder what the sports headlines were saying that day, and of whom they might be talking? Did they tell of a hat-trick scored sublimely at Wembley or a century, beautifully crafted at Lord's?

'Good luck to you, lads, well done,' he might have said, for he well understood the thrill of playing sport at the highest level; for this paperboy had played for England at Wembley and at Lord's.

This paperboy was different. This paperboy was Arthur Milton, Arsenal and England, and Gloucestershire and England, the last man to have been capped by England at our two national games, soccer and cricket.

This paperboy was Arthur Milton MA, proud recipient of an honorary Master of Arts degree awarded by his home city's university as a mark of high regard for his contribution to sport and to the life of Bristol.

And here he was, pedalling away on his cherished old bike (which he'd bought 'for a couple of quid') – a woman's bike at that and, like him, pensioned off from an earlier spell with Bristol Post Office – delivering papers with fat sports sections telling of the day's sporting heroes, the Gary Linekers and Kevin Keegans, and the Ian 'Beefy' Bothams, David Gowers and Allan Lambs – richly talented sportsmen, at the top of their game, but not one of them having earned England caps in both of the nation's major sports.

He might have been expected to be jealous of the fame and rewards accorded to modern sportsmen, but such thoughts were far from Arthur Milton's mind. A quiet, naturally modest and unassuming man, as ever happy to take life as it came, he saw little purpose, or benefit, in making comparisons between his sporting career and the careers and lifestyles of the modern sporting 'celebrity'.

The sports pages might dedicate columns to the sporting celebrities' successes (and be gunslinger quick, too, to gloat at their failures), while the news pages and diary columnists would tell of their vast earnings and their off-the-field lives. But the paperboy felt not the slightest sense of injustice or grievance. He happily considered himself as well off as any of them. Here he was, free to do as he wished – and what he wished was to go on enjoying the life that still got him out and about every day up on the Downs, among folk he knew and liked and who knew and liked him as Arthur Milton for who he was, as much as the sporting hero of earlier years.

'I loved the quiet of the early morning, looking at the stars. Sometimes people might suggest I'd missed the money of present-day sport, but I used to say that I was still a millionaire, out on my bike as life stirred so excitingly. It's such a beautiful area.'

Arthur had decided to become a paperboy when his post-cricket career as a postman had ended, all too soon for him, when he reached the official retiring age of 60 in 1988. He revelled in being a postman – for exactly the same reasons he later relished being a paperboy (though for paperboys there was the added advantage of no official retirement age). He was still out in the clear morning air, on those wonderful Downs in whose proximity he had spent so much of his life. Like a cow in clover, he was in his element.

As postman and paperboy he felt fulfilled. He had no need to work now, though the extra income was helpful; he pedalled the bike and delivered the post and papers as much for the real satisfaction it offered. The first delivery was usually finished in time to get home for breakfast, and with his second delivery completed he had time for golf, or to get to the 'office' – his designation for the local branch of bookmakers William Hill where he kept up with the form of racing greyhounds. Time, too, for his family.

His career as a postman had been delivered into his hands by chance. After his playing career had ended in 1974, and following a spell as coach of Oxford University, he was walking along the street in Westbury-on-Trym when a Gloucestershire cricket fan, Cyril Wood, stopped him. Ever ready to talk with those who love their sport, Arthur was pleased to stop and chat.

'What are you up to these days?' Cyril asked.

'Not a lot,' was Arthur's jaunty reply.

'Have you ever thought of being a postman?' Cyril fired back.

Whether or not Arthur replied or whether his face gave away his immediate response – of surprise – his friend compellingly outlined the advantages: 'As a cricketer you've always been outdoors, and you love that. And it would keep you fit and active.

'Oh, and by the way, there's a vacancy in our office now.'

As he headed for home Arthur chewed it over. The thought of being a postman had never entered his head. He didn't need to work, but he certainly couldn't face doing nothing. Cyril Wood's idea made sense. It would get him out, and it would keep him active. He began to warm to the idea and, with his wife Joan's ready support, he applied for the job, and got it.

'They made me spend a short time in the office first, in the sorting room,' he said, adding mischievously, 'I suppose they wanted me to know what an envelope looked like, and to learn the geography and postcodes.'

Before very long he was out on his rounds delivering the daily mail. Before much longer a vacancy posted on the sorting office noticeboard sought a replacement postman for the Sneyd Park round. Arthur fancied this. It was 'his' territory. But he was aware this was considered one of the best of the local rounds – 'especially at Christmas time' – and knew the office custom of the longest-serving being given the first chance.

A fortnight passed and no one had expressed an interest so, with something approaching a new boy's diffidence, Arthur asked if he could be considered. 'Yes' was the answer. The round was his.

All of this was a far, far cry from Lord's and Wembley, from Arsenal's Highbury home and Gloucestershire's County Ground, but for Arthur it proved to be an equally important, and greatly valued, part of his life, a life replete in sporting riches and, now, in other treasured non-material rewards. He had not expected life after sport to match the highlights his cricketing and footballing talents had yielded, or to be so fruitful. But that's life – and life had been pretty kind to him.

Such thoughts had stirred warmly within him many, many times, but in late 2006 they had again clearly bubbled up in his mind.

As I picked up the phone late one autumn evening that soft Bristol, south-Gloucestershire accent immediately gave away his identity.

After kindly enquiring about my well-being, he barely beat about the bush. 'Mike, I'm thinking of doing a book,' he said.

'About b----y time too, Arthur,' was my unhesitating reply, knowing full well that over the years he'd received (and yet constantly been surprised by) several invitations from publishers to write his story. With typical reserve he had turned them all down.

His riposte now was direct and equally brief: 'Yes, but I'm only going to do it if you help me.' It sounded unequivocally unequivocal.

Profuse protestations at the folly of that last suggestion did nothing to deter him. I rattled off a decent list of names of prestigious and well-known writers and sports journalists who would be thrilled to work with him, to no avail. The more I tried to persuade him, the more it became clear that (as in many things) Arthur had made up his mind. He was not for turning.

He was swayed, it seemed, by a piece I'd written about him previously for *The Cricketer* magazine's 'Second Innings' series (shortly before *The Cricketer*'s merger with *Wisden Cricket Monthly*, eventually becoming *The Wisden Cricketer*). He and Joan felt I had 'captured him'. Patently they hoped this would prove true of a book also.

Arthur's 'invitation' left little choice. Despite feeling wholly unworthy, I agreed we should start work together to 'see how things go'. And most definitely we agreed we wouldn't fall out with one another if either felt it wasn't working.

Seeing 'how things go' proved great fun, as well as an immense privilege. It was such a joy and a treat to visit Arthur regularly and to hear his story unfold. Once that initial decision about 'doing a book' had been taken (doubtless after much heart-searching), he needed little encouragement. Conscientious man that he was, he often did his 'homework' in preparation for my next visit, checking (in his own inimitable way) dates, facts and figures he thought I might need. His homework didn't always coincide with my agenda, but it was great fun as we covered an amazing amount of ground. Early notes and tapes were filled mainly with Arthur's soccer memories, as he assumed I knew all about his cricket and little about his football.

Neither was true but, chatting away, week by week, he unfolded the amazing story of his dual careers. I managed, too, gently to encourage him when he felt he might have said too much, and decided, 'We can't say any more about that.' That was usually a signal to move on to other matters, and then tactfully to tiptoe back towards that topic when we next met, to test the water again. Second time round he was often less diffident and, in reality, had needed only a little more time to think around the subject, especially if he felt he had been in danger of being critical of another player or of damaging their reputation.

Our morning sessions invariably ended with lunch provided by Joan, who joined us. Those lunchtimes always yielded their own bonus to what we had worked on during the morning. Too late did I learn that the recorder should have been kept running as we ate.

We worked happily away for a number of months. It was a real delight, and our morning's work on Tuesday 24th April 2007 proved as fruitful as earlier sessions. Only my notebook – with its retrospective scribble – reminds me, poignantly, that these sessions had come to an end:

We broke off to go to lunch with Joan – delicious Tuscan bean soup – and after a delightful and 'good fun' lunch I headed off, having arranged that when we next met we would look at Arthur's modest collection of memorabilia – most of which he hadn't collected but others had sent to him – and that we would try to meet up with Frank Keating at some time soon convenient to Frank.

Over lunch much lovely talk; persuasion that I should speak with Arthur Shaw; a recollection of Micky Stewart's story of Chelsea's 'take-no-prisoners' left-back; golf and greyhounds – occasionally his eyes welling with a tear or two as he gratefully recalled names and faces and memories of good friends.

And next day, Tuesday 25th April 2007 – oh so sadly – he was dead.

Chapter 2

Bristol Boy

TO HEAR THAT West Country burr, gentle and softly spoken, the words articulated in a relaxed, unhurried way (mirroring the easy style of his many wonderful innings), was to know that Arthur was, of course, a true and faithful son of Bristol. He was born in the city – of that he was adamant – at Bristol General Hospital, the first and only child of Violet and William Milton – William Clement Milton, hence Clement Arthur Milton.

But some sporting records claim Bedminster, Somerset, to be his place of birth.

Violet gave birth to her son in hospital. Home births were the custom at this time but she had suffered three miscarriages, so delivery with good medical attention at hand made sense.

'Mother often called me her fourth miscarriage,' Arthur recalled, his face creasing into a smile as he added, 'especially when I had been out playing cricket or soccer with friends and was late home for tea.'

Bristol General Hospital is city-side of the River Avon. Arthur insisted this made him a genuine Bristolian. For the Somerset qualification to have credence the hospital would have needed to cross the Avon.

Yes, he was a Bristol boy, though a wry smile came across his face when I pointed out the official record of 'Somerset' as his birthplace.

'I wonder what my career might have been like if I had been a Somerset player?' he asked puckishly, knowing full well that the pitches at Taunton's County Ground had proved to be the happiest and most successful of his hunting grounds, where he had scored plenty of runs – 1,490 in all with seven centuries – regularly putting Somerset's bowlers to the salix sword.

Arthur was born on 10th March 1928, when his parents – his father was invariably known as Bill – were living at Maple Avenue, Hillfields Park, on the eastern side of the city. Bill, an engineer, worked for the well-known firm of ES & A Robinson, cardboard and wax paper manufacturers and box makers, one of the largest and long-established employers in the city.

Robinson's opening of a new factory coincided with the city council building a fine new estate nearby. The company's key staff – Bill was one such – were each given one of these houses, which they paid for by deductions from their weekly wage.

Robinson's factory featured in one of Arthur's early boyhood reminiscences. 'On many a Tuesday evening, Dad often worked late, and as a very young boy I would wander down to the factory so that I could walk back home with him,' Arthur recalled, in memory delighting in that close company which cements the otherwise often unspoken affection between father and son.

An even earlier and more golden recollection of this time took Arthur way back to pre-school childhood. 'We had a lot of green fields around where we lived, which was very nice, and there was a lovely little area down the bottom, and Dad took me down there one Christmas morning, with a football. I was three years old.

'He played for Trowbridge Town in what was the semi-pro Western League, and to be there, playing football with him on Christmas morning is, I think, my earliest memory – and one of my fondest.

'He had his motorbike in the garage, which he used to travel on, because he loved his sport, playing cricket locally as well. But I remember that morning kick-around vividly and very fondly.'

It was the very first among a whole host, a treasury, of magical sporting memories to come.

Arthur's mother was one of 12 children. Her father was blind, having lost his sight during a mining accident. To outsiders, Bristol, or Gloucestershire, are not considered mining areas, but in Arthur's grandfather's time there were a good many coal mines in Bristol (the last closed in 1970) as well as across the Severn in the Forest of Dean. Arthur certainly remembered riding his bicycle over the humps and bumps – the 'diddly dumps' – around Hillfields Park, the aftermath of mining at Speedwell and Donkham.

Until her marriage Violet had worked, along with her sisters, either at ES & A Robinson or at another large Bristol employer, tobacco company WD & HO Wills.

Although the first and only child of Bill and Vi, Arthur had almost immediately acquired an elder 'sister'. Soon after his arrival, Vi took in her young niece Mary, the first daughter of Edie, her eldest sister, when Edie was about to give birth to her second child.

Mary became so much part of the family that she stayed on at Maple Avenue, to remain permanently with her aunt and uncle and new cousin. In Arthur's eyes, however, Mary was for ever his sister. 'It's strange Mum and Dad didn't officially adopt her,' he said. 'She was in every way part of our family.' As he recounted these memories his voice went to almost a whisper and cracked with emotion. And Mary, who was five or six years older than Arthur and would outlive him, remained very much 'part of the family'.

As a young lad, readily encouraged and prompted by his Dad, Arthur was seldom without a ball in his hand.

Playground games of soccer and cricket at Hillfields Park Infants and Junior School, a quarter-mile from home, extended his opportunities to develop his ball skills in an almost unknowing and yet natural way. It was just something that boys – especially boys like Arthur – did. Hillfields Park played against neighbouring schools which meant that, alongside the development of his innate ability with a ball, Arthur was also experiencing, from an early age, the challenges and the fun of competitive sport, and sport was already beginning to establish a hold on Arthur.

A different sporting experience came when, with fellow pupils from Hillfields Park Juniors, he competed in a Bristol Schools' sports day. The event was held at Bristol City FC's Ashton Gate ground and here, as a member of the school's relay team, he won his first sporting trophy.

Arthur himself, barely ten years old, then went on to win the 75-yard sprint. The competitive (and successful) sportsman in him was coming quickly to the fore. And alongside the playground games there was, of course, cricket and soccer with Dad in the back garden.

As well as soccer for Trowbridge Town, Bill Milton played cricket for Soundwell, a local Bristol club. Indeed, he was still playing for them well into his fifties.

During Bristol's blitzed war years, in which Arthur grew up, many formal cricket fixtures had to be set aside but on summer evenings the club often played 'pick-up' games – 'against the air raid wardens and that sort of thing, at Soundwell and Downend, where "WG" was born,' Arthur recalled. 'Downend – we used to play them, it seemed like, once a week. It's a lovely little ground.'

Arthur, who, as a schoolboy, did his stint as an ARP warden, was always ready to play in these games: 'Dad always encouraged me to take my kit along so I was ready to fill in when a team was a player short, or someone had failed to get home from work in time.'

He remembered that in those wartime years kit was in short supply, 'Bats and balls and pads and that, although they could get man-size bats all right.

'So Dad, I always remember, used to saw three or four inches off the bottom of the bat for me. In fact it was almost up to the "meat" by that time – but yorkers used to go really well, go for four off the bottom of that bat.' The gleeful delight in his voice echoed the still vivid pleasure of those times the ball rocketed off his shortened bat.

'Also, seeing a little lad coming out to bat they used to take pity on me and toss the ball up, you see, but after a while, without fail, they had to bowl properly to me and then they'd start trying as I got in. It just seemed to come naturally. I could always play – I don't know why that was.

'I always had a ball when I was a boy, playing against a wall, kicking it, and I used to play cricket in the garden with Dad, against the garage door with our wickets.'

Greyhound racing attracted him, too, from an early age. His father, through friends in the sport, had long run dogs, and Arthur quickly picked up his father's enthusiasm.

Bill Milton's great friend from Soundwell CC, Arthur Sutor, introduced Bill to greyhound racing. Arthur felt certain that Sutor and his father used to make a book at one stage, and were often at the track at Bristol Rovers' Eastville ground on Wednesday and Saturday evenings when the dogs were running. Arthur began to share his father's interest.

He could even remember his first bet. 'I was about ten or eleven, and the first two bets I ever had won. I remember I had 3/- to 1/- on *Jolly Good* [three shillings in 'old' money equated to 15p today, and was roughly the price of 20 cigarettes] and 3/- to 1/- too on one in another race, *Tree Jack* I think its name was.'

His appetite had been well and truly whetted.

Mind you, he claimed there was a time when he was deemed too young to be admitted to the track at Eastville, so he stood outside and, as his knowledge of the sport and of individual dogs increased, he would pass vital messages about a dog's recent form to his father, enabling Dad to assess his investments.

Arthur's keen interest in greyhounds continued right up until the end of his life, with Monday mornings often spent in the betting shop within an easy stroll of Arthur's comfortable home in a quiet residential cul-de-sac – checking the form of recent and upcoming runners.

But sometimes even sport had to take second place. His mother had a good voice, which she passed to Arthur, and together they sang in her Baptist Church choir. In 1939 Arthur was awarded a Certificate of Merit, First Class, by the Baptist Union Eisteddfod in Bristol for a Boy's Vocal Solo.

Around that time Arthur won a scholarship to Cotham Grammar School. In that era a boy's seniority often had a bearing on his selection for school sports teams. It was unusual for young boys to be selected ahead of their seniors. But such was Arthur's talent that Cotham set aside this custom. He had barely started there before his talent shone out and he was promptly called up to play for the school's first teams.

'I used to play outside half at rugby. Actually I started in the scrum – but I only ever played there once,' he recalled, laughing.

Tom Graveney, who would become one of Arthur's oldest friends as well as a Gloucestershire and England team-mate and one of the most successful and graceful batsmen of the post-war years, remembers playing rugby against Arthur in their school days. Tom, who at the start of his cricket career also played rugby for Bristol, was at Bristol Grammar School, near neighbours and rivals of Cotham.

'He was a superb rugby player, apart from his soccer, even then. At school we hated playing against Cotham. Arthur was one of those players rather like Cliff Morgan – you never got hold of him, he always slipped out of the way. So I knew him at school. David Allen and John Mortimore were both at Cotham as well, but a bit after him.'

Allen, like Mortimore a long-time Gloucestershire contemporary of Arthur's, recalls: 'John, who was just ahead of me, and I only joined the school as Arthur was leaving. His school reputation was second to none. He was a class above everyone else. He was equally talented in all three sports. Arsenal scouts were already watching him, and as a schoolboy he was good enough to play club cricket with adult teams.'

Mortimore had an inkling that Arthur was already beginning to make his way in the game: 'I'm not certain whether it's true, but I think in his last year Art may have played for Stapleton and not school, which was very unusual then. They were a pretty good local side. Jack Crapp had played there before Arthur, and David would play there after he finished at school.'

Years later, when Arthur was about to make his England soccer debut, a Bristol paper carried a photograph of him training alongside England team-mates Ivor Broadis, Nat Lofthouse, Eddie Bailey and Les Medley and, to show the path to Wembley had begun at Cotham School, the press photograph included insets of Arthur in the school's cricket, football and rugby teams, at the age of 13½.

When Arthur was at school it was an era of dedicated schoolmasters who encouraged boys to enjoy their sport, to value the healthy exercise and team spirit, and to learn hard-won lessons which would stand them in good stead in other spheres of their lives. Arthur came under the encouraging influence of Bert Crew, Cotham's English master and master in charge of cricket (who would later assist Gloucestershire as their honorary scorer).

Committed to sport though most schools and schoolmasters were, outside the public schools there were few former soccer pros or ex-county cricketers to help nurture boys' potential or develop their sporting brains. Those with talent – like Arthur, who throughout his time at school was known as Archie – just came to the top, naturally.

It was no big issue, not something he thought a great deal about: 'It was just how it was, I suppose. We didn't have any official coaching like so many do now; the masters used to take us for all our sport.' Arthur was just happy to be playing sport, and to be playing it well, without too much thinking about where the talent came from – or even what he might do with it.

I asked him about his memories of playing in representative schoolboy teams, thinking this would have been yet one more step in his seemingly effortless advance.

Initially his memory told him that he hadn't played in any representative teams – for city or for county – apart from appearing for Bristol Public and Grammar Schools' XV at the Memorial Ground, home of the famous West Country club, but he had little recollection of anything else about his representative appearances.

Research later uncovered the fact he had played soccer for Bristol Schools and for Gloucestershire Schools. 'Did I?' he asked, and then went straight back to talking about soccer at Cotham Grammar. That same research also revealed that Arthur had captained Cotham's teams at rugby and soccer as well as cricket – but not one word of this had passed his lips.

'We had a very good soccer side at school; we didn't get beaten very often,' Arthur remembered. 'And, of course, being rather precocious there was always someone, from the likes of Bristol Rovers and Bristol City, looking around for players.

'They came to see Dad to enquire whether I might be interested in joining them and then Dad passed it on to me. He obviously could see I could play, because he played himself.

'He said to me, "Look, we can look further afield here than Bristol Rovers and Bristol City" – they were not really fashionable clubs – and he found out that the Arsenal had a chap, Ted Davies was his name, who looked around for them in this area. Ted, who had formerly played for Huddersfield Town and Blackburn Rovers and also managed Bath City, had been a goalkeeper, with huge gnarled hands; his hands and fingers had been broken and dislocated and everything. He ran a side, Colston Sports, in the Downs League. Dad had a word with him and he said, "Bring the lad up next Saturday and I'll put him in the side, and we can take a look at him."

'That was 1944, and from there Ted arranged for me to go up to the Arsenal to play in a couple of friendly games because, you see, in those days at the end of the war the football leagues hadn't re-started; they didn't start again until '46.'

Allowing for a little understandable bias, Davies, who watched Arthur in his first trial game, reported: 'He was the outstanding player on the field.' It was a promising start.

Arthur's first appearance proper in Arsenal colours was in a wartime game at Maidenhead, on 12th May 1945. He was just 17.

'I played a couple of games up there at Highbury, and of course they were all coming back from the war – happy to be home. I first met Jimmy Logie there. Jimmy Logie was the same size as Alex James, about this high,' said Arthur – not the tallest man in the world – waving his arm around shoulder height.

Logie's name popped up frequently in Arthur's recollections, indicative of the great affection he had for his diminutive footballing partner, and his very high regard for the Scot's football skills. In part, too, it indicated his genuinely grateful recognition of how

Jimmy Logie's skills had fostered his own game, enabling it to flourish and blossom.

For those not steeped in soccer history, Edinburgh-born Jimmy Logie played 328 times for Arsenal in ten seasons from 1945–46, mostly at inside-right, very occasionally at right-half. A mercurial player, a 'schemer', his ability to do the unexpected – and, at the same time, make precision passes to the feet of his sprinting team-mates – made him a creative and inspirational force for the Gunners.

Logie had attracted Arsenal's attentions with his form for the Scottish junior side Lochore Welfare. Arsenal signed him in 1939, just before he joined the Royal Navy, and during wartime he made occasional guest appearances for St Bernard's in Edinburgh, Dunfermline and Grimsby Town when naval duties allowed.

Rejoining Arsenal in 1945, just as the young lad from Bristol was making his own first impressions on the Highbury hierarchy, Logie was to play a key part in all Arsenal's early postwar successes – the First Division titles in 1947–48 and 1952–53 and the 1950 FA Cup final win over Liverpool. Somewhat surprisingly he – like Arthur – was to play only one international, winning his Scotland cap against Northern Ireland on 5th November 1952.

One of Arthur's memories of Logie relates to that cup final. As the Arsenal players left the dressing room to cross the cinder track, Logie was nowhere to be seen. To considerable collective relief, he jogged alongside his team-mates just as they lined up for the pre-match presentations. The little wizard whispered in Alex Forbes' ear – 'It got beat, Alex.'

Immediately before taking the field for such an important match, in which he would play a key part in Arsenal's 2-0 victory, Logie's attentions had been intently focused on the success – or, as it turned out, otherwise – of a horse running that afternoon. His interest (pecuniary, and substantial almost certainly) had required Jimmy to make a last-minute phone call to verify the result.

Arthur recalled, with great joy, those early times in what was to be a fruitful partnership with Logie: 'I played at inside-forward then – later on I played on the wing. Jim was playing right-half, behind me, and whenever I ran anywhere the ball was there when I got there. That's how it was, honestly. Quite unbelievable. And of course we didn't know at that time we would have a happy combination in the first team, which of course we did.'

The way Arthur recounted the story, it sounded like the most natural of progressions. For a young lad with his talent, that is exactly what it was.

Equally instinctive to him was the need to finish his schooling. When the invitation to play in those friendly games came he had one more year to complete at school and, with it, his Higher School Certificate. This he achieved successfully in 1946, with passes in maths, physics and chemistry. 'I used to struggle with chemistry, but I did pass. But maths was my best subject really.'

Academic achievement at Cotham clearly sat easily alongside his sporting prowess, and gave an indication of the sharp intellect which would remain with him throughout his life. It provided an indicator, too, that he wasn't solely focused on sport; that he had, even at that age, a broader vision. Formal affirmation of this came with his appointment by the headmaster as a prefect.

In later life Arthur insisted that if he had his time again he would, despite the obvious and immediate temptations of playing sport for a living, go to university first – 'if I was good enough' – to study maths, or perhaps to train for a profession. Nonetheless, his maths skills remained a constant benefit, if only for calculating cricketing declarations, having a ready grasp of the odds (and his successes) at greyhound meetings, or totting up his golf score (though here the numbers invariably were very low).

When he was batting he often found himself doing mental arithmetic, particularly run rates, over rates, calculating runs required and time remaining, etc. and he found this a great help to his concentration. But for his total lack of interest in batting and bowling averages, his maths might have proved useful there, too.

As a boy, Arthur followed, at a distance and without any great passion, the fortunes of the two local soccer teams, but much preferred to spend Saturdays playing rather than on the terraces. 'For a time I thought Bristol Rovers was my favourite club – probably because their ground was nearer my home. Then I saw Roy Bentley playing some great football for the City, and I had visions of doing the same when I was old enough.'

Bentley, only four years older than Arthur, must have made a marked impression on him. He went on to play for Newcastle United, Chelsea, Fulham and QPR, as well as England, for whom he won 12 caps. He later managed Reading and Swansea.

Despite the fleeting inspiration provided by Bentley it's perhaps not surprising that, when the introduction to Arsenal came, Arthur had no particular boyhood footballing hero, no favourite club. Nevertheless, he was certainly well up with the form of most Football League teams. His regular Saturday evening task was to sit glued to the radio and to BBC's *Sports Report*, filling in the scores on the *Daily Herald*'s soccer pages so that Dad could check the success of his football pools selections.

Following his two friendly matches as an amateur in 1945, Arsenal invited Arthur to join them for the 1946–47 season, when the Football League resumed.

'I took a while to decide. I think what decided me was that, by this time, I was 18 and I was eligible for call-up for National Service. I knew that would happen sooner or later in 1946, so I thought, "Well, I'll go up and do the pre-season training with the Arsenal, see how I like it up there, and then take it from there."'

It was his first time away from home, but it was a time which conjured up happy memories.

'Arsenal went out of their way to help you settle in. They were a great club like that,' he recalled. 'They would find digs for you, and nobody – nobody – at the club had any airs and graces. They all understood that the club was bigger than any individual.'

The London club's pre-season training began in late July. That early spell at Highbury in the late summer and early autumn of 1946 was the only time Arthur undertook the full pre-season training programme with Arsenal. The club was always generous to cricketers and allowed them to finish the soccer season early and return from cricket late. 'They had about 40 players on the staff at that time, 40 pros, and they could have fielded three teams good enough to play in the First Division – which was why they could be so considerate to those of us who also played county cricket.'

To modern-day eyes that pre-season practice was hardly scientifically sophisticated or high-tech. 'We did about a month of training and regularly used to go for long walks in heavy boots,' Arthur recalled. Scientific or not, the players were fit, although it must be noted that Arthur was always one of those whippet-lean, whipcord men who was permanently and naturally fit.

'One early game for the third team,' he remembered, 'was up at Cheltenham in those days long before they had got into the League, and with my ordinary boots on, instead of those heavy training boots, I felt I was flying. I was never out of breath and could have run for a fortnight. I was pretty fit. Dad came to see that game, which was rather nice – for him and for me.'

Arthur stayed with Arsenal for August, September and October before the call came to undertake his National Service. Those autumn months in Arsenal's third team, playing in the Eastern Counties League, were shared with fellow Bristolian Don Oakes. 'If we got beat Oakesy and I got the blame, every time – probably because we were the boys from the "sticks". Sometimes it seems as if we got a bollocking every week,' he recounted, but the wry smile on his face suggests it was part of the team banter rather than any suggestion he couldn't play.

'One week they gave us a rollocking – I don't know why – and then next week we were up at Lowestoft. At half-time we're 2-0 up, and our team manager says, "Yes, that's the way to play" – and we hadn't played any differently from the previous week. But our 'keeper then let in two or three, and we got beat. Guess who got the blame?

'When we won, mind, they did stop and buy us a beer on the way home, though' – and fish and chips if they were lucky.

It was a good time to be at Highbury. With the return of players from war service and the resumption of the Football League, there was a feeling of overwhelming gratitude and joy that sport could again be given its rightful place, There was, too, a real desire to make up for lost opportunities and lost time.

As a junior Arthur was given a ticket to watch Arsenal play Derby County, the 1946 FA Cup holders. It was the first top-level football match he had ever seen. The names of the Derby forward line that day etched themselves in Arthur's memory. He rattled off their names like a ticker-tape machine: 'There was Frankie Broome and Raich Carter, and Jackie Stamps, Peter Doherty and Dally Duncan. It was a real "class" forward line, and it was my first episode of watching top-class soccer, and watching at one of the big grounds. I travelled in for that, mind, by tube from Hendon where my digs were, and there must have been 30,000 others going to the match.'

For the record, Arsenal's line-up that September day was George Swindin, Laurie Scott, Bernard Joy, Cliff Bastin, Leslie Compton, Jimmy Logie, Ian McPherson, George Drury, Kevin O'Flanagan, Bryn Jones and David Nelson. Arthur, as he recalled the match, was vague about the result (Derby won 1-0), but the names of all the players were indelibly written in his mind.

Then came the expected call to serve king and country and though he appeared rarely in friendly games for Arsenal during this period, he did make his debut for Gloucestershire County Cricket Club, in 1948.

Arthur by then had moved on from Soundwell. The club had been good to him but it was time to go up a grade, and Arthur joined Stapleton CC when he was 17.

It was here that he first attracted the attention of Gloucestershire and was invited to play for the county's Second XI. It was to Stapleton, too, that he returned every weekend, from Nottingham, National Service duties permitting.

By the time his two years' National Service was completed, he had become a professional cricketer on Gloucestershire's staff. The prospect of playing sport professionally, winter and summer, offered a wonderful vista, an opportunity most sports-minded young men would snatch. Thoughts about the wisdom of going to university or training as a quantity surveyor would only occur later.

Recalling that time he reflected, in part philosophically, in part wistfully, 'When you're 20, you never think about being 40, do you?' and so he took what seemed to be the obvious step – of playing for Gloucestershire in the summer and Arsenal in the winter – with no great thought about alternatives. Arthur's sporting progression continued. The Bristol boy was on his way.

Chapter 3

For King, Country, County and the Gunners

WHEN YOU HAVE just completed pre-season training with a top First Division football club, six weeks of square-bashing and initial training with the Army probably come pretty easily.

Not everyone, of course, could call on that advantage, but that was Arthur's experience. In any event, he was a man who just got on with life, very happily, without fuss. It was rare to hear him moan or groan, especially beyond the privileged confines of the dressing room. Rather, you needed to be in his company for but a short time to recognise that here was a man who was very happy with the cards that had been dealt him. 'I did my square-bashing at Brentwood, at one of the barracks there. I remember walking down to the barracks from the station and there were a couple of ATS girls walking along the other side of the road and they started to sing "You'll get used to it".

'Of course we were put in huts, and we had to make our own beds and things, you know. I remember the other lads in the hut had a good laugh the first night we were there, when I pulled out my pyjamas – I think I was the only one. I had a few funny looks, but they were all right, great.'

With initial training and drilling at Brentwood completed, Private 19086950, Milton A, was posted first to the Royal Engineers at Farnborough before a transfer to the Royal Army Ordnance Corps and their large depot at Chilwell, on the outskirts of Nottingham.

He arrived at Farnborough in the early months of 1947. To those of that vintage the very mention of 1947 conjures up an immediate picture of weeks of severe cold, frost, ice, and deep snow which, in the spring melt, would create horrendous flooding.

The metal Bailey bridges on which he was working were frozen, so ice-cold hands became even colder. No wonder the young recruits valued, as perhaps they would at no other time, their lectures. The warm and dry lecture rooms had a definite attraction. 'Mind you,' Arthur pointed out, laughing, 'we wouldn't be in there too long before everybody would be asleep and snoring away after being out in the cold.'

Easy access to the cookhouse also helped ward off the cold. In those Arctic conditions the chance to slip into the cookhouse twice, or even three times, for additional breakfasts or dinners was a distinct bonus. Soldier Milton remembers weighing 9st 10lbs – his natural weight 'wringing wet' – when he joined up, but three ice-cold and well-breakfasted months later he was tipping the scales at 12st 6lbs.

Arthur was vague – almost typically so in a sort of 'I'm not sure and in any event it's not important' way – about his transfer from the Royal Engineers to the Royal Army Ordnance Corps. He had no recollection of the reason. One thing was certain. Serving king and country at Chilwell proved to be more up his street.

'A chap called Bailey, Lieutenant Desmond Bailey, used to run the cricket. I was his sort of secretary and number two i/c, so that worked very well and so I played a lot of sport while at Chilwell. That was nice, very nice.'

Captain Desmond Bailey remembers his National Service colleague: 'He was a wonderful sportsman, of course. I got him to play some rugby for us, and sometimes folk would ring up and ask if he could turn out for this team or another and I'd say, "No – he's playing rugby for me."'

'I made him a Lance Corporal when he was with us, and also put him forward for WOSB – the War Office Selection Board – but he didn't seem that interested in a commission, he just wanted to play sport.

'He was incredibly efficient at his job, which was looking after our sports arrangements. I used to let him off to play cricket for Gloucestershire Seconds. National Service men had very little leave, so I tried to help him in this way whenever I could, though sometimes wishing he would appear on the scorecard as AN Other.

'In his time at Chilwell he proved excellent at table tennis. In fact he was good at all games, although I don't ever recall him playing hockey, which was a strong sport in the Army.

'He was always very smart, entirely reliable, a thoroughly good chap, and a nice man. He was good at everything he did – that seemed to be his way. We kept in touch over the years, not regularly but messages would go back and forward, depending on where I was based.

'We would sometimes go and watch the greyhounds at Long Eaton. I knew nothing about greyhounds, but he was well versed in the sport.

'Arthur was a lovely man. I'd have him on my side anytime, anywhere – a great chap.'

Arthur, when established in the Gloucestershire side, would later meet up again with by-then Captain Desmond Bailey when playing against Yorkshire on their home grounds, where his former service boss was for a time a convivial and hospitable member of Yorkshire's committee.

As far as one could be on National Service, Arthur was in his element. 'We had a good football side there,' he said. 'We used to play in the Notts Thursday League, and we won that. We had some good players, mind: several of the lads were on the books of League clubs. And of course I played quite a bit of cricket too, for the RAOC.'

There was another great attraction to Chilwell too. 'I shall never forget,' recalled Arthur. 'Do you know where Chilwell is near? Trent Bridge.'

The summer of 1948 saw him spending time at Nottingham-shire's lovely old ground, not then as thoughtfully or extensively developed as the splendid, yet friendly, Test match arena it is today but, of course, it abounded with history and atmosphere.

There, for the first time on the cricket field, he saw Denis Compton, cricket's 'glamour boy', in action.

At Trent Bridge, Lance Corporal Milton – lucky man – watched part of Compton's innings of 184 against Don Bradman's all-conquering Australians. 'It was during that Test that he got hit on the head, and then went back out with the cut stitched up.'

The way Arthur told this story was so typical of his charm and lack of pretension. That Trent Bridge Test was played on 10th, 11th, 12th, 14th and 15th June – less than a week after he had made his own debut in first-class cricket. Over the years players far less talented than Arthur might have been tempted to speak of that Test match with the lingo and swagger of an established cricketer, as one who had already made it, and to speak of Bradman, Compton and Miller as fellow performers.

Not Arthur. Nigh on 60 years later he told the story almost as a naïf, as one seeing the game played at the top level, and seeing the God-like players, for the first time. He told it with that sense of excitement which, for him, the tale never lost, and a sense of awe that 'I was there'. Perhaps he never fully lost that, although it is probably right and fair to say it metamorphosed into lifelong gratitude and appreciation that he shared the same stage and was of the same generation.

Looking back to that Compton second-innings century at Trent Bridge, watched by L/Cpl Milton (with England requiring 344 to make Australia bat again), it is fascinating to recall that it was made over three days as a result of 11 interruptions for rain, bad light and scheduled intervals, factors which made a fine innings even more remarkable.

The innings ended with Compton still taking the attack to the enemy. Essaying yet one more hook shot against a Keith Miller bouncer his leg broke the wicket. He was seventh out, by which stage England had scored 405.

Not that these figures and records had fixed themselves in Arthur's mind. No, it was the magical atmosphere of a Test match, played on a welcoming ground steeped in the game's best traditions, with real artistry and honest rivalry on display that he recalled.

'I used to go along to Trent Bridge to watch the cricket whenever I had a free afternoon,' Arthur recalled. 'I can see Denis Compton now, hooking Keith Miller to the boundary. I'm sat there on the side, looking out, taking it all in and loving every moment of it – never ever thinking that I would actually go out and play on that ground. It became my favourite ground when I was playing for Gloucestershire.

'And then, later, also to be at Highbury, where Denis was, and play football there – so there were some very good memories from my Army days.'

Arthur had first met Compton on his visit to Highbury for those two friendly, trial games in 1945 – 'He had just got back from India.' Denis had not quite finished with football, and would play for Arsenal until 1950. Their friendship would also later be extended on the cricket field.

Two largely uneventful years' service as a soldier of the King ended for Arthur on 1st January 1949. 'What a good New Year present that was,' he recalled.

While with the RAOC he had kept in touch with the Arsenal or, rather, they had kept contact with him. 'They used to invite me down, you know. They used to look after you very well, make sure you're going on all right, give you the "once over" and have a look at you.'

In writing these recollections of Arthur's I can hear again in his voice the pride of being an Arsenal player, and the gratitude that, even when he was away on National Service, the club retained its interest in him, a paternal interest rather than simply a proprietorial one. I hear again, too, his reference always to 'the Arsenal', never simply 'Arsenal'. With that definite article he conferred on the club a status which, in his eyes, with its records and achievements and its concerns for its players, placed it far above any other. 'They gave you a small retainer, of course, and when I rejoined them they found you digs, and they kept in touch with your parents – kept them in the picture. It was a marvellous club.'

Arsenal were not alone in taking an interest in 20-year-old Arthur. Gloucestershire County Cricket Club, too, were quickly developing theirs, which would lead to his career with them spanning the years 1948 to 1974.

As we have seen, Arthur's cricket development was encouraged by a sports-mad Dad, and by the Soundwell club's willingness to encourage those precocious talents and give him opportunities to play.

But even before his schooling had finished, and before his move to more senior cricket with Stapleton Cricket Club at Sleepy Hollow, not far from Hillfields Park, his prolific schoolboy form had been noted.

A cutting from the *Bristol Evening Post* states:

> *News has reached me of the activities of a young and most promising cricketer. He is A. Milton of the Soundwell club. Still attending Cotham School, being only 16 years of age, he had a most successful time in his Club's match against Downend.*
>
> *Milton took five wickets for 44, in addition to dismissing a couple of batsmen with smart catches, and then made 54 of his side's 150 runs, being undefeated.*
>
> *To use the words of Mr Jefferies, acting hon. sec. of the Soundwell Club, "Milton batted like a veteran."*

Even at this age, his talent was attracting the headlines.

On 11th May 1946 the *Evening Post* ran an article headed, 'School or Club? – A Problem'.

Post reporter Walter Hale, whose keen interest in club cricket found space in the paper's sports' pages, wrote:

> *Should the legitimate and understandable desire of a school always to field its strongest side, and uphold its reputation, be allowed to stand in the way of a brilliant young cricketer?*

This question is brought to my notice by the case of Milton, Stapleton's young star, who, I find, is still at school, and the school authorities have first call upon him for their games. I think it will be a great pity if this youngster is barred from playing for Stapleton, and it is to be hoped that the headmaster will be good enough to waive his claim and allow Milton to carry on with the Stapleton team.

He is 17 – just the right age to be in better-class cricket, where he will get the experience and confidence so necessary to gain him higher honours.

He wants all the encouragement he can get during this most vital season – probably the one which may set the seal on his future career.

The outcome of this public plea is not known. Arthur, one suspects, knew (or remembered) nothing about it, and would have preferred to know nothing of it. It would have embarrassed him, and he certainly wouldn't have relished anyone creating divisions for him between his school and his club.

In reminiscing about his early cricket not one word of this passed his lips. One felt that, even then, he was happier letting his bat do any talking that was needed.

And his bat did talk, superbly and prolifically, for his new club.

'I scored plenty of runs for them,' he said, as if it was the most natural thing in the world.

In June 1946 Reg Sinfield, the former Gloucestershire player, wrote in the *Bristol Evening World*:

One youngster stands out in my mind who I have had the opportunity of watching. I refer to young Milton, of Stapleton. If this boy develops as I think he will, I have great hopes of a second Denis Compton here, both in football and in cricket.

Evidence of 'young Milton's' prowess with Stapleton is seen in the club's records for the 1947 season. Of the First XI's 24 matches, eight were won. Arthur, who continued to be known as Archie at this stage (at least by the local press), played in just 11 for, by now, he was doing his National Service and it wasn't possible to get home every weekend. Eleven innings (with two not outs) produced 626 runs, and he headed the averages with 69.55, impressive form indeed for a young man in his first summer out of school.

His tally included three centuries: 105 not out against Weston-Super-Mare; 111 versus Westbury-on-Trym; and an undefeated 123 against Old Bristolians, the former pupils of Bristol Grammar School, a school with an excellent cricket tradition.

Arthur's name also appears in the club's bowling records. Twenty-four wickets at 17.29 declare unequivocally his all-round talents.

These facts and figures help paint a picture of Arthur's precocious talents in this teenage period before he became a professional, although I introduce them reluctantly, for Arthur was definitely not a man of stats – at least not in the normally accepted sense. He had little concern for his own averages or of those playing alongside him, or pushing to play alongside him. These all related to personal performances and what interested him more was the team's performance.

Where statistics did interest him was in comparing players of his own and earlier generations. Tony Brown, Arthur's great and close friend, Gloucestershire team-mate and, later, his county captain, recalls: 'He was interested in stats in a funny way – he used to like to muse over things like Hedley Verity's figures, or Wally Hammond's scores, and players like them for whom he had such a high regard, and liked to try and understand what made them tick and what they achieved.'

But those figures for Stapleton's new recruit help to show how talented he was. In that 1947 season those who followed him in the batting list were some way behind the gifted young serviceman, with averages of 34.58, 23.61, 19.91 and 19.31. The four team-mates who appeared above him in the bowling averages had figures of 12.44, 13.33, 14.36 and 14.51.

One broad-brush conclusion that can safely be drawn from those figures is that Stapleton must have played on a good many bowler-friendly pitches that summer. Had the severely cold and wet spring hindered pitch preparation and made them bowler-friendly?

In this context, and by any standard, Arthur's batting performances and average were mightily impressive. Indeed, apart from the 1935 season, when Jack Crapp (whom Arthur was soon to join in the Gloucestershire side) had proved even more prolific, such figures had never been bettered in Stapleton's history.

Arthur continued scoring runs for Stapleton during his National Service. 'It was easy to get the bus to Derby, and then you were on the main line down to the south-west. I used to come home and play for Stapleton on Saturdays.

'Some other cricket I really enjoyed around that time was playing for the Willows. They were a Sunday side and they were a team of fellows, most of whom had come back from the war. A great friend of Dad's, Jack Iles, played for them. He was a really talented chap, a lovely cricketer and a nice golfer, and he took me along.

'I made my first-ever hundred for them. It was at Almondsbury. A Dr Marwood was in charge of it all – they used to have their committee meetings in the pub – and we played in some lovely spots in those Sunday games.'

This prolific run-scoring led to Arthur being invited to play a few Second XI games for Gloucestershire. Again he scored well and made what, with typical reserve, he describes as 'a few runs' – plenty enough to deserve the award of his Second XI cap.

He was invited to play again in the following summer and the papers reported that he did well. The match against Surrey was reduced by rain to one innings apiece and the press reported on the effect Arthur had on the game after Cliff Monks had scored 64 in nearly two hours:

> Surrey's smart fielding reduced prospects of a big score by the home team but Tom Graveney and Archie Milton were beginning to find the gaps when the luncheon interval interrupted their partnership.
> After lunch the two added 50 in 30 minutes, and the 200 was hoisted 15 minutes later.

Milton reached his 50 with an off-drive, and was bowled by Surridge. His score included six fours.
His partnership with Graveney added 120 runs. The latter was undefeated on 82, which included a six and nine fours.

Surrey Seconds' 164 all out left them 113 short.

The next time Arthur appeared for a Gloucestershire team was his first-class debut just a week later, in early June. Charlie Barnett and George Emmett had been called up to play in an England Test trial and their absence created the opportunity for Arthur.

'In those early postwar years most county staffs were pretty small,' he recalled, 'and they were always struggling for players, numbers-wise, if any of their key men were called up by England or they had injuries. When Charlie and George were called up for the Test Trial it left Gloucestershire short. So I got invited to fill one of those places, and I made my county debut against Northants at Northampton, on 2nd, 3rd and 4th June 1948.'

The *Bristol Evening Post* had announced his selection:

Archie Milton in Glo'shire Team.
Archie Milton, who played for Soundwell before joining Stapleton, and who did well for Gloucestershire yesterday, is to make his debut in first-class cricket next week. He has been selected to play for Glo'shire against Northamptonshire at Northampton beginning on Wednesday next, the Glo'shire team being: BO Allen (capt), CA Milton, Goddard, Crapp, Wilson, Cranfield, Scott, Lambert, Cook, Graveney (T), Wilcox. Neither Barnett nor Emmett is available, as both are playing in the Test Trial.

Among Arthur's limited memorabilia was a small cutting from another (unidentified) local paper:

On leave from the Army, twenty-years old Bristol cricketer Arthur Milton has been chosen to play for Gloucestershire against Northants at Northampton this week. Arthur gained his Second Eleven cap last year, but this will be his first outing for the seniors. Product of the same Bristol club that gave JF Crapp to Gloucestershire, Milton will join the County staff in September when he is demobilised from the Army.

It was to be a truncated debut. Rain affected the game and the debutant was denied any worthwhile chance to make his name. He made eight not out in Gloucestershire's first innings total of 229-7 declared, and was not required to bat as the county closed its second innings at 48-2. The match was drawn, with Northamptonshire, who had been set 143 to win, clinging on at 99-9.

'George Lambert wasn't playing that day. I can't remember why. He was a Cockney. "Got any lices?" he used to say, when he needed to do up his boots and the old ones had broken,' Arthur said. He often referred to George as 'the Cockney' – overlooking the nicety that George was Paddington-born and would have needed highly tuned ears to have heard Bow Bells ringing out at his birth.

'Colin Scott was a good cricketer – he'd had a good season in '39 and they were looking to him to be one of the top bowlers as, apparently, he was quite quick, but of course he lost six years, the war took it away from him.'

How did the team react to a new young player?

'Well, they were good chaps, they welcomed you and encouraged you, and, of course, it was no different the next year when I was playing all the time; because Jack and George, they really looked after us youngsters.

'Charlie Barnett was still playing in 1948, but not in that match of course. He was pretty forthright, I think. His family had a biggish business in Cirencester; fish, meat and game and the like. And he used to go hunting.

'But later on that year, in August, they asked me to go and play again – against the Combined Services at Gloucester. Of course they were first-class games then and the Services could call on some very good players. I didn't get many in the first innings and in the second innings we had been left with about 300 to get to win the game and when I got in, about number six or seven I suppose, Tom Graveney had about 50 or 60.

'We put on over a hundred together, and I was with him when he got to his 100 – it was his first for the county – which was rather nice. I went on to get 58 not out, and made the winning hit. That was the first time Tom and I batted together in a first-class match, and I shall always remember that.'

Tom had a similarly happy recollection of that period: 'We were lucky, being youngsters, playing together.'

As we talked, Arthur looked up that season in *Wisden Cricketers' Almanack*. His *Wisden* originally had belonged to his long-time pal Andy Wilson, Gloucestershire's wicketkeeper for 19 years. It thrilled Arthur to have them for the mutual pleasure they gave him and, earlier, had given Andy. It pleased him, too, that in acquiring them he had found an acceptable way of offering the hand of friendship and support at a time when their previous owner welcomed this.

As he read from the cricketers' bible he laughed away as the good book reminded him: 'Look. I'm among the amateurs – BO Allen, CA Milton and Cliff Monk' – all listed with their initials before their surnames.

'Basil Allen scored 1,300 runs that season, so he must have been worth his place. They needed to be worth their place didn't they, the amateur captains, but it didn't always happen.'

Arthur was a bit of a favourite with BO Allen, but not everyone was. Tom Graveney felt it was often difficult to do anything right in Allen's eyes, even when he got runs. Tom recalled how he was 'awarded' his county cap in 1948, his first full season. He and Charlie Barnett had put on 140-odd to win a match.

'As I was sitting there taking my pads off this cap hit me in the face. It was BO Allen "giving" me my cap. "Here's your cap – if you hadn't been such a big-head you'd have had it earlier," he said. He was a horrible man, oh a horrible man' – a description one would rarely, if ever, hear from the genial and mild-mannered Graveney.

The Cricketer described the newcomer Milton as 'an attractive batsman and a useful medium-paced bowler (he had taken 3-16 in the Combined Services' second innings, all his victims being clean bowled) and a superb fieldsman.' The magazine's correspondent concluded, 'His all-round performance made a great impression.'

Gloucestershire were certainly impressed. He could play, of that there was no doubt. And so, in his words, they asked: 'How about joining us for 1949?'

That was how Arthur, somewhat nonchalantly, remembered it, but it is clear Gloucestershire had him firmly in their sights, and in their plans. At the annual dinner of BAC Cricket Club, at Filton, Gloucestershire's treasurer, Walter Giles, announced that the Gloucestershire committee were expecting Walter Hammond to lead the county again next season, and that, 'Archie Milton, the young Stapleton player, will be taken on the staff as soon as he has finished his military service.'

At that time there was but a limited overlap between summer and winter games, and so no real obstacles existed to Arthur taking up Gloucestershire's offer alongside his commitment to Arsenal. 'I loved my sport – loved it – so it wasn't a difficult decision to make.'

His first professional summer with Gloucestershire would earn him £200 – plus £2 expenses for each evening on county duty beyond Gloucestershire's boundaries and rail fares for matches (home and away) played outside Bristol, as his first county contract (see page 38) shows.

With all this talk of cricket for Gloucestershire, and Arthur's continuing links with Arsenal, it is easy to forget that he had still to complete his service to king, country and the RAOC.

So how had he enjoyed his National Service?

'I didn't mind it at all. It teaches you to look after yourself and all about being away from home. You have to succumb to the discipline, but I don't think that's bad, and plenty today could benefit from that. And it teaches you to get on with life, with its ups and downs, and to make do with your lot.'

And Arthur spent the rest of his life doing just that – and very happily so.

GLOUCESTERSHIRE COUNTY CRICKET CLUB

A N   A G R E E M E N T   made the first day of January 1949 between Lt.Col. H. A. Henson, the County Ground, Bristol, for and on behalf of the Gloucestershire County Cricket Club (hereinafter called The Club) on the one part, and Mr C.A.Milton of the other part, WHEREIN IT IS AGREED AS FOLLOWS:-

1. The Club agrees to engage and the said C.A.Milton   agrees to serve the Club as required from 1st April 1949 to 30th September 1949, and to play in all matches for which he may be selected during that period, and if not playing to assist therewith as may be required.

2. The remuneration of the said C.A.Milton   shall be the sum of £200.

3. The Club agrees to pay the said C.A.Milton   overnight expenses of £2 per night when playing for the Club outside the County of Gloucestershire, also railway fares when playing for the Club away from his home base Bristol.

4. The said C.A.Milton   agrees he will not correspond with the Press on any subject directly or indirectly connected with Cricket, or enter into any contract with the B.B.C. to broadcast any talk on Cricket either generally or in respect of any particular occasion without first obtaining the written permission of the Club.

5. The said C.A.Milton   also agrees that if through illness or accident not arising out of or in the course of his employment with the Club or through loss of form or other cause he does not play in the full complement of Club matches the Club shall have the right to re-adjust his remuneration in which case the substituted remuneration shall for the remainder of the term be paid to the said C.A.Milton   in lieu of the remuneration stated in para.2 hereof.

6. It is hereby mutually agreed between the parties that the Club shall not be held responsible for any accident to or illness of the said   C.A.Milton   not arising out of or in the course of his employment by the Club.

7. In the event of any dispute arising between the parties hereto upon any matter arising out of this Agreement, the same shall be referred to the sole arbitration of a person to be named by the Committee, whose decision shall be final and binding on both parties, such arbitration to be in accordance with the provisions of the Arbitration Acts for the time being in force.

AS WITNESS the hands of the parties

SIGNED by the said Lt.Col. H. A. Henson in the presence of

SIGNED by the said in the presence of

After being demobbed, Arthur returned to Highbury where he started 'in the usual place, in the third side', playing in the Eastern Counties League.

His terms with Arsenal were set out on the last page of his contract, which looked like this:

provisions and conditions of this Agreement, the said   Thomas James

Whittaker,   on behalf of the Club hereby agrees that the said

Club shall pay to the said Player the sum of £   Match fee when playing   per week from

1st August.,1948   to   7th May.,1949.

and £ 1:10:0   per week from 8th May.,1949.

to   31st.July.,1949.

10. This Agreement (subject to the Rules of The Football Association)

shall cease and determine on   31st.July.,1949.

unless the same shall have been previously determined in accordance with the

provisions hereinbefore set forth.

When playing for the Club the said player will be paid
the maximum match fee in compliance with Football League
Regulations relative to Service players.

Fill in any other provisions required.

If released from National Service during the period of
this Agreement the terms herein contained will be revised.

Usual bonuses as allowed by Football League Rules.

As Witness the hands of the said parties the day and year first aforesaid

Signed by the said   Thomas James

Whittaker.   and   Clement

Arthur Milton.

(Sgd). C.A.Milton.   *C. A. Milton.*
                              (Player).

In the presence of

(Signature)   (Sgd).W.J.Crayston.

(Occupation) Asst.Manager.   (sgd).T.J.Whittaker.
                                                    (Secretary).

(Address) 43 Byron Court,

Harrow.Middlesex.

The contract made allowance for the fact that he was undergoing National Service (at least at the start of the period). It had winged its way from Highbury's marble halls to 19086950 L/Cpl Milton C A, No. 2 Coy, 6th Battn, RAOC, COD Chilwell, Beeston, Nottingham.

Lance Corporal Milton was not the only cricketer on the club's books, of course. 'There were the two Comptons, Denis and Leslie,'

Arthur recalled. 'Don Bennett, who played for Middlesex, came a bit later; and Jimmy Gray, who played a lot for Hampshire – he and I later became very good pals, and so did our wives; Don Roper, who played for Hampshire too; another chap, Ernie Stanley, who played for Essex, and myself. So there were at least six or seven of us. And they let us stay with our counties to pretty near the end of the cricket season, too.'

One of Arthur's Highbury contemporaries, Arthur Shaw, who made 61 appearances for Arsenal between 1948 and 1955, mainly at right-half, but occasionally on the other flank, remembered the cricketers who played for Arsenal, and their informal contribution to team training and morale.

'Apart possibly from his first year on the staff Arthur, and the other county cricketers, joined us late in pre-season practice. Most of us had a month of training pre-season, and a month of lunches too [Shaw later showed me a photograph of Arsenal's staff at lunch in the players' dining room, very much a period piece, with the players properly attired in jackets and ties with not a tracksuit in sight] – no other club offered that – and, after lunch, training would take a different form and we'd often play some other ball game, tennis, cricket or the like.

'In that short period when the cricket boys had come back from their counties, we'd put up some stumps by the goalposts in the practice area behind the Highbury goals, it was no more than 60 yards by 30 yards. We'd get the cricketers to bat, and the rest of us lads – all of us young, fit and strong, and definitely trying to show them a thing or two – would hurl the ball down, and not always from 22 yards. You didn't always know where it was going or where it would pitch, but we certainly worked up a head of steam.

'And Arthur and Denis would bat one-handed. It was so magical to watch them. We hardly ever got them out. They seemed to be able to cope with whatever we bowled at them.

'And when they'd had enough, or it was time to pack up, they would hit the ball right out of the ground, still one-handed.

'In fact, so good were they – and frustrating to bowl at, although it was always good fun – that one time we asked if we could set up a game on the main playing area, which was normally sacrosanct and only used for first-team soccer. We decided we would play a game of baseball, using those Indian exercise clubs we had in the gym. Arthur and the rest had never played that so we thought that might put them at our level. But do you know what? Arthur kept smashing the ball many a mile and getting home runs. I don't think we got him out here either.

'That was typical of Arthur. He took up golf more seriously when he started cricket, but on one occasion some of us went to play with Dai Rees and when he saw Arthur hit a golf ball he couldn't believe it. "He's a natural," he said, which of course he was: a natural at any ball game as far as we could see.'

As a successful Ryder Cup player and captain Dai Rees, regarded by many as the best player never to win the British Open, was a national celebrity.

One talented soccer-playing cricketer, who was briefly a contemporary of Arthur on Arsenal's books, discovered there were occasional exceptions to the Gunners' intention of mutually harmonious relationships between football and cricket clubs.

Arthur explained that Yorkshire CCC's Brian Close had joined Arsenal for the 1951–52 season, after playing for Leeds United as a youth. After missing the previous soccer season for an outstanding reason – he was with England's cricket team for their Ashes tour of Australia, when barely 20 years old – Brian played mostly in Arsenal's Combination (reserves) side that winter and made a strong impression with his abundant goal-scoring.

Arsenal's reserves team had made their way to the Combination Cup final that season. It was to be played on the first day of Yorkshire's opening match of the cricket season, the traditional fixture between the county champions and the MCC at Lord's.

Brian arranged with Yorkshire's captain, Norman Yardley, to leave Lord's at around teatime to play in the final. Unfortunately Yardley had not consulted his wife. Mrs Yardley's timing in producing twins was awry and thus Yorkshire's captain did not travel to join the team at Lord's.

Don Brennan, the other amateur in the side, naturally took over the captaincy and he shared Yardley's view that Close might be released early to play in the final, but said, 'That's all right by me, but you'd better ask the secretary.'

John Nash was at Lord's for the game. When Close sought his approval he was very short, and, brooking no argument, insisted, 'You're a Yorkshire cricketer now, and you can concentrate on your cricket.'

Close stayed at Lord's until close of play, then raced to north London, where the match had reached half-time. Arsenal had fielded a third-team player in Close's place. With substitutes not then allowed Close had to watch the remainder of the game, frustrated and champing at the bit, at the same time knowing he was in bad odour with Arsenal.

Arsenal lost. George Male, one of manager Tom Whittaker's lieutenants, with ambitions to succeed him, told Close tersely: 'Ring me tomorrow morning.' Brian did as he was bid, from Lord's where he had resumed with Yorkshire, to be told by Male, 'You've got a free transfer.' Yorkshire's intransigence, in the form of John Nash, had cost Close his Arsenal career.

Bradford City took Brian on a month's trial after his summer with Yorkshire. Within a fortnight they had seen enough. He had scored so many goals they ended the trial and signed him. Nine games later, during which time he confirmed his goal-scoring ability, he was injured, his knee gave way, and that was the end of his soccer career.

I checked this unfortunate story with Brian, by then President of Yorkshire CCC, at England's Test match against South Africa in July 2008. Geoff Cope, the former Yorkshire and England spin-bowler, was sitting alongside us and reminded me of a tale about Close which linked Brian and Arthur, a story which Arthur had previously recounted to me.

At Arsenal, Close had scored prolifically for the Combination team. A phenomenal header of the ball (as one might expect of such a courageous and forthright character), he scored a notable number of goals that way, but had also missed a few.

Determined to remedy things, the reserves' manager, Jack Crayston, arranged for Close to do some extra training for a week. Arthur was called in to float the ball over to the goalmouth for Brian to head, like a human hammer, into the net.

The week's extra work went absolutely according to plan. Arthur would float the ball across with pinpoint accuracy and Close would head it, with the impact of a mule kick, and the ball would rocket into the net.

Come Saturday's game there came a moment early on when Arthur, with his customary ease and fleetness of foot, beat the opposing defence. With radar-like precision, he floated the ball across for Close to head in. Close hit it perfectly with great power – wham! As had happened all week the ball bounced in front of the goal and, as it shot goalwards, up went Close's arms to celebrate – at exactly the moment the ball rocketed way over the bar. Frustration everywhere – and not a little laughter too.

Brian was hovering nearby as Cope re-told the story, repeating, almost word for word, Arthur's version of it. 'That's exaggeration, gross exaggeration,' he insisted, but with a warm ebullient laugh that suggested it wasn't too far from the truth.

'Arthur was a great lad, a lovely fella – and by golly he could play. As a winger he was fast – no one could take him on,' added Close; a tribute offered with a Yorkshireman's economy of words, yet with genuine affection and sincerity.

Arsenal's customary magnanimity allowed Arthur to start the '49 season, his first as a professional cricketer, in good spirits. In looking back to this time he was grateful that the two seasons were quite distinct, and grateful too that Arsenal were generous and understanding employers, understanding especially of sportsmen with all-round skills. He recognised that some modern-day players, gifted at both sports, have found their cricket seasons very truncated (or non-existent) as football managers have been reluctant to release players early and have then chased them up for an early return before their cricket season had barely begun.

As we have seen at Arsenal, dual sportsmen of Arthur's generation were quite thick on the ground. Kent included Derek Ufton, Stuart

Leary, Sid O'Linn and Freddie Lucas, who all played for Charlton Athletic in the winter months. Surrey had Ron Tindall (Chelsea and West Ham) and Micky Stewart (another Charlton Athletic player). Ken Higgs of Lancashire, and later Leicestershire, played for Port Vale; Mike Barnard of Hampshire also played for Portsmouth FC and his cricketing team-mate Henry Horton appeared for Blackburn Rovers, Southampton, Bradford Park Avenue and Hereford United.

As well as Brian Close, Yorkshire had Willie Watson, the most successful of all double internationals, with 23 appearances for England at cricket and four at football, also playing the winter game, as did Gloucestershire's Barrie Meyer, Ron Nicholls and Harold Jarman; Derbyshire's Ian Buxton and Ray Swallow; Worcestershire's George Dews, Jack Flavell and Jim Standen; Sussex's Ken Suttle – the list went on and on. There was barely a county without at least one footballer on their books around this time.

Dual sportsmen of the generation after Arthur – like Phil Neale, who played for Lincoln City and captained Worcestershire so successfully in the 1980s (and is now the England XI's capable and efficient administration manager); Jim Cumbes, of Aston Villa and Worcestershire (in a career that also took in Tranmere Rovers, West Bromwich Albion, Portland Timbers in the USA, Southport United and Worcester City football clubs alongside Lancashire, Surrey, Lancashire again, Worcestershire and Warwickshire); Ted Hemsley, of Sheffield United and Worcestershire; Chris Balderstone of Huddersfield Town, Carlisle United, Doncaster Rovers, Queen of the South and Leicestershire CCC – and others would all say, in hindsight, that their cricket seasons were always far too short. Football, or football managers, held sway. And of course there are the soccer players who had cricketing talent but who committed themselves to the larger ball and never seriously pursued the summer game, among whom Bobby Moore and Geoff Hurst (both West Ham) and Gary Lineker (Spurs among others) readily come to mind as, among a more recent generation, do the Neville brothers, Gary and Phil (Manchester United and Everton).

Arthur's soccer obligations caused no need for him to look constantly over his shoulder when he was playing cricket, though there were reminders of his Arsenal links as the 1949 season unfolded.

In the county's match against Middlesex at Bristol, young Arthur had a hand in the dismissal of his Arsenal colleague Denis Compton. The *Western Daily Press* told the story:

> *Denis Compton, England's leading batsman, was out for a duck at the County Ground, Bristol, yesterday and disappointed a large crowd.*
>
> *The Middlesex player was dismissed by a brilliant catch by Arthur Milton, Gloucestershire's youngest professional and former Stapleton player.*
>
> *Compton played a defensive stroke to a ball from Goddard which popped up and went to forward short leg, where Milton dived forward, fell on his knees and then went full length to take the ball inches from the ground. It was a catch which gives further indication of the young player becoming a particularly good close-in fielder.*

Denis turned the tables in Gloucestershire's second innings when, after scoring 17, Arthur was dismissed 'ct & b Compton'.

Of the five half-centuries he scored in that first professional summer one stood out in his memory. It was the innings against Derbyshire at Chesterfield, in early August. He had earlier made passing reference to this; now he told the full story. His first-innings 92 not out did much to put the county into a winning position. He had joined Jack Crapp in the middle with Gloucestershire at 60-3. Crapp soon fell to Cliff Gladwin, as did the next three batsmen – all for ducks! Lambert too went without scoring and, from 60-3, Gloucestershire had descended to a cataclysmic 91-8. In company with those great stalwart bowlers (but sometimes precarious batsmen), Tom Goddard and Sam Cook, Arthur saw Gloucestershire to 192.

Arthur's recounting of the story contained a good dash of his typical underplaying of the details. 'I was batting at no. 6 or 7, I suppose [in fact he went in at no. 5]. I got in and started to get a few.

It was a wet wicket, and the ball was taking pieces out, and they had quite a good bowling side.'

Readers familiar with Derbyshire's bowling in that era will enjoy Arthur's marvellously natural, and wholly unwitting, understatement: '... they had quite a good bowling side.' The attack against which he made the top score included the seamers Bill Copson and Cliff Gladwin (who took 5-53 in 27 overs, 13 of them maidens, including ten overs in which he took four wickets without a run being scored off him) alongside Les Jackson and the leg-spinner 'Dusty' Rhodes. 'Quite a good bowling side' indeed.

Intriguingly, that undefeated 92 was to remain his highest score against Derbyshire.

Ken Graveney, Tom's older brother and father of David, a recent chairman of England's selectors, was another with good reason to remember the match. He took all ten wickets in Derbyshire's second innings as Gloucestershire won by 184 runs.

Run-scoring was not Arthur's sole recollection of that game. 'Walking down to the ground from the hotel on the first morning – because we used to go by train, so we were walking from the hotel – some painters, I remember, had got their ladders up against the buildings, sticking back out into the road. There were about four or five others, besides me, and I was at the back. And they all went out into the road, round the ladders – because it's supposed to be bad luck to walk under ladders – but I walked under them. They all got nought, and I got 92.'

By now Arthur was already a capped player. Basil Allen had earlier awarded him his county cap, barely two months after becoming a pro, in the match against Kent at Bristol. His innings of 49 – a frustrating score on which to be run out – had again rescued Gloucestershire, who went on to beat Kent by seven wickets.

Arsenal were aware of his good progress, and their delight is readily apparent in a letter from Jack Crayston, the club's assistant manager, writing on behalf of Tom Whittaker, the man he was later to replace as manager. He also saw similarities with Denis Compton.

ARSENAL FOOTBALL CLUB, LTD.

WJC/AFH.

TELEGRAPHIC ADDRESS:
GUNNERETIC. FINSPARK, LONDON.
TELEPHONE: CANONBURY 3312.

T. J. WHITTAKER, M.B.E.
SECRETARY-MANAGER.

GROUND ADJACENT TO ARSENAL STATION.
(PICCADILLY TUBE)

ARSENAL STADIUM,
LONDON, N.5.

8th July, 1949.

Mr A. Milton,
6, Maple Avenue,
Fishponds, BRISTOL.

Dear Arthur,

Mr Whittaker is at present having a brief holiday and in his absence I wish to thank you for your letter regarding the date you expect to report for training.

I will refer your letter to Mr Whittaker when he returns, when he will no doubt write direct to Mr Henson regarding this matter.

I noticed in the paper this morning that your cricketing successes have resulted in you being awarded your County Cap. May I personally say how pleased I am at these successes, and all at Highbury wish me also to say how pleased they are that you have done so well. Even this measure of success is only a start to something even better and in time I can see you reaching the heights that Denis Compton has.

In due course I will notify you regarding your accommodation which, of course, will be at the same place as Donald Oakes.

Kindest regards to your parents, and every good wish to yourself,

Yours sincerely,

Jack Crayston

ASSISTANT-MANAGER.

Gloucestershire's captain clearly thought a great deal of the county's newest signing. In a speech at the Bedminster Cricket Club dinner, before the 1950 season got under way, Basil Allen described Arthur and Tom Graveney as, 'two of the best young batsmen in the country,' before seemingly damning Tom with faint praise (doubtless colouring Tom's estimation of him in the process):

> 'Tom will go to the top, but whether he will stay there I am not quite sure. He has been lucky in that he has struck the years after the war when the bowling was not terribly good. I think he is apt to think it is a little bit too easy.'

47

He was far more glowing about Arthur:

Milton, I believe, was described as another Compton. That is, perhaps, a little unfair, but I believe that it may be justified, because he seems to have that uncanny ball sense which only comes to very great players. He is a brilliant fielder anywhere and, as regards his batting, he learns quicker than any youngster I have ever known.

At 21, and in his first full season, Arthur had quickly made his mark with Gloucestershire and with his captain, as well as with those who watched the county from the boundary edge and reported it from the press box. The future looked rosy.

Chapter 4

Up the Ladder
Wembley-Ward

CLOTHES RATIONING ENDED in Britain in 1949, and high summer gave way to a golden early autumn as Arthur tore himself away from Gloucestershire's Nevil Road headquarters to return to Highbury, feeling content after his first taste of life as a professional cricketer, grateful to be a sportsman for all seasons.

Winning his county cap in that first summer as a cricket pro had been more than he hoped for but, back with Arsenal, there was no chance for conceit to set in. Once more he was in the third team, still in the Eastern Counties League, keen to win selection for the reserves. All the while he was gaining valuable experience and nous and, after earning that promotion to the reserves in the Combination League, winning a few things on the way, such as the London Cup.

His admiration for Arsenal and his gratitude for the way the club looked after him, especially as a young player, constantly shone through reminiscences of his Highbury days. After a summer at home in Bristol with Mum and Dad, Arsenal's concern for his welfare, and digs (among them two sets of digs at Hendon and later at Muswell Hill) selected and vetted by the club, made for as near a home-from-home situation as a single young man might be entitled to expect. In any event the presence of Don Oakes, who had joined Arsenal in 1946 after leaving Kingswood Grammar School – 'about the only school side that beat us,' Arthur remembered with typical magnanimity – meant he wasn't cut off from all things Bristol.

Oakes was also a fine schoolboy footballer, but it wasn't until their time at Highbury that they got to know each other well. They shared digs, became very good friends, and Don would be Arthur's best man when he married.

But we're racing on.

'Don was a very good all-round games player, playing both games to a high standard. It took some time for him to make the first team at Highbury and then, frustratingly for him, just as he had made it, he contracted rheumatoid arthritis and had to give up the game. It was tragic. He loved his football. He was a good player. He was as thin as a rake but hard as nails, tough and hard – a bit like Joe Mercer – and it was such a surprise when he had to pack in.'

In fact Oakes, who played wing-half or inside-forward, made just two League appearances in 1952–53 and nine in 1954–55. But in Arthur's generous mind his good friend is indelibly linked with Arsenal FC.

Although arthritis ended Don's soccer career it didn't dent his love of the summer game and he continued to play London club cricket, with 'the Ally Pally', as Arthur called the club – Alexandra Palace CC. Arthur never missed the chance of inviting Don for a beer whenever county games took him to Lord's or The Oval.

Evenings reminiscing with Don, nostalgically re-living matches played together and chewing over all the foremost issues of football and cricket, sadly and all too soon became a thing of the past. Don died in his mid-forties. 'And I've missed him ever since. Very close we were,' Arthur said, his voice cracking with genuine sadness and affection. As he told the story he discreetly wiped away a tear, and took a moment to gather his thoughts.

That sadness embraced the understanding and sympathy for one whose talented career was arrested in its prime, from one who felt so privileged to have enjoyed every opportunity to fulfil his sporting gifts.

In reflecting on the fulfilment of his sporting prowess Arthur was honest enough to recognise it was not all headlines and hundreds. In the 1950 cricket season his form fluctuated so much that he, a capped player, was left out of the side at Cheltenham. After the rich promise of the year before it was frustrating. Arthur asked to attend the famed Alf Gover Cricket School in the New Year of 1951 to help him recover his form, something which fitted comfortably alongside his Highbury duties. Gloucestershire arranged it.

Mind you, if there were reservations about his form in 1950 it might have been a case of Arthur being hard on himself, as well as a case of 'a prophet without honour in his own land'. It might have been that his good form of 1949 had heightened expectations about his real potential, and he was being judged by his own already high standards. In truth his results in 1950 were not markedly different from those of his first full summer, and they were certainly sufficiently good to draw the praise of someone who knew what real talent was. Denis Compton said of Arthur's season: 'A fine fielder and my choice as the batsman of 1950.'

On his return to Highbury at the end of the summer, Arthur retained his place in the reserves, where he played for much of the 1950–51 season. Though he was away in London the local press continued to follow his fortunes keenly. The *Bristol Evening World* told its readers:

> *Twenty-one-year-old Gloucestershire cricketer Arthur Milton … is now doing his stuff as a professional footballer with Arsenal.*
> *Arthur, in fact, has struck excellent form in the Combination side, and some supporters of the Highbury club think he is going to prove one of the best Arsenal wingers since the retirement of Cliff Bastin.*
> *As an outside-right, Milton is expected to challenge strongly for a place in the league team.*
> *On Saturday last Arthur scored twice and paved the way*

for three other goals in Arsenal Reserves' 6-1 win over
Birmingham reserves in a Football Combination game at
Highbury.
Both in looks and style of his play, Milton is said to be very
much like Bastin.

Arthur's place in Arsenal's reserves created an opportunity in 1950 to play in his home city. On 9th December Arsenal were to take on Bristol Rovers' second string. Poor weather, however, led to the game's postponement. The *Bristol Evening World* expressed the disappointment of local fans, noting that Arsenal had pencilled in Arthur for the match. Lined up alongside him were fellow Bristolians Don Oakes and John Chenhall.

A few weeks later the match was rescheduled, but the local press expectations initially were not high:

One look at the deplorable pitch was enough to assure most
of the 1,500 crowd that they were in for an afternoon of
comedy in the Mack Sennett fashion.

The reporter's early prediction, fortunately, proved wrong:

In fact the game turned out rather differently. In spite of
ankle-deep mud, it was an enjoyable match to watch,
with Arsenal cantering home to an easy win, and what an
attractive side they were.
The Arsenal side again included three local boys – right-
back Chenhall, outside-right Marden and inside-left
Arthur Milton, the Gloucestershire cricketer.

Arthur Milton (no longer Archie) was made captain for the day and celebrated by scoring Arsenal's second goal in their 5-1 win.

A footnote to this press cutting told of another footballing cricketer, who was later to become a Gloucestershire team-mate of Arthur and a great pal:

Barrie Meyer, who leaves for Aldershot this morning to begin his National Service, scored for the Rovers.

Arthur Shaw remembers, 'I first encountered Arthur in the Combination side. I don't think he knew what to make of me at first, and I'm sure he thought that, as a London boy, I was a right scallywag but we were all good friends – Arthur, Jimmy Logie and I – all the time we played together. Mind you, we didn't spend a lot of time together away from the ground. I used to think I knew a bit about the horses, because I had got to know quite a lot of top jockeys, and Jimmy, of course, was a big gambling man. Dear old Arthur liked the dogs, the greyhounds – and he would quietly go off and watch them on his own.

'Arsenal played a 2-3-5 formation – as nearly every team did then, didn't they? – but we often adopted a V formation, with Arsenal players following a plan to back off rather than challenge the opposition unduly.'

Asked what he thought were Arthur's special skills and gifts, Shaw recounted, 'Getting the ball, facing his man, feinting, and then going past him on the other side – at speed.

'Strange as it may seem, it's probably the case that he didn't really go on and achieve all he should have done in the game at top level largely because that style, and his speed, didn't really suit the style of play Arsenal adopted in those days. Amazing really. Today all the top Premier League managers would be after him like a shot. He was way ahead of his time.

'And there's no doubt Arthur was very fast. I can see how he would have fitted brilliantly into the modern game, but I'm not sure his speed and style was always appreciated at Arsenal. Jimmy Logie said one day, "Arthur goes like the wind – but I'm not sure the guv'nor likes it."

'Obviously from my right-half position I was constantly linking with Arthur and Jimmy, and I enjoyed that and enjoyed the way they played – though they were far better players than me.

'I loved it when we pulled the opposition's left-back out of position. If I could get the ball to the corner flag, Arthur almost always would beat the full-back, and then he'd be in towards the goal, or float in a super pass.'

Arthur's speed, not least from a standing start (the sort of speed that made him such a good runner between wickets), was exceptional and frequently drew the approving admiration of his Highbury team-mates, as well as the fans.

Arthur Shaw recalls one occasion when, unknown to Arthur, they put him to the test – and what a test it was.

Arsenal's unique reputation meant that other stars of the sporting world sought to join them occasionally for training, men like golfer Dai Rees and the international sprinter McDonald Bailey.

Emmanuel McDonald Bailey is a Trinidadian-born British athlete, good enough to win the bronze medal in the 100 metres at the 1952 Olympics in Helsinki. From 1951 to 1956 he was the joint holder of the world 100 metre record at 10.2 seconds. He was no slouch.

Arsenal seldom trained on Mondays, and Arthur Shaw recalls a Tuesday practice session. McDonald Bailey was with them and he and Jimmy Logie decided to see just how quick Arthur was.

After lunch Shaw and Logie arranged a race among Arsenal's players, from one penalty box to the other, with McDonald Bailey very happy to be part of the fun.

'We had the players lined up', Shaw remembered, 'with Arthur at one end and McDonald at the other. And then it was "Ready, Steady, Go" – and off they all sped, but with the rest of our Arsenal players dropping out after 20 yards or so, as we'd asked them to, leaving just Arthur and McDonald Bailey racing.

'And I can see Arthur now, clearly. He flew down the field and beat McDonald Bailey by four or five yards.

'McDonald Bailey was amazed at Arthur's incredible speed and very generously suggested, "He would have beaten anybody."

'And what's more,' Arthur Shaw added, 'as we returned to normal training Arthur seemed completely unaware that he'd been set up, and unaware of his amazing achievement in beating an international sprinter.'

Next morning Logie and Shaw chatted about the previous day's test. Shaw remembers that when they eventually told Arthur, all he said was: 'I thought you were up to something.'

'It was no great thing for him,' said Shaw.

Another close friendship, one which extended well beyond their playing days, was forged at this time. Hampshire's Jimmy Gray met up with Arthur at Arsenal in 1948. He recalled his team-mate's ability: 'Art was a very talented footballer, very quick off the mark and he had excellent ball skills. Against Huddersfield on one occasion he was being marked by someone he considered a "thug" and when Art got the ball he kicked it past his marker, nipped off the field onto the cinder running track, sprinted down the track and came back on to the field to cross the ball.

'He thought football was a great game, spoilt by those who were not very good but good enough to stop you playing. I'm sure that, in the end, this was one of the reasons why he didn't play for as long as he might have. With today's lovely surfaces to play on, and a consistently bouncing ball Arthur would have been great – a star, as of course he was then. And he was a wonderful friend.'

Micky Stewart, who played football for Corinthian Casuals as well as Charlton, and cricket as an opening batsman (and, like Arthur, an insatiable close catcher) for Surrey and England, before later becoming England's cricket manager and, subsequently, Director of Cricket, relates a story of a group of county cricketers, two or three of whom had played both games, at a sporting social occasion.

Discussions sometimes touched fondly on days of yore. One of the company asked Arthur how many goals he thought he might have scored had he played a full season. 'Oh, perhaps ten, maybe 15 or 20, in 40 games.'

'But there were 42 First Division matches,' Micky protested.

'Ah yes,' replied Arthur, 'but Chelsea had that full-back Stan Willemse who kicked you off the park given the chance, so I might have missed those games!'

Despite such customary self-deprecating humour, few listening believed Arthur would ever have opted out of a game, even though he knew he might not enjoy the way in which it would be played.

Arthur's burgeoning form and reputation at Highbury meant that he now had a real, and justifiable, hope of promotion, and was giving rise to exciting expectations.

Those expectations came to fulfilment on 10th March 1951 – 'My birthday, would you believe. That's when I made my First Division debut. It was against Aston Villa, at Highbury. Not a bad birthday present, was it? My Mum and Dad came up, with a few people from his work.'

The Bristol press, faithfully reporting the young star's progress, announced on its sports pages the previous evening:

> *Tomorrow is Arthur Milton's 23rd birthday.*
> *Today the Arsenal manager, Mr Tom Whittaker, added a storybook touch to the occasion by choosing Arthur for a Division 1 League game.*
> *For this – his league debut – Arthur will be at outside-right against Aston Villa, at Highbury, in an Arsenal line-up of Platt; Barnes, Smith (L); Shaw, Daniel, Forbes; Milton, Logie, Holton, Lewis, Marden.*

Arthur picked up the story: 'It meant I joined up with Jimmy Logie again. I had been playing on the right-wing in the Combination side and it was on the wing that I was selected against the Villa. Jim was playing inside-right which was rather tasty. And we won 2-1.'

Had he expected his first-team call-up?

'I was certainly hoping I might get the call, but am not sure why it came when it did.'

In fact his debut might have come even earlier had he not talked Tom Whittaker out of selecting him.

Logie was out of the team, injured. 'Jimmy was half the side, you know,' Arthur recalled. 'They were certainly not the same without him. He was one of the greatest players I ever saw. We just knew what the other was thinking, you know, and we were a wonderful combination.'

Arthur was called to the manager's office to learn he would be making his League debut in Logie's place. By then he had begun to have reservations about Tom Whittaker's judgement of players, a conclusion he wasn't inclined to cast aside when the manager told him he would be in the first team for the match at Everton.

'Tom Whittaker said, "Jim's not going, he's injured." I was playing on the wing for the reserves by then and so was very surprised when the manager said, "We'd like you to play at Everton tomorrow and take Jim's place at inside-forward."

'I couldn't believe it, couldn't believe the sense of it. So I said to him, "I've been playing on the wing in the reserve team. I'm not used to playing inside-forward, it's a different game."

'I was aware we had a good young lad, a little fellow, Noel Kelly, who played inside-forward in the reserve side alongside me – I was on the wing and we were a nice combination – and so I said, "You've got Noel in the reserve team who's good enough to go and play." I didn't think I would be fit enough to play at inside-forward – you have to be a b----y sight fitter to play there than on the wing. Anyway, they realised. I don't know why they thought like that … but that's how they did it in the end. And he went and had a good game, this lad – but he never played any more. I couldn't believe it.

'And, of course, I soon got my turn and played on the wing to James Tullis Logie. And that's how I got to play on the wing for England. We had more inside-forwards at the Arsenal than wingers, and so I went on the wing.'

It is worth remembering that Arthur had almost made his Arsenal first team debut several years earlier. He had been chosen, as a 17-year-old, to play against Fulham (admittedly a war-time game and therefore not an official First Division match), but sustained an injury while playing for his school team. Tom Whittaker decided not to risk him sustaining further injury so Arthur's debut was put on hold until 1951.

'Before my Arsenal debut a chap called Ian McPherson was playing at outside-right. I saw him play a few times. He used to go with his head down, but he didn't seem to be really in control of what he was doing. He was very good at getting forward; he was very quick but I think they used to get a bit frustrated with him – especially Jimmy – because he never knew when he was going to get the ball, you know. I can only think that's why they made the change.

'We'd had some good games in the reserve side, and much of that goes back to Jack Crayston, the ex-player who looked after us there. He was a classic sort of fellow, was Jack. He was the one who always wrote to your parents to let them know how you were going. And when Dad wanted to come up Jack always used to send him the tickets – and Dad could never pay for those tickets. They were so good.'

Jack Crayston wrote to Bill Milton on 17th August 1949, enclosing two tickets for Arsenal's game with Chelsea which, he pointed out, were 'Guest tickets and I would like you to accept them with our compliments'.

He went on to say: 'We have all followed Arthur's cricket activities with very keen interest and it's a source of great pleasure to us all to know that this, his first season in county cricket, has resulted in him being established as a very firm favourite. We have always had a number of county cricket players on our staff and on no occasion have we had any difficulty in coming to a mutual understanding with the cricket authorities regarding the overlap of the two seasons.'

The start to Arthur's First Division career was short-lived. Towards the end of the match he went for a 50-50 ball with the Villa's Con Martin, and ended up the loser. 'I beat him to the ball, but that meant he came in over the top and I got six deep stud marks in my thigh. It put me out for the rest of the season. But I was lucky not to break anything or do the ligaments in some way. If they step on you that way you can be troubled with the old cruciate, can't you? Fortunately I'd got a bit of meat on me there from riding a bicycle as a lad.

'That was the only place I'd got any meat on me, and so it healed up pretty well,' Arthur recalled without rancour.

He could but look forward to the summer. Recovering his fitness, and the prospect of a new cricket season, were high on his personal agenda. This was just as well for he was wholly unaware, probably gratefully so, of what was going on behind the scenes in his absence, at Arsenal. Had Arsenal's plan borne fruit it would surely have had a marked – and disastrous – effect on Arthur's Highbury career.

Tom Whittaker had decided he needed new players. In fact he wanted one particular player – and went after him. In his book *Tom Whittaker's Arsenal Story* (published in 1957 by Sporting Handbooks Ltd), Whittaker wrote of the club's 1950–51 season: 'It turned out to be just one of those seasons, except that a fairly early Cup knock-out, and a position in the League which, while not to be sneezed at, meant that we were out of the running for championship honours, enabled me to blood a number of promising youngsters,' among whom he listed Cliff Holton, Jack Kelsey, 'and Arthur Milton, the young Gloucester cricketer, [who] played once.'

Then Whittaker recalled, 'In early August 1951 I tried to sign one of the greatest box office names in soccer, Stanley Matthews, the Blackpool and England right-winger.'

He had been looking at the advance sales figures for season tickets and, somewhat deflated, concluded: 'What I needed to put the name Arsenal back in the soccer shop window, particularly in north London, was a terrific box office draw.'

On the spur of the moment Arsenal's manager jumped in his car and, at high speed, set off for Blackpool. Unsurprisingly his bluff opposite number at Blackpool, Joe Smith, was amazed to see him, and even more amazed when Whittaker offered him, there and then, £20,000 for Stanley Matthews.

Smith was unwilling even to countenance the idea. 'I couldn't let him go,' Smith said. 'The board wouldn't agree to it. I'm not sure that Stanley would want to go, even to Arsenal – and the supporters would lynch me.'

Dejected, Whittaker returned to London but, unwilling to take no for an answer, a week later he was back in Joe Smith's office. Determined to succeed, he threw down Arsenal's cheque book on Smith's desk and said: 'Write your own price. I want Stanley.'

'Sorry, Tom, it's no use,' countered Smith – whose response to the whole issue appears to have been astonishingly good-natured, to the extent that when Tom Whittaker asked if he might speak with Matthews, Smith arranged for the most famous footballer of that era to come in. Whittaker succinctly outlined his reasons for being there, saying: 'Stanley, I've just offered the sky for you to sign for Arsenal. How do you feel about it?'

The 'Wizard of the Dribble' looked at him for a moment, then at his own manager, and then back at Whittaker, who heard his intended catch say, 'It is every actor's ambition to finish on the West End stage. I would like to play for Arsenal.'

But Blackpool stuck to their guns, and Whittaker reluctantly gave up his vision of a star signing.

Of course Arthur knew nothing of Whittaker's trips to the seaside. In any case, another summer of cricket was about to begin.

The 1951 season provided Arthur with more joy than its predecessor. 'I was more consistent, and began fulfilling my promise,' he recalled.

Batting usually at no. 5, he made 1,574 runs, at an average of 39.35, and scored his first championship hundred. And where did he achieve it? At Taunton, of course.

The *Western Daily Press* reported this maiden championship century thus:

> ... *Milton was Crapp's partner in the stand of 101 for the fifth wicket and the young player was responsible for 61 of them. He gave a grand exhibition of batting, especially in hitting his first 50 runs, which took him only 65 minutes.*
>
> *He played Lawrence* [Johnny Lawrence, Somerset's leg-spinner] *with apparent ease and confidence, and like a thoroughly seasoned player. Exercising a careful defence, he got the spinners in the centre of the bat and showed judgement in ignoring those leg-breaks turning away from the off. Anything on the leg-side – and the googly, which he was quick to spot – he hit very surely and gained many of his fours in that way.*
>
> *His best strokes, however, were on his back foot when he made forcing shots through the covers. Once or twice there was so much power behind these strokes that the tightly*

*packed field was pierced and he got several boundaries in
that way.*

*Milton mastered Lawrence – and the other bowlers – better
than any Gloucestershire player, and six of his nine fours in
his first 50 runs were off the slow bowler.*

*His last 20 runs to complete his century, Milton scored in
the last 35 minutes of play.*

He ended the day undefeated with 103. The following morning
Arthur went on to reach 125, helping Gloucestershire to a first-
innings total of 385, which they converted into a seven-wicket
victory.

By the summer's end Arthur had moved up the order to open
the innings with George Emmett when Martin Young, Emmett's
regular partner, was injured. It proved a fruitful partnership.

Had his birthplace provided a Somerset qualification (as has
been erroneously suggested), Taunton would have been his home
ground and undoubtedly, and by some distance, he would have
bettered his career tally of 32,150 runs and 56 centuries.

That maiden championship hundred was his first serious knock
of the summer. A week earlier he had made six not out in the second
innings of the county's customary pipe-opener against Oxford
University at The Parks, after not being required to bat in their first
innings.

Arthur's century set him up well for a prolific season. He scored
one more hundred that year, at the beginning of August – at Bristol,
also against Somerset, batting for part of his innings with the great
Wally Hammond, on his final appearance for Gloucestershire after
he had been tempted back having retired five years before – and made
six fifties, as so often with Arthur, when the side most needed them.

His first century earlier in that summer of 1951 had inspired
one of the Bristol papers to link Arthur's summer successes for
Gloucestershire and his winter sport with Arsenal:

*Summer or winter, you can't keep Arsenal out of the
news. No sooner had football boots been stored away than*

Arsenal's cricketers started hitting the headlines. Denis Compton (no longer an Arsenal player, but all his football was played with the Londoners) is again in record-breaking mood. Les Compton is also getting his runs for Middlesex and snapping 'em up behind the wicket. Arthur Milton has had a century for Gloucestershire. Jimmy Gray has made his highest score for Hampshire. Don Bennett has been bowling well enough for Middlesex to be talked of as an England prospect. Brian Close has scored 96 not out for the Army against Oxford University.

Batting surfaces at Bristol in that era left much to be desired, which is perhaps why so many of their batsmen enjoyed filling their boots at grounds like Taunton and Trent Bridge. 'Wickets at the County Ground were not good then,' Arthur recalled (with understatement very evident), 'which is probably one of the reasons why Tom [Graveney] was in and out of the England side around that time.

'Do you know, counties used to come and often they'd book out the third night because they knew it would probably end up a two-day game,' he added, smiling.

Over the years countless county cricketers have happily found that when one part of their game is in good nick, they often can't go wrong in the other departments too. Arthur, of course, was a brilliant fielder, one of the very best. Initially he was used as an outfielder (when, as a youngster, he had the legs to cover those parts of the 'outer' which some more venerable senior pros seldom saw) before soon being brought close to the wicket when the near infallibility of his close-catching became apparent.

And, liking to be involved, in 1951 he enjoyed his bowling too. It's typical of him that he was ready to bowl when others might prefer not to. 'I used to like to have a few overs, especially on a warm day or if there were lots of runs against us. I didn't mind having a bowl.'

Having told me this, Arthur, as if to emphasise the point, revealed he had taken 79 first-class wickets during his career. And that happy recollection triggered yet another balmy memory.

'When Tom Graveney celebrated his seventieth birthday, he had a party, up at Cheltenham, and he invited Joan and me, and asked if I might say a few words, which I did.'

Conscientious as ever, Arthur had let some thoughts run through his mind in the days before the party. 'I thought, "Well, he's always been just ahead of me: he's one year older than me, he got capped just before me, he scored more runs, he's better looking than me. I wonder if I can beat him anywhere?"

And then he remembered his bowling, and he remembered his 79 wickets.

'In speaking about Tom on the night it was very easy – and right – to point out that, great player that he is, he had always been one step ahead of me, in almost everything.

'But I thought I would tease him about his bowling. Feeling pretty sure he hadn't got more wickets than me because he didn't bowl a great deal – he used to bowl the old leg-spinners – I asked, "How many wickets did you get, Tom? I got 79."'

'"Well," said Tom, "I got 80 – and if you'd caught Don Kenyon off me at first slip at Worcester, I'd have had 81!"

'And damn me he was right, so he was still ahead of me.'

And laughing merrily away at the memory of it, Arthur then recalled that dropped catch.

'I'll always remember it, because he's bowling – and Don was a lovely player, wasn't he, a beautiful player – and I'm stood at first slip. Tom came up to bowl, bowls him a beautiful half-volley just outside the off-stump and I thought, "There's four," so I started to stand up, didn't I? And he stopped his shot, and nicked it, and I had to go back down again – and dropped it, you see.'

Later on Bomber Wells came on to bowl. 'Bomber was bowling to Don, and Bomber had a quick one. He was so strong, Bomber. He bowled one a bit short, and Don got back, gave it everything, but edged it and I caught it up here – one-handed way above my head, at full stretch. Tom laughed. "Look at that," he said. "You catch the buggers for him."'

The story also offered yet another insight into Arthur Milton. Here was a man, one of the best fielders in the history of the first-class game, and he was telling a story relating to a dropped catch. Mind you, since there were so very few of those over the years, perhaps – more than a half-century on – they were easier to remember. Keith Andrew, the former Northants and England wicketkeeper, was another of near-infallible class and I recall him, without an ounce of 'side' or arrogance (but, in all probability, with his tongue in close proximity to his cheek), once telling a tale which wryly began, 'That must have been the season I dropped a catch ...'

Despite that rare drop by Arthur, the 1951 season had been a good one, restoring his morale after the disappointments of the previous summer. Success with bat and ball and in the field meant that he returned to Highbury, in September, with a spring in his step and his short-lived Arsenal debut at the end of the previous season still fresh in the memory. It was time, as a footballer, to move nearer the top of the ladder.

'After the summer of '51, with the leg better after that injury, I went back up to Highbury, and got myself football fit – I was always pretty fit but needed just to go up another gear before starting back at soccer – and played a couple of matches in the reserves and then they put me into the first team again.

'I more or less went straight into the side; we were having not too bad a season' – yet another instance of Arthur's understatement. 'But I was quite surprised because it was not long after I reported back from cricket that I went in the side.'

He joined a team that was indeed in good form. Arsenal would finish in third place in the First Division, as well as winning a place in the FA Cup final.

If Arthur was surprised, so too – it would seem – was his manager.

In the breathless, racy style of his book (by now on Chapter XL) from which we quoted earlier, Whittaker recalled, seemingly to his own amazement: 'Lucky Arsenal they call us, and I must say that in the early part of season 1951–52, the season we went for the Cup and League double, we were lucky. Still searching for a winger, I watched many and varied types, until I found one right under my nose in the fair-haired Arthur Milton, who gained an England cap against Austria after playing only 12 league games.'

'I found one right under my nose ...' What that says about Whittaker's management style, and his awareness of the players his club had been developing, is not the subject of this story. But Arthur was delighted his soccer career with Arsenal was still firmly on track.

Was an England cap in the offing? Had he considered the possibility? Were newspapers and journalists canvassing for Milton for England?

'No, not at that time.'

Arthur's recollection was not strictly true but, as always, this probably owed much to his laid-back manner, and his 'happy to play the game but not be over fussed by all that goes on around it' approach.

In fact the *Daily Telegraph*, reporting on Arsenal's First Division game at Charlton Athletic on 20th October, some six weeks before his England debut, recorded Arthur's form in glowing terms. Arsenal had gone to the dressing rooms at half-time one goal down. They would go on to win 3-1. The *Telegraph* reported:

> *There must have been dressing-room debates. When Arsenal came out Forbes took the initiative.*
> *Disregarding his former purely defensive role, he went to get the ball. He soon had the Charlton defence dithering. He found a great ally in Milton and plying him with perfect passes the somewhat over-confident Charlton defence found itself in panic.*
> *Milton, who may soon be the answer to England's right-wing problem, danced his way through the defence as Finney might, but with less hesitation. Seven minutes after half-time he rounded the Charlton left-back, put over a perfect centre, and Holton nodded it safely home.*
> *Arsenal were level, Milton on top of the world, and Forbes still feeding him passes. Milton wove his way past half a dozen defenders and lobbed the ball over Bartram's head for a perfect second goal.*

A perfect goal? There were more to come.

Chapter 5

Capped First for England

'GO ON, PULL that one as well, Jimmy,' declared Arthur, stretching out his left leg. His pal Logie insisted he was not joking. Arthur was indeed about to become an England player. He was expected at Wembley.

Arthur was definitely disinclined to believe Logie. He knew him, and his leg-pulling, of old. The unexpected and unanticipated nature of the news convinced Arthur it was a practical joke. Indeed, when the newspapers hit the streets that day, 26th November 1951, they carried news of Tom Finney's absence and his injury and, without critical comment (a sign of the more respectful times), noted his replacement had not yet been chosen. According to *The Times*, 'The outside-right vacancy caused by Finney's withdrawal will not be filled until today.'

When the call came through to Highbury later that day, Tom Whittaker generously asked Arthur's great pal to tell him the good – and urgent – news of his call-up. With just 48 hours' notice he was to replace Finney against Austria at Wembley on Wednesday 28th November 1951.

Tom Finney – today Sir Tom Finney – is one of the giants of England soccer. In 76 games for his country he scored 30 goals. He was equally effective on either wing although, once Stanley

Matthews eventually found regular favour with England's selectors, most of Finney's caps were won on the left, with Matthews on the right.

Stanley Matthews might well have filled the place against Austria once Finney was injured. In the eyes of many soccer fans, especially looking back more than 50 years through rosy-hued lenses, Matthews – one of soccer's all-time 'greats', and a forerunner of the generously gifted soccer heroes of more recent eras like Bobby Charlton, George Best, and David Beckham – was an ever-present in the England side. But the facts tell otherwise. For reasons that maybe seemed unfathomable then – and equally so now – Matthews' face, earlier in his career at least, didn't always fit with the selection committee.

So it was Arthur Milton who received the call, not Stanley Matthews. Arthur's deeds for Arsenal – for whom he became the regular outside-right that season – his persistence, his speed, his footballing gifts had been noted.

'It was a bit of a shock,' he said. 'I wasn't expecting to play. There had been no press suggestions that I was in the frame or might be considered. I think I was very fortunate because Finney and Matthews were about two of the greatest you'll ever see.'

Arthur's 12 appearances for Arsenal had undoubtedly created an outstanding impression, not only with the England management but also with knowledgeable and experienced observers.

Bob Ferrier, forthright soccer correspondent of the *Daily Mirror*, said of Arthur on the eve of his selection by England:

> *In him Arsenal have found the complete natural footballer. He has superb control, a killing burst of acceleration, a shoulder swerve in the Finney tradition and a game of variety, originality and imagination.*

It was a glowing and deserved testimony. And, of course, it all came easily to him.

Nor, of course, had his matchless form gone unnoticed by his Arsenal team-mates. Nevertheless, Logie, the perpetual joker, was not going to give that any credence as he passed Arthur the news of his international call-up.

'It's only because you're the nearest to Wembley, and you've got your boots handy,' was his mischievous explanation, after just about persuading the Bristol boy that he was indeed in the England team.

What were Arthur's thoughts as he found his way into Wembley's home dressing room, to pull on that revered white shirt bearing the three heraldic lions?

And what were his thoughts as he ran out of the tunnel onto the rich greensward, to line up alongside Billy Wright (Wolverhampton Wanderers), Gil Merrick (Birmingham City), Alf Ramsey (Tottenham Hotspur), Nat Lofthouse (Bolton Wanderers), Jimmy Dickinson (Portsmouth), Eddie Baily (Tottenham Hotspur), Bill Eckersley (Blackburn Rovers), Jack Froggatt (Portsmouth), Les Medley (Tottenham Hotspur) and Ivor Broadis (Manchester City)?

Such thoughts needed teasing from Arthur's memory when others might have made it part of their constant conversation. He remembered, in a vague sort of way, heading along Wembley Way to the stadium, almost unrecognised among better-known team members.

He wasn't unrecognised in the dressing room, of course, but he knew most of his new team-mates only by reputation. He had met few personally, and his short First Division career had given him little direct on-field contact with most. It wasn't quite a case of introducing himself to them, but it wasn't far off. And, of course, as a late replacement he would have missed most of what limited training sessions there had been (it was an era when First Division players were expected to fulfil the normal League programme, with none of the present-day breaks and training camps before internationals).

What was very clear in his memory was the real sense of privilege of being called up to play for England. His Arsenal colleagues were, of course, thrilled for him. From Tom Whittaker: 'I'm very proud for you, that you've been selected to play for your country. Well done.' And from his teammates, encouraging words: 'Get out there and show them what you can do.'

The pride felt by Arthur and his Arsenal pals was shared delightedly by his family and friends, although they had no opportunity to turn that into support from the terraces. Joan, his landlady's daughter – and by then his fiancee – had been sent on a course by Baring Brothers, her banker employers, and so could not get away, and Arthur's call-up notice was insufficient to allow his Dad to get up from Bristol. It was, in those ways, a low-key international debut.

One who was among the capacity crowd was 15-year-old Tony Brown. 'My Dad took me to that match,' Arthur's Gloucestershire colleague and great friend recalled, almost 60 years later, 'the first time I visited Wembley. Little did I know then that I would be playing cricket with Art three years later.'

Sharply clear in Arthur's recollections was the fact that England might have – should have – scored early on in the game. 'We should have scored three goals in the first 20 minutes, you know. We never got one of them and then – you know how it is – if you don't get a goal you begin to struggle a bit,' he said.

The Times, on the intervening day between Arthur's selection and the game itself, had said, 'Milton, too, a true games-player, progressive and intelligent, for all his inexperience, should not be overawed by the experience. He has the temperament, one suspects, for the big occasion.' It added the hope that, 'Milton will play his natural, progressive game.'

For those who don't mind being diverted briefly, that preview in *The Times* was followed immediately, with barely a sub-heading gear-change, by a brief report relating to another hugely gifted sportsman, Peter May, who would feature later in Arthur's career:

Cambridge Blues – The Cambridge University Association Football captain, PBH May, has invited GG Tordoff (Normanton GS and St. John's), left-back, and CFM Alexander (Woolmer's School, Jamaica, and Caius), centre-half to play [in the Varsity match] against Oxford at White Hart Lane on Saturday, December 8.

At Wembley, England's early untaken opportunities were rued by The Thunderer:

> *But one great save by Zeman four minutes after the kick-off, when Broadis was sent clean through a wide area and straight up to the goalkeeper by Milton's pass, almost certainly had as much bearing on the afternoon as anything else. Had Broadis shot low then it is easy enough to write that England might have marched on to victory instead of finally having to fight for their lives against brilliantly scientific opponents.*

It seemed, though, to *The Times*' soccer correspondent, that his previous day's optimism about Arthur's temperament had not been fully borne out. Yet he was perceptive enough to realise that, despite his undoubted rich potential, here was a player still limited in top-flight experience:

> *Milton certainly did two or three things in the game to show his undoubted quality, but the occasion and tension generally were too much for him.*

Arthur's own reflections on his performance? 'I drifted out of the game a bit after that opening spell. The ball seemed to keep going over to the left side of the field too – Billy Wright had a strong right foot and kept booming the ball over that way. Perhaps I missed Jimmy Logie, drifting the ball in right to my feet.

'If I was a bit more experienced I would have gone looking for the ball, but I didn't, and drifted out of the game.'

Arthur drifting out of any sporting contest is difficult to imagine, for he was – and always had been – an honest, conscientious man, committed to the task in hand, with a real and overriding desire to play his part in the team effort.

Might there have been – however subconscious – a recognition that no matter how well he played Finney would be back for the next game? Perhaps it was indeed inexperience and yet, when he looked back on his cricket career, he recognised that even as a young inexperienced cricketer he was often at his best when there was a real challenge. Some of his best performances came when a pitch was 'doing a bit' or Gloucestershire had lost early wickets and were up against it.

Others were perhaps able to view his England game more objectively. Those watching from the press box noted that he started superbly, confidently. In the fourth minute he had put Ivor Broadis through for that shot at goal saved brilliantly by Austria's goalkeeper, Walter Zeman, and a second high-speed dribble down the line enabled Arthur to fire across another chance for Broadis. This also went unrewarded.

Arthur's own shot extended the goalkeeper shortly afterwards but, as the game unfolded, he found himself stranded out on the wing. Recognising his talent of speeding down the touchline, beating his full-back and floating in his cross, England's manager, Walter Winterbottom, had earlier told Arthur, 'Stick to the line.' The new cap adhered firmly to the directive. But as the game went on he found himself isolated, and didn't have the confidence or the experience to override (or ignore) his manager's instructions.

Jimmy Logie was disappointed for Arthur and was frustrated on his behalf by his unusually diffident performance – and told him so at end of the game: 'You didn't come off your line at all. What were you up to?'

Ivor Broadis, also making his England debut, having been called up to replace Stan Mortensen, recalled: 'I thought Arthur did well against a good Austrian side. He burst on to the Arsenal scene like Theo Walcott has today, and he could well have earned more than one cap had a Sir Alf Ramsey or a Fabio Capello been in sole charge of selection, but in the '50s an FA selection committee had a big influence on the line-up of an England side.' Offering these thoughts, he wondered if club directors serving on that committee often plumped for 'their man'.

Talking with Arthur about his England cap was to listen to a man who, though quiet and unboastful, was justifiably proud to have played for his country. Had further invitations come he would doubtless have taken them in his stride, for that was his way as well as being the response of the natural sportsman, always ready to test himself against other top players.

Yet he needed to be prompted to talk about the occasion. Many others might talk incessantly about their one game as if they had played numerous times, and might well bore for England about it: 'Alf said this ...'; 'Do you know what Billy Wright did ...?' and more. That was not Arthur's style.

In all of this it's worth remembering that he had been given little more than a day's notice to prepare himself for the big occasion, although Arthur never held this out as any sort of excuse. Barely time to put his kit together, let alone to get mentally prepared. No time to think of match strategies – indeed barely time to discover if England had a strategy. Barely time to get excited.

It's also worth remembering how fate had played its part. Had Tom Whittaker's mission to Blackpool to sign Stanley Matthews proved successful, Arthur's England cap might have been simply a dream. So, too, might have been his Arsenal career. His promotion from Combination League to First Division football and his meteoric ascent to the England team was an astonishing progression.

England ended on level terms with Austria that November afternoon, thanks to an Alf Ramsey penalty and a late Nat Lofthouse goal. The critics generally felt England had played well. Four months later, when England selected their side for their next international – against Scotland at Hampden Park – Tom Finney was back in the no. 7 shirt. Arthur was not chosen again.

There were, though, other times when Arthur felt he might have been within shouting distance of again being selected for his country. He recalled a match against Tottenham Hotspur early in the 1952–53 season when he, along with the rest of the Arsenal team, was definitely on top of his game.

Scottie Hall, reporting for the *Daily Graphic* on 22nd September 1952, waxed lyrical about Arsenal and Arthur Milton:

Arsenal, just like spinach, jellied eels and Miss Tallulah Bankhead's mist-wrapped voice, are an acquired taste. If you like them, you love 'em, and type your letters with a red ribbon. If you don't, and they happen to win, which is an old trick of theirs, you attribute credits to the groundsman, the ball boys – almost anybody but Arsenal.

All of which is beautifully fair in ye olde English manner of agreeing to disagree about such important things as governments, where to spend next year's holiday – and soccer.

But sometimes it is a question of being absolutely fair. Of sprinkling the truth freely, as Mr Arnold Bennett once almost put it.

This is such a moment. Arsenal's 3-1 win over Spurs at White Hart Lane was clear and correct and convincing. It had the thoroughness of the game itself, a sweeping, soaring match that immediately gripped you by the lapels and never let you go.

What a boon to those dollar and sterling credits, about which we hear so much and, personally, know so little, if we could export in quantity such unchallengeable quality.

A light, lean chap with buttercup hair and looking like the 69,000 crowd's kid brother was the top attraction of the topping afternoon.

To an almost poetic Miltonesque beat, and coaxed to his artistic impudences by Jimmy Logie, who refutes the suggestion that the Scots are niggardly about their possessions, Arsenal outside-right Arthur Milton made a brilliant comeback to big-time soccer.

His 'comeback' to football followed a successful summer of cricket. At the beginning of that very same month when he was entrancing the 69,000 crowd at White Hart Lane, he had scored 75 not out and 53 not out for Gloucestershire against Northants. Trumpeting away, Scottie Hall declared:

We thought him a really good player when England picked him against Austria last season, and we kept on thinking

*so despite the Dyspeptic Dismals who flailed him for his
tentative, somewhat apprehensive performance.*
*Milton, despite picking up two bruised ankles, set the mood
of this acquisitive, attacking 'new-look' Arsenal, whose
accuracy and professional crispness really made Spurs look
as if they'd only got as far as chapter one of 'Soccer – How
She is Played'!*

Hall's florid prose might seem to be over-egging it, but those
fortunate enough to see Arthur play in those seasons with Arsenal
when he was on top of his game – and even in his brief spell with
Bristol City – would firmly and happily echo those sentiments. That
was the memory many had captured for posterity, of a truly gifted
player – a 'class' player, an outstanding footballer – whose talents
were thoroughly deserving of Hall's technicolor description.

One of Arthur's memories of that match was the goal he scored.
'Jimmy Logie and I had a fantastic combination and in that game
it produced the best goal I ever scored. I've got a picture of it
somewhere – it shows Ted Ditchburn at full stretch, you know, and
the ball's gone in the top corner.'

He showed me the picture and it's included in this book.
Ditchburn is indeed at full stretch and Bill Nicholson, the Spurs
defender, looks on in amazement. But Arthur is not in the
photograph. His shot was from so far out that the photographer
could not capture both him and the ball hitting the back of the net.

'We always seemed to have it over them, funnily enough, in
those days, and they were great matches to play in. It was the old
local derby. You couldn't beat it, and yet it was all friendly stuff.
Wonderful, wonderful.

'There was a funny story about a time when we played them at
Highbury once – I think it was Highbury. When it was 1-1 – or
maybe it was 2-1 – I got passed the ball coming up the byline, and
l pulled it back and Jimmy popped it in the net. And going back to
the middle and the centre spot again, he came over to me and put
his arms around me in a great bear hug. Well of course no one did
that in those days, no goal-scoring celebrations like that, we just

got on with it. I thought it was bit funny, but didn't say anything then.

'Then, later, when we were towelling down after getting out of the bath, I said to him, "What was all that about?"

'Jim was well known as a snazzy dresser. "Well," he said, "my tailor said that if we beat Spurs – and I scored a goal – he'd give me a new suit, so you've helped me win a new suit. That's why I grabbed you."'

Arthur's telling of that story was so typical. The venue, and the scoreline, were not entirely sharp in his memory but the human element of the story was crystal clear.

More equally illustrious, headline-grabbing and fan-enthralling performances would follow that against Spurs which had so dazzled Scottie Hall and the *Daily Graphic*. But there was to be no England recall for Arthur.

When I tackled Arthur Shaw on this point and asked whether Arthur might have played more for England, he said, 'I don't know – that he was certainly talented enough was not in doubt, but his fast, direct style of play was so far ahead of his time and the thinking of many of those running the game then. Do you know, there were ordinary businessmen picking the England side then – and they didn't know much about the game.'

It would, of course, have been amazingly difficult to take that no. 7 shirt from Finney or Matthews who, between them, won 130 England caps and stood among the game's true 'greats'. To have worn that shirt just once for England, and to have worn it in their place, was indeed a very special feeling for Arthur, one of his sporting high-spots. But he had to be encouraged to share his memories.

One man who needed little prompting to reflect on Arthur's standing in the sporting world was Sir Tom Finney himself, now president of Preston North End FC: 'It is a great honour, and achievement, to have represented his country at both football and cricket, one of the very few to have done it, but then Arthur was a great player at the highest level.'

Praise indeed.

Looking back to Arthur's appearance in an England football shirt we now know – as did Sir Tom Finney when he paid tribute to Arthur – that later, when winning his England Test cap in 1958, he joined that very select group of double internationals. We can say, with virtual certainty, that as the twelfth of that honoured brotherhood, he will also be the very last. It is improbable that anyone – other than the most gifted genius – will ever repeat that feat of being capped by England at both cricket and soccer. In the words of one of Arthur's favourite sayings, 'There'll never be another.'

What can also be said surely is that no England player will ever again win selection after just 12 League games. There will, indeed, never be another like Arthur Milton.

Back at Highbury in 1951–52 Arsenal, with Arthur playing regularly, were enjoying a good season. Until quite late in the campaign they were chasing the League and Cup 'double'. Arthur scored six times and – as always – made many more for others to hit home.

Arsenal's continuing success won them a place in the FA Cup final, to play Newcastle United at Wembley on 3rd May, where they were beaten 1-0. Amazingly, and almost unbelievably, Arthur, after all his dazzling contributions to the team's results, was not selected.

Even now, at this distance in time, it seems remarkable that he had been good enough to play for England in November, and make 20 League appearances for Arsenal that season, and yet the club felt they could go into the FA Cup final without him. He watched the game from Wembley's terraces.

His sole FA Cup appearance that season was in the quarter-final, away to Luton Town. Arsenal won 3-2, and Arthur played well enough, albeit out of position.

'I played in Jim's place in the quarter-final, at inside-forward, and felt I had played pretty well, and the team went well, and then in the semi-final against Chelsea we won 3-0 in the replay. And so we had reached the final, and I got left out. They didn't even want me on the wing.'

Tom Whittaker, not surprisingly, had a different slant on Arthur's non-selection: 'Unfortunately, after an injury Milton did not pick up and by the time we had qualified for Wembley Freddie Cox was back in full possession again.'

Arthur thought there might be another reason. 'Perhaps they thought that, going back to Wembley – because I hadn't had a good game with England there – might affect me. That was daft. Also they looked on Freddie Cox as a bit of a lucky mascot as they'd had some good results when he played. And of course Jimmy had more or less walked out of hospital to play.'

Billy Milne, the club's physiotherapist, had massaged Logie's injured thighs so much and so robustly in attempting to get him fit that, in the process, he put him in hospital.

'He was not a great masseur,' recalled Arthur. 'In trying to "pick up" the muscles, which had a deep-seated bruise, and massage them he pulled the hairs on Jimmy's legs so much that the hair roots became septic.'

The blood poisoning spread within Logie's thigh and he was packed off to hospital for the sepsis to be drained. He was there for five days before being discharged on the Tuesday immediately prior to the final. A walk around Highbury in the sunshine, with an operation wound in his thigh 'big enough to put an apple in', was hardly ideal preparation for a Wembley final.

'And then in the final itself, unfortunately for the club, Wally Barnes did his knee in, in the first five minutes as well, and there were no subs then, of course.'

All this Arthur recounted without a hint of criticism or rancour in his voice – disappointment and surprise, yes, but no criticism of 'the Arsenal'.

The following season, 1952–53 – 'the highlight of my football career when we won the First Division championship' – he played in 25 League games, scoring seven goals. In a close-fought Coronation year championship Arsenal clinched the title at the eleventh hour with a 3-2 victory over Burnley in their final match. Equal on points with Preston North End, Arsenal won by virtue of their better goal average. It was the narrowest victory in the Football League's history – just 0.099 of a goal – and it gave them their seventh title. By then, though, Arthur had returned to Bristol for the start of the cricket programme, but he had made his splendid contribution to the Gunners' success and deserved his League Champions' medal.

As we shared some early thoughts and talks about this book Arthur read to me a newspaper cutting of the day, which said the 1952–53 season 'was a glorious one as Arsenal won the League title for the first time in five years. Arsenal had one of the finest sides in Europe.'

That same newspaper article listed all the key players in Arsenal's Championship-winning side that season. Of those who played more than 20 games there were the celebrated names of Joe Mercer, Jimmy Logie, Alex Forbes and goalkeeper Jack Kelsey; Joe Wade, Lionel Smith, Arthur Shaw and Ray Daniel, who comprised the backs and half-backs; with Don Roper, Doug Lishman, Peter Goring, Cliff Holton in their forward line and, of course, Clement Arthur Milton, all of them members of 'one of the finest sides in Europe'.

Arsenal fans cheered their team as again they progressed to the quarter-finals of the FA Cup. Arthur appeared four times in that campaign, adding one to his FA Cup goal tally.

In the following winter, 1953–54, Arsenal signed Tommy Lawton. A centre-forward famed for his pace, heading ability and two-footed effectiveness in front of goal, Lawton had lost some of his speed at 34, but he put his name on the score-sheet when Arsenal beat Blackpool 3-1 in the FA Charity Shield at Highbury.

Arthur said: 'It was a great experience to play with him. He was past his best when he came to Arsenal but he was still a brilliant player. Joe Mercer was already there, of course, so we had two elder statesmen from the same era and the same area – Liverpool way. They were grand characters. We all looked up to Joe and Tommy.'

That early-season boost for the Gunners proved deceptive, for they finished twelfth in the League. Arthur had missed the Charity Shield match but played in half of Arsenal's 42 First Division games, as usual missing the beginning and end of the campaign because of his cricket commitments. He scored three League goals, with another coming from his two FA Cup appearances. Only Jack Kelsey, Jimmy Logie, Alex Forbes, Don Roper, Doug Lishman, Cliff

Holton, Len Wills, Bill Dodgin and Bill Dickson played more games for the Gunners that year.

But towards Christmas 1954 Arthur began to feel that the great days of Arsenal were fading. His pal Jimmy Logie had left the club by then, under circumstances which Arthur considered unfortunate and dubious. The big playing staffs of which he had been part were not being maintained – big staffs which meant stacks of competition for places, but also high-quality cover when a key player was injured. And, of course, it was this large number of players that allowed the manager to be generous over the comings and goings of his cricketing footballers, whose summer exploits Whittaker admired and which, in his mind, offered Arsenal an added and decided commercial benefit by keeping the club's name to the fore even in the summer months.

Those who have enjoyed good times and tasted success with a club find it hard, and possibly unacceptable, to see standards and ambitions slipping. Arthur felt this to be the case at Arsenal. Logie's departure, which was to spark off Arthur's reflection about his own place in top-class soccer, came about because of a handshake – or rather a handshake that wasn't.

Arsenal were in the vanguard of inviting teams from Europe and further afield to play at Highbury and, in November 1954, they invited Spartak, one of the Soviet Union's top sides, to north London. The Gunners were also among the first of the English clubs to install floodlights, in September 1951. Arthur remembered, 'The lights – it was the early day of floodlights – were fixed to the roof of the stands; they were all along the top of the stand and they didn't offer the same brilliant lighting which current-day floodlights offer. If you punted one up high nobody had a clue where it had gone.'

Whether Spartak's centre-half lost sight of Arthur and the ball, or whether he had evil intentions, will never be known. 'It was near the end of the game and we were getting beat 2-1, with about five minutes to go. I hared past the full-back, and the centre-half had to come out. I was jinking past him,' Arthur recounted, 'and he just took me out with a bad foul.

'The Russian referee, Nikolai Latychev [who would later referee the 1962 World Cup final in Chile] awarded an indirect free kick, but it should truly have been a penalty. It couldn't have been anything else but a penalty.'

The Times shared that view, reporting that when 'the Russians were 2-1 up … Arthur Milton, the dashing winger, drove into their penalty area and was blatantly brought down. Latychev refused a penalty.'

Tom Whittaker recalled events thus: 'Arthur Milton, the fair-haired international winger and top-line cricketer, hared downfield, and roared into the Spartak penalty area at top speed, only to be hurled to the ground by a Russian defender.'

Arthur remembered the next moments clearly: 'What they did was to stand on the goal-line, you know, and so we failed to score. Within a few minutes the ref was blowing the final whistle and walking off.'

The disputed penalty later caused a public slanging match between Whittaker and his Spartak opposite number in the press box at their post-match press conference.

If Whittaker was feeling frustrated, cheated and annoyed he was not alone. Jimmy Logie was livid, and when the referee went across to shake hands with him at the end of the game the Arsenal captain turned away. As he told this story Arthur's voice slipped into quieter mode, suggesting he didn't really approve of Logie's action and yet, at the same time, his regard for Jimmy was not diminished and he understood why he did it.

'That didn't go down well in the boardroom,' Arthur remembered. 'That sort of thing was looked down on. It didn't fit with their public school way of doing things. I understood how strongly Jimmy felt we had been cheated – but he hardly played for the Arsenal again. Jim was transferred to Gillingham shortly afterwards …' – by February 1955, Arthur explained, Gillingham being then a non-League side.

Lionel Smith had been appointed manager at Gillingham after leaving Highbury, where he had been a contemporary of Arthur and Jimmy Logie. 'He was very keen for Jimmy to join them – but so were a few other clubs because he was still such a talented player. Anyway, he had a fistful of pound notes in a suitcase to go down there, so he did all right.'

The recollection of his pal Logie and a case full of pound notes had Arthur chortling away. But there was anguish in his voice too as he recounted the tale and, after a long pause for reflection, ruefully added, 'He had a rather sad life after that.'

Arthur's voice revealed his unease, too, as he remembered the feelings of injustice; frustration that his pal's illustrious top-level career should have been ended in such a sorry and inglorious way; and disillusion stemming from his disgust – albeit voiced with typical understatement and puzzlement that folk could behave in such ways – that those in the boardroom should take such draconian action against a captain who had acted in support of a player he believed had been unfairly treated by centre-half and by referee.

The sorrow in his recollection came, too, in part from the fact that Arthur himself was never a man to question publicly the decisions of umpires or referees; for him to be party, albeit indirectly, to an incident which had far-reaching results and which arose from inept refereeing, was another cause of sadness and hurt. And for a man who could only talk highly of Arsenal – *the* Arsenal – in the warmest and most loyal of tones it was a hard memory to recall.

The incident – and the loss of his team-mate – upset Arthur more than most might have imagined. Only in words left unsaid was there a hint of a rare and reluctant criticism of the Arsenal.

On the cricket front Arthur was, by now, established in the Gloucestershire side. Summers were spent at his parents' home in Bristol and then, in the autumn, he would 'up sticks' again and head for north London, and his Arsenal 'digs' in his early days or, after his marriage to Joan, to his new family home at Brookmans Park in Hertfordshire. It was time to settle down. Here was yet another reason to wind up his soccer career at the end of that 1954–55 season.

'By this time I had been playing both games for five or six years and so I decided I would finish with my football at the end of the '54–55 season while I still had a good pair of legs – even if they were bent and bowed – and concentrate on my cricket.'

In recent times Tom Graveney has remembered, with some amusement, Arthur telling him of that time. 'He said, "Once I got in the side at the Arsenal I had the most magnificent inside-right – Jimmy Logie. When Jimmy left we got a mad Welshman, who ran around like a headless chicken for 90 minutes and I never got a decent ball." And that was part of his decision to finish up there.'

So, just before Christmas 1954, he shared his thoughts with Arsenal's manager. 'I went up to see Tom Whittaker and told him that I was not going to re-sign for the following season.' Whittaker wasn't surprised. Arthur was already facing keen but not unwelcome competition for his place in the League side from Danny Clapton and Derek Tapscott. Having shared these thoughts about his future, he wasn't then greatly surprised or frustrated to find himself in and out of Arsenal's League side for the remainder of that campaign. He played in two FA Cup rounds and eight First Division games, adding three goals to his club tally.

But then, after appearing for the Gunners against Luton Town in a Football Combination match early in the year, 'The manager called me up and said he wanted to talk to me. He'd had a phone call from Bristol City manager Pat Beasley, who was enquiring to see if Tom had any players who might want to come down to the City and give them a hand because they were doing quite well in the Third Division South. They thought that a bit of help from somebody up there at the Arsenal might help them get somewhere and possibly win it. Anyway, I said yes, I was interested.'

Arthur was happy to take up the challenge, especially when his suggestion that he should continue living at home, at Brookmans Park, train locally and join the Robins on match days, gained ready approval from Beasley and his chairman, Harry Dolman. Arthur was transferred to City on 16th February 1955. The transfer fee – for the remainder of that season – was £4,000. It was a fee which carried a rider, of which more anon.

Bournemouth and Boscombe Athletic's Dean Court ground could not match Highbury or Wembley; a crowd of 9,888 was modest enough compared with the thousands upon thousands who had watched him play in Division One; but Arthur's goal there – the only one of the match – allowed Bristol City to hold firmly on to the hopes of a title, the title they went on to win on the last day of the season. It was his last goal, his last game, and a good – and happy – note on which Arthur, a proud son of Bristol, could end his career.

Arthur played 14 games for Bristol City – during which the side was unbeaten. So he finished his soccer career in the medals again, with a Third Division League winners' medal, although under the rules he shouldn't have been given one.

'I think I played 14 games for the City – just one short of the 15 I had to play to qualify for a medal, but they did one especially for me anyway. We finished up comfortably on top – and by scoring in my last match I finished in style. It turned out that was the end of my football days, helping my home city club win the League. It was a nice way to finish my football.'

Football had given him some wonderful memories. His time at Arsenal had won him many deserved plaudits, many friends among fellow players and admiration from legions of supporters. Of all of these, and of the benevolent way the club had looked after him, he had scarcely anything but the happiest recollections. To all of this he could add the privilege of wearing the no. 7 shirt for England, and then rounding off his career by helping his home team win honours. This all counted for a lot.

He had made his mark, on team-mates, opponents and others of his peers; on the vast crowds who thrilled to the skill, the style and the joy of his play; and on countless youngsters who had idolised him and been inspired by him, whose memories of Arthur were fixed in the increasingly valued cigarette card collections from which his fair-haired 'kid brother' image ceaselessly, yet shyly smiled.

But from now on he would concentrate on his cricket. That was his firm intention. It was, however, an intention that faced an immediate challenge.

Joe Mercer, his former Arsenal captain and pal, sought to tempt him to stay in football. It was an offer hard to resist – especially when the offer came from a friend he respected so much and whose company he enjoyed.

Mercer had signed for Arsenal midway through the 1946 season when Everton, believing he was past his prime, treated him less than sympathetically. As is often the case, the change of club re-invigorated his career and he enjoyed a splendid Indian summer with the Gunners. If his game was slightly less adventurous than in his halcyon Everton and England days, he continued to show all the gifts of a distinguished left-half. More importantly, he was the most inspiring of captains.

Mercer, who played 275 times in all for Arsenal, had decided to retire at the end of the 1952–53 season. Second thoughts sidelined that plan and he returned to Highbury for one more campaign. Towards the end of that final season, with retirement now imminent, he was particularly keen to play for the club in their game against Liverpool at Highbury on 1st April 1954. Alas, he broke a leg and was carried off on a stretcher. Still showing natural courage, with a cheery wave he bade farewell to the fans who had admired him so long and who now cheered him loudly and with warm affection as his glorious playing career came to its end in this unfortunate and unanticipated way.

Mercer had certainly inspired Arthur. 'We seemed to share the same values and play the game with the same outlook. Joe was a great fellow. He didn't always train with us at Highbury, he trained at home, because he had married into quite a big business family, I think. Anyway, he used to come up on a Friday, and do a little bit, just to stretch his legs and get loosened up, and the thing was that he always used to come and grab me' – Arthur still sounding incredulous and surprised some 50 years later – 'to train with him. So I used to do a few laps and a few sprints with him, that sort of thing. And he kept doing it, so one day I said to him, "Joe, why is it that you ask me to come out with you?"

'"Well," he said, "You're the only chap who's got legs as bandy as mine."

'On Saturdays, match days, we used to have a light lunch down at the Kings Cross Hotel and then go up to the ground, on the coach, up to the match. Very often they used to have a chat, the manager and the powers-that-be, about the game coming up, about how we were going to play and what-have-you. We'd go up and get changed, get ready and, when it was time to go out on to the field, Joe would have the ball, and he'd lead us out. We'd be going down the tunnel before we got out on to the pitch, and just as we got to the bottom he'd turn round and say, "Right lads, forget all that – let's go out and enjoy ourselves." Amazing.'

Of Joe's career-ending injury, Arthur recalled, 'They said it was like a gun going off, you could hear it the other side of the park.' It was bad break, but it led to Mercer taking the first steps on a colourful and successful managerial career, which would reach its pinnacle in 1974 with his seven-match spell as the popular and admired caretaker-manager of England.

The first rung of this managerial ladder was at Sheffield United, and so great was Mercer's admiration that when he heard Arthur was thinking of packing up the game, he implored him to join him at Bramall Lane. And he suggested Arthur could name his own salary, and offered to let him train at home (so long as he turned up fit and ready to play on match days). That was some compliment from an excellent judge of a player and an outstandingly good man-manager.

Arthur's recall of that offer also says something about his high regard for the avuncular Mercer and for the generosity and enthusiasm of his approach, although we need to remember that the professional footballers' maximum wage of £20 per week was still in place, and would remain so until the end of the decade when the campaigning of the Professional Footballers' Association, led by its dynamic chairman, Jimmy Hill, led to the removal of this outdated restriction.

The offer was tempting – for Arthur principally because of the man who made it, rather than the opportunity itself. But his head was not turned. Young though he was – too young for retirement, some might argue – he had made up his mind. Cricket it was to be.

Even so he was rather surprised – and amused too – not to receive some sort of offer from Bristol City. After all, he had helped them win promotion, he was in his prime and an international player and this, added to his First Division experience, could have been worth its weight in gold to the Robins. Then Arthur remembered the rider clause in his transfer fee. Shrewdly, Bristol City had negotiated a 50 per cent reduction in the £4,000 fee if he did not play for them beyond the end of the 1954–55 season. It seemed City's board, clinging to that shrewdness, had decided finances held sway over footballing considerations – so no invitation came from Ashton Gate. And a little later a cheque for £2,000 was winging its way back to Ashton Gate from Highbury.

I asked Arthur Shaw if he was surprised that Arthur had given up soccer so soon at the relatively young age of 27.

'Well, not really. That was him. After his early years, and his regard for the high standards which the club then had – you know, with 40 or so players on the staff – he began to feel frustrated that those standards were allowed to slip. Good players were not replaced in the same way, and the size of the staff got smaller. Arthur sensed that things were not going to be the same again – as did one or two others of us. But he'd got his cricket, and decided to concentrate on that.

'It might have been different if they'd known better how to harness his special talent. Do you know, with the modern soccer ball, the lighter plastic one, instead of that old leather one we used to have – which got heavier and heavier as it got wet and muddy – he'd have been the best of the lot, Thierry Henry included, and he's a great player of course.

'Arsenal have always handled these things in the right way. It was very rare for someone to be sacked or simply be transferred. It was always one of Arsenal's principles – and I believe it may be the same today – that players left on their own terms rather than being sacked. There was a real family feel to the club. A lot of other clubs think they have it, but it's not quite like Arsenal.'

And so, with thoughts of soccer at Highbury, at Ashton Gate, and (almost) at Bramall Lane with Joe Mercer now firmly behind him, the 'light, lean chap with buttercup hair ...' waved farewell to his illustrious soccer career.

Having graced the game so handsomely it does seem truly remarkable – and maybe surprising – from our vantage point today that, at 27 and arguably at the zenith of his footballing prowess, with potentially four or five more good soccer seasons ahead of him, Arthur felt it was time to move on. The summer game would now be the focus of his undivided attention and his immense natural talents. Cricket it was indeed to be.

Chapter 6

Capped by Gloucestershire and Nearly by England

WINNING AN ENGLAND soccer cap after just 12 First Division games was truly remarkable. On the other hand, a wait until his tenth season as a cricket professional to win an England Test cap was not unremarkable.

The honour came Arthur's way when England picked him to play against New Zealand at Headingley at the beginning of July 1958. His Test cap immediately conferred another honour – that of joining that most select group of gifted sportsman who have been capped by their country at both soccer and cricket.

He recognised his good fortune in playing at a time when soccer and cricket seasons barely overlapped. It was a time, too, when benevolent goodwill existed between most sports, and between their players and administrators, as well as with the sporting public at large. Multi-talented sportsmen and women were widely admired and greatly encouraged.

As always, Arthur happily took each step as he encountered it – all part of his continuing and unstudied sporting progress.

It was as if these opportunities came to him, fell into his lap, for there was little sense of his actively seeking them out. Indeed, playing two sports professionally at the highest level from 1949 until 1955 seemed to him nothing more than the natural and obvious thing to do.

And that wait until 1958 to win his England cricket cap conveys no suggestion that here was a slow developer. Far from it. Arthur's talent was apparent from his earliest years. A good few who watched him playing for Soundwell or Stapleton, or for Gloucestershire Seconds, must have predicted: 'Young Arthur (or 'Archie') – he's an England player in the making.'

Rather, his climb to international honours perhaps reflected the slower, more contemplative nature of cricket, which had – and has – in England, at least, little tradition of players rocketing to international recognition. It reflects, too, the greater competition there was among young county cricketers to shine and grab headlines.

As right-wing for Arsenal Arthur would have been compared with the 20 or so other outside-rights in the First Division. However, with five, six, and sometimes seven English batsmen in each of 17 county sides – overseas stars were then a rare exception – many more sought to catch the eye of selectors. As county staffs grew larger after the immediate postwar years the competition was even greater.

In the late Forties and early Fifties many young batsmen like Arthur were expected to start 'down the order' and work their way up. That depended, of course, on their own talents, coupled with an ability to display that talent consistently.

Established players played longer, too, in that era. It was by no means unusual for professional cricketers to play on into their forties. They were seldom willing to give up their careers prematurely – many knew little else – for a young pretender. 'Dead men's shoes' was undoubtedly a facet of the game then.

Whenever talking cricket with Arthur, especially talking of Gloucestershire cricket, it wasn't long before two names revered by the county's fans would trip admiringly off his tongue: 'Jack' and 'George'.

Jack Crapp's and George Emmett's names were spoken with a note of reverence, and almost awe, by Arthur, and invariably with the warmest admiration and appreciation. Making tuneful harmony with those sentiments was the high regard of one who felt immensely privileged to have grown to know them as respected team-mates and solid friends.

Jack and George were senior pros, established players when Arthur joined the county staff. From them he learned a great deal – perhaps all the essentials there were to know about county cricket. He might have expected them to be like other gnarled old pros – keen to encourage talented young players, but recognising the upstarts had their place – their proper place – and needed to win their spurs in the heat of battle. Gnarled old pros often felt young players were granted no favours by being given a too-easy promotion.

But Jack and George were different. Or perhaps it was that they saw in young Arthur something decidedly different, something special.

And they would not be the first – nor the last – to warm to this delightful man and his sporting gifts. Talented sportsman though he was, there was indeed something else, something about Arthur which people genuinely warmed to. His gentle good nature was endearing; his seemingly eternal, youthful looks were appealing; his unassuming lack of 'side', and his willingness to listen to others' stories rather than tell his own made others feel comfortable and relaxed in his company.

Even a sporadic off-day in the dressing room if he was being a 'right royal pain' or showing a propensity for being wise after the event (which some hinted at) – he was human after all – was almost always forgivingly discounted as a once-in-a-while contrast to those more accustomed qualities which made Arthur Milton a valued and respected team-mate and good friend. Rare was the individual who did not feel infinitely better for sharing his company.

Batting at the top, or early order, of Gloucestershire's line-up, as George and Jack had done for years with immense success, they also recognised a national need. England, in their view, needed a young opening batsman, for no one had made that position their own since Len Hutton – and, for much of his time at the top of England's batting order, he had no settled partner, apart that is from a spell when Cyril Washbrook opened with him. There was a place to be filled.

Arthur, they thought, had a good chance of playing for England – especially as an opener. Jack and George encouraged Arthur to take this step – and in some regards they made way for him. Their altruism for ever made Arthur think as generously of them as he thought of Arsenal and the beneficent way the Gunners had looked after him (and other young players). His gratitude knew no bounds.

Chatting with Arthur about his career made one immediately conscious that statistics and records had little interest for him. 'Oh, I was batting at six or seven …' or 'I probably scored 80 or so …' or 'I'm not sure whether I got more than one wicket in that spell …' or 'Did we play them at Clacton or was it Leyton …?' were typical *en passants* as he told his story. That might have suggested a sometimes less-than-sharp memory in a near-80-year-old recovering from a mild stroke a few months earlier, but much more was it due to his characteristic, natural trait of valuing the human dimension of cricket and of the countless incidents and stories forming the rich treasure-house of his memories.

It would be unfair, then, to him and to his memory to pepper his story with unnecessary stats. It would have been the last thing he wanted.

Nevertheless I felt a need to get an overview of his career. A brief recourse to the records was required – and in a way that would, I sense, have appealed to the mathematician in Arthur.

When compiling the season-by-season aggregate of his runs scored in first-class innings, it became obvious that for 20 seasons – apart from a decided case of 'second seasonitis' in 1950 – each summer's results showed an improvement on its predecessor.

Such a pattern of inexorable improvement would, of course, produce a profile like a single high mountain peak, with a rapid and sustained climb to the summit or high mountain plateau followed, probably, by a slope slipping away gently from the summit towards his career's end.

In Arthur's case, what broke up this single high-mountain pattern of year-upon-year improvement was the appearance of four 'valleys' among his seasonal aggregates. Each, it must be noted, coincided with a significant injury which set him back, albeit temporarily, before the season-on-season improvement was resumed the following year.

Tony Brown reflected one day: 'The poor old bugger was always injured.' An element of poetic licence and 'sportsmanese' lies within this recollection from an admiring but objective friend. Arthur was not always injured. Indeed, he was very seldom injured in the sense of bruised fingers, pulled muscles, muscle strains, back or hamstring problems or other 'niggles' experienced by many others. Such indispositions featured rarely in his career. Serious injuries apart he hardly missed a game, and he recognised his good fortune, as well as the blessings his natural athleticism freely offered.

But Tony's 'always' pointed more to the fact that when Arthur was injured, it was often a more serious injury, and one which kept him out of action for a while. Frustratingly, those injuries invariably seemed to come when he was in really good form.

That was true of 1953 (groin strain), of 1957 (damaged wrist), 1960 (broken thumb), 1964 (broken arm), and 1970 (fractured arm). In 1953 he also missed Gloucestershire games when on twelfth man duty for England.

But let's not race ahead.

There he was, just 21, a capped player in his first season as a county cricketer, with his National Service behind him, and on the threshold of what was to prove a meteoric soccer career.

At the Cheltenham Festival that year he fell victim to Tony Lock, the first of 16 occasions on which the Surrey left-arm spinner captured his wicket, making Lock the bowler who took Arthur's wicket more than any other in his first-class career. Derek Shackleton dismissed him 15 times, and Lock's spin twin, Jim Laker, succeeded on 14 occasions.

All three, of course, were very fine bowlers but, when asked about bowlers who had the 'fluence' over him during his career, Arthur was gloriously (and typically) vague. None particularly sprang into his mind. 'I really didn't mind who was bowling when I was in good form.' A second or two's further thought prompted him to offer the names of bowlers who brought out the best in him: 'Lindwall and Miller, Heine and Adcock.' A few other top-class batsmen must have shared the same thought.

By the end of the 1949 season – his first as a professional – he had scored 960 runs in the county's first-class matches. *Wisden* noted that he had 'played many excellent innings, often when conditions helped the bowlers, and fielded splendidly'.

As he recalled his early years, his thoughts darting here and there, each memory triggering another marvellous tale, it was fascinating to hear still in Arthur's voice and words a sense of the almost impressionable, eager-to-learn youngster who, like many new young pros of his time knew his place – to be seen and not heard. The freshness of it all, the excitement and novelty of the new experiences – which in many ways he never lost – shone through his memories.

Two years with the Army had made him streetwise, and his pleasingly successful first season as a pro verified he had no need to doubt his cricketing skills. At every level at which he had played, those skills amply affirmed he was a player of remarkable gifts; not that they seemed anything but natural to Arthur. But his boyish charm and demeanour and his never-dimmed appreciative delight at his lot rang out constantly, as did his lack of pomp – features that many swiftly and cynically lose but which, by and large, Arthur Milton retained wholeheartedly throughout his life.

Those memories reflected – faithfully, I believe – how he felt at the time. And yet, in the eyes of team-mates he was no typical wide-eyed rookie. His place as an Arsenal footballer, alongside his obvious and undoubted cricketing talents and rich potential, certainly gave him a certain status in the eyes of fellow cricket pros even in his earliest seasons.

Tony Brown, who joined Gloucestershire's staff in 1953, recalls his early memories of Arthur: 'Having seen him play against Austria I knew who he was but the thing was, he wasn't there at the start of pre-season practice when I first played, as he was still playing soccer. He usually stayed with Arsenal until nearly the end of their season and then would come back to us, perhaps with time to get a bit of cricket pre-season training in, but he would be available usually by the time of our first game at Oxford.

'We always played Oxford University the first game of the season – always Cup final Saturday – so you'd see Arthur then. But for all us youngsters around that time, Arthur Milton, and Tom Graveney, who was an international cricketer – and Arthur, of course, was an international footballer – were something special, someone inspiring, and someone you aspired to be like. Neither of them had any "side" on them, or was in any way unapproachable. In fact they were good guys and friendly, even if you sort of waited until you were spoken to.

'And then gradually – particularly after my National Service – I got to know Arthur. My parents lived just round the corner from where Arthur and Joan lived and we, Judy [Tony's wife] and I, started to baby-sit for them sometimes, and so I got to know him almost more through off-the-field contact at that stage. And of course we became really good and close friends, as did Joan and Judy.

'I played for the RAF and some Combined Services cricket, but I didn't play for the county during my National Service – though I did play some Second XI cricket for them. So it wasn't really until 1957, when I became a regular in the side, that I really got to know Arthur, and then to realise what a brilliant performer he was.'

There would be many more summers when, to echo *Wisden*'s words, Arthur 'would bat excellently' – especially, it seemed, when conditions helped the bowlers or when Gloucestershire, one way or another, were up against it. And, of course, he could only ever field superbly.

In his second summer, 1950, Arthur did not excel quite as had been anticipated. A second-season setback is a common enough experience for many young players, and some more mature ones, too, in their second summer in the game. It might come from a player resting, subconsciously, on the laurels of a promising first summer. More likely it comes because bowlers, to whom the first-season tyro was an unfamiliar quantity, have retained an impression of the player and realised how to counter their strengths and exploit their weaknesses.

His long-time Arsenal pal, Jimmy Gray, a stalwart and high-scoring opening batsman for Hampshire, remembers the first time they were opponents on the cricket field. It was in June 1950, and it offered an insight into why Arthur was known to moan about the Bristol pitch. 'This match is, perhaps, an example of why Art didn't play more games for England. Thirty wickets fell in the match, 24 of them to spinners. The Bristol wicket was renowned for being prepared for spinners. The sand, which must have been washed into the surface, helped their spinners Goddard, Cook, Mortimore, Allen and Wells. Fair enough, it won them a lot of games, but it has to be remembered that Arthur, Tom and the rest had to bat on those pitches, a far different situation from that faced by Surrey's batsmen or Nottinghamshire's.'

Whatever the reason, Arthur's second season was deemed 'disappointing'. This, in retrospect, seems harsh for, in weight of runs, this summer was barely less productive than its predecessor when he had created such a favourable impression. Perhaps his first summer had raised expectations unduly. Perhaps he had been expected to 'kick on' more in 1950. As might be assumed with such an exceptionally talented player there were, however, some definite high spots.

In a hard-fought match against Yorkshire at Bristol he battled away for more than three hours to avoid the follow-on, scoring 59 in the process, and followed this with 77 not out in a second-innings knock of two-and-a-half hours which saved the game for the county.

Against Glamorgan, at the Wagon Works, Gloucester, in mid-June he took five first-innings wickets for 64 runs in 27 overs as Glamorgan made 400. His victims were Emrys Davies, Allan Watkins, Jim Pleass, Len Muncer and Haydn Davies. It would remain his career-best bowling figures and a career-long highlight.

Nineteen fifty-one was the season when he passed 1,000 runs for the first time (a milestone he passed in 16 of the following 24 summers). His maiden first-class century was one of two he scored that summer against Somerset, who would see him hit eight more hundreds against them before he finally put his bat away in the cupboard. He followed that first century at Taunton by rattling up 120 almost three months later at Bristol. In both games Gloucestershire went on to win.

It was in 1951, of course, that he first opened the innings for the county. Arthur joined George Emmett at the top of the order when injury sidelined Martin Young. To a player who was always happy to talk about the game, and to assimilate yet more from watching others' techniques, what a valuable education that must have offered.

It was a pairing which – in its short life – prospered. They shared three century opening partnerships that summer, including one of 193 against Somerset (out of Gloucestershire's first-innings score of 299-9 declared) in the game where Arthur posted his second century.

Another relished partnership was with his other mentor, Jack Crapp, when they added 158 against Hampshire, at the Wagon Works ground.

At the same ground, in late July, he gamely resisted the spin and the combined wiles of Laker and Lock, battling to keep Gloucestershire in the game – though Lock ultimately would get his wicket in both innings (and Surrey would win the match). Conditions proved abundantly helpful to Surrey's renowned spin duo in Gloucestershire's second innings, but Arthur's innings of 55 displayed the full palette of his batting talents as well as his typically stout and obdurate response to a challenge.

A few days later he took his season's tally of wickets, in a season when he was seldom called on to bowl, from eight to ten when, against Lancashire, he twice captured Cyril Washbrook's wicket, one with the help of a memorable 'caught and bowled'.

'We were playing Lancashire at Blackpool. Washy was playing; I'm not sure whether he was captain, perhaps he was. They batted first. I used to get on a bit with the ball, and I finished up bowling to Washy. I bowled him one and it swung a little bit, and he hit the deck a bit, as you do, and the ball went off the edge to Jack Crapp at first slip. And Washy stood there because he wasn't sure; you don't realise you've hit it as well, so the umpire had to give him out.'

In Gloucestershire's first innings Arthur had suffered one of his very rare run outs. 'I was "in" and we were going well, and I hit one towards extra cover. Washy was at cover, and he picked it up and threw the bowler's wicket down.

'In their second innings I'm bowling to him again, and he'd got a few on the board. He was a very on-side player. And I bowled a full toss to him. Now I knew where he was going to hit it – he was going to hit it mid-on way. So I started to go over there to field it really. But it was airborne – and I finished up catching it out there somewhere' (indicating a long way out).

'After the match he comes up to me. He said, "Do you always catch those?"

'I said, "Do you always hit that one wicket?" and we had a good laugh together.'

This story was triggered by my asking Arthur about his best, or most memorable catch. 'Well, I suppose I could nominate quite a few. Obviously there were some sharp ones at slip or at short leg, and some out in the deep, which were pleasing, but I do remember catching Washy in this way. I always remember this one because of the circumstances of it.'

When he returned to his summer sport in 1952, with that Wembley international and another successful season for the Gunners behind him, his spirits were high and he enjoyed his most successful cricket season to date. Playing in all Gloucestershire's 28 championship games, his 1,922 runs at 43.68 put him in tenth place in the national averages. Hundreds against Kent (at Bristol), Nottinghamshire (at Trent Bridge, where the off-duty L/Cpl Milton had earlier enjoyed free afternoons), and against Sussex (at Hove, where he also held eight catches in the match) contributed to this total.

Every aspect of his game was well oiled that summer. His 55 catches put him second in the catchers' table, just behind Stuart Surridge, Surrey's inspirational captain and voracious fielder. And 15 batsmen found his bowling more deceptive than it looked.

Such form prompted some commentators to pen their most lyrical phrases. The *Playfair Cricket Annual* reflected:

> *Milton advanced surely along his primrose path with an urbanity and a cultured ease that belied his toughness in adversity.*

Arthur once read this quote to me, and laughed, amused and still not believing the purple (or even primrose) prose even after all the intervening years.

A more restrained *Cricketer* magazine declared him,

> *... the most dependable batsman in the side ... always at his best when the team was in a tight corner.*

It was in 1953 that Arthur received his first call from England's cricket selectors. Perhaps he recognised promptly the need not to raise his hopes too high for, when the call first came, it was to invite him as twelfth man for England's first Test against Australia at Trent Bridge. But clearly he was in the reckoning. *The Times* wrote:

> *The England cricket team to play Australia in the first Test match, which will be begun at Trent Bridge on Thursday, will be chosen from the following players: L Hutton (Yorkshire) (captain), TE Bailey (Essex), RT Simpson (Nottinghamshire) PBH May (Surrey), DCS Compton (Middlesex), AV Bedser (Surrey), TG Evans (Kent), R Tattersall (Lancashire), TW Graveney (Gloucestershire), JB Statham (Lancashire), GAR Lock (Surrey), DJ Kenyon (Worcestershire). Twelfth man, CA Milton (Gloucestershire).*

Their cricket correspondent then went on to debate whether the side should be packed with batsmen: Hutton, Kenyon, Simpson, Compton, May and Graveney, leaving four bowlers (plus wicketkeeper Godfrey Evans) to contain the Australians on a wicket notoriously unfriendly to bowlers, or whether one of Peter May, Tom Graveney, Reg Simpson or Don Kenyon should be omitted. What an immense embarrassment of riches – and what a selectorial choice to make.

Arthur's position was highlighted by The Thunderer:

CHOSEN FOR FIELDING
Now they have invited 13 players to gather at Nottingham under the captaincy of Hutton. One of these, Milton, on the threshold of joining the select band who have played football and cricket for England, will remain twelfth man irrespective of weather and wicket. He earns this opening distinction in his summer career on his magnificent fielding alone. Thus we are left with 12 men – six batsmen pure and simple, five bowlers, and Evans behind the stumps. Who will be discarded?

Arthur's 'magnificent fielding' – a part of the game he always loved – was perennially of the highest class, from his earliest days until he played his very last game. 'Without a doubt – looking back on it – my fielding was the best part of my game. And the main reason would be, especially from the batting point of view too, that you were doing it for the bowlers. They sweat away all day, and they don't get many chances to get people out in a day's play, do they? So if anything goes astray, that doesn't help them very much. So you really want to catch 'em when they come along if you can. "Taking catches wins you matches" is a great old adage, and I'm a great believer in that. So it used to sharpen my concentration.'

That was clearly in the selectors' minds when they called him up (in itself a measure of the good impressions he had already forged). However, as *The Times'* cricket correspondent perceptively recognised, Arthur's progress in all departments of his game, in four seasons as a professional cricketer, had brought him to 'the threshold of joining the select band who have played football and cricket for England'.

It was as twelfth man that he was called up again for the second Test, at Lord's. Much as the selectors valued his fielding, they recognised that, on Test duty as a substitute fielder, he was missing games when he should be playing, so he was allowed to rejoin his county. Here he scored three centuries during the summer: against Somerset – again – at Taunton; against the Combined Services, for whom Doug Padgett (Yorkshire), Mike Ainsworth (Worcestershire), Roy Swetman (Surrey and Glos), John Mortimore (Glos), 'Bomber' Wells (Glos and Notts) and Terry Spencer (Leics) represented stiff opposition at Bristol; and against Nottinghamshire at Trent Bridge.

How he relished playing at Taunton and Trent Bridge – but he still scored his centuries, too, at Bristol.

He seemed always to play his best when Gloucestershire were up against it, as demonstrated by three of his seven half-centuries, made in low-scoring games against Nottinghamshire (at the Wagon Works) and against Warwickshire and Essex, both at Bristol.

'Now that summer of 1953 was when I missed a few matches for Gloucestershire – for two different reasons, the first being I was selected as twelfth man for England versus Australia, which meant I missed two championship matches each time, and then, later on, I had a groin strain which meant I missed six or seven games altogether. So my total was not as good as in previous years.'

He played in only 19 of Gloucestershire's 28 championship matches in 1953. Nevertheless he scored more than 1,000 runs for the county. If he rarely bowled that summer, his near-infallible catching ensured 36 batsmen returned to the dressing room earlier than they had hoped.

Looking back on his selection as England's twelfth man, Arthur recalled, 'Any twelfth man will tell you there's no fun in doing that job. Yes, it's nice to be caught up in the atmosphere and see the cricket at close quarters but there were always hundreds of autographs to get done and drinks for players and suchlike – and in that first match I didn't get on the field at all.'

His call-up definitely raised his hopes of being capped by England and these were given a further boost at the start of the following season when he was chosen to play for MCC against Surrey, the champion county. England's selectors then had an input into the MCC side, more so than today, when the tradition of blooding potential England players seems largely to have been dispensed to the past.

But we're racing on, and we should let Arthur recall his memories of those early days with Gloucestershire, and of his team-mates, and also of another major landmark in his life.

Chapter 7

Don't Get Tangled Up with your Landlady's Daughter!

THOSE OF A certain vintage will readily recall 1953, a year that stands out brightly in warm and affectionate remembrance. The Queen's Coronation was undeniably the highlight of an amazing year in which Edmund Hillary and Tenzing Norgay became the first to reach the summit of Everest, Francis Crick and James Watson's inspired science unlocked the detailed structure of DNA, and Len Hutton's England side regained the Ashes after 20 years. Moved and cheered by the Coronation and by its new young Queen, the nation and its people again began to blossom confidently. The sacrifices, restrictions and dowdiness of the war years were being left behind.

As we have seen in Arthur's two parallel sporting careers, 1953 provided notable landmarks of its own, with a League Championship winners' medal won with Arsenal and his call-up to England's cricket squad. It would provide, too, one other landmark, one that in his eyes overrode all the others and remained of paramount importance for the remainder of his life.

On 22nd August 1953 he and Miss Joan Gore were married.

Arthur and Joan had first met some three or four years earlier, when Arsenal arranged for Arthur and Don Oakes to lodge with

Mr and Mrs Gore, Joan and her younger brother, Peter, at Muswell Hill.

Arthur was never less than warm and appreciative when talking of the 'digs' Arsenal arranged for him. He had been very happy at Hendon prior to moving in with Joan's parents. All had provided a home-from-home for Arthur and for Don.

His new Muswell Hill digs, with the Gores, were equally welcoming – and a little different. Joan's father was a man of many parts. An electrical engineer, he was able to make or mend almost anything, including constructing the family's first television. He was a talented signwriter too, commissioned by universities to create laboratory-sized wall charts of the periodic tables. He loved music, played the saxophone and clarinet, and took his family to concerts. There was always music in the Gore home, and Joan's enduring love of music stems from this.

Arthur dates his love of classical music and concert-going to this same period, and ascribes it to Joan's encouragement. Their son Richard later threw some light on this: 'Although he excelled academically, access to "highbrow" music and the arts would have been limited for Dad growing up and it was Mum who opened the door for him to these things.

'Although Dad was not a musician, he had good rhythm – which he always said you needed to play sport, particularly golf – and he could certainly hold a tune when he sang.' His choirboy's training had not been for nothing.

Multi-talented though Joan's father was, in other ways he was decidedly conservative, which makes it surprising that he readily agreed to accommodate young professional footballers. Perhaps it was Joan's mother's keen love of soccer, and of Arsenal in particular, that provided the key.

In an age when few women supported football both Joan and her mother regularly watched the game. Joan recalled: 'Mum and I went to every match at Highbury, whether it was the reserves or the first team – and we sometimes got to away matches as well.'

Her reminiscing had Arthur quipping mischievously: 'When I was playing and they came to the game I had to be on my best form, mind, otherwise they'd be yelling at me out of the West Stand. They were great days.'

It was a sentiment Joan spontaneously and warmly endorsed: 'Oh, they were wonderful, they really were.'

With her love of football it was not surprising that Arthur had 'star' appeal in Joan's eyes, not least because he was 'very handsome, and a lovely, gentle, kind – and good – man'. But it was in fact Arthur's more cerebral skills which first appealed to Joan.

She was in the middle of her School Cert exams, finding maths hard, and needed help. Dads may be the obvious, but not necessarily the most fruitful, port of call for such help for teenage daughters. Maths was Arthur's subject, something he enjoyed, and so it was a pleasure, and certainly no great chore, for him to exercise his mind by helping his landlady's daughter prepare for her exams.

Mr Gore was doubtless grateful for the help their young house guest gave his daughter in this very practical way but when – and no one is quite sure when it was – the mathematics gave way to deeper feelings he wasn't quite so enthusiastic.

Joan takes up the story: 'He was a lovely man, my Dad, but he was very conventional. Dad played golf himself but he wasn't interested in any other sport.' While Joan was recounting this, Arthur was amused and good-heartedly interjected: 'Mind you, his own father was quite a games player.'

'That's right,' affirmed Joan. 'My Dad's dad … he and Arthur would have been absolutely on the same wavelength in every way because he was a clever man, an accountant, good with figures, a racing man and a sportsman – he played billiards and won many trophies, swam and sculled. He was a "bit of a devil" in a way.

'Grandad would take us to the pub sometimes. I sat outside – I was quite young then – and would have some crisps and he would sometimes come out to give me a sip of his beer! But my Dad was not at all like that.

'Dad had high hopes that I might marry someone from an office, or from a bank; someone "conventional". Having a sportsman for a son-in-law was completely out of his realm. My mother, of course, was more in favour, and not only because she liked her football. Dad and Arthur really became quite close later on but, at the time, he wasn't keen on me marrying a sportsman who played football.'

As an accomplished musician Mr Gore was a cultured man, and it may be that this, and a certain 'class' feeling (which still prevailed in the Fifties when soccer would have been perceived in many quarters as working class), made him feel uncomfortable about the prospect of a footballer as a son-in-law – even if he was an England player, and had excelled academically.

By this time Arsenal had found other digs for Arthur– not for any sinister or style-cramping reason, although it was, as Arthur laughingly recounted, 'an unwritten and very firm Arsenal rule that you didn't get tangled up with your landlady's daughter.' By then he and Joan had become an 'item' but, to spare her father's apprehensions, they would meet secretly. They rapidly recognised they were made for each other.

In Arthur's case it seemed so obvious that he never actually got round to asking Joan to marry him. Smiling affectionately, Joan explained: 'We got engaged in 1952, although he never actually proposed to me. He simply said, one day, "When are we going to get married?" In Artie's mind it was very much a question of "when" not "if".

'That was Artie. As in so many things he was laid back. He didn't even buy our engagement ring. I liked to do things properly, but he was quite relaxed about all those sort of things. I thought it was the right thing to do to have an engagement ring, so Mum came with me one day to choose my ring, when Arthur was playing football.'

Arthur takes up the story again, 'We got married in 1953, on 22nd August. I should say that around the time we decided to get married I went up to see Tom Whittaker, because the Arsenal had a number of houses on their books to use for their players, especially when they were making new signings. I was at Highbury when Tom Lawton arrived and he was given an Arsenal house.

'As I was playing both games at the time, I thought it might be handy for us to have a home at the London end because, at that stage, I always stayed with Mum and Dad when I was in Bristol.

'So I went up to the office and asked the manager about it, about using one of the club houses if one was available. I shall never forget what Tom said to me. "Well, Arthur, you're playing both games now and I think you're in a position to start buying your own house."

'And for once in my life I listened to somebody – and of course never regretted it, never regretted it for one moment.'

This seemed a strange remark for Arthur to have made as, to those who knew him well, he was never an obvious 'know-it-all'. Invariably he was his own man, happy to make up his own mind, happy to make his own decisions, not one to unthinkingly follow the crowd, but he never came across as obviously pig-headed. In fact, he always seemed open to the knowledge and experiences of others. In telling the story, had he recalled a hint of such a trait in himself when he was a young man?

Mind you, family, team-mates and friends knew he had a canny knack of avoiding doing something if he didn't want to do it, or felt uncomfortable about it. He wouldn't make any great scene, or throw a tantrum, there would be no rows or raised voices; he merely closed his mind to it and simply never got round to it. It seemed to him the prudent thing to do.

Tom Whittaker's advice was heeded. 'We bought our house in Brookmans Park, a nice area not too far from North Mymms, Hertfordshire, just off the old A1.

'We got married there, in North Mymms Church. It was nice, very small, a lovely little church. My Mum and Dad came up from Bristol, and Joan's family were there of course. And Don Oakes was my best man, yes, dear old Don,' and not for the first, or the last, time in our memory-trawling Arthur's voice choked momentarily as he recalled both his wedding day and the part played by his great pal.

As he shared this part of the story, it was Joan's turn to laugh and contribute another memory. 'The vicar was one of the old school – he wore a monocle, I remember. He was quite horrified, because of what he saw as our "peculiar" circumstances. As we'd already bought the house he insisted on putting our Brookmans Park address down for both of us on the forms. I don't know why he did that, because Arthur's permanent home address was still Hillfields Park and home for me was still Muswell Hill. We didn't want to be married there at home, so he said, "Well, I know you're not married, but you've got the same address." That seemed to make him very anxious. That was really frowned upon in those days. It's all changed now, hasn't it? He was very dodgy about that but eventually said, "We'll have to do it."'

Joan's father gave her away, happily reconciled to having a gifted and international sportsman as a son-in-law.

Those with a keen eye will have noted that 22nd August falls in that period when the cricket and soccer seasons overlap. The dual sportsman faces a challenge in finding a free date for many things in his seemingly continuous seasons, even for once-in-a-lifetime matters like weddings. But marriage was important to both Arthur and Joan. A date had to be found.

Gloucestershire's yearbook for 1954 records Arthur playing – they still had four further championship matches to play – in their match against Middlesex at Lord's on 19th, 20th and 21st August. It was as close to his wedding venue and date as the county cricket circuit allowed. In Gloucestershire's only innings he scored 8 (was his mind perhaps on other things?) as they went on to win by an innings and 82 runs. His six catches in the match suggest he clearly still had his wits about him. Joan recalls that his 'stag party', typical of its time and his own situation, was 'a few drinks' – and a modestly sore head or two – with team-mates and friends, including Don Oakes, one evening after play.

Tom Whittaker, in his *Arsenal Story*, records: 'Milton, who had played cricket all summer for Gloucestershire, had been given a fortnight's leave in order to get married,' carefully avoiding indicating whether it was Arsenal or Gloucestershire who had allowed him the time off.

And no matter whether it was the cricket season – or the football season – they were married.

Arthur and Joan set off on their honeymoon, still not entirely divorced from sport, for in the car with them as they headed for the West Country was their Arsenal chum and best man, Don Oakes.

'We went to Mousehole, in Cornwall, to The Lobster Pot, for our honeymoon – a lovely old spot, totally unspoilt,' Arthur recalled. 'Don was still playing and, as it was a Saturday when we got married he was due to play in the reserves' evening game at Brentford. So on our way out of London we dropped him off at the ground' – and not surprisingly some 53 years on Arthur and Joan were still laughing away happily at that memory, Joan still wryly amused that even on honeymoon, 'Artie managed to fit in a game of golf.'

They returned to Brookmans Park, which was to be their home for four years, as Arthur began a new campaign with the Gunners. Come the summer months he would head to Bristol, again staying with his Mum and Dad at Maple Avenue. Joan remained at home, 'but she used to come down now and then to stay with Mum and Dad, and around the time I finished playing soccer, she would go looking for a house as well, for us here in Bristol.'

Joan's house-hunting proved successful and they moved to a quiet part of Henleaze, one of Bristol's numerous 'villages'. By the time of their move Robert, the eldest of their three boys, had arrived and had just celebrated his first birthday. 'We moved into this house on our wedding anniversary in 1957,' Arthur recalled, and just to make doubly sure he went off to check with Joan; 'Joanie, Joanie ...'

It was a simple, everyday habit, but one which embraced the depth of the affection they shared. It embraced, too, the reliance Arthur readily placed in Joan. There was no doubting that Joan was central to Arthur's life. Theirs was yet another splendid half-century partnership. It was a truly sparkling one too, one in which so much had been shared. Yes, there had been challenges, as there are for most couples, but it was a partnership which certainly had its share of fun, laughter and joy and which had given fulfilment to them both.

It was a partnership cemented by the arrival of two more sons, David and Richard, to join Robert. Arthur had few aspirations to be a 'modern-day' Dad, adept at nappy changing and bath times or preparing children's meals, but nevertheless considered himself very much a family man. His family came at the top of the list of the things that were important to him – though they could readily be forgiven if they felt that sport sometimes squeezed them into a close second place.

Joan was entitled to feel that way concerning the birth of their boys, for Arthur managed to be absent on all three occasions. At the start of the 1956 season he had just returned to Bristol for Gloucestershire's pre-season practice, leaving a heavily pregnant Joan dividing her time between their home in Brookmans Park and her parents' in Muswell Hill, when Robert arrived. Robert was determined to make an unexpectedly early entrance, so his arrival brought a delighted Dad scuttling back from Bristol, albeit after the event. As Joan put it: 'Robert arrived three weeks early and Arthur 24 hours late.'

When, two years later, number two son, David, was born, Arthur was thousands of miles away, Down Under with England on their Ashes tour of Australia. Expectant dads – especially Test-playing dads – had no thoughts of rushing back to be at the birth in that era, so Joan was very much left to her own devices.

Although by now used to coping at such times, she fully anticipated that Arthur would be about for the birth of their youngest. Richard was due in April 1962 and, with Gloucestershire undergoing their pre-season training at the County Ground, barely a crow-flying mile away, Joan understandably supposed Arthur would be at hand. That was certainly the expectation – until the county captain, Tom Pugh, decreed that Gloucestershire would be better served by undertaking a tour to Bermuda. Pre-season tours were rare exceptions for counties in the Sixties, and Gloucestershire's unanticipated trip meant, yet again, Arthur was absent on cricketing duties overseas. Joan, once more, was on her own. Some years later she firmly but good-naturedly ticked off Tom Pugh for his ambitious but ill-timed pre-season programme. They could both laugh about it then and remain good friends, but at the time Joan understandably felt miffed.

A delightful, attractive and immensely capable woman, with an appealing and bubbly personality, Joan shares Arthur's ability to take things in her stride and get on resourcefully with what life puts in her way, as seems to be expected (from necessity) of many sportsmen's wives. If it was perfectly understandable to look for her husband's moral support at key times, such as the successive arrivals of three boys, Joan also recognised that Arthur's laid-back and sometimes non-interventionist approach to life meant he would probably contribute little in any practical or effective way. And, in his mind, wasn't it better not to get in the way?

Their Dad's sporting commitments often made the boys feel he wasn't around very much. He was never one to push them hard, beyond encouraging them always to do their best. Schoolfriends and teachers expected them to have an advantage at sport, particularly cricket, assuming they would be constantly coached at home. Encouragement they got, which probably accounts for their continuing to play club cricket and follow their other sporting interests as they moved into adult life but, in general, away from the game Arthur tended to keep a low profile, even with his own boys. As one of them said: 'Dad rarely did anything with us as children in his playing days, and I can see why.' At home he was – by choice – not a sporting star or celebrity and, as Joan one day commented, 'When he came home we never knew whether he'd got nought, 41 or 101.'

Many with nine to five occupations take to the golf course, attack the gym, cheer on their local soccer or rugby team, head to the pub, or maybe go to the races the moment their working duties release them. Arthur was no different, other than his 'office' happened to be Highbury and the County Ground; his 'work', very much 'high-profile' and in the public eye, extended far beyond nine to five, Monday to Friday. But when he left the office he, too, was happy to unwind by heading for the golf course, the dog track or the snooker table. It seemed the natural thing to do. And, because of who he was and what he was, he was in demand on the fairways, at the track or with a cue in his hand. There was no denying he lived a sporting life.

Robert touched sensitively on this after Arthur's death, in the moving and perceptive address he gave at the Service of Thanksgiving for his father's life. He recalled: 'I began to understand his celebrity as my peers at the grammar school sought me out to purloin his autograph for them, and my teachers, fruitlessly as it happened, hoped to extract from me the sporting genius they felt must surely have been genetically transmitted my way.

'Gradually seeing more of his professional world I was beginning to appreciate the circles in which he operated and felt genuinely privileged to be a small part of it, shaking hands with a touring Gary Sobers and being given a personal guided tour of Maine Road [Manchester City's ground] by the great Joe Mercer to name but two of many wonderful experiences.

'I stepped onto a cricket field with Dad, in a competitive sense, only once,' Robert continued. 'He was due to play in a Sunday charity match at Westward Ho! The day before the game the phone rang at home with a message that one of the team was unable to play and could Dad think of anyone as a replacement. I was passing through the hall at the time and received a tap on the shoulder – the next day Dad, Roy Swetman and I were wending our way to the Devon coast.'

On arrival Robert blushed to see a billboard outside the ground trumpeting the participation of a Gloucestershire XI – of which he apparently was now a member, albeit a late stand-in.

'The home side, complete with guest professionals, batted first. Given a chance to bowl and determined to live up to my billing, or at least not get carted all over the park, I set about a damage limitation strategy and turned in what I thought was a respectable 0-23 from six overs.'

Robert thought he had performed creditably enough to earn a pat on the back from Dad during the tea interval, only to get an insight into how charity matches were meant to be played. Arthur, ever the focused professional, suggested he might have tempted the batsmen a bit more had he shown more faith in his own bowling. It was one sportsman talking to another and, in this way, it bore the hallmarks of a compliment too, even if that wasn't immediately apparent to a young lad.

'It was a gentle reminder that, in sport, the team and entertainment value take precedence over individual aspirations,' Robert supposed. 'As a teenager I didn't always readily take Dad's words of wisdom to heart, but I have never forgotten that piece of advice.

'We batted and Dad strolled in at number three. The ball, to the bowlers' consternation and the crowd's delight, proceeded to disappear, on the deck, to all parts of the ground. On 107 and with an imperceptible, but surely premeditated, swish of the bat he struck the ball over mid-off, out of the ground and, with one bounce, into the gents' public convenience on the opposite side of the road. The ball narrowly missed a twice-relieved gentlemen emerging into the daylight, who returned it to the field with a round of applause ringing in his ears. With that Dad turned on his heels and retired his innings, to give some possible respite to the bowlers and the rest of the order their chance in the middle. Being really inside his world for those brief few hours began to open my eyes to what Dad was all about – a true sportsman with boundless talent but, moreover, absolute respect for the game and all those who played it.

'Ironically it was not until I left home, first to university and then on into my chosen career, that I really got to know Dad. He retired while I was at college and this, coupled with the 450 miles between St Andrews and Bristol, signalled a deepening of our relationship. With the sporting thrust gone and the competitive edge worn down a bit he had the time to point up his underlying values and to appreciate the sides of life that single-mindedness of career sometimes blots out. We became the greatest of friends.'

With his football days behind him the winter months allowed Arthur to play a more dutiful part in sharing the school runs and doing those things that were part of the year-round duties of most fathers, and Robert, David and Richard valued this. They were proud of their Dad, and loved him even more when he did the things that other dads did.

David recalls that he, Robert and Richard were often at the County Ground as youngsters. 'That was great fun, as we got to know the children of the other players. We got to know Tony Brown's son, Neil, well that way. And we would go into the pavilion, and meet the players in the other teams. We thought those times were pretty special.'

When the boys had been a little younger Joan had taken them to the ground, but found that keeping three little ones entertained, and stopping them upsetting or annoying the members by their exuberance, took the edge off their visits.

As with nearly all boys, there was cricket in the garden (with the odd broken window too). 'We enjoyed that,' says David, 'especially when Dad joined in but, without anything ever being said – and certainly not by him – we quickly became aware that he was pretty special.'

One of David's fondest memories of this time is of playing in a charity match alongside his Dad, at the County Ground. 'I was 15. I had probably gone in early. A wicket or two fell and Dad came in, and we were batting together. I loved that; it was a great experience to be batting with him. We put on a hundred or so – of which Dad made 83 in next to no time.

'What I do remember is that even then, at that age – and I reckoned I was pretty quick – I couldn't run fast enough to keep up with him. If we ran two, he'd almost be at my shoulder as I was turning after the first run. And we seemed to do a lot of running that day. A wonderful memory.'

Away from cricket or out of season Arthur was happy to tackle car maintenance and general DIY, happily calling on skills learned from his father, as well as painting and decorating and gardening. 'Artie was good at painting and with colour schemes,' Joan said, 'and he enjoyed gardening,' though she qualified the latter by adding: 'He did the green bits and I did the brown.'

Indirectly Arthur had already admitted this when I asked if he had green fingers. 'Well, Joan is the keen gardener, very keen on the flowers, and I look after the grass. We've got a Bramley in the garden, which has been there since the house was built, so it's about 60 years old. And it's the most prolific and beautiful Bramley you could ever wish to have. When I go out on my rounds I take apples to my customers, you see.' Yet again, he smiled at the memory. 'They're a beautiful flavour.

'During the war years it was "Dig for Victory", and Dad used to grow stuff in the back garden. We had a greenhouse as well, and we had a couple of apple trees – but the soil wasn't a lot of good; it was very clayey, and he was always trying to do something with it.

'But during the war, a market garden down the bottom of the avenue was split into ten, and it was beautiful red soil and it used to grow stuff … beautiful. We used to take leeks home and have them for supper.'

On the subject of Arthur's DIY, Joan recalled it wasn't all plain sailing. 'Artie could be a bit cavalier where ladders were concerned (shades here, perhaps, of his career-best innings against Derbyshire!). He would just stick the ladder up against the wall or the roof without putting anything under the feet to ensure it was stable. On one occasion he slipped down the roof and only managed to avoid falling off by grabbing the guttering, before somehow eventually getting his feet back on the ladder.

'He wasn't entirely practical. Another time he went up the ladder to paint some guttering and, rather than constantly going up and down to re-fill his paint pot, he decided to take the big tin up with him. Well, the plastic handle gave way and broke. There was paint everywhere. That took some clearing up.'

Being the wife of a top sportsman certainly provided bonuses, and Joan recalls enjoying numerous splendid cricket and soccer social occasions with Arthur 'from the Dorchester downwards'. She enjoyed, too, the company of other players and their wives in the years when Arthur played for Whitbread Wanderers after he had finished with Gloucestershire. The team regularly played charity and fund-raising games, many around the West Country.

Summer holidays *en famille* are nigh impossible for county cricketers. Days together, short breaks, have to be grabbed, and treasured when they can. For the Miltons 1971 provided one such opportunity.

Cricket aficionados will recall that year as the summer of the remarkable record-making Gillette Cup semi-final between Gloucestershire and Lancashire at Old Trafford. An epic game set a record for late finishes. Lights around the ground and at the adjoining railway station shone brightly against the late-July evening sky as Lancashire's David Hughes walked to the crease at 8.45pm, to hit 24 from one over in near darkness to win the match. For Joan it is remembered as the year when they were able to enjoy a summer break together. Arthur was in the Gloucestershire squad for the Old Trafford game (although he didn't play) – and when the match finally finished he and the family (who had been at Old Trafford for the game) set off for a short break in the Lake District. It was a rare summer treat for them all.

As the boys grew up Arthur's relationship with them burgeoned. Joan remembers Sunday evenings – when Robert, David and Richard were in their teens – 'sitting around the dining table playing cribbage; quite often the port would come out – and a cigar would be lit'; though one imagines the latter, if not the former, applied to Arthur only.

Rounds of golf shared with Dad are still fondly remembered today by the boys, and Robert, David and Richard all retain a love for the game, doubtless recalling as they stroll around the course all the helpful advice Arthur shared with them. And it would have been his style and his way to share his advice and tips with them, as with others, as if they were his sporting equals. 'All the boys play,' he told me. 'The younger two, David and Richard, hit a golf ball well. I enjoy playing with them. They're my best pals really.'

When the boys married or found partners the family extended in a way Joan and Arthur joyously welcomed. Then came a whole hand of delightful grandchildren: Stephanie, Nicholas, Kathleen, Michaela and Clara; along with a young family friend, Matthew, treated by Arthur and Joan as if he, too, was a grandson.

Ironically for one who had managed not to be present at his own children's birth Arthur was very much to the fore when Richard and Dympna's twins, Kathleen and Michaela, were born. Joan happened to be away at the time, holidaying with a friend, so Arthur buckled to and stood in for her, offering support with pram-pushing, cradle-rocking and the like. And he delighted in it. The birth of their first granddaughter had fixed itself firmly in his mind too. 'Stephanie

– the first girl in the family – was born on my 60th birthday, in the week I retired from the Post Office. What a week that was.'

Of Arthur as a grandparent, Richard recalled: 'He was very generous to us in later life, when his playing days had finished, and that perhaps made him a better grandparent than parent. The things I admire about him the most were his pure approach to things he was passionate about, his non-materialism and straightforward honesty.'

Arthur's sporting gifts, as well as his unassuming response and approach to sport, must have been firmly in the genes, something Richard unassertively sensed within the family: 'I have seen just glimpses of some of these abilities in my brothers and even in myself, and in our offspring. A couple of years ago, Clara [Richard and Dympna's youngest daughter] went to try badminton with a friend who played. She started to play once or twice a week. One day, a couple of months later, she asked for a lift to badminton, but it wasn't at the usual time. When pressed, she said she had a county trial for the Under 17s' – she hadn't let on – 'and she played for the squad that season. She and Kathleen are both very competitive, whereas Michaela is the more creative one.'

Like most grandparents, Arthur and Joan never tired of talking of the joy their grandchildren brought them, and they revelled in their company and in their achievements and aspirations.

Grandson Nicholas turned out to be a keen Arsenal fan and, as a birthday treat for him, Arthur and Joan planned a visit to Highbury. Young Nicholas unfortunately fell ill, and the visit had to be re-arranged. 'Joan had suggested we take him up to Highbury. I'd never been back since 1954, and I was doing an interview with Brian Moore for Sky TV, and I happened to mention our plans to go to Highbury. Brian suggested I should get in touch with Bob Wilson, which I did, and Bob kindly arranged it for us.

'Poor Nicholas, who was then 10 or 11, was ill on the morning so it ended up with Joan and I going on our own. We had a fantastic day.

'The commissionaires on that first visit – we got there and they were outside – they greeted us with 'Good afternoon, Mr Milton' – I think they were almost as old as I was. They must have known we were coming. I'm sure they wouldn't have recognised me after all those years. Anyway, they went and got Bob, who looked after us so well.

'The two big stands at Highbury, they were like grand hotels. They had been built before the war on the back of the success in the Thirties, and they were just the same as I remembered them when I went there in 1946.

'Before the game Bob took us down to the dressing rooms and they were just the same; the kit laid out for the players. You go past the visitors', and into the home dressing room, and it brought tears to my eyes when I went in there because I looked round … and I could see them all, our team: George Swindin, Wally Barnes, Lionel Smith, Joe Mercer, Alex Forbes, Ray Daniel, myself on the wing, Jimmy, of course, and Cliff Holton, Doug Lishman, Don Roper – I could see them all, and it brought tears to my eyes.

'And on my peg, where I used to change, there was a shirt which had number 14 on it – my number was 7, you see – so I said to Bob, "I used to be there; whose is that shirt now?"

'"Oh," he said, "that's Patrick Vieira" – and, making a point of the different number, added, "He's twice as good as you!"' Arthur giggled away merrily as he recounted the story. He knew, too – though deigned humbly to even suggest it – there were others who reckoned Bob's tongue-in-cheek assessment might well have been the wrong way round.

'But we had a fantastic day. They made us so welcome and treated us royally. At one point Bob said "The chief exec – who's just retiring – wants to see you, because he knew you when you first came here to Highbury." And he introduced us to Ken Friar. Ken was pleased to see us, and he said, "You won't remember me, because when you first walked through the door in 1946 I was the little lad who used to run messages for the commissionaires." And he went from there to be chief exec for all those years when they were so successful. It was such a delight to meet him again – all part of a great day.'

Having broken the ice, Arthur, with Joan, paid return visits to Highbury, ensuring that Nicholas made up for that first aborted trip. They were there, too, for the last game at Highbury before the move to the Emirates, and Arthur along with other former players was part of a celebratory procession around the pitch before play got under way. 'We were treated like royalty, like celebrities,' he recalled.

His career at Highbury might have been relatively brief, but he had certainly made his mark. Many present who had seen his amazing right-wing wizardry roared their delight and appreciation, while others cheering in the capacity crowd knew him by his unsullied and enduring sporting reputation – not least as a double international. It was indeed a great day, which created many happy memories for them both, though Arthur, with typical reserve, could barely believe how they had been feted.

If Joan's love of soccer had allowed her a window into her sportsman husband's career, she claims to have only a modest understanding of cricket. Certainly, she never wanted to be the sort of wife whose own interest added pressure to a sportsman's life. Rather, home was an oasis of calm and good sense, a steadying and feet-on-the-ground retreat from a sporting life lived out in the public view. The *Guardian* crossword was a shared delight, as was their love of good music enjoyed at Bristol's concert halls. In later life, when Arthur had more time, they visited the theatre, being frequent and enthusiastic patrons of the renowned Bristol Old Vic.

In that era, too, when Arthur had retired from his sporting career, they were able increasingly to fulfil their love of travelling, of experiencing and enjoying new places and, especially, meeting new people.

Europe featured often and pleasurably in their travels, and their explorations were given an added joy in that many were shared with old friends. Jimmy Gray shared a good many Milton holidays along with his wife, Betty.

'Jimmy and I of course had known each other at Highbury, but it was when we started playing cricket against each other that we became the best of pals,' Arthur recalled. 'And it's a friendship that's just gone on and on.

'From about the time Joanie and I got married the girls became just as good friends as Jim and I, which was very nice. Betty came from the same Muswell Hill area as Joan and yet funnily enough they didn't know each other before they got hung up with us.'

Those later holidays with the Grays were remembered with great happiness by them all. Not that it seemed – to Arthur at least – the most obvious thing to do. As Jimmy recalled: 'During his cricket career, Joan and Arthur did not holiday much. Summer was dominated by cricket, and the autumn coincided with the running of the greyhounds. Betty and I, on the other hand, went regularly to the continent, often for a month at a time, and we thoroughly enjoyed it.

'The two girls must have got together and hatched a plot, thinking it would be a good idea for the four of us to go to America on a fly-drive holiday, and this we did. It was a great success and we ended up going to the States two or three times together. We got to California and Florida, and New England for the Fall.

'The girls sat in the back to chat. Art wasn't over-keen on driving so I was the driver, which I quite enjoyed. Art would navigate – when he was awake – but Joan kept an eye on him from the back seat as assistant navigator, so we never got lost – well, not really lost.'

Joan remembered: 'Artie was not very keen on holidays at first. He was never very keen to go abroad, while I was dying to go, and he stayed in so many hotels during his cricket career that staying in another one at holiday time had little appeal to him. So, at first, he had to be persuaded to get away.

'The first joint holiday we had with Jimmy and Betty was to Vale do Lobo in Portugal. Artie and I had gone down to Southampton for some cricket function and Betty and I got our heads together about going to Portugal, where we had the chance of staying in a villa belonging to some friends of the Grays. Jimmy worked on Arthur – and we went and had a fantastic time. It wasn't so difficult persuading Artie to go away again after that.'

One of the joys of these holidays for Joan was that she had Arthur to herself. 'It was marvellous to have his undivided attention, and he was lovely. He was fine.'

Once they had opened the door to regular holidays Arthur loved seeing other places, seeing the tourist sights, and especially enjoyed getting a feel of the countryside, to understand how these places and their people worked, and to learn something of their history and culture. Mind you, he wasn't too clever at languages and happily left this to Joan. Her great love is Italy and the Italian language, but she also speaks 'schoolgirl French and Spanish – and I find that if I'm not very confident or don't know too many words you only need one or two words to be able to communicate with others'.

Joan's linguistic skills suited Arthur, as he had earlier declared. 'Joanie's very good, so when we're abroad she likes to talk with the locals, and the good thing about it is that I don't understand either of those languages, so when she's rattling away I don't have a clue what's being said – sometimes not even in English!

'Taking my wife on holiday was a big plus. To do that and to go more or less where we wanted, that's given me as much pleasure as anything.'

In retirement Arthur and Joan had invested in the major transport company for which Robert worked – he had earlier been part of a successful management buy-out – and the shares took off soon afterwards. That enabled them to be more adventurous regarding holidays than they might have been.

Arthur's involvement with Whitbread Wanderers and the Old England XI, as an observer for the Test and County Cricket Board (predecessor of the England and Wales Cricket Board), and as a man-of-the-match adjudicator for Gillette and NatWest also offered added opportunities for short summer breaks, which both greatly appreciated; Arthur always faithfully fulfilling what was expected of him in the cricket sense, and enjoying the time away with Joan. For her part there was the pleasure of meeting up again with the other players' wives, many of whom she had come to know over the years. He played for Whitbread Wanderers and occasionally Old England, 'until my late fifties. I got my hand smashed up a bit trying to stop one in the field one day and I thought "It's time to give up – I've got to be able to hold a golf club!"'

Arthur with his mother Violet and father Bill, and his cousin
Mary who he regarded as his sister.

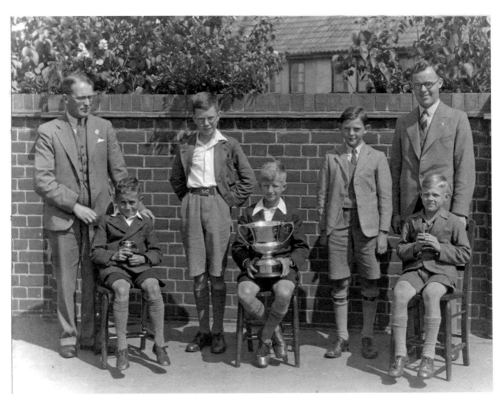

Arthur, fleet of foot even at the age of seven, holding his first sporting trophy.

COTHAM SCHOOL A.F.C., 1943.

Veale & Co.
Bristol.

M. I. HAWKINS   R. G. JONES   C. A. MILTON

Mr. E. R. COOK   J. C. ANDERSON   B. A. I. DAVIS   R. J. LONG   A. D. TOVEY   Mr. A. E. CREW

W. A. DUTTON   A. J. GUY   Mr. S. R. WOODS   R. B. D. HARRIS   J. G. MacDONALD
               (Capt.)   (Headmaster)

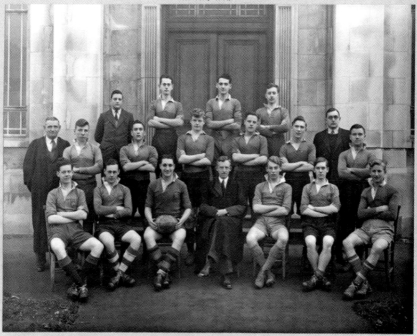

COTHAM SCHOOL R.F.C.
1st XV., 1944.

L. G. Parkhouse   D. Dudbridge   D. Williams   D. Jenkins
(Linesman)

Mr. A. E. Crew   K. E. Matthews   J. B. Norman   G. Dobbs   J. Handford   C. Jacobs   Mr. E. J. James   J. L. James

D. Porter   D. B. Payne   W. A. Dutton   Mr. S. R. Woods   J. G. Carr   J. Troon   C. A. Milton
(Captain)   (Headmaster)

COTHAM GRAMMAR SCHOOL.
1st XI. 1945.

D. G. Lyne.   R. R. Kelly.   A. White.   K. E. Matthews.
(Scorer)

Mr. A. E. Crew.   D. G. Jenkins.   D. A. Downer.   D. A. Harris.   D. B. Payne.   G. Chippendale.

R. B. Wood.   C. A. Milton   Mr. S. R. Woods.   G. C. Smith   D. W. Porter.
(Captain)   (Vice-Captain)

Arthur (third from right, back row) as a member of RAOC Chilwell's successful soccer team.

A young Arsenal recruit with a Gunners' legend, Alex James.

A packed Highbury watches Arthur in action.

Arsenal's massive squad in 1949–50 included five county cricketers. Left to right, (back row) E Collins, L Pilkington, J Gray, C Holton, R Barr, C Grimshaw, E Davies, W Duffy, A Horsfield, W Healey, N Kelly, F Grosvenor. (fourth row) G Male, E Stanley, J Chenhall, J Babes, N Uprichard, G Dunkley, E Platt, A J Kelsey, G Swindin, D Oakes, J Ollerenshaw, L Delaney, W Milne (trainer). (third row) A James, J Crayston (asst manager), D Gripps, C A Milton, D Farquhar, J Wade, R Daniels, A Fields, T Vallance, A Shaw, F Cox, B Sexton, E J Holland, H Owen (asst trainer), J Shaw (second row) D Roper, A Forbes, L Scott, J McPherson, J T Logie, D Lishman, L H Compton, A Macauley, W Barnes, R Lewis, L Smith, H Goring, D C S Compton (front row) M Ryan, F Marlow, B Griffiths, C Carson, A Batsford, R Prouton, B Walsh, W Quinn, N Smith.

First Division debut against Aston Villa, with Arthur (on ground) going for goal.

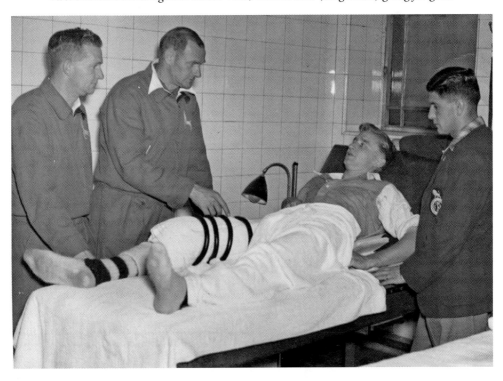

Receiving treatment after his debut came to an early end.

Arthur (out of shot) scores what he considered 'my best goal', beating Spurs goalkeeper Ted Ditchburn. Bill Nicholson can only look on.

HRH Duke of Edinburgh's XI versus Duke of Beaufort's XI for the National Playing Fields Association, of which the Duke was President. (back row) Reg Sinfield, John Mortimore, RES Wyatt, Billy Griffith, Hopper Read, Tom Graveney, Jack Crapp, Laurie Fishlock, George Mann, Jim Parks (Snr), Sam Pothecary. (middle row) Errol Holmes, Jack Cheetham, HRH, Duke of Beaufort, Sir William Becher, Jackie McGlew, Lord Cobham. (front row) Jim Sims, George Lambert, Martin Young, Cdr Mike Parker (HRH's Private Secretary), Arthur Milton, Bomber Wells.

England captain Billy Wright greets Arthur before his England debut, against Austria.

England v Austria November 1951.
(back row) Walter Winterbottom (coach), Nat Lofthouse, Alf Ramsey, Jack Froggatt, Gil Merrick, Jimmy Dickinson, Bill Eckersley, Jimmy Trotter (trainer); (front row) Arthur Milton, Ivor Broadis, Billy Wright, Eddie Bailey, Les Medley.

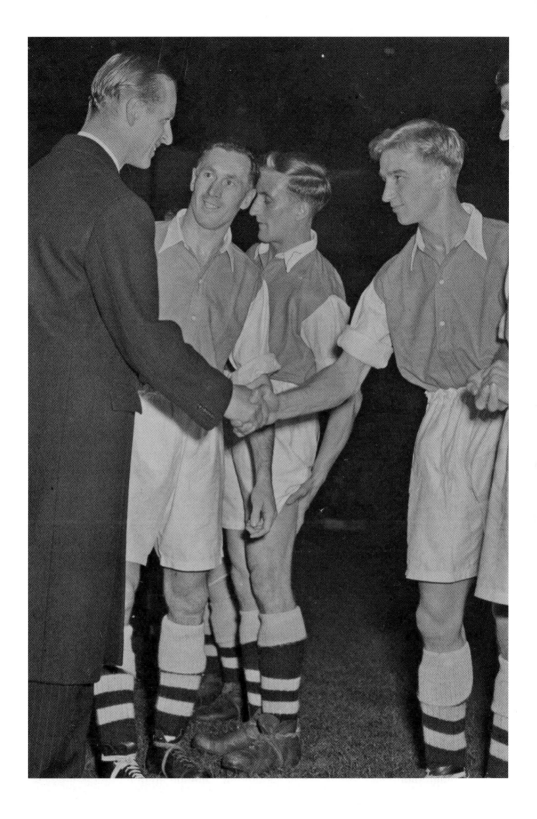

Meeting the Duke of Edinburgh again at another match staged for the National Playing Fields Association. Arsenal skipper Joe Mercer introduces Arthur to HRH.

The Old Master and the Young Master No. 1. Arthur batting with Wally Hammond, in 1951 at Bristol, in the only County match in which Arthur played with the great man (and, as shown here, nearly ran him out).

Arthur's Dad, Bill Milton – a sporting inspiration to his son - is seated second from right in this photograph of Soundwell CC.

Dressed for the course, of course. Arthur and fellow Bristolian and Arsenal clubmate Don Oakes enjoy a round of golf during the soccer season. (Getty Images)

Mr and Mrs Milton. Arthur and Joan on their wedding day.

A bashful Arthur with his bride, and best man Don Oakes.

Arthur lines up with his Bristol City team-mates who he helped become Third Division South Champions 1954–55.
(back row) Wilf Copping (trainer), Arthur, Ivor Guy, Bob Anderson, John Atyeo, Cyril Williams, Mike Thresher. (front row) Ernie Peacock, Jimmy Rogers, Jack White, Tommy Burden, Jack Boxley.

Double internationals both. M J K Smith, who played rugby and cricket for England, was Arthur's opening partner against New Zealand at Headingley in 1958.

Arthur batting on his Test debut, against New Zealand, when he made a century, and was on the field throughout the match.

The same Test, and Arthur shows why he was one of the game's best-ever catchers (here catching Bill Playle), while Godfrey Evans looks on confidently.

One endearing trait of Arthur's was his little 'ways', his eccentricities. At lunch, when we were working together on the initial stages of this book, he would always offer a glass of wine (we might perhaps also have enjoyed a sherry together earlier). White wine would be taken from the fridge, properly chilled, as any good host would do, but one of Arthur's foibles was that he didn't enjoy cold wine himself. So he always first poured hot water into his glass, warming it before pouring in the wine. He also introduced me to a red wine he had first encountered in Sicily on one of their holidays. It was certainly imbibable, and he was delighted to discover it was stocked by their local supermarket – at a most attractive price. In this, as in many matters, Arthur was his own man. He was no wine snob; he knew what he liked and enjoyed, and if it didn't cost an arm and a leg so much the better – and good reason too for sharing the information with friends.

Another foible was his way of avoiding doing something if it didn't appeal to him, didn't seem strictly necessary, or didn't seem right. On the other hand he wouldn't mind at all doing something if he felt it was right, even if others thought it odd or unusual.

David Brown, a former Gloucestershire team-mate, called to see Arthur one day and found him gardening. He was wearing his old England blazer, and when his visitor expressed surprise, Arthur explained: 'Well, it was only taking up space in the wardrobe so I thought I'd wear it. It keeps you lovely and warm.' As in so many things, great and small, Arthur was happy to do his own thing.

Particularly endearing was his inherent lack of vanity and boastfulness. It was possible to be in his company for a while for, say, lunch, or an evening meal and never know that he had been a professional cricketer, that he had played soccer for Arsenal and England. Seldom would a word pass his lips to suggest he was one of Gloucestershire's greatest cricketers, that he had played cricket for England or, indeed, that he was the last to be capped by England at both soccer and cricket. He knew his worth and recognised his proper place in the sporting lexicon but in later life this was not something always at the forefront of his mind, not something he felt obliged to foist on others. On the other hand, if the company was of cricketers – or footballers – sharing reminiscences, then he would delightedly enjoy the company and join happily in the lively discussions almost always generated in such circles. But even then it was his nature to let others tell their stories; he needed prompting to share his.

Such traits and his natural insouciance probably accounted for Arthur determinedly overlooking Arsenal's unwritten rule. He had become 'tangled up' with his landlady's daughter – very happily so, and never for one moment did he regret that.

Joan, and Robert, David and Richard, and their families, meant so much to him. They in turn were devoted to him and immensely proud of who he was and all that he was, as well of what he had achieved. At home he was husband, Artie; and Dad; and grandad. They knew he was a sporting star, because the media told them so, and their friends readily made that plain, but at home there was no sense of that and that was the way he liked it. Arthur never sought adulation.

In typical Arthur style he would sometimes seek out those who saw him as a sporting idol, but this was no searching for adulation or hero worship. Rather these were instances of Arthur's immense interest in others, and in what makes them tick, and also of his unassuming, un-grand nature and his genuine kindness.

John Brookes was a case in point. Born in London in 1920, he had worked his passage to Australia in 1939, arriving with two shillings and sixpence in his pocket. When war was declared he walked from Broken Hill to Melbourne – 700 miles – to join up. He served with the Australian forces in the western desert and Greece, before being taken prisoner in Crete. During the four years he spent in prisoner-of-war camps, he took to writing poetry, of which 'Thermopylae 1941' is perhaps the most compelling and best known. Others of his PoW poems were irreverent and anti-establishment.

After the war Brookes returned to England and lived in the Cotswolds. There he wrote articles for the local newspapers and began writing poetry again. He was keen on cricket and loved Arthur's way of playing the game. A correspondence began and, in later life when he had more time, Arthur visited John Brookes at his home purely as a result of the bond they had created. Arthur was just as interested in John's background as John was in Arthur's cricket. They became good friends. On one such visit John presented Arthur with a signed copy of his book of poems, which included 'Resurrection at Lord's', a work Arthur was very taken with.

All this Arthur recounted at one of our later sessions together, not long before he died. As he recalled the poem his eyes moistened. He leapt up to find it – he had to share it with me. It is a splendid poem, quite long, and so on that occasion Arthur read just a small part:

> *When summer's green has turned to gold*
> *and dreams are done and we are old.*
> *When knees grow stiff and eyesight fails*
> *and Father Time removes our bails,*
> *then let us pray Almighty God*
> *in his great wisdom gave the nod*
> *to pitching wickets up in heaven –*
> *Christ the Skipper: God's XI.*

It seemed entirely appropriate that these words should be included in the Service of Thanksgiving for Arthur's life at Bristol in May 2007.

The link and friendship he had established with John Brookes was not a one-off. Friendships developed with others who, initially, had contacted him as Gloucestershire or Milton fans – but, for Arthur, there was always the interest in other people's lives, and in their abilities and achievements.

Correspondence with a Gloucestershire supporter in Weston-super-Mare led to the possibility of their meeting up, until Arthur found that his correspondent was severely disabled and could not drive. This, he decided, was no bar and so he jumped in his car and went to meet his new acquaintance in Weston. Other visits would follow. All of this stemmed from Arthur's interest in those around him, most certainly not through any hankering for stardom or for gilding his ego or his reputation. It was his way.

Blissfully for a man who was so naturally fit, Arthur's health generally remained good apart from having prostate cancer diagnosed late in life and until that mild stroke slowed him down some months before his all-too-early death. His cancer treatment was debilitating: 'I wish they had told me beforehand how rough I might feel,' he once said, and yet it brought out some of his best traits. He would take himself off to Bristol Royal Infirmary's Oncology Unit by bus, to save Joan driving him there and also to save her waiting for who knows how long. On those bus trips and at the unit he got to know three or four other men undergoing similar treatment. They became a team around Arthur, offering each other encouragement and mutual support, making the most of their circumstances, and squeezing what fun they could out of their shared journeys. Not quite *Last of the Summer Wine*, but you get the drift.

He valued his family, home, his health and his careers, contrasting though these had been. His gratitude for all of this was real and unqualified. He found it difficult to find words which expressed this fully. That, in any event, was not his style. In his unpretentious way what was unsaid felt equally compelling and deep, and he hoped and believed his family understood this.

Life had unquestionably been good to him; that he knew – and was grateful. One sensed also, without him ever saying it, that genuinely he hoped he had been good to life too. Few would doubt that.

Chapter 8

Early Cricket Summers, Early Memories

BY AND LARGE today's citizens adjust, albeit sometimes reluctantly, to the vastly increased and sometimes insane tempo of our modern world. Cars, trains and aircraft travel at high speeds, bringing us more swiftly to our destinations – or allowing us to leave later and travel faster. Mobile phones, computers, laptops, Blackberrys, iPods and iPads, blogs and tweets and the rest mean that messages, urgent or not, are instantly despatched, with expectations of immediate responses. The world seems to move only at a breathless pace, leaving some in its wake; some of us clinging defiantly to the view so eloquently expressed by the Welsh poet WH Davies: 'What is this life if, full of care, we have no time to stand and stare.'

Not surprisingly, today's generation considers itself more sophisticated, too, and, with greater scientific knowledge and experience, to be better informed and better enabled than those that have gone before.

Sport is not immune from such changes in our culture; it was ever thus and ever will be. The constant breaking of established records; the more scientific, structured and detailed preparation which sportsmen and women now undergo; changing views about what's sporting (and what is not); the influence (for good or bad) of huge sums of money; all attest to this.

Listening to Arthur recalling his early days as a pro was to be taken back to a less frenetic era and, doubtless, a more idyllic one. That's not to say that cricketers, footballers and other sportsmen and women of Arthur's time were in any way amateurish or lackadaisical in their approach to training and preparation, or had life easy, but rather they performed and prepared as thoroughly as they could, according to the best knowledge and practice then available. And they did so with great joy.

It's important to remember, too, that when Arthur was first a professional he – along with so many others – had just come through the war years. Many playing alongside him had lately returned from active service. Many, through no fault of their own, had sacrificed the best years of their sporting careers. Others, like Arthur, had grown up during those six war years, and had known and experienced the restrictions and deprivations this brought. But seldom was a complaint heard.

What was heard, and experienced, was the joy and pleasure that 'normality' had returned – different though that normality now was. The joy and delight of taking up their sporting lives again was overwhelming, something to be celebrated, wholeheartedly welcomed, enthusiastically relished, and greatly enjoyed.

And, in his recollections of those early days as a young pro, all of this shone through Arthur's charming and affectionate memories.

'I remember coming back in April – the Arsenal used to let us come back for pre-season practice, or part of it. We'd practise, usually in the nets and then, at lunchtime – we used to take our own sandwiches for lunch – we'd play cards, and then get back to practice until about 4 o'clock.

'Then we'd come in and have a shower, and Tom [Graveney] would then take me home – he lived in Coombe Lane, a lovely part of Bristol. Their house backed on to Bristol University's playing fields. It was a lovely spot. We'd go back there and have tea.

'I will always remember going into the house, and smelling the cakes cooking. I've never forgotten that. His Mum was a good cook, good at the baking. She was a typical Geordie, with a real Geordie accent, because the family originally came from Riding Mill, before Tom's Dad had died.

'The Graveneys were quite a big family – three boys and two girls – and his Mum had married again, you know. Mrs Gardner she became. Tom's Mum would give us tea and then we'd go up to Henbury Golf Club and play round there until it was dark.

'I remember, too, that at that time Tom was playing rugby for Bristol. He was a good player, but I think in the end he decided to give it up, in case of injury, and concentrate on his cricket.'

I asked Tom Graveney about introducing Arthur to golf. 'Yes, that's when we were living up at Stoke Bishop. Father had died when we were in Newcastle. A distant cousin of my mother was on leave from Shell in Singapore, and he came to the funeral. He clearly took a shine to mother, as they got married and he took us all on – five kids. I was only six then, and was the middle one of the five – with two brothers and two sisters. Bob Gardner did a good job,' Tom recalled with warmth and gratitude.

'We came down to Bristol in 1938, via a brief spell in Blackpool. Henbury Golf Club was my club all the time I was in Bristol. I would later become champion there, and won all the trophies in my time.

'I remember the first time Arthur got seriously interested in golf. We were playing Somerset at Taunton, and they had a nine-hole short course in the middle of Taunton, and Ken, my elder brother – he was a wild golfer in those days, he hit it hard, but anywhere – and I got Arthur started.

'Of course he was on Arsenal's books then, so he spent many an afternoon playing on Dai Rees's course at South Herts, where he got to know Dai very well. And he became a very good golfer straight away.'

The after-tea golf followed a day's practice and pre-season nets. Arthur recalled them: 'Mostly we had nets, and we'd have some practices in the middle, but also we'd have a game or two of football to get the legs fit. Of course, even in my later days, that came pretty easily.

'I tell you what – we might not have won the county championship but we'd have done well at a counties' football championship,' he recalled, amused. 'I reckon we'd have won it! We had Barrie Meyer, who played for Bristol Rovers, Plymouth Argyle, Newport County and Bristol City and who had scored more than 200 goals in the Football League; Ron Nicholls – a goalkeeper for City and Rovers; Bobby Etheridge – another who played for Bristol City – he was a good player but perhaps just lacked a yard of pace. And then there was David Smith, who had played left-wing for the City; and Browny, Tony Brown, was a very good player in the Downs League, and Harold Jarman too – a little fellow who played for Bristol Rovers and Newport County.'

Tom Graveney remembers some of those pre-season work-outs. 'We used to play 20 minutes each way football in pre-season practice, Arthur was in a class of his own, and made everybody look idiots.'

Those who play professional sport over a long period are frequently keen to find ways to keep practice routines and sessions fresh and constructive. Arthur recalled one way of doing this. 'Later on in my career, after I'd been playing quite a long time, I liked to put the gloves on and keep wicket when we had middle practice games. I always recognised what a difficult job it was and these sessions helped me keep aware of that and keep the old reactions as sharp as possible.

'The first time I put them on, we were out in the middle, and the seam bowlers were on. I decided to stand up to the wicket – so they couldn't have been too quick that day. Things were going along all right and then, after a few overs, one of the bowlers came up and bowled a beautiful half-volley. I thought, "That's four runs for certain" and started to stand up, didn't I? The batsman missed it, and it hit me straight in the box. By golly that woke me up,' he said, laughing away, without any apparent tear-inducing sympathetic recollection of the acute discomfort it must have caused!

'But I do remember catching one off an inside edge, which rather chuffed me. Of course, in my time I stood alongside a few good keepers. Swettie – Roy Swetman – who I'd toured Australia with on that trip in 1958–59, came to us from Surrey and was with us for two or three years. I thought he was as good as any. He knew how to keep wicket.

'Peter Rochford – yes, he was another good 'keeper, as was Bobby Etheridge. Bobby was a really good games player, but for some reason George Emmett didn't rate him. I used to think sometimes that he might nearly have been a better 'keeper than Barrie Meyer, and he was rather useful with the bat. In fact, they were all pretty good with the bat, and were good for me, often giving me great support in partnerships lower down the order. Barrie was very good that way.

'We played Yorkshire once, at Cheltenham, and it was a typical Cheltenham wicket at that time – difficult. We had to get 80 or 90 and were losing wickets all the way down the order. We got a bit closer and Bobby came in to join me, and he got the odd few runs.

'Anyway, he gets down to the end to face Johnny Wardle and – I always remember it – Wardle was bowling from the College end, with the short boundary up towards the pavilion. He bowled one up there, about middle-and-leg, and Bobby hit it up into the stand. Wardle turned round to me and said, "Who the hell's that?" "Oh," I said. "You wouldn't know, but don't worry about it – he doesn't know who you are either."' And as his memory repainted the picture Arthur rocked back and forth in genial, gentle laughter.

'Do you know, the match finished up with us winning it, and we'd all come off, and then the scorers decided they'd made a mistake and we still needed one run to win. There was only another one or two wickets to fall, so we all had to go out again for this one run. I forget who bowled then, but I can see him now, he came up and bowled, it turned a lot, beat the wicketkeeper and all, and went for byes.

'Andy, Andy Wilson, of course, was our wicketkeeper when I first played for the county. He was a useful bat too. Andy used to follow me in, especially in my early days, very often. We had a lot of nice partnerships.

'I think it might have been my first game for the county – against the Combined Services at the Wagon Works ground. We must have travelled by train from Bristol, and then we got a bus up to the ground. We played spoof to decide who was going to pay the fare. Anyway, I was walking from the bus stop up to the ground and Andy was behind me, and for ever after that he called me "Steve". He reckoned my legs were as bandy as Steve Donoghue's, the jockey.

'So when we were batting together – and we had quite a few good stands, he and I – he used to call "Come on, Steve" or "Come one, Steve."

'We were playing the West Indies at Cheltenham one time and, everybody … we were all watching Sonny Ramadhin, because none of us was confident about being able to pick him very well. Anyway, we got into the second innings and dear old Andy said, "I've got him. I can tell.'"

'He went out to bat and about his second ball he shoulders arms, and over they go! Actually I could pick him at the end, but reckoned he threw it – like Muralitharan.'

On another occasion Arthur remembered, 'I'm not sure if it was the same match when I got five-for, against Glamorgan at the Wagon Works or another match against them. We were batting and it must have been in my early days as I was in the middle order. Andy Wilson came in to join me.

'And Wilf – Wilf Wooller – was bowling. Andy was only about 5 foot 6 inches or something like that – a little puller and cutter, wasn't he? He kept chopping Wilf down through the gully. Eventually he nicked one to one of the Davies's at slip, who put it down. Wilf was livid.

'He stood in the middle of the pitch, by me, hands on hips, with his arms bristling out of those short-sleeved shirts he used to wear – do you remember? – and he looked down the wicket at Andy and said, "You lucky little f****r."

'Andy, not in the least disconcerted, looked up at him, took off his cap, and said, "Is that what they taught you at Cambridge, Mr Wooller?"'

And Arthur was away again, laughing at the merry reminiscence, and rejoicing too in the memory of two good friends, and of how the pros still referred to their amateur colleagues at that time.

His recounting of the story gave yet another insight into Arthur Milton the man and the sportsman. For in telling this story about Andy Wilson and Wilf Wooller, he had mentioned, only in passing, his career-best bowling, 5-64. He hadn't allowed the landmark to sidetrack him from the story of his two friends. Nor did he return to it when the story was told, until prompted.

Arthur made legions of friends throughout his life, within his chosen sports and far beyond them. Not for him any airs and graces, or concerns about status. He simply loved genuine, honest, good people, and once you were a friend, you were a friend for life. Of course, among his closest friends were those he played with and against.

A lovely, and typical, story about Arthur came to light, long after the event, of him phoning Andy Wilson at his home at Redmarley D'Abitot on the Gloucestershire–Worcestershire border, late in Andy's life. Deep snow had hit the West Country, and Arthur was anxious that his by-now elderly team-mate and good friend was able to manage. Had he plenty of food in the house? Did he need any supplies? Could he get his car out of the drive?

Andy happily offered positive responses to Arthur's concern. Even so it took all his powers of persuasion to prevent Arthur driving up from Bristol through the snow to clear Andy's drive or do anything else that was necessary.

But let's return to Arthur's recollections of his early Gloucestershire seasons.

At various times in our reminiscing Arthur surprised me by referring to the Bristol pitch in less than complimentary terms; at least, that is, until David Bridle became head groundsman and things improved significantly. This seemed ironic, especially for someone whose reputation as a high-class batsman had, in part, been built on the countless successes he achieved when the going was tough and challenging. It was patently contrary to his general and genial nature, too, most unlike him.

Perhaps it was simply a case of familiarity breeding contempt (like school dinners). Perhaps it was a frustration of recognising that the soil, with its high clay content, had real potential – given a greater familiarity with the heavy roller – to provide more pace and bounce. Perhaps it was a voicing of an inner frustration on behalf of fellow batsmen who knew that, over many years, Bristol pitches frequently were prepared with the county's legion of prolific spin bowlers in mind, from Tom Goddard to Sam Cook to Bomber Wells, David Allen and John Mortimore.

Bristol's pitches, 'slow and low' for much of Arthur's career, undoubtedly frustrated many a batsman, not least those free-scoring players like Arthur himself who relished the ball coming on to the bat.

Over the years Tony Brown and John Mortimore had suggested to Arthur a possible solution. As the latter recalled: 'Art was forever saying he couldn't bat at Bristol because the ball never came on, and for years Tony and I used to tell him he ought to use a heavier bat. Eventually we got him to use one in one particular game. He played forward and blocked it – and it went past mid-on for three, and he gave us a little flourish of the bat. But I can't say he went out and got a heavier bat.'

Arthur, as always, was his own man. 'Do you know we – Tom and I – averaged more than Bradman at Bristol during his visits to the County Ground. That must say something about the wickets,' Arthur suggested, with an impish grin.

'Before I started playing for the county, Gloucestershire had a tied match with the Don's Aussie side. Charlie Parker was one of the greatest left-arm bowlers who ever lived, I should think – quite a character. He was the county's coach when I went there. And he did for Bradman that day.

'Bradman had a very strong right-hand grip and the people who used to do him when the wicket did a bit were the old left-armers, like Hedley Verity who did him in the famous match at Lord's, when they got on a turner. Bradman wouldn't have seen much of that sort of pitch, because when their pitches got wet in Australia they were hopeless.

'When I think about Bradman's average at Bristol, and Tom's and mine,' he volunteered, laughing, 'I often wonder how it would have been if Bradman had been born in Bristol and Tom and I had been born in Bowral.'

It's a lovely thought, and it points to Arthur's love of the game and his enchantment with its many facets, but it's a memory only tenuously supported by the facts. For one thing Bradman played at Bristol only once, in that famous tied game in 1930. He scored 42 in his first innings – 'caught Seabrook bowled Parker' – and 14 in his second when, again, he fell to Charlie Parker. As this was Bradman's only appearance against the Glosters his average was 28. Arthur's average, it is true, was over 33 for Nevil Road innings, and Tom's was just over 42 but – a little whimsical thinking apart – Arthur wasn't really suggesting any significant overhaul of the relative merits of the Don, Tom Graveney and himself or of their respective places in cricket's Hall of Fame!

Gloucestershire folklore contends that Bradman hadn't enjoyed those battles with Parker and his fellow spinners (perhaps it was also the 'slow and low' pitches he didn't relish) so he managed to 'rest' himself whenever the Australians visited Bristol subsequently.

But these particular memories did not detain Arthur for long. An earlier mention of Tom Graveney, and the fun and friendship they shared as young players – which continued to their mutual delight to the end of Arthur's life – set him off on a tangent of memories about TWG.

'Back to Tom. He was tall, and a beautiful driver, but he certainly wasn't afraid of the short stuff.'

This reminiscence led Arthur to yet another memory, of a Worcestershire innings at Cheltenham (in 1965) when Graveney and Basil D'Oliveira batted against John Mortimore and David Allen, then at the peak of their powers and with a pitch that was offering considerable help. In knocks which both batsmen have recalled with pride, each placing it among the best of their innings, Arthur could picture Tom typically playing virtually everything off the front foot, while Basil, again characteristically, played comfortably off the back foot or, as John Mortimore himself remembered it, 'Basil played the length – he did that superbly, that was a great strength of his.'

Arthur described it as a joint master-class of how to play high-class spin bowling. Almost gleefully he recalled: 'Basil was a good player on a wicket like that. He was such a good hitter over the top – he'd wait and wait and wait and then, if the ball was up to him, he used to let it go bump, just like that, and just hit it down the ground, and Tom of course was pure class, playing forward as only he can.' It was a reminiscence rewarded with a long and respectfully appreciative pause.

Arthur himself was a fine player of spin bowling, as Tom Graveney reminded me. 'Arthur had a great talent, a great talent. He played so well on turning pitches and of course the pitches were uncovered then. You had to have a decent technique when you played on a turner, and Arthur was masterful in these situations.'

But we have interrupted Arthur's memories of his pal Tom. 'Anyway, I was delighted for Tom. We never lost touch with each other, and we have always been great pals, really, right from the beginning. He took me up to the Test, my first Test match, at Headingley. He took me up by road and looked after me. I appreciated that as a new boy.

'Later on, of course, Tom was elected President of MCC, which I thought was a terrific gesture – he was the first old pro to be honoured in that way, which was marvellous.

'When he was president he very kindly invited us – some of his old cricket mates and our wives – to a day's cricket with him in the President's Box at Lord's. We were looking forward to that and were all due to go up for the England–Bangladesh Test – we were going up as his special guests on the Sunday. And England had the blooming match over and done with on the Saturday!'

As we have seen, Arthur had batted down the order early in his career. 'That was the way things were then. As a youngster you started down the order, and worked your way up.'

He recalled that, in 1951, the chance came to move up. 'I opened once or twice, when Martin Young was injured, and showed that

I could do it and enjoyed it really.' By 1955 he had established a fruitful opening partnership with Young; 'I then started opening regularly when Jack Crapp and George Emmett thought I might make the England side.'

This seemed an immensely generous – and visionary – gesture on their part, as it meant one or other of them moving down the order to make way for Arthur. One wonders how easily some modern-day players would offer such altruism, and I made this point to Arthur.

'Well, they obviously thought I was worth it, was worth a place in the England side. I always got runs when they were needed even if, sometimes, I played best when I'd had a metaphorical kick up the arse to make me concentrate, you know. And the fact was, part of that challenge came with playing on our wickets at Bristol. Anyway, it showed they thought I had enough in me to make it, to make the grade.

Jack Crapp probably had it in mind that retirement was not far off (in fact he retired in 1956, to become a respected and long-serving first-class umpire good enough to stand in Test matches). While there might have been a sense of grooming a potential successor, there was also the realistic realisation that Arthur had what it took to be an opener, and to open for England. George Emmett played on until 1959, by which time Arthur Milton and Martin Young had firmly established themselves as a consistent and high-scoring opening partnership for the county.

'Playing in Australia on that 1958–59 Tour really sharpened me up because, the next season, I was opening as usual – with Youngy – and we each made six hundreds. We made a lot of runs together. Two of my hundreds were against Somerset – my favourites – and there was 99 against Essex, at Leyton in that match we tied.'

Arthur retained a natural youthfulness almost throughout his playing days; for a long time, he retained, too, his youthful appearance. Photographs of Gloucestershire or England teams in which Arthur played look as if a schoolboy – albeit a senior school cricketer – had sneaked into the line-up. This eternal youthfulness added to his appeal, and there were countless young followers of

Gloucestershire or England who felt a natural affinity with him for this very reason.

When Arthur looked back to his earliest days on the Gloucestershire staff, and when together we looked at team pictures of this era, it wasn't difficult to create that vision of a young lad who had just walked off the school playing field and been invited to turn out for the county side – a young lad with the natural diffidence of youth, until his cricket bat skilfully and confidently proved his entitlement to be alongside his seniors.

Was it a big staff? 'No, no – that's why I got the call to go to Northampton, when I made my debut. There were probably only 12 to 13 pros in those seasons just after the war, if that.'

Who were those seniors when he first played for the county?

'Jack Crapp and George Emmett, Colin Scott, George Lambert – he was a good bowler, George, he should have gone to Aussie sometime or another. Andy Wilson and Tom – Tom Graveney – of course, he'd played one season before I arrived. Sam – Sam Cook.'

Over the ages so many others, team-mates and opponents alike, have spoken warmly and affectionately of Sam – the 'Tetbury Plumber' as Wally Hammond christened him. Arthur often spoke similarly of Sam, his long-time contemporary and team-mate, who enjoyed nothing better than to bowl – and then bowl some more. And Arthur's simple, sincere summing up of Sam – 'What a bowler, a great lad' – said it all.

'I remember the first time I saw Cooky. It was in a sort of a trials pre-season practice match, North of County versus the South, up at Gloucester, and Tom Goddard was captaining the northern side – can't remember who was captaining our side or very much else about the game. Tom didn't have anyone to take the new ball, so Sam had to come up and bowl. I was opening. I suppose I must have been quite young and not on the staff then, and he got me out for not very many. He came and apologised afterwards. That was the first time I met Sam.

'When he retired it wasn't the same for us, bowling sides out, because we'd lost the old slow left-armer, and you need one of each, the left-armer and the off-spinner. We had plenty of off-spinners, perhaps one or two too many.

'BO Allen – Basil Allen – was the captain, of course in my first two or three seasons. Then came Sir Derrick Bailey, another amateur of course, for a couple of seasons in 1951 and '52 – quite a character. He had been brought up in South Africa, where his father was a very wealthy industrialist and something big in the diamond mining industry. I got on quite well under Sir Derrick.

'The boys used to moan about him a bit – some thought he was a bit aloof and seemed conscious of his position. That never worried me and I decided just to get on with it, and make the most of what I could do. But at the end of one season – I can't remember which it was, probably 1952 – some of the senior players let the secretary know how they felt, but Jack and George didn't go. As senior players they wouldn't have anything to do with it.

'When he was captain, though, I did have quite a nice run of form, even though it was still my early days – and he himself did get the odd hundred. I remember he used to wear all his father's old shirts. His father had been in the army and Sir Derrick used to wear his old khaki shirts and things. He was odd in those sorts of ways.'

Arthur recognised there were moments of good humour, too, during Sir Derrick's time as captain. He shared a lovely story of an over bowled by Bomber Wells in 1951. It was the Falstaffian bowler's debut for the county and Sir Derrick's first year as captain. So they knew little of each other.

'The skipper walked in as Bomber bowled the first ball, and then turned and walked back to his mark ready for Bomber to bowl his next delivery. But Sir Derrick hadn't switched on to the fact that Bomber had virtually no run-up. Occasionally – very occasionally – he might have a run-up of six or seven paces but mostly he bowled with a one-pace, or no-pace, run-up. Anyway, by the time the skipper turned to walk in again, Bomber was already on the third ball of the over!'

Sir Derrick quickly became aware that a Bomber Wells over took little time. He also became aware of Bomber's sometimes quirky, almost always joyful approach to the game, even if he didn't always go along with it. Arthur went on to tell the delightful story, part of cricket's folklore, of Bomber bowling to Roly Jenkins – something of a chip off the same block, another good spin bowler and good-natured, good-humoured comic – at Worcestershire's beautiful Severnside ground, and completing the over within the time the cathedral bells chimed 12 noon.

'What do you think you're doing?' Sir Derrick enquired.

'Not a lot,' came Bomber's reply.

'You're making the game look stupid,' was the captain's testy rejoinder.

'I'm not,' insisted Bomber. 'That's what I normally do.'

'I want you to go back ten yards further, and then come in from there.'

'Well,' Arthur continued, 'dear old Bomber walked back an extra ten yards, and then decided he would bowl from there. So, with his usual no-run run-up, he bowled it from there, ten yards further back. We were in stitches. George Emmett was doubled up at short leg, but the captain went berserk. He dropped Bomber for a couple of matches after that.'

Mention of Roly prompts two stories worth recalling, if only to remind ourselves that many dedicated professionals were determined the game was there to be enjoyed. Arthur would firmly include himself in their number.

At Cheltenham one year, George Emmett hit Roly for four successive fours. Above the home crowd's mounting approbation, Roly shouted down the wicket: "George, if you don't like me, say so – but for Christ's sake don't take it out on the ball!"'

On another occasion, at The Parks, a promising young university batsman found himself batting against one of the wiliest and most competitive of leg-spinners. It seemed he had encountered little of this kind of bowling before. Unavailingly he kept lunging forward to Roly's deliveries, making no contact whatsoever, unable even to nick a run off the edge. Eventually Roly stood, hands on hips, and said to the perspiring batsman: 'Laddy, if you give me that bat, I'll go and get some edges put on it before you bat again on Monday.'

In any talk of this era the names of Jack Crapp and George Emmett were seldom far from Arthur's thoughts. As senior pros and later captains of the county – Jack in 1953 and 1954 as successor to Sir Derrick Bailey, and the first professional to captain the county, and George from 1955 until 1958 – they made an immense impression on Arthur. It would be a lasting and valued appreciation.

The regard he had for both of them was summed up splendidly one day when Arthur said, 'Well, George and Jack would teach you your cricket – and they taught you your manners, too. You knew if you nicked it you had to go, or else you would be in trouble.'

That unambiguous and unwavering distinction between right and wrong, in cricketing matters and in other aspects of the players' lives, was made very clear to those who played alongside Jack and George. This was apparent in what they said and in the example they set for their team-mates. It was a creed Arthur followed all his playing days.

'But they were different altogether from each other. George could win you a match in an hour; they couldn't bowl at all at him sometimes. He got 90 against the Aussies and he got picked for a Test match, at Old Trafford I think.'

George Emmett, a slight and short right-hander, was one of those whose armoury included every shot in the book. Quick and well balanced on his feet against the spinners, and a fearless hooker and cutter of the quicks, Emmett held the bat high on the handle and employed a flowing back-lift to drive wristily on either side of the wicket. With such gifts he played countless attractive and memorable innings, as almost 23,000 runs for the county and 34 first-class centuries would suggest. If his penchant for taking the attack to the opposition occasionally led to an early downfall, it was seldom without providing entertainment on the way.

'George was a beautiful player,' Tom Graveney recalled, 'but a funny fella, mind.'

The adventurous spirit seen in Emmett's batting was often evident in his captaincy, and it came as something of a surprise to learn from Arthur that, as skipper, George was a firm disciplinarian.

But undoubtedly Emmett was awarded the team's respect. It was a respect and regard Arthur never lost: 'George, on his day, was liable to take anyone apart. Jack was a very solid, a more stolid player.'

Crapp, with all the bearing of an unhurried countryman, was a sound and prolific left-hand batsman. Batting usually in the early middle order, his record matched that of George Emmett; his 23,615 first-class runs including 38 centuries. Jack was also a high-class and brilliant slip fielder, something which would have endeared him even more to Arthur.

'Jack got a hundred against the Aussies at Bristol in 1948. I remember seeing part of his knock. I used to call in at the ground often on my way home from school, on my bicycle, and see the last hour or so's play, but I guess I must have been on leave from the Army to see Jack get his hundred.'

Arthur's sharing of this particular memory offered an insight into his affection and regard for those who had helped him in life, those he was proud to say he had played alongside. For in that match the Aussies scored a phenomenal 774-7, Arthur Morris making 290, Sam Loxton 159 not out, and a young Neil Harvey falling just short of a century, with 95. Bradman was not playing. But it was Jack Crapp's knock, undefeated on 100, that stayed at the forefront of Arthur's memory.

'Jack was a good skipper – and he used to talk to me a lot about the game. He had an amazing background too. He lived locally, of course, when he played for Gloucestershire but he was born, and brought up as a lad, in Cornwall. He lost his father in the First World War. And the family apparently didn't have any money and so his mother – she must have come originally from Bristol – and the children walked all the way from Cornwall up to Bristol.

'Jack was too nice in many ways, but it was a very happy side. He, George and the likes of them looked after you all right. They'd pass stuff on to you, bats and such-like. We used to get bats, a couple of bats from Stuart Surridge or other bat makers. He was very good. If you bought one, he gave you one, which was very nice. I guess most of the bat-makers did that.

'But I did finish up playing with Gray-Nicolls bats. They used to supply me. I used to get fed up at Bristol where the ball didn't bounce, and it was difficult to drive.' As we know, Tony Brown and John Mortimore had been trying to persuade Arthur to use a heavier bat – 'and one year – I'm not sure which one it was – Tony Brown had got a heavy bat from Gunn and Moore. In fact I've still got it – well, our grandson has got it now.

'We were up at Ashby de la Zouch and Browny said, "You ought to try this bat." We opened the innings and I got nought and Browny made 80-odd with the bat. So I used his bat in the second innings and made a hundred. It was the one I used when I got two hundreds in the match against Kent – at Bristol! – when we won the match off the last ball. So I kept that bat.'

Today's players are embarrassed for choice of kit provided by their sponsors and by their counties. This is not something that ever caused Arthur to feel any retrospective envy, but he gave a wry smile when he recalled that, when he became a pro, players had to provide for themselves. Apart from bats there was no sponsored gear. 'My Mum made my socks,' he remembered. 'Nylox she used to use. They were really good. My Mum was a great knitter. She used to knit all my stuff at school, for football and the like – and Joan carried on the sock knitting when we were first married.'

Arthur's undiluted regard for Emmett and Crapp was readily endorsed by Tony Brown. 'Absolutely, quite right, they were fantastic. George could give you a rough ride but all for our own good. Arthur would say exactly the same, although obviously he was treated differently from us younger lads. But if George said something then you listened, and even years later you'd know that what he had said then stood everybody in good stead.

'Jack was captain when I first started playing. I can remember sharing a room with Derek Hawkins and we'd gone to bed – the senior men used to stay up a bit later than the younger guys – and we thought we'd play a trick on them.

'Derek put a call through to the hotel reception, asking for Jack Crapp of Gloucestershire CCC. When Jack came on the phone Derek said – using a disguised accent: "Oh hello, is that the captain?

Would you like to buy a battleship?" and swiftly put the phone down.

'Anyway, at 7 o'clock in the morning the phone went in our room, and a slumbering Derek Hawkins woke blearily to pick up the phone, to hear a voice say, "Oh, by the way, how much is that battleship?"

'And nothing more was said – or needed to be said. He didn't give us a bollocking or anything. But they could do what they had to do.

'George, who was a superb striker of the ball, would often say "Don't play the lap shot, don't play this or that," but it was very much, "Do as I say, not as I do." They were both excellent and there's no doubt Arthur was quite right, they taught you how to behave as well as sharing their experience about how to play.'

It wasn't long before Arthur's heart and his memory took him back to some of the others he played alongside, and from whom he learned much about the game.

'George Lambert was not the worst. He had quite a family, George. He was a very good bowler, and he always bowled well on a good wicket, but when he got a wicket that helped him he never seemed to be able to make the best use of it. Jack and George used to moan about that,' Arthur recalled.

Lambert had been 20 when the Second World War started and his engagement in that tougher, more demanding campaign denied him six vital years of his career and reduced the prospect of winning an England cap.

The Paddington-born, MCC-trained fast bowler would take 917 wickets for Gloucestershire with an action of which 'Bomber' Wells once said, 'If ever a fast bowler had a better action than George Lambert, I have yet to see him.'

Arthur recalled another player of that era. 'We also had a chap called Billy Neale and 1948 was his last season. He wasn't an amateur but Wally Hammond used to stay with him. He used to go to Billie's when he was at school in Cirencester. His parents lived in Kent, so Wally didn't often go home. He lost his Dad at the end of the First World War, did Wally. I watched Wally a bit when I was still at school.'

It is said that when Wally Hammond first saw the young Milton his appraisal was brief – and unqualified. 'He'll do,' he said, and then swiftly added: 'But don't try to change him' – praise indeed from such a distinguished quarter.

To that point Arthur and Wally had noted each other from a distance, but then came the moment when they appeared together in the same county side. 'Wally's last season for Gloucestershire was really 1946, but in 1951 – as a sort of PR job to bring in the crowds – he played in the bank holiday match against Somerset, and I batted with him.

'George [Emmett] and I opened the innings. We each got a hundred. George got his before me, of course. When he got out, Wally came in. Of course he was quite old by then' – in fact he was 48, just a tad older than Arthur would be in his final season for Gloucestershire. He hadn't played first-class cricket for five years – 'and he didn't seem too fit, which was sad for someone who had been such a fine athlete and a fine cricketer, one of the true greats. He wasn't too good on his feet either. I suppose I hadn't properly registered this when I called him for a short single. Oh dear – he had no possibility of getting in.

'I forget who the fielder was, but he bowled the ball in underarm, and the 'keeper thought it was going to hit, so he stood up. The ball missed the wickets and Wally got in – to my great relief. Golly, the crowd would have lynched me otherwise, wouldn't they?

'Anyway, I got my hundred when Wally was still at the wicket, but he never said a word' (this proffered without any rancour). 'Perhaps he was a bit puffed. He didn't get many, about five. But it was a mistake – a generous one mind you – for him to agree to play. He should never have accepted the invitation to play.'

Also in the Gloucestershire side that day was John Mortimore, who remembered the enthusiasm among the crowd who turned out to see Hammond again: 'Mind you, quite a few spectators seemed reluctant to watch until Wally had got his first run. And Somerset were not going to make it easy. One or two of them remembered him coming out to bat against them at Bristol in '46, when his face had a look about it which said, "This might be the last time – and here's something to remember me by," and he got 200 odd. They'd suffered on many occasions. Of course, there wasn't a side that hadn't suffered at some time from Wally's bat, and some had suffered more than others.

'He used to come back to play in benefit games or charity games at Badminton where the Duke of Beaufort used to run a game for the beneficiary,' Arthur recalled. 'It was a very good Sunday, plenty of people there.

'I remember Wally making a hundred there the first time he came. I had to get him off the mark though.

'I also had to get the Duke of Edinburgh off the mark in one game. He was playing in a game for the National Playing Fields Association, which was his big project. He was its president, I think. I was a bit worried I might get him out, but dear old Reg Sinfield was umpiring. He said, "Don't worry, leave it to me, I'll call no-ball if necessary."

'Not long after that Prince Philip came to Highbury where the Arsenal were playing against Hibernian, the Scottish League champions, in a game for the National Playing Fields Association – I think we beat them six-something. We were introduced to the Duke before the game and as Joe Mercer accompanied him along the line, introducing us, the Duke said: "Ah, this is how you keep fit for cricket, is it?" so perhaps it was just as well I didn't get him out at Badminton.'

After these delightful meandering reminiscences Arthur returned again to thoughts of his team-mates in those early summers.

'Monty Cranfield was an off-spinner, although he missed out quite a lot because of Tom Goddard being in the side. Colin Scott, a fair-haired young quick bowler from Downend, who converted himself into an off-spinner for a while, was a very good fielder; he taught me a lot about my fielding.'

High praise from one of the outstanding fielders of his own era; indeed of any era. 'Cooky always used to have somebody on the drive – not silly mid-off, you know, but on the drive, to be able to pitch the ball up and let them drive, and Scotty … he'd catch anything there. It could be hit as hard as you like but he'd catch it. Never a doubt.

'As young players we used to field out all the time. Then they decided to bring me in because they were lacking close catchers, lacking in the gully, I remember. And Colin knew what the story was.

'He'd say, "Get down and stay down. You need to get down, because it's easier to come up than go down. If you have to go down again, you won't catch anything – and stay down and don't do anything until you see it."

'It was good advice. I passed that on to a few. I remember "Kipper", Colin Cowdrey, talking to me and asking lots of questions about fielding, when we were on the boat to Australia. He was pretty nifty at slip for a biggish fellow, and he always wanted to know about the game and talk about it. On that trip he used to come and find me, to do some catching practice on deck, and he'd hit me catches and see if he could make me miss one or two. I loved him. He was a gentleman.'

And as the memories flooded back, the tears welled up in Arthur's eyes. For someone so down to earth, who took life in his stride, things like this – a genuine regard for someone sadly no longer with us – moved him enormously.

This led to us both reminiscing about Colin Cowdrey's legendary note and postcard writing. Arthur recalled writing to Colin when the latter was quite ill, 'and saying a few nice things, about how much I had enjoyed playing with him and against him – and also for his being there in our salad days, so to speak. I had a card back with just one or two lovely words from him – I've got it upstairs somewhere – and he died the next week.'

And then, after a long reflection, he added, 'He was an amazing batsman, a beautiful driver of the ball, wasn't he? Colin called in here once or twice. He was a good friend of Brian Huggett, the golfer. Colin used to go and visit him, and called in here on his way through to see him.

'I could have played for Kipper, you know, without any doubt,' Arthur said, and turned to wondering how things might have been had Cowdrey skippered the 1958–59 tour to Australia rather than Peter May. In typical Arthur fashion he was loath to criticise the tour management, but simply added, 'Well, it might have been a better choice in my view.'

What about those Arthur played against? Who had he enjoyed facing?

'Glamorgan, the Glamorgan lads – I always loved it in the evening after play, especially when we played at Swansea. We used to meet up at the top of the pavilion, often with the rugby players as well, and Don Shep [Don Shepherd] who, along with Roger Davis, came on tour with us to Zambia in my later Gloucestershire days. Alan Jones, the opener, the left-hander who played for them all those years, he was a beautiful player; Jim Pressdee; Wilf (Wooller) of course; Allan Watkins …

'Later, after I had finished playing, when I was doing the rounds for TCCB as an observer, I was due at Glamorgan on the day when they had their old players' do, and they invited me to join them – and Joan too. It was the first time a girl had ever been there. We had a lovely day with them. And Allan Watkins had come back for the first time since he had finished playing, as he'd always been coaching at Oundle before.

'And Derbyshire. I liked playing against them. Donald Carr was such a lovely man' (said with real affection and warm regard in his voice). 'Donald was a nice cricketer. Another good "copper". And Alan Revill; he and I, we used to have our own competition to see who could take the most catches in the season. Arnold Hamer [who joined Derbyshire at the age of 33, having made two appearances for Yorkshire], with his red, round face. He got a lot of runs for them.

'Hampshire. I enjoyed playing against them – and of course the Worcester lads too, they were a great bunch, and Somerset.' And as Arthur's memory slipped into this particular gear I recognised it would not be many seconds before he had recalled all the counties and all those players whose human qualities especially, as well as their cricketing skills, had fixed them for ever in his mind.

'EDR Eagar – Desmond – he was the "cash man" on the trip to Aussie in 1958–59 you know, and later became Hampshire's secretary when he gave up the captaincy. He and Ingleby [Colin Ingleby-Mackenzie] were a good pair. Jim [Gray] could sometimes be a bit critical of certain things, cricketwise that is, but he was a great friend and a good one. Neville Rogers I liked, and Shack [Derek Shackleton] of course.

'The stories they used to tell about Shack. Apparently he never really bothered to look after himself fitness-wise much in the winter, so it used to take a month of the summer before he bowled himself fully back into shape. And Leo, Leo Harrison, he was a grand guy. And Arthur Holt …' and, as always, as the names tripped off his tongue it was invariably accompanied by that warm and affectionate chuckle which said almost as much as the words, sometimes more.

Arthur's reminiscences reminded me that I once watched Leo Harrison running an MCC coaching course. In the process of demonstrating the basics of bowling, the long-serving wicketkeeper had placed a folded newspaper on a good length. With a virtually seamless, black-and-white halved coaching ball he then proceeded to pitch the ball on the paper every time. Not satisfied with that he then demonstrated the bowler's grip for the out-swinger and made this seamless ball arc away from the bat, followed by the in-swinger which ducked in to order. Had he not captured 681 victims behind the stumps he might well have got them from the other end.

It was yet another cricket reminiscence which set off Arthur's memories and thoughts. 'If you're interested it's not difficult. I used to have a ball like that. I could bowl both. It took me a while to get the in-swinger – I could bowl out-swingers naturally. I used to do the left-handers in our nets; used to get Andy [Wilson] out for a pastime.

'Crumpy – Brian Crump, who played for Northants – he used to bowl unplayable balls at times. And when we were playing Northants I'd had a bet with somebody that I'd get a 50 at Gloucester. I was on 48 at lunchtime and thought, "I'll win the bet." And we came out after lunch and he pitched one on leg and hit the top of the off. He did me a few times.

'Anyway, we were playing them up there. Tom [Graveney] was captain – and we had to get the last couple out. Tom had left a gap in the slip field and, damn me, the ball went through there – if it had gone to hand we'd have probably won the match. Crumpy was in and time went on and I said to Tom, "Tom, come on, I'll have a bowl, let me have a go." Crumpy was well set as I ran up and bowled the first two, and then I bowled him one that did quite a little bit, away from him, and he missed it.

'So I thought, "Now's the time for the inner," and I bowled the old inner and he went back, shouldered arms …' and, chuckling at the recollection, Arthur finished the tale, '… he went back and over went his stumps. Oh, I did enjoy that. He'd had me so many times himself.'

Chapter 9

In the Reckoning

ARTHUR'S CALL-UP as England's twelfth man in 1953 was followed, at the start of the following summer, by his selection for MCC against Surrey, the champion county. Here were sure signs that his continuing progress and promising form was being noted by those beyond the county's boundary, importantly by those charged with selecting the national side. He seemed to be in with a definite shout.

In the three summers from 1954 to 1956 Arthur showed the season-by-season continuing advance which was the general pattern of his career, each season offering more than its predecessor.

Of the five centuries he made in 1954, three came in successive games, lifting his fortunes in a season which began unpromisingly. In his opening first-class game Jim Laker struck twice, restricting Arthur to single-figure scores.

A 71 in mid-May against Kent at the Wagon Works ground, a venue which frequently saw him in his best run-scoring form, was remarkably his sole half-century in his first 18 knocks but then, in the return match (return match, note) with Oxford University at Bristol, in mid-June, he scored 142 before falling 'c. Cowdrey b. Fasken' – and it re-opened the tap. Runs again began to flow.

Against Nottinghamshire, at Bristol, in early July he scored 111 in his county's only innings as they won by an innings and 45 runs. This he followed with another century, 163, against Northants, also at Bristol.

He was on a roll, as Surrey discovered in their home match at The Oval where he made a hundred in Gloucestershire's first innings, before falling caught and bowled Laker. Three centuries in a row helped make up for that frugal start to the season.

And, to sign off the summer, in the county's home game against Warwickshire he notched up another century, 135, before being caught behind the wicket by Dick Spooner off Jack Bannister's bowling.

Intriguingly, four of his five hundreds had been made at the County Ground. Clearly he didn't always find it difficult scoring runs there – or had the pitch, or the circumstances of the match, created that challenge which brought the best from him?

Arthur's century against Nottinghamshire was described in Gloucestershire's yearbook as 'his finest innings to date'. Nottinghamshire's Bruce Dooland, an Australian-born all-rounder, was a batsman of immense class and a leg-spin and googly bowler, considered by many to be the best of the postwar generation until the emergence of Shane Warne. In this match he showed redoubtable form, aided by a helpful pitch.

Dooland had played three home Tests for Australia in 1947 and 1948 but was omitted from the party (Don Bradman's 'Invincibles') that toured England in 1948. Nevertheless, he came to England that summer and played the first of four very successful seasons with East Lancs of the Lancashire League. His form encouraged Nottinghamshire to sign him for the 1953 season, at the age of 30. In that first summer he just missed the cricketers' double of 1,000 runs and 100 wickets, but was to achieve that feat on two subsequent occasions, including 1957, his final season with Notts.

Dooland had already taken his first wicket when Arthur came to the middle with the score at 86-2, soon to become 96-4. At this stage he was joined by his captain, Jack Crapp, and, with a fine display of batting, they added 130 for the fifth wicket. Crapp's share was 30.

In the Reckoning

How did Arthur rate that innings? Was it among his best?

'Yes, yes … I remember we were having a drink in the bar, after the first day. We had bowled Notts out [for 166] and I'd watched how Joe Hardstaff played Sam Cook. I was fascinated to watch how he played him. Well, after the day's play we were in the bar and I talked with Joe about how he played the spinners. And then next day against Dooland and the others I finished up with 80-odd not out at close of play, after we had bowled them out.

'The Notts boys used to bet like hell among themselves, and Joe said, "I've bet our fellows your lot are not worth a hundred. We reckoned we only had to get one man out – you! – and now you look like making a hundred on your own."'

And next morning that was what Arthur did, leading Gloucestershire to a first-innings total of 289, to bring them their victory. The county's spinners – Sam Cook, Bomber Wells and John Mortimore, along with pace bowler Frank McHugh – played their part too.

From a slow start, Arthur had blossomed into his best form. After six summers as a professional cricketer Arthur had scored 8,130 runs, taken 57 wickets, and held on to 202 catches.

As we know, by the summer of 1955 he had become Martin Young's regular opening partner. Altogether, between their first pairing and Young's retirement in 1964, they would share 21 century partnerships, 14 of them for the first wicket.

Arthur was also continuing to win selection for representative sides. Following Gloucestershire's traditional season-opener against Oxford University at The Parks, he was again called up by MCC to play the champion county – Surrey again, by now in the middle of their seven-year reign – and, at the season's end, he played for England XIs against the South Africans and against a Commonwealth XI, both at the Hastings Festival. He was, it seemed, still in the reckoning.

His highest score that summer, 150, came in the championship match against Worcestershire – 'I remember that, at Gloucester, Youngy and I put on an opening stand of over a hundred.' The Wagon Works ground yet again had proved a happy hunting ground, as had the County Ground at Taunton, where he scored yet another hundred (138), and where he was undefeated on 44 in his second innings of a drawn game. Ten half-centuries accompanied those two centuries and contributed to his season's aggregate of 1,821 runs.

Arthur may have firmly persuaded himself that the Bristol wicket did not favour his style of batting but his perpetually tenacious response to a challenge was again seen in the county's low-scoring match with Lancashire at Nevil Road.

After their first innings of 198 (the highest total of the match), Gloucestershire bowled out their visitors cheaply, giving themselves an advantage of 73 runs, a useful lead. However, a second-innings scoreline of 74-8 suggests the home team had not gained unequivocal control of the game. In truth, that scoreline offered a significant improvement from their earlier unhealthy position of 8-3 (when Martin Young, Tom Graveney and Jack Crapp had all returned to the pavilion having scored 4 between them). For this recovery they owed much to Arthur who, after going in first with Young, carried his bat for 51. By sensible nursing of the tail, and with their support, he led an embattled Gloucestershire to a lead of 190. It was sufficient to earn the county a win by 88 runs as Lancashire succumbed to the bowling of Frank McHugh and Bomber Wells.

'They had done some pitch repairs, and there was a turf in the middle of the wicket on a good length – it was the last match of the season I think. Wickets fell steadily – this was another match at Bristol where it was such a challenge, especially with that patch there – and I batted through the innings. It must have been quite a challenge, mustn't it?' Arthur recalled, smiling away at the memory.

As a sign of the times it is perhaps worth noting that he batted 64 times in first-class matches that summer, a fairly typical workload for a professional in that era. Fifty-one of those innings were for Gloucestershire in championship games. The consistency and quality of his run-scoring, coupled with his nigh-infallible talents as a fielder, ensured that his name continued to be in the frame in the following summer.

His 1956 season brought two early appearances for MCC at Lord's. In their traditional opener against the champion county he played alongside his Gloucestershire partner Martin Young. He was also selected for the club's following game, against Hampshire.

MCC's 'bacon and egg' colours were donned again at the end of May, when Arthur was chosen to play against the Australians at Lord's. His star was indeed in the ascendant.

The Hastings Festival saw him in action again at the summer's end, for an England XI against the Australians – his third meeting with them that summer – and for an England XI against a Commonwealth XI. Against the Australians he made 94 (out of 222-7 declared), a good end-of-season reminder to the selectors that his star was burning brightly.

An appearance for the Rest of England versus Surrey at The Oval was Arthur's final outing of the season. Of his batting there *Wisden* reported: 'On the first day Milton defended admirably when the pitch was probably at its trickiest.'

With a pitch at its 'trickiest' the batsmen found themselves up against bowlers who knew full well how to harness such trickery. Between them, Surrey's four-man attack in this game – Peter Loader, Alec Bedser, Jim Laker and Eric Bedser – had captured 444 wickets during the course of the summer. They knew what they were about.

Arthur's scores of 36 and 24 need to be set in the context of the game as a whole, in which the Rest of England made 192 and 72-3 declared and the champion county 71 and 72, this for a Surrey side at full strength apart from Tony Lock. The bowling figures suggest a 'sporting' pitch, and Surrey's quartet of bowlers were all among the wickets, as were those firing for the Rest: Frank Tyson (Northants), Fred Trueman (Yorkshire), and Lancashire's Roy Tattersall and Mervyn Hilton. Remarkably the most expensive of the eight bowlers in action was Alec Bedser, in the Rest's first innings, yet his 4-78 was a worthy return from 28 overs.

Surrey may have lost to that Rest of England XI, but they had earlier beaten a powerful Australian side (Jim Burke, Colin McDonald, Ken Mackay, Neil Harvey, Keith Miller, Len Maddocks,

Ray Lindwall, Ian Johnson, Alan Davidson, Pat Crawford and Jack Wilson) – and did so by ten wickets. And if that Australian side, with a number of the game's greats, was memorable, so too was the Surrey side: David Fletcher, Tom Clark, Bernie Constable, Peter May, Ken Barrington, Roy Swetman, Dennis Cox, Jim Laker, Stuart Surridge, Tony Lock and Peter Loader.

There was no reason why that particular Surrey versus the Tourists match should have registered with Arthur (apart from his customary perusal of scores when opening the next day's papers) for he was playing against Warwickshire at Bristol at the same time. But it was, and is, firmly and indelibly fixed in my own memory. It was the first first-class match I saw, having travelled to The Oval with a group of fellow pupils from my school in Newbury, to sit on the benches beneath the shadow of the gas-holders. How it whetted my appetite. And what special delight there was for a Berkshire boy to know that May and Barrington, as well as the Bedser twins (not playing that day), were Berkshire boys too.

During this glorious introduction to the great game I never, for one second, thought (dreamed might be more appropriate, and what wild dreams they would then have been) that a decade and a half later I would begin a career with Worcestershire which would bring me into contact with many of them as colleagues and as friends.

One of those good friendships established through the great game of cricket was, of course, with Arthur, whose memories were now taking him back to that particular summer. 'That year, 1956, was an interesting one for me,' he reflected. 'One of the things I remember was making a hundred against Yorkshire, which is always something, at Bramall Lane.

'A week or so before that we were playing Notts at Stroud. Joe Mercer had been on holiday down in Cornwall somewhere, and on his way back saw that we were playing at home and he called in at Stroud to see me and to watch some cricket.

'So, you see, I said to him: "Joe, we're coming up to Bramall Lane soon. It would be good to see you again and I'll leave you some tickets on the gate, shall I?"

'He said, "Fine, that'll be fine."

'So we go up there and win the toss and bat. I'm still not out at lunchtime, on the way to a hundred, and when I come in for lunch Joe's in the dressing room – and I can see by the fun and hilarity that he's been entertaining them all, all ruddy morning.

'I was, of course, really pleased to see him again and so I said, "Nice to see you Joe. Did you get the tickets I left for you on the gate?"

'With a lovely look on his face, and the smile that so many people got to know, he said, "My office is only up there," pointing up in the stands there at Bramall Lane. "I don't need tickets to get into the ground."'

Arthur laughed gleefully away at the memory of his old pal. Here, yet again, was an Arthur Milton story which, if not exactly told against himself, swiftly bypassed a landmark or two of his own.

In that match at Stroud he had made 70 not out, again with the support of the lower batting order and John Mortimore in particular, and guided Gloucestershire from 95-5 to 214 all out. His old Arsenal mucker would have been proud of him.

Telling the tale of Joe Mercer's visit to Stroud and then of Gloucestershire's game at Bramall Lane, might – in other players of a different mindset – have triggered another story about himself concerning the return fixture with Yorkshire at Bristol, played a week later. But it needed a trawl through the match reports to highlight the story; no word came from Arthur, though it deserved to.

At Nevil Road, Yorkshire won the toss and batted. Brian Close made 42 out of Yorkshire's paltry 95 (George Lambert took eight very inexpensive wickets that day). If this disheartened the men from the Broad Acres their spirits were given a fillip on bowling out Gloucestershire for 88. Yorkshire's second innings was another low-scoring effort as Wells, Mortimore and Cook ran through them, leaving Gloucestershire needing 99, the highest score of the match, to win.

This was just the sort of challenge that inspired Arthur. He made 31 not out and with his opening partner George Emmett, (62 not out) scored 100 for the first wicket – so win Gloucestershire did, by ten wickets.

My reminding Arthur of this knock fired his memory about yet another innings – and also about his fielding that summer. 'And then there was a hundred, too, against the old enemy at Taunton – and 63 catches, which meant I won the Brylcreem Cup, the award for the most catches in the season.

'Brylcreem – do you remember they used to sponsor Denis Compton, the "Brylcreem Boy"? – only did the award for three years, and I won it in two out of the three. I think I won it in 1954 as well, and Stuart Surridge must have won it in the year between.'

Arthur told this story, with its reference to Denis Compton, without ever mentioning that he too was a 'Brylcreem Boy' – as was Johnny Haynes, Fulham FC and captain of England – and his fresh-faced wholesome image appeared on adverts and posters at that time: 'Men of Tomorrow use Brylcreem Today'. One so associates Denis Compton with the Brylcreem image that it is easy to forget the company also used Arthur and Johnny, with their images as successful, decent, honest and upright sportsmen, to promote its wares. Happily Clara, Arthur's granddaughter, found a poster showing Arthur – one of the 'Men of Tomorrow' commending the use of Brylcreem. Years later David Beckham would also take on the mantle.

Arthur's fielding record is truly remarkable. In six of his 26 seasons he held on to 40 or more catches, his best being the 63 victims he dismissed in this summer of 1956. In 1959 he held on to 56 catches. In all first-class cricket he took 760 catches, an amazing record, which only seven players (Frank Woolley, WG Grace, Tony Lock, Wally Hammond, Brian Close, John Langridge and Wilfred Rhodes) in the history of the game have bettered.

'They were nice cups. I've got one in the cupboard here at home in our dining room and, as I had two, I gave one to my golf club, Long Ashton, to play for.'

The cup did indeed sit, unostentatiously, in a corner cupboard in the Miltons' dining room. It was one of the few visible reminders that his home was that of an international sportsman who had enjoyed a gilded career in two major sports. It was intriguing to note too, on the occasions when we met to work on this book and to look at some of Arthur's memorabilia, how little he had collected. Indeed, much of what he possessed had been sent him by others. Some of the newspaper cuttings of his youthful club cricket days must have been kept by his father, Bill.

The brilliance and reliability of Arthur's fielding required help from no one but, as was the way within cricket's freemasonry, occasionally a fellow player would offer a helping hand, as Tom Graveney disclosed: 'Arthur was a great catcher and – I shall never forget it – he was leading the catcher's table one year when we were playing Kent here at Cheltenham.

'Godfrey Evans walks in to bat and I could see he didn't want to hang about, he wanted to get off on the way home – it was the last day – and I said to Godders as he came in, "Don't forget Arthur's leading the catching."

'"One off the mark?" he asked. "Yes, I'll fix that," I told him. He got his one off the mark and the next time he took strike he turned to Arthur at slip and said, "Just a bit straighter, Arthur," and he went bang, and straight in it went,' Tom demonstrating Godfrey's chip to slip as he told the story.

As Arthur reminisced about his fielding he recalled: 'When I was one of the young 'uns and in the outfield I caught everything that came, of course, and got to some that nobody would ever think I could get to. Anyway, the thing was that they realised ... they thought that I would make a very good close-to-the-wicket fielder and so I began to field at the bat-pad position – you know, very short square. Jack [Crapp] used to field at leg-slip and I used to field here – that was pretty often. And then when Cooky was bowling, slow left-arm, we were the other side of the wicket – Jack would be at slip and I would be in the gully and we caught most of what came our way.' A memory offered, as so often, with typical Milton understatement and reserve.

Although Arthur had finished his football career in April 1955 he was occasionally tempted back to play in charity games. It was in one of those that he suffered an injury which cost him half a season's cricket, and that at a time when his form was being noted by England's selectors.

'During the winters I played a few friendly games for an All-Stars side. We used to go and play to raise funds for charity and other good causes. You would be given a few quid in your boots for expenses but, that apart, after I finished with the Arsenal and at Bristol City I didn't play any serious soccer.

'I'm sure it must have been in one of those games, in the winter of 1956–57, that I fractured my wrist. I went down on it, the one you break when you put your hand out to stop yourself hitting the ground, the scaphoid. Those fractures can take a long time to heal.

'I remember that, while I was having trouble with my wrist and could "feel" it after a while, it didn't really bother me that much at first. But I played some golf one day and it finished up that I couldn't hold the club properly, so I thought, "There's something wrong here." I went to see my doctor, who said, "Well, you are going to have that x-rayed but I know what it will be." He was sure it was the scaphoid. After six weeks it wasn't doing well enough, so I had to go and have another plaster put on, and so I was in plaster for about twelve weeks in all.

'It meant that I didn't start the next summer, 1957, until near the end of June when we played Cambridge University at Bristol. A 50 there was a good way to get back into the swing of things, and I still managed to score 750 runs in the remaining weeks of the summer. I was back at no. 5, of course, because by that time Martin Young was opening the innings with George [Emmett] again.'

There was, too, a brittleness about Gloucestershire's middle order, so his return lower down the order was welcomed.

That summer was one of the four 'valleys' – created by injury – in his career, when he missed out on scoring 1,000 runs. Nevertheless, his high batting average (42.11) showed all the old magic was there. In his foreshortened season there were no hundreds but he made ten half-centuries.

Four of those half-centuries came in Gloucestershire's games against Nottinghamshire. In the match at Trent Bridge he was undefeated in both innings, with 59 and 58. In the return at Bristol he was heading comfortably towards his century when Bruce Dooland bowled him for 89. Sixty-four not out in Gloucestershire's second innings took his aggregate against Notts that summer to 270 for once out. He was making up for the belated start to his season.

In his 17 championship matches, Arthur amply demonstrated that the wrist had recovered well and that he had retained his taste for run-scoring.

George Emmett, then in his third season as captain, was unavailable for the away fixture with Yorkshire that summer and, in Arthur's words: 'He gave it to me, when we played at Scarborough.' That first taste of captaining the county would remain special among whole hosts of games which stood out in Arthur's memory.

'We won the toss and bowled them out for not too many, 122, and only Closey [Brian Close] got runs. They were at one another,' he recalled, even a half-century later scarcely believing this hallmark of Yorkshire teams of that era. 'There were one or two, I think, who were prickly and a bit of a problem, but anyway ...

'At the end of the day we were in front, with about five wickets down. I was 84 not out, and I remember Youngy had scored 50 or 60 with me. Anyway, we had 'em by the short and curlies, didn't we?

'And it didn't rain but, you know, we didn't bowl a ball on the second day.'

Why was that?

'It was one of those sea frets. It hung about this high, four feet off the ground, and it never moved all day long. I felt really frustrated because it was not often you got the Yorkies in that sort of position, not in those days.'

Thwarted though the stand-in captain and his team may have felt, the sea fret lifted, allowing play to resume on the last day. Gloucestershire had declared with a first-innings lead of 90. By the close of that last day Yorkshire, with 117-5, had barely nosed into a lead, but it was enough to secure a draw.

If a few Gloucestershire players had things to say about Yorkshire's coastal weather as they headed south to New Road, Worcester, for their next championship game, it was unlikely their acting captain was of their number. As Tony Brown has recalled: 'Arthur wouldn't get upset about things like that. He was always so good like that. He wouldn't make a big issue of it.'

He later recalled, sea fret or no sea fret, that he had enjoyed his first chance to captain his county. 'And we had such a good match.' It was another high spot in a summer which, after his delayed start, had offered much satisfaction.

Selection in early September for an England XI to play a Commonwealth XI at Hastings offered further encouragement. A first-innings top score of 74 did his burgeoning reputation no harm. Such an encouraging and optimistic note would be good for the spirits in the winter months – especially as now there would be no football.

Yes, he was still in the reckoning.

Chapter 10

Another First – Capped Again for England

THE MCC CREST on the letter dropping on to the Milton household's doormat became a regular signal for the arrival of a new cricket season. Arthur's selection for the club's annual season-opener was becoming something of a custom.

The 1958 season was no exception. It began with an invitation from 'HQ' to play in the summer's opening fixture against Yorkshire – at last Surrey had been deposed – where his knocks of 47 and 48 were among the best performances in the game.

Arthur's fielding, however, first caught the eye. *The Times'* correspondent reported:

> *Close and Wilson (were) in possession, but not for long. Close, who might have been caught at backward short leg in Tyson's second spell, called for a sharp single but reckoned without Milton's power of return from the gully and Wilson, not the most nimble of men between wickets, was run out.*

His batting, too, made its mark on the man from *The Times*:

> *MCC's innings was not launched without incident, for with the total at 24 Hallam was dropped by Close at first slip off Pickles, who also came near to making Milton play on. But Pickles was out of luck, and Milton and Hallam made the most of it. Hallam sent up the 50 by pulling Trueman for six, a shot to warm the heart, but unwise as it turned out, for next ball Hallam was caught by Wilson at short leg at the second attempt. Then we had rather more than half an hour of Milton and Graveney which produced just 30 runs and much the best batting of the day. Unfortunately, Graveney, to whom all the bowling seemed to come so easily, was in a little too much of a hurry and a towering drive off Illingworth was held by Padgett in the deep after anxious fumbling. With the 100 up for the loss of two wickets Close was given a turn with the ball and promptly bowled Milton, whose departure must have been as much a disappointment to the onlookers on this first day of the season as it was to MCC.*

In the second innings he batted for some time with Roy Swetman, then Surrey's reserve wicketkeeper; later, of course, to join him at Gloucestershire. Swetman went on to make 107, his first hundred in first-class cricket. *The Times* told its readers:

> *Most of the time Milton was Swetman's companion, and a very accomplished companion he looked with his square and cover driving. He is obviously in good heart and if the evidence of this match is anything to go by a good season should lie ahead of him. He was out three short of the 50 he deserved, caught at mid-wicket off Wardle with the total 127.*

If a run of good innings, consistently made, make for a good season, then that is indeed what lay ahead of Arthur that summer.

Then, as if knowing when to pick his moment, he scored a century for Gloucestershire at Lord's in mid-June. As he recalled, 'It's always good to get runs at Lord's, and put your name in front of them.'

It was timely, for England's selectors were still seeking openers to fill the gap created by Len Hutton's retirement. Peter Richardson, of Worcestershire, had established himself in this slot but without a regular partner. In the first two Tests against New Zealand (both of which England won) Warwickshire's MJK Smith had been given the chance to make his mark as Richardson's opening partner. But the search went on.

In order to give opportunities to others who might partner Richardson on England's winter tour of Australia, the selectors took the most unusual step of 'resting' the Worcestershire man for the third Test to give other openers a real examination at international level.

Throughout his life Arthur always seemed ready to accept the cards that were dealt him and – to stick with this analogy for but a moment longer – one senses that he didn't often feel tempted to influence the dealer of the pack.

So we can assume his England selection was taken calmly in his stride; delighted himself, gratified shyly by the public recognition of his talent, and determined to do well – for his own sake, as well as for his new England colleagues, and for his family and friends, his Gloucestershire team-mates, and for all who had supported and encouraged him, for Arthur never liked letting anyone down.

He himself made little, and thought little, at the time of becoming a 'double international'. It was 'nice' – a simple word, but from his lips invested with rich abundance – to have been honoured by his country and been acknowledged as among the best at two sports, but that did not make him a better cricketer or prompt him to think any more highly of himself.

Nor did the press make a great song and dance about it then, at least not in the way it would be covered now. Can you imagine the hyperbolic, outrageous headlines if, say, David Beckham showed sufficient talent with the bat to be part of England's line-up for an Ashes Test, or if Freddie Flintoff had the ability to lead England's goal-scoring at Wembley?

To be a double international was a distinct and extremely rare honour. But it must be remembered that, back in 1958, it was not considered beyond the realms of possibility that another sportsman – or sportsmen, even – might follow in Arthur's footsteps. The limited overlap of the soccer and cricket seasons did not preclude the possibility, and there were a number of talented individuals who played at top level in both sports.

But as the years have advanced, the soccer season has become longer (now always overlapping seriously the summers of cricket), and as soccer clubs and their players became more mono-focused (blinkered, if you like) it has become apparent that any repetition of Arthur's achievement was less and less likely, indeed improbable.

So, with a stealthily increasing awareness of this improbability has come the recognition that Arthur, unquestionably, is the last of the double internationals, a realisation that has turned the spotlight more closely on his feat.

It is thus with a degree of irony that one notes that as Arthur went out to open the innings for England for the first time, alongside him was another dual international. Like buses, they don't come along very often and then two come together!

Mike Smith – MJK – had been capped by England at cricket and at rugby, and yet dual recognition in those two sports never seems to have captured the public's imagination, or the attention and regard of the press – the popular press, at least – in the same way as the cricketing soccer players. MJK, a fly-half and occasional full-back, played for Oxford University and England and, as befits a good all-round games player (he was a good squash player too), he had a wonderful pair of hands and a good eye.

In terms of sporting esteem, what a unique and remarkable distinction it was to have two double internationals opening the batting for England – and one of them was Arthur Milton.

The Times announced his selection thus:

Another First – Capped Again for England

Milton has been on the edge of the England team for several seasons, and he is probably no better a player now than he was two or three years ago. I believe, too, that, like Smith and Watson and Cowdrey, he is seen to more advantage in the middle of the order.

But the selectors were naturally anxious to try someone new to Test cricket, and by being chosen Milton will become one of the few men who have played both Association football and cricket for the full England side. He appeared at Wembley on the wing against Austria when a professional with Arsenal. Now he has given up serious football, preferring, instead, to make the most brilliant catches near the wicket for Gloucestershire, and bat off the back foot in his own casual way. There is no doubting his natural ability, and it remains to be seen whether he can sharpen his spurs sufficiently for Test match cricket.

Alongside Arthur in the England XI were Peter May (Surrey, captain), Trevor Bailey (Essex), Colin Cowdrey (Kent), Godfrey Evans (Kent), Tom Graveney (Gloucestershire), Jim Laker (Surrey), Peter Loader (Surrey), Tony Lock (Surrey), Mike Smith (Warwickshire) and Fred Trueman (Yorkshire).

His ten years in the county game, and his spells as England's fielding twelfth man, meant that all the players were familiar to him – a far cry from his arrival in the England soccer team's dressing room.

Nevertheless, he was pleased to find Gloucestershire team-mate Tom Graveney in the side, and was grateful that Tom was happy to drive them both to Leeds. There's little doubt that cricket talk came high on the agenda and, by the time Tom's car turned into the hotel car park, Arthur undoubtedly had a better insight as to what Test cricket was all about.

Tom saw in Arthur, 'a fine player. If he'd played anywhere other than Bristol – and perhaps if he'd had a bit more "devil" in him – he would have been one of the game's greats. He was a hell of a good player. He was a wonderful player off the back foot, and when the ball turned. He was a great talent, a good judge of a run, and a great catcher. And he was very intelligent. He did the *Daily Telegraph* crossword before anyone else in the dressing room.'

But let Arthur himself remind us about his Test debut.

'We had a wet day that first day.'

In fact the second day was rained off too and play started only on the third day, 5th July, continuing on the 7th and 8th, Test matches then being played (as they always should be!) on Thursdays, Fridays, Saturdays, Mondays and Tuesdays. Sunday was a rest day or often, for those inclined, a relaxing golf day.

After Jim Laker and Tony Lock had bowled out New Zealand for 67 it was time for the debutant to make his mark.

'We went out and opened the innings and I got off the mark off a bloke called Hayes. There's a photograph of him in *Wisden*, he bowled one halfway down and I tried to hit it … and it gloved me and went over the top of the wicketkeeper. That was my off-the-mark shot! And I finished up getting a hundred.

'Ken Barrington wasn't playing in that match, Tom Graveney got a few and eventually PBH [Peter May] came in. I had about 50 or 60 but he still got to a hundred before I did. But I did get to a hundred, which was rather nice.'

'Rather nice …' – no overweening histrionics or boastful ball-by-ball recounting of his first Test innings. That, of course, was Arthur: quietly rejoicing in the opportunities his talent – and destiny – had opened up to him, and genuinely grateful.

In making a hundred, Arthur became the first Gloucestershire player to score a century for England in his first Test since WG Grace in 1880. By the end of the match he had become, too, the first England player to be on the field of play throughout a Test match (although, as Arthur readily pointed out, 'rain restricted play to three days!').

His own recollections of what most would consider a major cricketing milestone were – typically – unsung, unassuming and completely lacking in any undue preoccupation with his own contribution or success.

Perhaps we need the conclusions of an independent observer to remind us of his first Test match. *The Times'* cricket correspondent reported:

> *Yet when the time came to leave the ground at the end of that third day there was something else to puzzle over apart from New Zealand batting, for Smith had failed again at the start of England's innings. When he and Milton went in thirty-five minutes were left, and the latter has no doubt earned himself a bonus mark by seeing out the day. He might just conceivably have been caught in the first over hooking at Hayes and deflecting the ball to Petrie's upstretched hand. After that he was quietly confident. Smith, however, was caught low down at slip playing back to an out-swinger from MacGibbon, and England unfortunately are no nearer to finding a partner for Richardson. Smith, it seems is not the answer after all, and to-day Milton has a chance to prove who is.*

Despite *The Times'* supposition about Mike Smith's prospects as an opener for England, he would make 50 Test appearances for his country and captain them in half of those games.

He was a good leader, popular, and respected by those who played alongside him and against him. His laid-back, unflappable demeanour and the bright sparkling eyes peering somewhat owlishly through his spectacles gave an impression of an absent-minded academic. It was an appearance which masked an astute cricketing brain, and a great love of the game.

Mike was a prodigious run-scorer, especially in county cricket (where in each of the six seasons from 1957 he scored 2,000 runs, with 3,245 coming from his bat in 1959). At Test level he would average 31.63. Arthur had a high regard for his fellow double international. 'MJK was a good captain you know. I liked him. I could have played for him, you know.'

The game resumed on the fourth day, giving Arthur, 5 not out overnight, the chance to prove he was the solution to England's search for an opener to join Peter Richardson. *The Times'* report unfolded the day's events:

> *The vast disparity between the England and New Zealand teams was underlined more heavily than ever in the third Test Match at Headingley yesterday, when England declared at 267 for two and New Zealand in their second innings made 32 for three in the face of a deficit of 200 runs.*
>
> *Now indeed, as has not happened before, New Zealand's bowlers were mastered on a day that was unbelievably fine and warm and blue, and two centuries were made for England, by May and Milton. For a batsman to score a hundred on his first appearance in a Test Match is an achievement at any time. For Milton to do so when England are engaged in such a desperate search for a partner for Richardson is a considerable event. A successful combination of opening batsmen has not been found since the firm of Hutton and Washbrook was dissolved in 1951. Since then something like 16 players have been tried, most of them without success, so that Milton's performance is obviously of much interest.*
>
> *A century on a first Test appearance was last achieved by May on this same ground against South Africa in 1951 and it was May who yesterday shared a stand of 194 with Milton. At the end of it there can have been little England's captain did not know about this 30-year-old batsman who has stolen a march on all his rivals for the Australian tour. His record, May must have known, consisted of 19 previous hundreds in ten seasons, five of them against Somerset, one against Oxford University, one against Combined Services, three against Nottinghamshire, and two of more significance against Yorkshire and Surrey.*
>
> *Now he was able to see Milton's technique at close quarters, to sense his philosophical approach, to admire the way in which he achieved what he set out to do and to observe his*

repertoire of strokes which, one is told, he has cut down
since he started to go in first for Gloucestershire.
Luck is bound to play some part in the ascent of a cricketer.
Some batsmen, for instance, get their chance in a Test
Match when an Australian attack is at its peak, others
when the tension is unbearable. Milton, for his part, found
everything in his favour when he resumed his innings
yesterday morning. Not only was the weather completely
reformed but the wicket also was slow and amiable. If it
favoured one particular type of bowler it was the spinner,
and New Zealand's strength lay elsewhere.

But Arthur still had to make the most of his good fortune, knowing that failure to do so would jeopardise his chance of going to Australia and revive the selectors' search for another opener.

At least 80 batsmen have made a century in their first Test innings but that number cannot mask the fact it is a remarkable and commendable feat. Was *The Times'* correspondent being guarded and sparing with his praise? Perhaps he had seen a number of pretenders to the opener's role come and go, and did not want to hail yet another false dawn?

The Times declared:

In an innings lasting five hours Milton laid bare his
limitations and revealed his stronger suits.
If he made more than a dozen runs off the front foot I
should be surprised. Just before luncheon he drove Reid for
two past cover point and he reached his 50 at a quarter
to three with a lofted drive over mid-on. But almost all
his scoring strokes were made off the back foot for his first
movement is to go back, and when, against his will, he is
drawn forward he seldom pierces the field.
There have, of course, been some great back-foot players in
Australia. Indeed they mostly fall into this category, with
certain notable exceptions over the years. But it seemed
yesterday as though it would be quite a simple matter to

silence Milton by pitching the ball up outside his off stump, and even when hooking or cutting his strokes hardly had the punch of a man who sees the ball so early in its flight. This may seem rather carping criticism, but the impression one gained was of a player with a first-rate temperament and a placid disposition. Small, fair, he seemed reluctant, except when in a hurry, to put one leg in front of the other, yet he has the look of one of Nature's games players and he played very few false strokes during his innings.

The day began with Gloucestershire in partnership and it was close on one o'clock by the time Graveney was well caught and bowled low down by Sparling. By then England were six runs ahead and a near neighbour [presumably in the press box!] *had taken his pullover off for the first time this year. The two best strokes had come from Graveney, both of them straight drives for four, but somehow he never quite looked like taking full advantage of the situation.*

May's innings was as chanceless and charming as it was inevitable. It lasted for less than three hours and Milton could not have been more blessed in his partners. He began with a close friend and then had the world's best batsman proceeding so smoothly that he himself had no scoring rate to worry about. At luncheon May was 20. Forty minutes afterwards he went to his 50 with a six and a four off successive balls from Cave; and at five past three, when he was 63, he overtook Milton whom he had given a start of 32. May's ninth Test century came five minutes before tea, scored out of 161.

Milton's progress was dictated by the number of short balls he received and a chart of his innings would show that his runs came when he had the chance to step away and steer the ball backward of cover point. The morning brought him 31: the afternoon a further 55. His first 50 he reached after just over three hours and when, at the tea interval, he was 91 not out May decided to bat on afterwards long

*enough to allow him the chance of a century. This he duly
reached at 4.50pm with, appropriately enough, a stroke
towards third man. He had hit twelve fours against May's
twelve fours and two sixes and as soon as he attained his
landmark May declared.*

New Zealand, faced with scoring 201 to win, again found Laker
(3-27 from 36 overs) and Lock (7-51 in 35.2 overs) in unassailable
form and they went down limply by an innings and 79 runs.

As a member of a victorious England team, and a century-maker
to boot, Arthur left Headingley with understandably high hopes of
playing in the fourth Test at Old Trafford. But Lady Luck doesn't
seek popularity and doesn't always stick to the script.

Arthur returned from Leeds to rejoin the Glosters at the
Wagon Works for the home matches with Northamptonshire
and Nottinghamshire. And then it was off to Lord's for the
traditional – and prestigious – game between the Gentlemen
and the Players. Surprisingly it was the first time that Arthur
had been selected for the Players in this historic annual fixture.
It would prove, too, to be the only occasion on which he played,
quite remarkable for a player who was among the most prolific
and consistent run-scorers in the county game and was highly
regarded by his peers.

His right to be there was more than justified when he made
101 in the first innings. But ambitions of cementing those good
impressions were quickly thwarted.

As he explained, 'When the Gentlemen were batting, Johnny
Wardle was bowling to my old mate Peter Richardson, a left-hander,
and I was fielding short square, here,' and, in that way so many
cricketers have, he began to show his own proximity to me as a
measure of how close he was to the batsman. 'They were all trying,
and trying to impress, because of the forthcoming tour to Australia
that winter.

'Wardle is bowling to Richardson, and I'm fielding here, and
he's telling me to get in closer, you know. Eventually he pitches one
up, and he was a great lapper, was Peter Richardson, and I used to

walk in quite often, a little bit, and Peter gave it the old lap and hit it straight into my face. I can vaguely remember coming back on the roll up, but he must have knocked me out.

'You can tell how bad it was as they had to get sawdust out to mop up the blood! It's the only time I was ever knocked out in my life. I just remember coming to, that's about all I can remember. Apparently I was in a bit of a mess around my mouth and cheek and they had to take me to hospital to get me cleaned up, and have some stitches put in.

'And do you know who looked after me overnight? EW Swanton. Jim Swanton took me in. He lived just round the corner from Lord's, and he took me home and asked his wife to look after me for the night, which was very nice.'

Arthur's appreciative tone here amply illustrated the warm gratitude he felt for the Swantons' spontaneous kindness and hospitality, perhaps recognising that, despite Jim Swanton's reputation in the cricket world for aloofness, there was indeed another side to him.

'I didn't take any further part in the match. Then Tom, Tom Graveney, brought me home I remember, and came in first to warn Joan not to worry about what I looked like!

'I always remember I had a mouthful of ulcers come up and the old doc gave me some tincture of myrrh to treat them because they used to hurt like hell. Oh dear, that brought tears to my eyes.'

As we sat there, with Arthur reminiscing away, we recognised that had he lived Jim Swanton would have been 100 the previous weekend. And off went Arthur with further reminiscences. 'Jim on TV had a very distinctive and well-rounded way of describing the day's play at the end of each day, didn't he? Yes, I used to love his summaries of a day's play.

'His wife, Ann, was a lovely lady. She was a wonderful, gifted pianist too. She used to play the piano in the evenings when we were away on tour in Australia in '58. It was very kind of her to look after me on that occasion when I got whacked.'

With his hundred against New Zealand and another good hundred for the Players Arthur might well have expected to see his name on England's team sheet again, but that injury at Lord's meant he was out of action for two weeks, until the end of July.

His keenness to get back meant he turned out for Gloucestershire against Sussex at Bristol at the same time as the fourth Test was being played. He was relieved that neither his form nor his confidence suffered. His knocks in Gloucestershire's remaining games were, if truth be told, relatively modest, although scores of 35 and 46 at Blackpool were significant contributors to delaying their innings defeat by Lancashire. They showed clearly that his relish of a challenge, and his ability to battle things out, remained undiminished.

Once he was match fit again, and with his Headingley century to his name, his recall for the final Test of the summer, at The Oval, was assured. Here Arthur opened with Peter Richardson in England's only innings. His knock of 36 was the side's top score, until Fred Trueman, coming in down the order, made an undefeated 39. As England pressed for a 5-0 whitewash they were seriously hampered by the weather, rain permitting only 12 hours' play over the five days.

It had, nevertheless, been an eventful and gratifying summer for Arthur and he had showed he could make scores when it mattered and when those who needed to be impressed were there to see them. He had made a notable contribution to England's 4-0 series win over New Zealand and, to cap his good form in 1958, he was nominated – along with Roy Marshall and Derek Shackleton of Hampshire, Derbyshire's Les Jackson, and New Zealand's captain and all-rounder, John Reid – as one of *Wisden's* five Cricketers of the Year.

When the 1959 *Wisden Almanack* greeted the new season their accolade read:

> *As a fielder, Milton is worth his place in any team. A fleet-footed footballer, he was quite happy at first in the outfield, but Gloucestershire gradually brought him in closer and turned him into one of the best short-leg and gully fieldsmen in the country. His agility and anticipation, in addition to*

very safe catching, twice brought him the County fielding award for most catches in a season – 44 in 1954 and 63 in 1956. He made eight catches in the leg trap against Sussex at Hove in 1952 when, before the awards were offered, he held 55 catches.

Standing just over 5ft 9ins, and weighing 11 stone, Milton makes up for any lack of brute strength in his stroke-play by splendid timing. He has a repertoire of stylish – often elegant – strokes all round the wicket, with the drive, square cut and hook his favourites. While realising the danger of hooking, Milton stands firm by this stroke, in England at least, because he is not often out through it. Many people thought Milton more attractive when he batted lower in the order, but Milton himself is not aware of any change in is style, except that he now declines, as a matter of basic policy, to take risks at the start of the innings until the shine is off the ball.

He believes in restraint in the morning when the ball is swinging and attack in the afternoon when the bowlers have lost some of their bite.

Arthur, being Arthur, ever ready to take things as they come, was most unlikely – even with such a fulfilling and productive summer behind him – to look out his passport, book his injections and smugly get out the tourist's guide to Oz the moment the season ended. But he must have harboured hopes of selection for the Ashes tour.

Might he be spending Christmas under the southern sun?

Chapter 11

Ups and Downs
Down Under

AS THE P&O liner SS *Iberia* set out from Tilbury for Australia, on 20th September 1958, Arthur was on board, an England player and part of Peter May's team setting out to retain the Ashes. Long before Christmas 1958 Arthur was indeed enjoying the southern hemisphere sun and adjusting happily to the wholly new experience and challenge provided by the pace and bounce of white, sun-bleached Australian pitches.

His summer's form had deservedly earned him selection for the Ashes tour, a great accolade for any cricketer. England, it should be remembered, toured as MCC in those days. Indeed, on tour they played in MCC's colours, with the cap and blazer badges bearing the crest of St George slaying the dragon, rather than the three lions and crown. Of course, when it came to the Test matches the team metamorphosed, in name, into England. One peculiarity of these arrangements was that players who appeared for England only on tour never won the traditional England cap bearing those three lions and the crown. Such idiosyncrasies were far from the thoughts of the touring party's members as they boarded the *Iberia*.

Peter May captained the tour party, with Freddie Brown, the former Northamptonshire and England all-rounder and something of a popular hero in Australia, as the tour manager. Other members of the party were: Colin Cowdrey (Kent, vice-captain), Trevor Bailey (Essex), Godfrey Evans (Kent), Tom Graveney (Gloucestershire), Jim Laker (Surrey), Peter Loader (Surrey), Tony Lock (Surrey), Arthur Milton (Gloucestershire), Peter Richardson (Worcestershire), Brian Statham (Lancashire), Roy Swetman (Surrey), Raman Subba Row (Northamptonshire), Freddie Trueman (Yorkshire), Frank Tyson (Northamptonshire) and Willie Watson (Leicestershire). Desmond Eagar, Hampshire's secretary, was assistant manager, and the veteran tourist and former Lancashire and England wicketkeeper George Duckworth was the team's scorer and baggage master.

Willie Watson injured his knee when getting out of a deckchair on board the *Iberia* and was flown ahead to Perth for an operation. Raman Subba Row sustained a fractured wrist just prior to the first Test, and so Ted Dexter (Sussex) and Arthur's Gloucestershire team-mate, John Mortimore, were added to the party. It was a touring party that was to be plagued by injuries.

Theirs was the last team to travel to Australia by ship. As a mode of travel it offered numerous advantages, not least the chance to unwind after the English season, which was barely behind them as they took to the seas. Those, like Arthur, making their touring debut, had ample opportunity to meld into the touring party and to get to know, in a leisurely and relaxed way, how their team-mates ticked.

There was time, too, for on-deck games and activities, gradually building up fitness levels. As they sailed ahead players adjusted to the different climate and increasing temperatures. Today a team can leave freezing, snowbound London and, not many hours later, find themselves suddenly in southern hemisphere high summer. But that more leisurely mode of travel meant players were away from home for far longer than many current-day players would readily tolerate. Indeed, those 1958–59 tourists to Australia and New Zealand would be away for almost six months.

The stately voyage out was an eye-opener for Arthur. 'One of the best things about the tour, for me, was the boat trip. We had a wonderful trip – just over three weeks in all, through the Med and down through the Suez Canal.'

John Woodcock, *The Times* cricket correspondent, was among the press corps travelling with the team. He remembers Arthur's on-board sporting gifts. 'On the boat going out to Australia he could possibly have swept the board at deck games, and, for all I know, was a beautiful dancer!

'Come to think of it, I wonder whether he would have beaten Godfrey [Evans] at deck tennis; I never saw anyone do that when Godfrey was trying.' And looking back to an earlier generation, John added: 'I believe WRH [Wally Hammond] was another who could turn his hand to any game with the same facility as Arthur.'

John, himself a keen golfer, suggested: 'There were several very decent golfers in that side in Australia. Ted Dexter, Tom Graveney, Colin Cowdrey and Arthur. It is often said that if Ted had chosen golf ahead of cricket he would have become a Walker Cup player – but I'd still have backed Arthur to give him a game.'

Such memories take us ahead into the tour, but Arthur was keen to relive the voyage and recall his thoughts. 'Colin never captained in Australia, you know – I was a bit surprised by that. I think he would have been much more sympathetic to people. He played the quicks well, possibly better than PBH [May].

'We went through the Bay of Biscay, which was at its most furious, and then into the more quiet Med. I can't quite remember how many stops we made but we often seemed to go into port during the night or in the very early hours of the morning. We almost always stayed up to watch the ship going into ports like Aden and suchlike. Actually I think Brian Statham missed the boat at Aden. They brought him out on a pilots' boat which had to catch us up.

'And, of course, we went down through the Suez, which was quite unbelievable really, going down there with this narrow strip running through the countryside and out into the Indian Ocean and the Arabian Sea.

'When we reached Bombay [now Mumbai] – from where we were going to fly down to Madras [Chennai] and then on to Colombo in Ceylon [now Sri Lanka] to play a couple of one-day games – it was early morning. Well, as we got off the boat in Bombay, it was about six o'clock, there were bodies beginning to rouse themselves up off the pavement; they'd been sleeping there all night. That was an eye-opener.

'We flew to Madras and the fans seemed to know we were coming. They were all there, the autograph hunters, at the airport … and then we flew down to Colombo, while the boat was coming on round, you see.

'Anyway, the monsoons arrived, and that put paid to the cricket. But public relations was to the forefront. We were each invited to have dinner with the tea planters in that area. That was quite interesting. And then it was on to Fremantle. By that time the boat had come round to Colombo to meet us, so on we got and headed off across the oceans. It had been a very interesting and educational voyage.

'We began the tour in Perth. We stayed there, and practised and played a couple of matches. We were staying in the hotel there for just about a week or so, I expect, and … you've heard about people getting their sea legs and all that – well once you'd got off the boat every now and then you used to veer off.' Arthur's hand signals indicated swaying to the left and right, accompanied by much gentle laughter. 'One night I was going in to join the boys for dinner. I was walking across the hotel lobby, and finished way up somewhere else. I think the boys thought I was paralysed or had had one or two to drink – except many of them were in the same boat.'

Western Australia, admitted as full members of the Sheffield Shield competition only two seasons earlier, provided the opening opposition. Arthur was included in the tourists' side for the four-day game. He was glad to be in action – and to adjust to the pace and bounce of Australian pitches, and to the bright light which always seems to make the ball arrive earlier for fielders and batsmen unaccustomed to the southern hemisphere sun – but his scores in this opening game did not set the world alight, nor did they in the following game against a Combined XI.

Recalling his first knocks on those Western Australian pitches, Arthur reflected: 'I would have loved to go and play on those wickets when I was a boy. I think at that time the Perth wicket was the quickest in Australia – without any doubt – and had plenty of bounce in it. I was pulling good-length balls. They were going down to fine leg – and I top-edged a couple. After Bristol, you can imagine how it was for me. So the boys spent half a morning in the nets bowling me ruddy long hops off 19 yards, so I could hook.

'I think I would have liked to play a full season in Australia at some stage, to get used to those wickets because it was the complete opposite of Bristol.'

From Perth the caravan moved on to Adelaide. 'I enjoyed Adelaide – the lovely beach at Glenelg and the trams running up and down from the city.'

By now Arthur was moving into good form. A second-innings 63 not out against South Australia was followed by a century against Victoria at Melbourne. Here he made 116 before falling lbw to left-arm quick bowler Ian Meckiff.

Meckiff was to feature constantly in the minds of the tourists' batsmen and, indeed, in the press reports of the tour. This was the so-called 'chucking' tour in which the bowling action of Meckiff – whose almost casual approach to the stumps gave no hint of the searing pace he could generate – that of his fellow quick, Gordon Rorke, and those of off-spinners Keith Slater and Jim Burke, were decidedly questionable. It is said that at Sydney, where Peter May, then perhaps a batsman without equal, made excellent hundreds in both innings (allowing England to beat an Australian XI by 345 runs in three days), a wag on the Hill yelled out, 'Put Burke on – he can throw straight.' It's a witty story, made even more amusing by the fact that Burke was not even playing in the match. It seemed his advocate was calling for reinforcements.

'Richie Benaud captained the Australian XI in that match,' Arthur remembered, 'and that started the great run and the success which he had, which was right as he was a very, very good captain, without any doubt.'

Rorke was not only a suspect 'chucker' but a pronounced 'dragger' as well, frequently dragging his back foot several feet over the bowling crease. To face a tall, 6 foot 4 inches giant of a bowler, who let the ball go at great speed from around 18 or 19 yards, was a considerable challenge for even the tallest batsmen. For batsmen like Arthur, brought up on the slow, low pitches at the County Ground, Rorke posed a real test.

Harry Gee, a respected pressman who covered this tour for Reuters and for the Press Association, later wrote a reflective piece on the tour, in which he said:

> On this very controversial tour ... perhaps the most vexed question was related to the delivery action of some Australian bowers. Not once in Tests or in other first-class matches did the umpires no-ball a man for throwing or jerking.
>
> Had they, as I saw things, strictly carried out the Law they should have called on many occasions Burke, Meckiff, Rorke and Slater, of the Test bowlers, and several other men of lesser reputation.
>
> The actions of the bowlers concerned varied from a bent elbow or a poised upright arm to a bent wrist – movements difficult to analyse even with the help of a film camera – but all had in common a look admitted to be doubtful even by a good proportion of Australian cricket enthusiasts. As the Law stipulated that umpires should call no-ball if they were not entirely satisfied of the absolute fairness of a delivery, there seemed to be something radically wrong. Some Australians, including umpires, stated that a universal definition on the point of what exactly constitutes a throw or jerk would help towards interpreting Law 26.
>
> The Australian Board of Control denied the existence of a throwing problem.

Rorke's dragging was to be a contributory factor in the imminent introduction of the front-foot no-ball Law.

The bent-arm merchants weren't restricted to the Tests. Arthur recalled: 'Yes, we encountered not only Meckiff and Rorke, but there were two others playing for South Australia at Adelaide, Hitchcox and Trethewey – "Pitchcock" and "Trethrowy" we nicknamed them.'

Dubious actions were not, however, restricted to the Australians. It was after seeing film of his own bowling on this tour that left-arm spinner Tony Lock re-modelled his action. There were others in the English game, including Arthur's fellow tourist Peter Loader, whose actions raised occasional doubts. Before the start of the 1959 season MCC instructed umpires to take the necessary steps to call bowlers of doubtful propriety and encouraged counties to offer remedial support for such bowlers.

Of his approach to Meckiff's bowling, Arthur said: 'The thing is – with the "chuckers" – certain things are apparent if you know what you're looking for. I mean … the left-armer, the ball comes at you and goes that way [down the leg-side] when it pitches, unless he's going to get it to cut back. You know, Meckiff had to bowl out there somewhere [gesticulating wide of the bowlers' stumps] to hit the wickets.'

The immense size of Melbourne's MCG stood out among Arthur's recollections of that hundred against Meckiff and the other Victorian bowlers: 'It was vast, it seemed to me. I'll tell you how big the ground is at Melbourne; when I made a hundred there I couldn't reach the boundary – because it was so big. I had 15 threes in that hundred,' and off he went into delighted laughter at the memory, of all the running they had to do. It was a tale which – wholly unintentionally – emphasised Arthur's artistry as a great timer and placer of the ball. He was not one of the game's big hitters. 'Anyway, I did manage to get a hundred in that game – but it wasn't easy.'

That century was followed by a second-innings 81 against New South Wales. He was getting himself in nick. Of that NSW game Arthur recalled: 'They won the toss and batted, and Neil Harvey made a good hundred. He was one of the greatest players I've ever seen in my lifetime – not only as a batter but as a fielder.'

As Arthur unfolded his memories of the tour they were accompanied by much clearing of the throat, as if – even 50 years later, and even though these matters had been well documented and publicly commented upon subsequently – he was still averse to say too much about the 'chuckers'. The England players had been reluctant, indeed had been advised to be reluctant, to say much at the time. There was, too, part of Arthur which never wanted to criticise fellow cricketers, even those who, in his view, 'didn't play the game'.

'Anyway, I was getting to come to terms with it [the 'chucking'] a bit. I'd made a few in the first match against South Australia on that lovely Adelaide wicket. Then came the hundred at Melbourne, and we went on to New South Wales where this fellow Gordon Rorke opened the bowling. I remember being at the non-striker's end when he bounced one at Peter Richardson and I thought it was going to go over the sightscreen without bouncing again. That's how quick it was.

'A bit later on I got up to that end and had difficulty getting the bat on the ball. Eventually I nicked one, and nicked it on to the off-stump and it broke it clean in half. And they're hardwood, their stumps.

'When we were bowled out we were 200 or so runs behind them, and so we followed on. Well we get out there, and they've got the new ball of course, and Rorke comes on – and suddenly he's bowling about my pace. It turned out he'd thrown his arm out in the first innings – literally [Arthur's clear implication here being that Rorke had done this bowling] so we finished the day 88 for no wicket, Peter Richardson and I. I went on to make 81 and we saved the match pretty well.'

His form after almost six weeks Down Under won Arthur selection for the first Test, at Brisbane, to open the batting with Peter Richardson, with whom he developed a warm friendship on the tour.

Peter recalls: 'Arthur was the straightest, kindest person I've known. The tales of his honesty on the cricket field are legion.

A more selfish and self-centred person would have been a more successful cricketer. His was a rich talent, but I wondered sometimes if he was ambitious enough. I don't think he realised how good he was – or could be.

'He was great company – as was Swettie [Roy Swetman], who was the third member of our "enjoy the tour" brigade. We were very close and, looking back, I think we needed to be in that team, where there were one or two disruptive individuals.'

Frustratingly, the mutual rewards of their friendship were not echoed on the field. The opening partnership of Richardson and Milton never really found its feet. England's Test batsmen, apart from Peter May and Colin Cowdrey – and Tom Graveney as the tour advanced – struggled generally against Alan Davidson, Meckiff, Rorke and Australia's new captain and gifted all-rounder Richie Benaud.

Various permutations of openers were tried: Richardson and Milton; Richardson and Trevor Bailey; Bailey and Milton; and Richardson and Willie Watson. This last combination put on 89 in England's second innings of the fourth Test (at Adelaide). It was the only opening partnership of the five Tests which exceeded 30.

England lost that first Test, by eight wickets, and Peter Richardson felt it coloured much of the rest of the tour. 'When you look at the side we had you would have to conclude that it was a very good side, and potentially a great one, but the slide in confidence after that Brisbane Test was there for all to see. Perhaps that resulted from bad decision-making. Certainly batting first, by choice, was a disaster from the outset. Or so it seemed to me.'

Despite the defeat, Brisbane offered some charming memories for Arthur. 'Lindy [Ray Lindwall] was a delightful bloke, I thought, and a great bowler as well, of course. He looked after us well when we were in Brisbane, took us playing golf and that. I was very taken with him.

'And another good memory: it was during the Brisbane Test match that our second son, David, was born.

'In that first Test match, where I didn't do well at all, we were beaten fairly comfortably. They're the best competitors I've ever played against, the Aussies.

'Another clear memory of that Test was of Trevor Bailey scoring not very many in a very, very long time. It was horrible,' he recalled, smiling.

In England's second innings, which they began 52 behind Australia in a relatively low-scoring game, Bailey made the slowest recorded half-century in all first-class cricket. In making 68, out of England's 198, he batted for 458 minutes, scoring at just less than nine runs per hour and, out of 425 balls received, he scored off 40 of them, with four fours, three threes, ten twos and 23 singles.

Arthur's memories of Trevor's rearguard action set him thinking too about Neil Harvey's fielding in the covers: 'He was absolutely brilliant. Whenever he tried for a run out he hit the wickets almost every time. Later in the day he said, "Would you believe it? The only time I had him out of his ground I missed the bloody wicket, didn't I?"

'I said, "I wished you had hit 'em, for all our sakes."

'Neil fielded out most of the time then. But when Richie Benaud became captain, he had Neil as his vice-captain and wanted him closer to the wicket, so he put him in the slips. He caught everything there. He was just a wonderful fielder. Pshhh – he didn't miss anything. And a wonderful bat. He made a wonderful hundred against us at Melbourne, I remember.'

Arthur's firmly-tongue-in-cheek comment about Bailey's batting and Harvey's failure to run him out, and his admiring compliments about Harvey's batting, were so typical of a man who saw cricket in the round – who recognised and valued the skills and artistry of other players, whether playing alongside him or within the opposition. 'Neil Harvey was one of my favourite Aussie cricketers, a real top-class man.'

A game against a Combined XI at Launceston in Tasmania followed a break of a few days after the confidence-denting result in the first Test, and offered the players some relief. Arthur's innings of 85 confirmed his continuing good form but then, when he must have felt he was in good shape, he received an unwelcome Christmas present.

Arthur in 1958. This is the photograph Arthur had taken to leave with Joan while he was away in Australia for the 1958–59 Ashes tour, in the days before mobile phones, e-mails and Skype and when even 'phone contact was not reliable and so contact relied mostly on airmail letters.

England's Tour Party in Australia 1958–59. Left to right, (back row) R Swetman, CA Milton, FS Trueman, PJ Loader, W Watson, JB Mortimore, PE Richardson; (middle row) G Duckworth (scorer and baggage man), JB Statham, GAR Lock, ER Dexter, R Subba Row, TW Graveney, FH Tyson, DE Montague (masseur); (front row) FR Brown (manager), TE Bailey, MC Cowdrey (vice-captain), PBH May (captain), TG Evans, JC Laker, EDR Eagar (asst manager).

Arthur facing Ian Meckiff during England's second innings in the third Test at Sydney, January 1959. Trevor Bailey is backing-up. (Keystone/Hulton Archive/Getty Images)

With England opening partner Peter Richardson.

Gloucestershire, at Worcester, May 1950. Left to right (back row) CA Milton, JK Graveney, TW Graveney, CJ Scott, M Cranfield (scorer), GE Lambert, CS Cook, DM Young; (front row) GM Emmett, TWJ Goddard, BO Allen (captain), JF Crapp, AE Wilson.

Gloucestershire at The Oval 1956. Left to right (back row) DM Young, JB Mortimore, BD Wells, RB Nicholls, CA Milton, PD Rochford; (front row) TW Graveney, GE Lambert, GM Emmett (captain), JF Crapp, CS Cook.

Gloucestershire 1960. Left to right (back row) RB Nicholls, AS Brown, DA Allen, B Crew (scorer), DR Smith, BJ Meyer, CTM Pugh; (front row) JB Mortimore, CS Cook, TW Graveney, (captain), CA Milton, DM Young.

Gloucestershire v MCC at Lord's 1961. Left to right (back row) DG A'Court, DR Smith, RB Nicholls, FJ Andrew, F Dudridge (scorer), DA Allen, D Carpenter, BJ Meyer; (front row) JB Mortimore, DM Young, CTM Pugh (captain), CA Milton, DG Hawkins

Great friends, on and off the field. – Tom Graveney, Andy Wilson and Arthur ('Scobie', as Andy called him).

The Old Master and the Young Master No. 2. Mike Procter batting while Arthur, backing-up as always, watches intently.

Arthur with Surrey's Stuart Surridge in 1956, receiving their cups, the Brylcreem Awards, for the most catches in a season.

The newspaper advert showing Arthur as a 'Brylcreem Boy' – a campaign which also included Johnny Haynes, the England footballer, and in which Denis Compton, Arthur's cricketing and footballing colleague, featured prominently.

Captain Peter Pan. Gloucestershire 1968, at Lord's. Left to right (back row) M Bissex, BJ Meyer, DR Shepherd, D Hobbs (scorer), MJ Procter, DM Green, DA Allen; (front row) RB Nicholls, JB Mortimore, CA Milton (captain), DR Smith, AS Brown.

Gloucestershire 1969. This was, effectively, the county's same playing staff as in 1970, the summer Arthur had intended to be his last season. Left to right (back row) RW Phillips, JP Sullivan, M Bissex, DA Allen, BJ Meyer, J Davey, G Pullar, DM Green, MJ Procter, GGM Wiltshire (coach), DR Shepherd; (front row) F Dudridge (scorer), DR Smith, JB Mortimore, AS Brown (captain), CA Milton, RB Nicholls, GW Parker (secretary-manager).

Arthur with Richard, Robert, Joan and David, relaxing during a Benefit match.

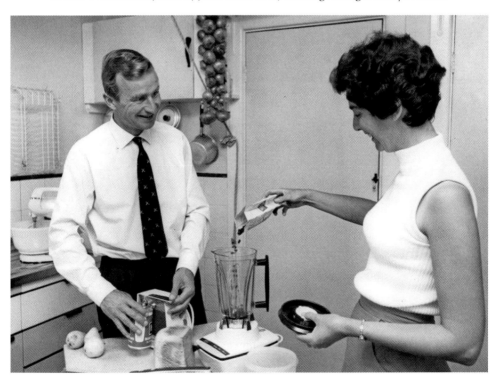

*Joan's delight, when Arthur's splendid run-scoring form in 1967 won them
a number of kitchen appliances.*

Arthur, 'Mr Cloth Bat', again on the back foot and scoring square of the wicket.

The Players versus the Gentlemen. Lord's, 1958. Left to right (back row) RA Marshall, JB Statham, CA Milton, DV Smith, JM Parks, GE Tribe; (front row) FS Trueman, W Watson, TG Evans (captain), JH Wardle, TW Graveney.

Coach to Oxford University – at Lord's for the Varsity match 1976. Left to right (back row) Arthur, R LeQ Savage, RDN Topham, DR Gurr, K Siviter, SM Clements, JA Claughton; (front row) PB Fisher, CJ Tavaré, VJ Marks, (captain), AR Wingfield Digby, G Pathmanathan.

Arthur with his 'trusty' bike on his Post Office round.

Arthur on Gillette Cup Man of the Match adjudicator's duty, with Joan, Gordon Ross ('Mr Gillette Cup') and Mrs Ross.

Greyhound racing was a life-long passion for Arthur. He knew a winner when he saw one.

Golf was another sport at which Arthur was a 'natural'. Even when recovering from a stroke near the end of his life his clubs were readily at hand so he kept his swing well-oiled.

A man's allowed to take a breather and recall happy memories at the end of a long, successful career. Arthur is wearing his England cap, and one of his Brylcreem cups is visible over his right shoulder.

Master of Arts – 'There'll never be another'. Arthur after the graduation ceremony where he received his honorary Master of Arts degree awarded by Bristol University.
(photo by Martin Chainey)

The tourists had returned to Adelaide to play South Australia, and almost pulled off a thrilling last-over win. The match began on Christmas Eve, and continued on Boxing Day and the two succeeding days, but any seasonal cheer was marred for Arthur when he was hit on the top joint of the middle finger of his right hand and sustained a fracture.

It meant he missed the second Test at Melbourne. There Alan Davidson's left-arm seamers had England's scoreboard reading 7-3 after 17 balls, as he dismissed Peter Richardson, Willie Watson and Tom Graveney with the first, fourth and fifth balls of his second over. England recovered to make 259 but, after Australia made 308 (of which Neil Harvey's contribution was 167), their batting again succumbed to Davidson and Meckiff (who, apart from one over from Benaud, bowled throughout England's innings). The Tourists were dismissed for just 87, leaving Australia to make 38 to win. It was, perhaps, a good game for an opening bat to miss.

The broken finger was not sufficiently incommoding for Arthur to miss the third Test, at Sydney, but he was again out of luck, scoring eight in each innings. He was in the side, too, for the following game, against Victoria. His second knock there indicated he was about to go on and make a decent score, redeeming his briefer first innings. He had reached 35, and was going along comfortably, when he was hit again on that middle finger, just three weeks after the initial blow. The fracture re-opened. His tour was over.

'I came home early – with Colin Cowdrey's wife, his first wife, Penny. She was lovely. Although I went out with the team by ship, we flew back. We had some engine trouble at Singapore and were going to be delayed for quite some time, so we went for a taxi ride around Singapore and all I remember is the washing hanging out, hanging from the houses and the flats and all that, and it looked a really run-down place. It has changed a bit since then, but it was a quite different place in those days, with a real flavour of the East.

'Anyway, I got home and Tony Brown brought Joan and Robert up to the airport to meet me. I think Billy Griffith from Lord's might have been there too, and I was advised not to say too much about the Tour when the press came in, you know. Not that I would have said much anyway.'

Then, chuckling, he added, 'Actually you probably couldn't have printed what I would have liked to say.'

The suspect bowling actions, which seemingly had become embedded and unchallenged in Australian cricket at that time, were creating more tensions and sensitivities than were being publicly acknowledged. Best say nothing rather than upset the apple cart.

'It was disappointing that the fractured finger ended my tour. However, such is life and you have to make do. But I was pleased to get home and see Joan again and the new arrival, David – he was a bonny lad. Joan had had a bit of a rough time when David was born, and was also having difficulties with his feeding, but once that was sorted out he was a beautiful baby.

'When I was back at home I remember thinking I wouldn't mind over much if I didn't go on a tour again. Family-wise it wasn't good. It's hard for the wives, isn't it, when husbands are away on tour especially if – as in Joan's case – they're expecting and due to give birth when their husband's away. Mind you, Joan never made a fuss, and simply got on with life.

'There was no missing the cricket and flying home for such things in those days, and certainly no emails or mobile phones or what-have-you. I did get to call Joan very occasionally by phone, but mostly we kept in touch by letter. I used to write the old airmail letters, once a week, something like that, let them know we were still alive.

'Also we played a lot of cricket in the summer and I think that you need a break from the game after a full summer. I'm sure you benefit from a good break, and then you come back refreshed, don't you?

'I was quite happy and always used to look forward to the start of the cricket season, and that first cut of grass on the lawn, the smell of the grass ... I still get that memory now.'

Had he enjoyed his first major tour? 'I have no doubt that, given the right circumstances, I would have loved touring. But I'm not sure I enjoyed that particular trip.

'One thing I was disappointed about personally was that we never went up country. Our itinerary took us only round the coast and the big cities. It would have been good to have time to get up country. Rural areas are always the best places to get a feel of a country, aren't they?

'I do remember, though, the fun and games I enjoyed in the company of Peter Richardson and Swettie [Roy Swetman], and that did help. Peter was bloody funny.

'What a character Swettie was. He had some funny ideas about the game, but what a good 'keeper he was. He was the best 'keeper I've ever stood by. When he was with us at Gloucestershire, I can't remember us ever dropping one, although one went through between us one day. He said it was mine, and I said it was his. I saw him catch a couple stood up on the leg-side. Incredible.

'He loved playing; he'd have a game anywhere. He loved to bat and used to get loads of runs. He batted down the order mostly. I don't know why he didn't score more in first-class games, because he had a lot of ability.

'He was a well-made lad. I think he used to do a bit of boxing. When he finished he ran a pub in Bristol. In one pub he had the Graveney Lounge and the Milton Public Bar. That was probably about right. That was another thing where Tom was ahead of me!

'Unfortunately that Aussie tour wasn't the best of tours, and we lost the Test series four-nothing. That was the start of Benaud's reign, and we always seemed to be struggling. PBH [Peter May] had Virginia, his fiancee – a lovely girl, mind – and his future in-laws on the trip, so we didn't see too much of him away from the cricket. And Freddie Brown, the manager, always rather drank too much, I think, and never … I really don't like saying it but, as a new tourist, I didn't think they seemed a real part of the team.'

As a late call-up John Mortimore joined the trip for the state game against Queensland before the first Test. He offers another slant on May as a captain, although it may have been coloured for him by a briefing from a fellow member of the off-spinners' union.

Yorkshire's Johnny Wardle, a candidate for the trip, had been left behind following his highly publicised fall-out with Yorkshire.

England opted to rely on Surrey's spin duo Jim Laker and Tony Lock, plus Mortimore, who recalled: 'I thought Peter May was fine as a captain. Jim Laker had said to me, very early on, "Peter May's all right; he'll look after you," and that certainly proved to be the case.' Laker's advice must be seen as an unalloyed compliment from one who was, by reputation, taciturn and not a natural advocate of the establishment.

Harry Gee's post-tour conclusions seemed to resonate with Arthur's own thoughts, when he noted that a number of England's batsmen – May and Cowdrey apart –

> *were ill at ease against the ball moving from leg to off – the main form of attack by the left-arm fast-medium bowlers, Davidson and Meckiff, and the stock delivery of Benaud. The dominating part these men played in the Tests is shown by the fact that, between them, they took 72 of the 94 wickets credited to Australian bowlers.*
>
> *May, as a player – probably the finest batsman in the world – ranked as high as his rival, but there the comparison ended. Whether or not his policies were decided by others – his tour selection committee consisted of himself, Cowdrey, Evans, Bailey and Brown, the manager – the fact remained that May never seemed to communicate to his team the driving force which Benaud gave to Australia.*
>
> *May's field-settings were stereotyped, especially in the placings for his fast bowlers with the new ball. Benaud, in contrast, backed up the efforts of Davidson, Meckiff, Lindwall and Rorke with the most intimidating fields he could devise.*
>
> *May had a fairly reasonable excuse, when England's batting deficiencies became clear, that he could ill-afford to throw runs away, but his semi-defensive outlook when Australia were batting was not calculated to keep his opponents on tenterhooks.*

Jim Swanton summed up the Tour as one,

> *which saw all sorts of perverse happenings – from an injury
> list that never stopped (and culminated in only 12 out of
> 18 being fit to fly to New Zealand), to the dissatisfaction
> with umpiring and bowlers' actions that so undermined
> morale. From various causes England gave below their
> best ...*

Fifty years later, as Arthur looked back and re-lived his memories, most of which were happy despite the poor results of the tour, he took a quick look at the Association of Cricket Statisticians' informative profile about his own career and quoted:

> *This was Milton's first and only overseas tour and it was
> something of a disappointment from a personal and team
> point of view ...*

As he read this Arthur looked a little rueful for a moment, and then smiled and said, '... which was quite true.'

And then he read on: 'He played in 12 games including the Test matches at Brisbane and Sydney and scored 650 runs at an average of 31.33,' which put him fifth in the Tour averages, behind May (57.0), Cowdrey (45.57), Graveney (44.33) and Subba Row (34.88).

Continuing to refer to the ACS booklet he remembered that two well-regarded Australian journalists had taken a more sympathetic view. Jack Fingleton, a good player and former Australian Test batsman himself, suggested in his book of the tour that Arthur 'was not used to batting on good pitches'.

'Fingleton's comment was fair,' Arthur concluded, 'and probably said something about the pitches we regularly played on at Bristol. Besides Fingleton's comments, AG Moyes, wrote that I "might have benefited from a move down the order to his favourite no. 5 position". Yes, I suppose that might have been true.'

Others too felt these were shrewd and supportive comments. John Woodcock concluded: 'Arthur found the bounce in Australia in 1958–59 something of a problem, not to mention the questionable bowling actions that were prevalent there at the time.'

In this Arthur was not alone.

Just before leaving Arthur's reminiscences of the tour it might be instructive to share his thoughts about another great fellow pro, Alec Bedser. When earlier Arthur had been recalling the names of all the England party who boarded the SS *Iberia*, I asked if Alec Bedser was among them.

Big Al was not a member of that 1958–59 side, but mention of his name sent Arthur's thoughts back to England's previous tour of Australia (in '54–55). Bedser, for so long a stalwart of the England side and the flag-bearer of England's bowlers of that era, had been left out of the side by Len Hutton after the first Test, after contracting shingles.

Arthur said, 'I've often wondered whether that was used as an excuse for leaving him out. The reason I say that is because during the previous summer, the 1954 season, Gloucestershire had been playing Surrey at The Oval. Alec came on to bowl when I had been in a while and was beginning to make a score.

'To my amazement I found I was able to hit him off the back foot through the covers, which had been impossible when he was in his pomp. And I thought, "He's gone, he's lost that zip," because it was his pace off the wicket which was one of his great strengths.

'He was a wonderful bowler, mind you, and his pace off the wicket was quite extraordinary. I couldn't believe I could now get back and cut him. It made me wonder whether, because of his previous efforts in Australia, he'd lost just a bit of that zip. But he was remarkable, wasn't he?'

With his thoughts focused on that earlier tour of Australia, Arthur came up with reminiscences of another England bowler, Frank 'Typhoon' Tyson, who had remarkable success against the Aussies in that same 1954–55 series.

'Frank was at his best at that time, wasn't he? It was his one great year – jeez, he was quick,' Arthur's whispered words signifying an immense admiration for a bowler who was one of the fastest the game has known.

Arthur recalled a game at Bristol in July 1954, shortly before
Frank's remarkable tour to Australia, when he was particularly
quick. The score was 16-2 when Arthur went to the wicket. 'I faced
Frank straight away, and I thought, "I won't lift the bat up very
much here." I had my foot behind it ready to be on the back foot,
and I was down his end for three overs before I got off the mark.
And eventually I got off the mark and got down the other end to
face Nobby Clarke.'

RW Clarke had succeeded another 'Nobby', EW Clark, who was
also a left-arm seamer and a legendary and long-serving stalwart
bowler for Northants. 'He came on to bowl, and I stood there at
the crease as he lets the ball go. I looked at it and thought "Where's
this going?" – and I hit him for four fours in that over. He looked
like a slow bowler to me after facing Frank for a spell. It's just the
difference, and it's incredible how it sharpens up your reflex, you
know. But he was a lovely person, Frank.'

Tyson, of course, was one of Arthur's team-mates in Australia in
1958–59, though he too suffered on this injury-hit tour, missing all
but the last two Tests.

Typically, in recounting the story Arthur didn't let on that he'd
scored 163 (lbw b George Tribe) in that innings at Bristol. Tony
Brown was later to value Arthur's advice about how to play the
Typhoon. 'I do remember Art telling me at Northampton in 1958
much the same, when I faced Tyson for the first time: "Stand in
front of the stumps, don't pick the bat up at all to start with. Once
you have faced a few balls, if you survive, you will pick up the speed,
your brain will speed up your reactions." And, of course, he was
quite right as usual.'

With those memories shared of his time Down Under, Arthur
suddenly declared, 'I don't think there's much more to say about
the tour now.' In truth there was a lot more that might have been
said, and as this story was being written there were plenty of further
questions I would have wished to ask – but by then, sadly, he was no
longer with us. For the moment, Arthur had shared his story – his
guarded and diplomatic account – of the trip. In part his reticence
to discuss the 'chucking' issue, which had been very controversial

at the time, had become ingrained and had coloured Arthur's thinking on the matter, then and since. He had to be nudged to share the thoughts recorded here. Besides he always – and typically – showed a reluctance to criticise fellow players, even when his great respect and affection for the game was offended by those who, in his eyes, breached its laws or its spirit.

Although he was disinclined to say more about the tour, and his part in it, Arthur was undeniably in good heart in the early months of the new year as his injury healed.

Chapter 12

Mid-Career
Merry-Go-Round

WHEN THE 1959 season got under way Arthur was again invited to play for MCC against the champion county, Yorkshire, at Lord's. He was still very much in the frame.

Following scores of 2 and 39 against Yorkshire, a century against Oxford University eased Arthur quickly and purposefully into his stride. The Parks was always an idyllic place to play cricket, and it was a heartening way to begin the new season. Yet another early-summer century came against Somerset at Taunton. The premature end to his first England tour clearly had dented neither his form nor confidence.

Then came a second invitation from MCC, on this occasion to play against the touring Indians at Lord's. Here he maintained his century-making form. His first-innings 104 (he didn't bat in the second innings), backed by Ted Dexter's 100 not out, helped MCC to notch up a comfortable win over the Tourists. The selectors confidently retained Arthur for the first two Test matches.

In the first, at Trent Bridge – often a happy hunting ground for Arthur – England gained a handsome innings victory after making 422 in their first innings. Arthur's contribution was 9.

In the next Test, at Lord's, England required but three of the five days of the match to record another comfortable win. In both innings Arthur fell to Ramakant Desai, India's right-arm fast-medium out-swing bowler, whose pace was considered 'lively', making 14 and 3 respectively.

'Although it was a good season for me, I didn't do very well in the Test matches,' was Arthur's succinct recollection of that summer. He was left out for the third Test. That second Test would prove to be his last. England's search for opening batsmen went on.

'I didn't get many,' Arthur recalled. 'It's very strange, looking back on it, but it wasn't doing much for me. It wasn't stirring me in any way. I much preferred to play with the boys I knew. That's one of the difficulties, you see, and the football side had the same trouble. You're playing with different people. You get so used to playing with your own boys. You know exactly what they're going to do, and what they're capable of.

'Surprisingly, I found I wasn't too disappointed when they left me out. I wasn't sorry about that. And I didn't miss it at all. I was always a bit that way inclined. I needed something to sharpen me up, sharpen up my concentration more than anything,' said Arthur dispassionately, looking back on this chapter of his life.

It seemed an odd and startling conclusion for one who rose naturally to most cricketing challenges. Indeed, with a bat in his hand he seemed an even better player when encountering a challenge. Yet here he appeared almost relaxed, certainly unfazed, at missing further chances to test his skills consistently at the highest level.

Might this have been simply the subconscious protection many of us throw around ourselves when things don't work out as we expect? Possibly. If so, it would have been a normal and natural reaction. It might also have been his way of rationalising the circumstances so that there was minimal disappointment when, or if, selection did not come his way again. It's worth remembering, too, that Arthur had the great gift of being able to take things in his stride.

On the other hand, it is perhaps important to recognise also that his thoughts on non-selection for further Test matches gave a strong measure of just how importantly he rated county cricket, and how much enjoyment and fulfilment this bedrock of the game gave him.

There is no doubting that he saw the county championship as the game's blue riband. He felt very much at home there, and felt privileged to play the game in that way.

Gloucestershire certainly benefited from his return to the colours. He made 24 championship appearances that summer, and in all first-class matches scored 1,984 runs at an average of 40.48. It was form that helped Gloucestershire to enjoy one of their most successful seasons for many years. It was form that should have continued to press his case with England's selectors.

His pal from Arsenal days, Hampshire's Jimmy Gray, was one of many who felt he should have played more for England: 'One reason he didn't play more for England was that, unlike Tom Graveney, he didn't flourish, in the style of his play. He just played. But he was even better than he looked.'

Gloucestershire's successes in that summer of 1959 owed much to the consistency of Arthur and Martin Young, by now regular opening partners. Each made six centuries for the county that season and they rarely failed together. 'Yes, I had a good season after coming back from Aussie. I'd been playing on good, bouncy wickets there.'

What was Martin like to play alongside?

'He was fine. A funny thing was, for an opener, he was not greatly fond of the quicks but he managed to cope. Hampshire's Derek Shackleton got me out quite a lot, but Youngy always used to get a hundred against them, quite extraordinary. That year we played Hampshire over on the Isle of Wight, at Cowes. It was a beautiful summer, and we won the match.'

In an evenly balanced game Gloucestershire were left to score 130 runs to win and, through Milton and Young, they got them without losing a wicket.

'If he had the chance, Youngy always used to like finishing it with hitting a six or a boundary at least. Someone, you know, always seemed to bowl a slow one up to him to hit. I think it was Ingleby

– Colin Ingleby-Mackenzie – on this occasion, and Youngy hit it for four.'

Yet again memories of happy times among fellow county cricketers, on delightful grounds, had Arthur chuckling.

'Youngy wasn't the worst player, by any means. Very "public schoolboy", I'd say, you know.'

But good to bat with?

'Yes, [said very emphatically] yes.'

The county was also continuing to benefit from Arthur's consistently brilliant fielding as well as his batting, and the 56 catches he had to his name put him second to Peter Walker of Glamorgan in the season's list of successful catchers.

Arthur's championship hundreds that summer were crafted in the games against Somerset (no surprise there) at Taunton and Bristol, as well as against Warwickshire, Lancashire and Glamorgan.

When the Indian tourists headed westwards in August to play during the Cheltenham Festival, Arthur's good form continued and his innings of 77 and 57 helped Gloucestershire beat them by an innings and 192 runs.

One other match of 1959 stands out firmly and glowingly in Arthur's memory. As he began to recall the match, he reached out just to check the scores one more time in the ACS booklet: 'Here we are,' he said. '"Milton made 99 in an exciting tied match with Essex at Leyton."'

'That was a fantastic match. It was Tom's – Tom Graveney's – first year as captain, but unfortunately he was out of the side. I think he'd injured a finger and George Emmett had been standing in for him. But for some reason George wasn't available so I was in charge again.'

To help him put the encounter freshly in context in his mind, Arthur looked back to his own part in the game. This was unusual in the discussions we had, as more often than not he was wont to tell you what happened in a game, and to describe what other players had done, before recounting his own deeds.

'I was on 99 when they took the new ball, I remember, and Barry Knight bowled. He always used to bowl in-swingers. I played this like an in-swinger; it didn't do much, it sort of straightened off the wicket, and got a nice little edge, a little dolly to gully, and so I was out on 99.'

Essex had batted first, he remembered, and scored 364 before declaring with six wickets down, Doug Insole making an excellent 177 not out. Martin Young fell quickly, but Gloucestershire then made steady progress to find themselves almost on par with the home side. Arthur's had been a captain's innings.

'Who was Essex's captain? Dougie – Doug Insole – was captain. He played beautifully in the first innings. Anyway, we got up close to them and had 'em in some sort of bother in their second knock, when Dougie played another brilliant innings – I think he made about 280 for once out in the match. He was out not long before lunchtime on the third day. Being captain I walked from our dressing room into theirs to go into lunch with them. Trevor Bailey was sitting there chatting with Doug, and I could sense they were probably talking about a declaration. So I said to them, "Are you thinking what I think you're thinking?"

'"Probably," says Doug.

'"Well," I said, "I'll tell you what – if you declare now we'll go for them the whole of the way through the innings. We'll have a result." That's how we used to play.

'I think Trevor said, "Haven't you got to phone the county to see if you can do that?" Apparently it was the practice in some counties, especially if a stand-in captain – and a professional to boot – was at the helm, to check with their county hierarchy before taking such a step.

'I said, "No, don't be daft. We'll have a game."

'And Doug readily said, "Yes, OK" and so after lunch we started. How many did we have to get? Was it 212 to win? Yes, that was it.

'We again lost Youngy quickly, with no runs on the board, so Ron Nicholls and I effectively opened the innings. We'd put on more than 50 when I got run out – I slipped up as I turned, and was sat there on the deck when I was run out.'

Arthur recounted that dismissal without feeling a need for added reference, even though 'Milton, run out' was such an unusual dismissal. There were many times in his career when fielders thought they had him well and truly stranded in mid-pitch. But so fleet-of-foot was he, with deceptively swift acceleration over the first few paces (which had been key to much of his success on the soccer field), that almost always he made his ground, often at a stroll it seemed. Even more infuriatingly for the fielders, he was such a good judge of a run that, after the initial acceleration, he appeared to ease off, but always got in, apparently without breaking sweat.

Indeed, in 1,078 innings over 27 seasons he was run out only 26 times, less than once a season. A notable run-stealer throughout his career, this skill kept the scoreboard ticking and his own, and his partners', score mounting. Quite remarkable.

The Times' esteemed cricket correspondent, John Woodcock, estimated that Arthur's skill at running between wickets must have been worth 'a good 2,000 runs to him over his career. As a judge of a run Arthur had few equals, missing nothing, and yet never in an apparent rush.'

'Anyway,' Arthur continued, 'we kept chasing but also lost a few wickets. I'm upstairs on a little balcony we had outside our dressing room looking out over the ground. Keith Miller, the great Australian all-rounder, was writing for the *Daily Express* then, and he always liked a bet. He kept offering me odds about winning the game, because I said we were going to try and win it.

'We got to about 130-something for eight and he said, "Well, I reckon you're 20 to 1 now", so I had 20 shillings to 1 shilling [£1 to 5p] with him.

'The next wicket fell at 209, and we wanted 212 to win. Tony Brown had made about 80 or 90. He'd hit about four sixes, a good few fours, and he'd played really well, but then got out when we were so close. He was livid – livid with himself. Trevor Bailey had come on with the new ball; he'd bowled a wide in the previous over, and I reckon the ball Tony got out to would have been a wide if it hadn't hit the toe-end of his bat. Old Tonker [Brian Taylor], their 'keeper, caught it, and we're 209 now, needing three to win.'

For the record, and as a measure of Arthur's often understated way of assessing events, Tony Brown had gone to the wicket with the score at 82-4. When he was out some 85 minutes later Gloucester were within touching distance of victory. A win was still possible, as was a loss, or a draw – or even a tie. It all now depended on Sam Cook hanging on with Barrie Meyer, as Arthur described:

'Sam Cook joined Barrie Meyer, and they must have already got a run somewhere when Barrie played one down to third man. The outfield down there was awful, it bumped everywhere – and Barrie was quick. He went up and looked for the second run but decided against it. I think he would probably have got back in – anyway, he regretted it after,' Arthur recalled.

'But you can't do anything about that – he'd decided not to go for that second run. And then they've got to get one to win and Barry Knight was bowling to Cooky. There was a bit of bounce in the wicket, and he bowled it a bit short and it bounced. Cooky nicked it – and Milner caught it in the leg-trap. So it finished a tie. A wonderful game.'

With those happy memories going round in his mind, Arthur mused on: 'I found Dougie interesting. He was a very good all-round games player. He played some good football [in a distinguished career as an amateur Doug played for Cambridge University, Walthamstow Avenue, Southend United, Pegasus, and Corinthian Casuals for whom he played in the 1956 FA Amateur Cup final, as well as making some wartime appearances for Fulham] and captained Cambridge at both soccer and cricket. I really got on with him well. He wasn't the worst bowler and he was a very good slipper.'

Tony Brown, Arthur's long-time travelling companion, remembered returning from Leyton. 'We were driving back in the van after the match, and I was beside myself because Barrie and I had got to the point where we should win the game.

'I'm so upset, saying, "I shouldn't have got out, we should have won," and Arthur insisted, "You mustn't, you must not, take it out on yourself."

'He was always so good like that. He was never critical or inclined to say, "Well, you should have bloody hit that."

'I should have done, I know I should have done – but he wouldn't make a big issue of it. And I remember him speaking similarly to others time and time again like that.

'He would be a bit cross with himself, mind. Oh dear – towards the end of his career he padded up to one against Yorkshire in the Benson & Hedges Cup, and lost his off-stump, and he would come in, and say, "That beat me."

'He used to get bowled quite a bit playing there … "I didn't get it quite right there," he would say. He wouldn't create a situation where he said, "I mustn't play any of these." He was always prepared to back his own judgement.

'He was a very, very, very fine cricketer. He was an excellent batsman. And he wasn't the worst bowler; he could swing it. He was a fantastic fielder. He wasn't just a great catcher. In his younger days especially he had a good enough arm – he used to run people out, because he could reliably hit the stumps.

'He was a very good judge of a game, tactically and field-placing and all that. A hugely talented cricketer, wonderful player, great ability. And we need to bear in mind that, for most of his career, he played on uncovered pitches, which makes a difference with such things as career stats – it lowers batting averages, and bowlers' figures are a bit more impressive.'

With a knowing and appreciative smile, Tony remembered Arthur's speed about the field – both the cricket field and the soccer pitch – and his speed between wickets.

'Art had terrific speed. You'd never believe how quick he could be. You couldn't actually judge how fast he was going. If you were running with him or against him, you would only know he was fast because he would beat you by only a couple of yards – but do it easily.

'He never had to run at his fastest. I don't think anybody ever saw how fast he really was.'

As Arthur's memories of this part of his career unfolded, it was apparent that Gloucestershire's captaincy upheavals of the early Sixties were marker posts along his sporting way. Arthur being Arthur, he undoubtedly wished those issues hadn't come so much to the fore, especially as, in general, they involved good friends as well as fellow players.

This is not the right place to rake over the carcass again in any detailed way, or to spend time reflecting on what those changes meant for the county. However, it was a period which had fixed itself in Arthur's mind, and his reflections are relevant.

Tom Graveney had been appointed captain for 1959, to succeed George Emmett on the latter's retirement. In following Emmett and Jack Crapp, Tom was the third professional in succession.

Some, at that time, felt Arthur would have been a good and obvious choice. Might he have been the ideal person to follow George Emmett when Gloucestershire were a good unit? Almost certainly Tom Graveney would happily have accepted such a move, as it would have allowed him to play for England and come back into the side as a batsman first and foremost, without needing to worry about all those things captains have to take on board. Arthur, as mentioned earlier and as he readily affirmed, had learned a huge amount from George Emmett. Almost certainly George Emmett would have supported that, and, as a contemporary pointed out, 'We had a good side at that time and with Art's guidance I'm sure we could have done well.'

Gloucestershire's committee opted for Tom Graveney and the results that summer certainly seemed to verify the wisdom of their choice. They ended the summer as championship runners-up.

Championship runners-up. Championship runners-up. Since the County Championship's formal constitution in 1890, Gloucestershire had reached such exalted status on only three previous occasions, in 1930, 1931 and 1947. But this, arguably, was Gloucestershire's most successful and stirring campaign since William Gilbert Grace was at the helm for their title-winning season in 1877 or, possibly, Bev Lyon's title challenge in 1930. Frustratingly for the new captain, Tom missed a number of games through injury. George Emmett, helping young players in the Second XI, was recalled to deputise and, as we have seen, Arthur also led the side. The shared leadership did nothing to hinder the county's progress in this spirited season when Gloucestershire pressed hard to deny Yorkshire their title. One particularly pleasing result for the new captain and his team came when they beat the eventual champions at Bristol, by the commanding margin of an innings and 77 runs after bowling out the Tykes for 35 in their first innings, courtesy largely of Tony Brown's 7-11. In what was a glorious summer for cricket, Gloucestershire had enjoyed one of the most exciting, and best, summers of their history.

Arthur recalled: 'Tom had broken a finger, I think. George even stayed in the side for a game or two when Tom came back to pick up the reins again. I don't know whether that was because George had his suspicions things weren't going entirely smoothly, or whether it was the committee. But I believe it was through that – though he never said as much straight out – that, a year later, they finally decided to change the captain.

'It was a sad time, I remember,' said Arthur, lowering his voice to a whisper as he recalled the episode.

Alongside the successes of 1959 an undercurrent of disquiet had begun to filter from the dressing room, and criticisms were voiced in the committee room, much of it focusing on the leadership of the side.

'There was one particular match, we were playing at Kent, and Tom changed his mind three times in about ten minutes as to what to do, when to declare.

'There was a feeling, too, that Tom was likely to be away frequently, playing for England, and together these things must have decided the committee to take it away from him.'

But that would not be until after the 1960 season had ended. By contrast with its predecessor, that proved to be a disappointing summer for the Glosters. The upshot was that, after the behind-closed-doors rumblings and despite many protracted close-season meetings (where Machiavellian actions and decisions of committee and senior officers brought little credit to the county's name), Tom Graveney left Gloucestershire during the winter of 1960–61 – almost certainly against his natural desires and inclination – to begin a new career with Worcestershire at the age of 34. For 13 seasons he had been Gloucestershire's leading batsman, batting as only he could, with immense class and grace, and with great distinction.

Happily for him and the cricket world at large, Tom's career blossomed again; he won back his England place, and it was during this period that he notched up his 100th hundred and was awarded the OBE for his services to the game.

'One of the reasons he went to Worcester,' Arthur recalled, 'was because he lived in Winchcombe, not too far from Worcester, just down the lane from the pub, The George, where Jackie's sister married the proprietor. When we were going north, we always stopped off there on the way up for a few sandwiches; it was a regular watering hole for us.

'Anyway – he went to Worcester and he had to qualify – Lord's wouldn't allow him to play straight away, and he played in all those non-championship matches and Second XI games that year.'

Regarding his great long-time friend, Arthur says: 'It was the making of TWG, that move to Worcester. He was a very fine player, but the thing was that our wickets weren't at all helpful to him. Anyway, he found it hard to accept having the captaincy removed from him.'

Although sad to see Tom leave, Arthur recognised a positive benefit for his pal. 'When Tom started again I always felt he had something to prove, a point to make, didn't he?

'Worcester was a good place for him to go. The wicket was much better for him than at Bristol – the pitches there had more bounce. And he was such a talented lad that I knew he was going to get a lot of runs. And Worcestershire had a good side then, with Don Kenyon and Martin Horton, Jack Flavell and Len Coldwell, Norman Gifford and Dougie Slade, Roy Booth keeping wicket. And Basil [D'Oliveira] came a bit later. And Tom felt he had something to prove.

'I was pleased for him because he played so well and got back in the England side, and he really enjoyed cricket at that level. He proved what a really good player he was and really made a name for himself.'

In one of the many ironies sport throws up, if it was the travails surrounding the captaincy that led to Tom Graveney joining Worcestershire in 1962, he was joining a county where a relatively new skipper had resolutely established himself, but only after recovering from a start that hadn't pleased all his masters.

It was the fourth year of Don Kenyon's reign as captain from 1959 until 1967. Kenyon was to prove a towering figure in Worcestershire's history, and its most successful captain (until Phil Neale came along and led the county to six titles, including two championships, in five seasons in the late Eighties and early Nineties). Yet Kenyon had come very close to being sacked after his first season at Worcestershire's helm because of committee-room criticism.

Back at Bristol, as one of Gloucestershire's senior pros, Arthur might himself again have been in the reckoning to succeed Tom Graveney. Indeed that seems to have been the case, for the committee took him into their confidence. In typical Milton style, with that kind of objectivity which seems to border on a naivety based on his ability (or desire?) not to get involved in political in-fighting, indeed of seemingly being unaware of it, he suggested to the committee a more democratic approach.

'One of the committee, the deputy chairman I think it was, came to see me and outlined to me what they wanted to do, and asked if I would support them. They might have been sounding me out too, but that wasn't very clear.

'I remember writing back to them, writing a letter to the club – and I also wrote to Tom too – and what I said was that, over the years, I had always felt they – the committee – didn't know enough about the game to pick the right bloke as captain. I suggested they elect a captain by putting all the players in a room before the beginning of the season, and then we could have a democratic vote to see who the lads wanted.

'I have always felt the players always knew who should be captain. That would take all the hassle off the committee and off their selection. And the thing is, you see, if we chose the wrong chap then we just had to live with it, to get on with him, and make sure we made it work.

'Very often the committee used to pick the best player without thinking over much about their leadership abilities or their relationship with the rest of the side, and that player might not turn out to be the best captain.

'It wasn't that Tom was in any way unpopular as a bloke; far from it. As captain he used to miss things in the field a bit. We might have a chance to win a game and it wouldn't matter about runs – wickets were the most important thing. But Tom didn't always look to fill the slips, and the ball would go through the gap where a slip fielder ought to have been in my opinion. It was more that – tactical things – than any questions about personality. Yes, because he's a really nice chap. We've been good pals all our lives.

'I always felt Tom would have preferred to stay and, at first, that seemed the most likely outcome. But as things went on, the committee handled it badly, or with less than good grace, and Tom's position was undermined. He became determined to leave. There were a few players here who felt that Tom's wife, Jackie, felt very affronted on Tom's behalf too, and in the end probably didn't discourage him from getting away.'

In his recall of the rumblings of that 1960 summer, Arthur was typically circumspect, feeling that time effectively had drawn a veil over the events of nigh on 50 years ago. He certainly sought to recall those events accurately before sharing them with me, feeling a need to check his facts as far as this was possible. In any event – and, again, very much in his nature – he never looked to dent a fellow player's reputation.

Tony Brown's recollections of this time are worth noting, and echo Arthur's opinion. 'I don't think anyone had a problem with Tom himself. It was probably more what the players felt about tactical and strategic matters than Tom's relationships with them as players. As one of the younger members of the team I was certainly not aware of any animosity towards Tom.'

Tony agreed, too, that Arthur enjoyed captaincy as such but when it arrived in 1968, 'It came too late.'

Tony also suggested that, while Arthur would have enjoyed captaining the side earlier in his career, he would have felt reluctant to step into Tom's shoes. 'I don't think Arthur would have liked to have been put in that position in 1961. But I certainly think the rest of the players would happily have accepted Arthur as captain then.

'Sam Cook was the senior cricketer, but Arthur was the senior pro. Sam was marginally senior in the sense of his length of service, but he wasn't senior in his knowledge of the game. He was a lovely man, but tactically he couldn't really care less; all he ever really wanted to do was to bowl. If he could bowl he was happy.

'But he had a well-developed sense of cricket discipline. He would tell a young player if he stepped out of line, whereas Arthur didn't like giving anyone a ticking off in that way. It would be Sam who would remember to say, "Don't forget your bloody blazers at lunchtime, lads." He might not want to wear one, but he made sure everyone knew the form. But he would never expect to step into the breach if the captain was injured or ill, whereas Arthur did this superbly.'

A match in mid-summer 1960 provided a good example of how Arthur felt the game should be played. It also showed his esteem for and understanding of his fellow professionals, not least those who were facing real challenges.

Gloucestershire were playing Somerset, at the Bath Festival, and Eric Bryant, from Weston-super-Mare, was bowling his left-arm spinners for the home county. A jerkiness in Bryant's action had raised eyebrows in other games. Here, at Bath, he was 'called' by umpire Hugo Yarnold in Gloucestershire's first innings. When his captain Harold Stephenson brought him back, Arthur was on strike.

Four times in the over Yarnold called 'no-ball' from square leg. In the midst of his opponent's distress Arthur made no attempt to take advantage of the bowler's misfortune and embarrassment. Each ball, legal or otherwise, was played back to the bowler and, with real sympathy for Bryant, he said: 'Let's get this over finished with, Hugo.' That regard for a fellow player in trying circumstances did not go unnoticed.

If alleged 'dressing room unrest' did indeed lead eventually to Gloucestershire's change of captain it is likely that the views of the senior players would have been given some heed, but it is worth noting here that Arthur was out of the side for much of that summer of 1960.

After 11 championship games his season had come to an abrupt end. In the final days of June, Gloucestershire were playing the South African tourists at Bristol. The scorebook tells us that Arthur 'retired hurt' in the first innings and 'did not bat' in the second.

'They had left a lot of grass on the wicket and it was very dry. There were cracks in it as well. It was horrendous,' he recalled.

'South Africa made 116. In our first innings I had made 16 when a ball from Adcock flew from the pitch, and bent back my thumb sharply, bent it right back. It broke it. It was a boxers' fracture – the type they commonly suffer if they mishit their punch.

'Neil Adcock – he was quite quick. He and Heine, they were quite a pair – they always seem to hunt in pairs, the best bowlers, don't they? The ball missed the hand on the bat handle but took the thumb.'

Arthur had gone to the wicket with Gloucestershire's score at 8-3. 'After I'd retired hurt with a broken thumb we made 81, and then we bowled them out for 49. You can tell what the wicket was like from the scores.

'We were 87 for 7 when we finished up winning, and I remember they got me padded up ready, you know, with a so-and-so broken thumb, intending I should just go out there and stand at the wicket if the ninth wicket went down, which was fair enough.

'Anyway, it didn't get to that. Ron [Nicholls] was still in at the time and we finished up scrambling home. We beat them, we beat South Africa,' this last said with great intensity as he re-lived the memory, 'and I was out for the rest of the summer.

'That was frustrating as, although I hadn't made a hundred at that stage, I felt in good nick,' he recounted, with relish. 'I can certainly remember making 75 against Surrey, at Stroud, a bit before that. That was against Bedser, Lock et al, too – that couldn't have been a bad knock, could it?'

Around this time Gloucestershire, like a number of counties, were taking cricket around the county, as well as playing regularly at Bristol, Cheltenham and the Wagon Works. The Stroud ground belonged to the Erinoid Company. It was small and its pitch favoured bowlers more than batsmen, so much so that some referred to it as Death Valley. Others called it a turnip patch. Arthur had again risen to the challenge offered by a sporting wicket.

The scorecard of that Stroud match showed that Arthur was batting at no. 5, as he did for much of the 1960 season. This is where he claimed to most enjoy batting, even though he opened the innings for much of his career. Two things make this change particularly noteworthy: the move back to the middle-order spot in 1960 followed the county's successes of the previous summer when Arthur had formed such a consistent opening partnership with Martin Young; and his place at the top of the order was taken by CTM Pugh, the amateur and top-class rackets player.

It was Tom Pugh who was appointed as Tom Graveney's successor for the 1961 season – and he promptly nominated Arthur as his vice-captain or senior professional.

David Allen, a shrewd and successful off-spinner (one of the most successful in the county's history) and a useful middle- or lower-order batsman for Gloucestershire from 1953 to 1972, was firmly established in the side by the early Sixties. When asked in recent times whether there was any feeling among Gloucestershire's pros that Arthur might have been appointed to succeed Graveney at that time, a one-word answer sufficed: 'Plenty.'

Allen – good enough to have played in 39 Test matches for England, including that oft-remembered Lord's Test of 1968 when, with Colin Cowdrey at the other end with his broken arm in plaster, he gamely played out Wes Hall's final over of the match to earn England a breathtaking draw – expanded on his spontaneous response with the following insight: 'When TWG's successor was appointed the dressing room was very surprised by the appointment of Tom Pugh, a young man with limited experience of first-class cricket, let alone of captaincy of a professional side. There was no doubt the senior professionals wanted Arthur as their captain but the committee ignored them.'

The committee, which had been happy to appoint professional captains since 1953, was again hankering after an amateur, even though by 1961 the amateur was a swiftly disappearing and increasingly rare species in the county game. And so, not quite out of the hat, they pulled Old Etonian Tom Pugh.

Pugh had played occasionally for the county in 1959 and, in a full season in 1960, he made just over a thousand runs.

Arthur's designation as Pugh's deputy is intriguing. As has been noted, Sam Cook was slightly senior to Arthur in length of service. He might have seemed a candidate, if only on the basis of 'Buggins' turn'. But as Tony Brown pointed out, Sam – a dedicated Gloucestershire man through and through, and a lovely, gentle character – was happier simply bowling (and bowling and bowling; and what a great bowler he was) before switching off by finishing his day sitting quietly with a beer or three or four, accompanied by a cigarette, and maybe even a thoughtful word or two about the day's play. Of course, had he bowled a bad ball that day that might require rather more of a post-mortem. Arthur, as a thinking cricketer, with a good cricket brain (surprisingly not always a given for all professional cricketers), proved the sound, reliable man and experienced player an amateur captain – particularly one learning the ropes – needed.

Speaking about Arthur's role, Tom Pugh explained: 'When I was asked to be captain I made seven stipulations to the committee, one of which was that Arthur should be vice-captain. Before I became captain, Arthur couldn't have been kinder or more encouraging. I've a great deal to be thankful for to him.

'In 1960 I hadn't been doing well for a spell of four or five games and thought Tom Graveney might be about to leave me out of the side. We were up at Chesterfield to play Derbyshire where, unusually, I was rooming with Arthur – it was normally poor old Barrie Meyer who had to put up with me. We were talking cricket in our room and Arthur said, "I want to show you something," and he picked up a bat and told me to hold it. And he just changed the grip of my left hand a bit, at the top of the handle. He reckoned I'd been playing across the line a bit, and that's why I had been getting out.

'Next day Tom Graveney and I put on 256 for the second wicket – which I think still stands as a Gloucestershire record today. I think that 137 saved my career, and I have Arthur to thank for that.

'I loved Arthur. Later that same summer he, Morty and I were invited to play at Lord's for MCC against Cambridge University and as my home was in London I invited them to stay with us. To her dying day my mother said she never had a more polite or more appreciative guest than Arthur. She was very taken with him.

'Of course, I had enjoyed watching him playing for Arsenal before I joined Gloucestershire. In fact, when I was signed from Middlesex, one of the great attractions for me in joining Gloucestershire was that I would be playing alongside him. It was incredible I should end up captaining him, because he was such a star – not that he seemed to recognise this.

'Whenever I watched Arsenal I tried to be near the touchline, as I loved watching Arthur on the wing. I remember once at White Hart Lane, Spurs versus Arsenal. It had snowed heavily, and to get some play they rolled the snow to make the surface good enough to play on.

'Arthur was involved in the game a good deal that day, up and down the line, beating his opponent and getting his crosses in. At one point, he must have been momentarily knackered as he had his hands on his knees, catching his breath when Alex Forbes sent over a cross. Someone shouted "Arthur" and he looked up when the ball was only five feet or so from him, took the ball, beat three men as he raced down the line, and sent over a wonderful cross.'

In talking of Pugh's spell as captain, Arthur had initially, and with decided reluctance, commented, 'Tom Pugh didn't get on too well at first,' implying that the new captain perhaps wasn't yet sufficiently experienced in the county game to be at the helm of a team of professionals – 'but we soon trained him.'

If any had doubts about Pugh's right to hold down a place for his batting alone, they all recognised he was a fine games player, as Arthur readily acknowledged. 'Tom was, of course, a brilliant rackets player, world class.'

What did Arthur mean by 'we soon trained him'?

'Well, you know, he was captain, he was there, so we knew we had to get on with him. He used to listen to you, but then he didn't always do what you advised. He used to make his own mind up, though very often it turned out right – funny that.'

Arthur played much of his cricket in an era when the senior pro's role was unique and distinctive. Some ruled the dressing room taciturnly with a rod of iron; others would readily share their experience and wisdom with younger players, especially those keenest and most willing to listen and to learn, as Arthur had to Jack Crapp and George Emmett.

Many an amateur captain, too, owed a great deal to the nous, tactical knowledge, and much more besides, offered by their senior pros. 'Oh yes, the senior pro used to keep it all together. If the boys had something to say they could go and talk to him and if he thought they were in the right he would go and talk to the captain,' Arthur suggested.

The summer of 1961 was to prove one which focused Arthur's thoughts and activities in other ways too. It was the year of his Benefit, awarded 13 years after he had first played for the county and 12 years after he had won his county cap. And Tom Pugh's wisdom of appointing Arthur as vice-captain was seen after the captain was injured in May. As a result Tom Pugh missed the next 17 championship games, for all of which Arthur was in charge.

'By May in that '61 season, we were third in the championship,' he reminisced. 'Then in the game at Peterborough, against Northants, Pughie ducked into a ball from Larter – he was very tall and had a long arm. Pughie must have thought it was the bouncer, and he ducked, and it turned out to be a full toss and it hit him full in the face, broke his jaw.

'I had to take him down to hospital, where they wired up his jaw. He had to have food and drink through a straw. I really felt sorry for him at that time and during that season, because it wasn't easy.'

To add insult to his injury, Pugh was given out lbw for 0, and that from a ball that had hit him direct on the face!

Again in reliving these memories Arthur failed to recount his cricketing part in the game. It needed recourse to the record books to discover that, following Pugh's departure, Arthur – with his bat and his captaincy – had led the side to victory. Needing 304 in their second innings to win, he and David Allen had come together at 137-5. By the time they were parted, at 257-6, Arthur had made 80. Allen, who went on to make 87 not out, and Barrie Meyer saw Gloucestershire to victory by four wickets. It was an encouraging and positive start for the stand-in captain.

Arthur's recollection of Tom Pugh's unintended injury at the hands of David Larter took him off, reminiscing about other similar situations. He remembered Fred Trueman had once felled Trevor Bailey, and then apologised: 'Plenty more I'd rather have hit than thee, Trevor.'

Arthur recalled that the Surrey bowler Peter Loader could sometimes be a handful. 'I remember a game at The Oval, when I was in and facing Loader. Peter was very suspect, really, both with his bouncer and his slow ball. His slower ball, he bowled it like an off-spinner. It was a terrific ball, really. He used to go right through with it, and the ball didn't arrive.

'Anyway, he bowled a bouncer to me, which I hit through mid-wicket, and the next one he threw. I knew he was going to do it and I was ready, and I hit it for four through mid-wicket.

'When I got down to his end I said, "You throw another one at me and I'll hit you with this bat" – and I never had any trouble with him after that, you know. Perhaps he was a bit chicken underneath, but he was a good bowler. He didn't need to "ping" it. 'He did the hat-trick in a Test match – at Headingley [against the West Indies in 1957] – with his slower ball, I think. That was one of the problems with the throwing business. It was difficult to pick the line and the pace.

'He hit people too. He hit Ken Suttle twice. Dear little Ken' (said with incredulity in Arthur's voice at the recollection of it, even after all the years).

'Ken played a record number of matches in succession for Sussex didn't he, around 400? [It was, in fact, a remarkable 423 consecutive county championship games between 1954 and 1969.] And he played a bit of football too. He was a good lad.'

And then his thoughts were back with Gloucestershire and Tom Pugh, and the horrific injury he had sustained so early into his spell as captain.

Pugh recalled his own memories of that incident: 'When I was injured and Arthur went with me to hospital, he was as kind to me as the kindest father might be in that situation,' and as he recounted this Tom had tears forming in his eyes.

'He couldn't have been sweeter. And he stayed with me until I decided I needed to get back to London to one of the best hospitals for further treatment, and so went off in a minicab.'

As an amusing footnote to the incident he remembered: 'When I was out of the side I went off to America for three weeks courting my American girlfriend. Not a good idea when your jaw and mouth is wired up.

'Do you know, I have always wondered whether Arthur expected to be made captain when Tom Graveney left. I don't know the answer to that, but what an amazing cricket brain he had, and he was such a brilliant close-to-the-wicket fielder.

'He helped me sort out the batting order too. Either I had been opening with Martin Young or, occasionally, Arthur did but it was he who suggested we might try Ron Nicholls there, and that he might drop to no. 4. He reckoned Ron had the right technique, and not having to sit around and wait to bat would suit his temperament far better. It was Arthur's idea, which I got the credit for.

'He also suggested that he might be more valuable at first slip rather than at short leg. That, of course, proved to be the case. It was a good move, and he trained Tony Brown and encouraged him to field well in his place at short leg.'

'An example of how he was so helpful was at Canterbury in 1961. In Kent's second innings they needed to get 247 to win and we'd got them 93-4, or something like that, and then Stuart Leary and Alan Dixon started to cream it about. "What do we do, Arthur?" I asked.

'"Get Sam on the field pretty smartish," was his cryptic reply. Sam had been off because of a groin injury, but Arthur saw that the ball was beginning to turn quite a bit, and the ball turning away from the bat would be dangerous.

'My first reaction was to protest that, as Sam had been off for a good while, he couldn't come back on and bowl straight away, but Arthur assured me that the laws, playing conditions, what-have-you, allowed that. He was obviously right. I called our twelfth man and sent a message to Sam to get changed and get on the field as quickly as he could.

'Colin Cowdrey, who I'd known well since we were very young through playing rackets as well as cricket against each other, wasn't as sure and when he saw Sam take the field he came on and consulted the umpires – but Arthur was right. Sam could bowl.

'I got Sam on and in five overs he had Leary caught and bowled and then dismissed Dave Halfyard who, with a few clubbed blows at no. 9, looked as if he might win it for Kent and, with David Allen mopping up the tail, we won by about 20 runs.'

If that was typical of Arthur's perceptive reading of the game, he also had a hand – literally – in Kent's demise, by catching Derek Ufton for 0 off Allen's bowling, when the latter tightened Gloucestershire's hold on the game by taking two wickets in the 64th over.

Tom Pugh's voice gave ample evidence of his warm regard and affection for Arthur as he re-lived his memories of this exciting result: 'Arthur was a real help to me in that period, and in my second season we had a run of nine wins in my last 15 matches as captain. I reckoned in Arthur I had the best cricket brain in the game working with me.'

The new captain and his seasoned senior professional were beginning to understand and respect each other.

Chapter 13

And Such a Talent

CAPTAIN AND SENIOR professional were indeed beginning to understand one another. Arthur's kindly assertion that, by the start of his second season, Tom Pugh was 'trained' provided ready proof of this. 'He would listen to us more by then, and we became a good side,' said Arthur.

Other team members also offered their perspective. John Mortimore, then 28 and established in the team by the time of Pugh's appointment, commented: 'Someone in the committee must have had a view that Tom Pugh was the right sort of leader. My view about that, in general, is that it's great to be a leader, but it doesn't half help to have a compass to tell where you're meant to be going. It makes you think of the Grand Old Duke of York, doesn't it – but then he had an altitude problem rather than a directional one.

'Pughie was very brave in the sense the physical courage was there. I personally didn't get on badly with Tom Pugh – as was the case with most of the players – as Tom Pugh, a bloke playing.'

Tony Brown added his recollections: 'Some found it a considerable surprise when Tom Pugh – "Pug H" as some of the lads called him – was appointed captain. I liked Tom Pugh and got on well with him. Somehow I seemed to end up as his car passenger for lots of away match journeys – don't ask me why, although I think it was because I didn't object to his way of driving, which was pretty quick most of the time! You wouldn't have described him as a top-class batsman, although he did have a great eye, as you would expect from a world-class rackets player.'

After half a century, reflections about the 'political' issues hovering over Gloucestershire's appointment of their various captains in this period detained Arthur but briefly and, after circumspectly sharing some thoughts on the matter, he was soon back to the cricket.

'We played some good cricket in that 1961 season, when CTM got hit,' he remembered. Anxious that memory did not play tricks on him, he read from a contemporary record: 'After Pugh's injury Milton found himself captaining the side for the next 17 matches, five of which were won and six lost.'

With that record to hand, memory could not deceive him but, typically and endearingly, Arthur was prompted to tell of one of those defeats.

'We suffered two losses in one week, I remember, one of them being the famous game against Middlesex at Gloucester. Ian Bedford was the Middlesex captain, and we had three great days. We made 144 – of which I made nought – and they came back at us with 336 for 5. We declared on 432 in our second knock, I think I made 85, and we declared, six down.

'They batted, and they were a good side to play against. They used to have a game of cricket with you. I caught two or three, out and about, and anyway the last pair were in – a little fellow called Mickey Sturt, and Ian Bedford.

'Ian hit the biggest dolly you've ever seen up to me at mid-on, off Cooky – just a little donkey drop, you know. And I must just have taken my eye off it and it went bomp, bomp, bomp, right on the floor. They still wanted 76 to win – and they got 'em.

'As we walked off, Ian – he was such a lovely chap – came across and said, "Thanks for the game, we've had three lovely and delightful days cricket with you."

'So I went into their dressing room to thank their lads for the game and, of course, Don Bennett, from my Highbury days, was there. I went and sat by him. We talked about the match a bit and then he said to me, "Art, it's very good of you to come in and see us and have a chat, and it's good to have your company, but shouldn't you be going to your dressing room and seeing your guys?"

'I said to him, "I think I'm a damn sight safer here than going into our own dressing room at the moment"' – and the memory of it had him amused yet again.

Another game that slipped away from Gloucestershire has fixed itself in Jimmy Gray's memory. 'We played Gloucestershire at Portsmouth in mid-June and, with Tom Pugh absent, Art was in charge. We bowled them out for 176, and batted the rest of the day to make 96. I had made 23 and Roy Marshall 71, both of us not out. The second day was lost to rain, so Colin Ingleby-Mackenzie declared behind. Art had talked him into the declaration – not a difficult task with Ingleby. Gloucestershire batted again to establish a lead of 199, requiring us to score at 88 an hour. We got to 162-8, with the odds probably on Gloucestershire at that point, and in came Butch White, batting average 12. He slogged 33 to win us the game, as I say against the odds. That was the summer we went on to win the championship for the first time in our history, and we drank Art's health, among others, at the end of the season.'

This was the way Arthur felt cricket should be played, and he believed that if you played this way you would get the right results, albeit not every game.

The burdens of captaincy did not affect his own play one jot that summer. Against Sussex, at Eastbourne, he scored a century in both innings, 150 in the first and 100 not out in the second, with Gloucestershire winning by 109 runs.

Arthur's Benefit was a success, too, raising £3,235. By comparison with today's standards it was certainly not a princely sum, but he was happy, and truly grateful for the supporters' generous recognition of his cricket.

He didn't find it easy to be the focus of a Benefit: 'Of course, we didn't have anything like the number and variety of events players do today. We mostly relied on a Benefit match, the odd Sunday game and social event, but it still felt like going round with the old begging bowl, and I have to say I didn't feel altogether comfortable about that.'

Nevertheless, in a Gloucestershire context, it was a good and popular result. It allowed Arthur to pay off the mortgage on the house he and Joan had bought four years earlier. It would be their home until his death, and he was for ever grateful that the Benefit funds had made this possible.

The following summer, 1962, started slowly for Arthur. Unusually, his first 15 knocks produced only one 50 (against Derbyshire at Derby) and then, according to the record books, he suffered a 'break for injury in June'.

'Injury, my foot!' Arthur exclaimed. 'Pughie left me out of the side for a couple of matches. 'And he left me out because he felt I'd been laughing at him, when we played Somerset, so he said: "You'd better not play for a couple of matches." I hadn't been laughing at the captain – I'd been laughing at Bill Alley.

'Bill was in good form, was striking the ball well, and making nonsense of our bowling and field-placing – almost for fun – he was in such good nick. Bill kept hitting the ball to Pughie, too, and running, and laughing. He was laughing at the fun and joy of it and I suppose, because I was someone who enjoyed enjoying the game, I was laughing away at Alley – but Pughie obviously thought otherwise.'

Tom Pugh, a warm-hearted man, whose immense, sincere and enduring affection for Arthur is so readily apparent, has an entirely different view on the reason for Arthur's omission from the side. Honourably he chooses to keep his thoughts to himself. It might properly be acknowledged though that, great and fierce competitor that he was, he also enjoyed immensely the fun and laughter of the county circuit. To drop someone for enjoying themselves would not have seemed his most likely course of action.

He does recall, however, that Arthur accepted the decision manfully. 'On the last morning of the match I walked out on to the outfield with him before play, and said to him, "Art, you're not coming to Lord's with us for the next match." For someone who had never been dropped before, he took it like a gentleman and simply said, "OK, captain, you're in charge."'

Arthur missed the championship matches against Middlesex and against Warwickshire at Bristol. But on his return, against Warwickshire at Edgbaston, he was soon into his stride, scoring a first-innings hundred. 'I had something to prove, I suppose. It really got up my nose that I'd been left out.'

That accords with Tom Pugh's own recollections. 'When he came back into the side at Edgbaston, I asked him to come in the car with me from the hotel to the ground and I said to him, "Arthur, I want you to make your runs, take your catches, and be quiet. I want you to shut up about the Bristol wicket" – he was for ever moaning about the pitches at Bristol being too slow – and I pointed out that if he, as our best batsman, went on and on about those pitches, it was demoralising for the rest of the team. For the rest of the season he batted like a hero, and was very, very helpful to me.'

The episode of Arthur's omission certainly seems to have heightened both their respect and their regard for each other and they remained good friends thereafter.

Arthur finished the season with 1,617 runs (averaging 43.70) in all first-class matches. 'Pughie always said he did me a favour leaving me out of the side. He said, "When I left you out you were averaging 20; after I left you out you were averaging 60."'

Tom Pugh fondly recalled another Milton memory from years later, when he had invited Arthur to a cricket match and a picnic lunch with some chums in the car park. 'Arthur said immediately he would be pleased to come to lunch, but said he would have to slip off afterwards as he had arranged to play golf. Well, he hadn't arranged to play golf; it was just his own polite way of having an excuse if he felt a need to slip away. That was Arthur for you. In fact he stayed all afternoon and we had great fun.'

After his successful return to the side three more centuries followed, notably against Kent at Bristol when he scored 110 and 102 without losing his wicket. As I pressed him for more details he immediately went on to talk – lyrically and movingly – about Colin Cowdrey: 'What a beautiful player he was.' He then shared several cricketing and personal recollections, not least of Colin just being 'a very nice man, a great man'. Tears were forming in his eyes as the memories flowed from him.

To refresh his recollection of those two hundreds against Kent, Arthur once again referred to his ACS booklet: '… two not-out hundreds against Kent at Bristol where he steered the side to victory with a boundary off the last ball of the match.'

'That was a good way to win the match,' Arthur recalled. 'Browny was in with me at the end, in that second innings, and we'd got to where we wanted two to win and one to tie. Anyway, Browny was on strike and we got a leg-bye off it, and so we were left with one to win – and I hit it for four. Less than a boundary would have won us the match but I wouldn't have got to the hundred. So that was something special.

'I remember John Mortimore and I both had good matches with the bat, where we put on a lot of runs together, in both innings. Colin Cowdrey played beautifully – he made runs in both innings too – and declared and left us 247 to win. Morty and I put a big stand together in our second knock and, as I was getting up into the eighties, Morty came down the wicket and encouragingly said, "There's a hundred for you here."

'And of course, as soon as he said that, I found I started hitting the ball at the fielders and, in the end, we struggled to get there when we had seemed to be winning it comfortably.

'I always remember when I came in, I was walking up the steps and Morty was at the top applauding us in, and I said to him, "Don't you ever say that again." If we hadn't won the match I would have been livid.'

John Mortimore can readily and happily recall the incident. 'The captain had changed the batting order a bit in order to get us quick runs, but we still needed to get something like 140 in 80 minutes. We got to a stage where it was apparent we had a serious chance of winning, and there was a good chance Art could get a hundred. Well, I half said that to him, and half played a bit that way, and then missed a straight one, which left Art there with two overs to go, I think. He hit them off the last ball.'

And Such a Talent!

Tony Brown readily confirms these memories. 'When Arthur came in, he said the hundred – getting another hundred in the match – didn't matter. What was important was winning the match. It was more important to him for Gloucestershire to win than for him to get a good score. That was him, that was his way.'

Arthur may have been a bit self-critical that he had cut it fine in taking Gloucestershire to victory, but his captain was more generous. Tom Pugh readily recalled: 'That second hundred of Arthur's was made at a speed which allowed us to win the match. He paced it beautifully.'

Mortimore remembered a first-innings discussion with Arthur about the run rate. 'In those days we got additional points for getting a first-innings lead, having scored faster than the other side. Well, Art, as you know was a great push-and-run merchant, and I'm not very athletic so, if I've got to push it on, the ball has got to go for four.

'He came down the wicket at one point and said, "We're just a bit behind on the run rate." Alan Dixon had been bowling for an hour-and-a-half into a stiff breeze, so I hit the next five balls for four each – I'd decided it was worth giving it a go – and Art wouldn't talk to me at the end of the over. He turned his back on me' – and as John recalled this he laughed at the memory of Arthur perhaps feeling his partner had taken a hammer when a subtler approach might have sufficed – or that he might have wielded it earlier.

Tom Pugh's memories of Arthur revealed a touching incident. 'At our end-of-season party, probably at Lord's, it was getting near midnight and I took Arthur aside and we had a quiet chat. I told him, "Arthur, I want to thank you for all you have contributed this season in so many ways. It wouldn't have been the same without you." And he looked me in the eye and said: "Captain, it's me who should be thanking you. You told me if I didn't pull my finger out I wouldn't get another contract, and that did me a power of good." Do you know, that had never been – definitely had not been – part of my earlier discussions with Arthur, but Arthur seemingly had seen it in that light, and had responded positively and purposefully.'

As he shared these thoughts Tom's voice unashamedly broke with emotion as he recalled treasured memories of a good friend and valued colleague. 'I've been so lucky to have known him and played with him.'

As the memories flowed, Pugh recalled another match in which Arthur's cricketing brain and nous had allowed his captain to get to a family wedding which he expected to miss because it clashed with his cricketing duties.

'This was another game where Arthur had a major impact. I'd been up to see my Uncle Geoff, who lived in the Cotswolds, and was staying with him around February time, and he told me about his daughter, my cousin Dinah's wedding. She was due to marry David Nicholson – then a top jockey and later a successful National Hunt trainer – in mid-summer. Uncle Geoff very much hoped I would be there. I looked at the fixtures, saw it clashed with our game against Sussex at Stroud, so began to make my apologies, but Uncle Geoff said, "You've just got to beat them by lunchtime on the second day, and you can be there" – a suggestion that seemed so unlikely that I roared with laughter.

'Come the match, when we looked at the pitch on the first morning we thought it was going to be a war of attrition-type pitch. Sussex chose to bat and I immediately set out with the idea of strangling them. The fields I set would probably be called Sunday League fields now, but that's how we started. I said to David Smith, "I want a couple of maidens from you and then we'll get the spinners on," and at the other end I said the same to Browny and set a similar field. He wasn't happy – and said, "You might as well put Arthur on."

'I persuaded Tony of what we were about, but brought in a short leg and a gully, and he started bowling. Alan Oakman popped one up to short leg and they were 0-1. With Tony's fourth ball he caught-and-bowled Ken Suttle and, not many balls later, trapped Jim Parks lbw. They were 0-3.

'I still had it in mind that the spinners would perform well and was planning to get them on but, in a way, although the ball was turning a lot, it was doing it too slowly. Arthur strolled up and said,

"Captain, you want to get Browny bowling his off-cutters." In truth I didn't know Tony could bowl off-cutters, but I followed Arthur's suggestion and kept Tony on, but now bowling those off-cutters. At one stage Arthur also pointed out Tony was doing too much with the ball and suggested I got him to go round the wicket, which I did. And Tony finished with 7-24, and we bowled Sussex out for 41 in next to no time. And who did I have to thank for that?

'We made 174, and then got a couple of Sussex wickets before close of play that first evening. Next day David Smith took seven wickets as he and Tony Brown bowled them out for 58, and we won by lunchtime on the second day. And I got to my cousin's wedding, largely through Arthur's help and cricket brain.'

Arthur's wise cricketing head was the subject of another John Mortimore memory.

'Having played a long time with Art I knew he had a good cricket brain and he had a very clear view about where fielders ought to stand. By later in my career I had a very firm view about where fielders ought to stand when I was bowling.

'In one game Harold Jarman, who was a good fielder, was at extra cover. I've got three on the off-side, one square, extra cover, and mid-off. And Arthur thought Harold ought to be a little bit squarer, not very much, about three or four yards. But I knew where my fielders ought to be, so I would turn at the end of my run and if a fielder wasn't in the right place I would move him.

'I didn't know that Art, who was captaining that match, was moving him and, after three overs of this, Harold walks towards us and says, "I wish you two silly old buggers would have a word instead of keeping moving me about."

'I don't know whether any of our other bowlers would have moved him but what I do know is that, by that time, I knew where I wanted them. David Allen used to say not only did I know where I wanted them, I knew which ones I wanted in which positions.'

Tom Pugh's standing with his players had risen in the two seasons of his leadership, in the second of which the county finished fourth in the championship.

John Mortimore recalled discussions with Pugh on the question of captaincy and leadership. 'I've debated with Pughie about the difference between a good captain, and a captain who's lucky enough to have a good side, and tried to persuade him that it's a combination of a number of things. Pughie has his own view about his captaincy – as he's entitled to have. He did it as he saw it, and we didn't do too badly.

'He has a theory, which is tenable in many circumstances, that it's the leadership that matters, and over the years we've debated that. Yes, there is a point in that, but if you are lucky and your good players play well that season things begin to happen. Was Stuart Surridge the best-ever captain, or did it have something to do with Surrey being a very good side at that time? It needs to happen altogether – and when it does you're unstoppable.

'Coincidentally, Pughie demonstrated to Lord's – I was never sure whether by accident or design – that there was a fallacy in their proposal that the first innings had to stop after so many overs. Pughie, fair enough, bowled seamers, effectively all the way through. Great as a demonstration of what was up with that particular suggestion, but bad for the side, because we ended up with not many fit seamers.'

Pugh saw Gloucestershire as having a strong bowling side, both in the seam and spin departments, and he knew they were a very good fielding side. But he had concerns about the depth of the batting and so shuffled the order around to get the best out of a weaker batting line-up, often dropping himself down the order for that purpose. In so doing he might well have shot himself in the foot. By the season's end there were some who felt he was filling a key batting place but his supply of runs (741 from 51 innings) was insufficient to hold down a regular spot.

'By that time,' Arthur recalled, 'we'd became a good side, and then – lo and behold – the committee took the captaincy away from him. I couldn't believe it.'

Tony Brown shared Arthur's surprise. 'There had been lots of amateur captains and former public-school players in more than half the county sides in those days so Tom Pugh's appointment was, perhaps, not unusual, and of course we in Gloucestershire had been captained in pre and postwar years by two of the best, Bev Lyon and BO Allen.

'Obviously Pughie wanted to impress, and he was always positive in striving for a win in a match. He was brave and willing to listen to the advice of the senior players and, while not always following their thoughts, he managed to win nearly 50 per cent of the games he captained – aided by some good efforts from us of course.

'However, he was discarded by the committee at the end of that '62 season. That had the feel of a poor decision about it because he was by then getting the idea of how to achieve his aims as a captain. In fairness, he never did come close to being the next PBH May – an unreasonable expectation for anyone, of course – but that is what PGH Fender had told the Gloucestershire committee when recommending Tom Pugh to the county.'

One interesting footnote to this saga came long afterwards, when the two Toms, Graveney and Pugh, were golfing together and chatting over old times. As Graveney remembers: 'Pughie told me they had informed him he was going to be captain in '61. That was even before my first season as captain – when we came second – or when we came seventh the next year.'

So with Tom Pugh departing, one amateur captain gave way to another. Indeed, such seemed to be the committee's profound belief in the ideal of an amateur captain that it is unlikely Crapp, Emmett or Tom Graveney would ever have been appointed had a suitable amateur appeared at the right time. Overtures to Desmond Eagar (Hampshire), Donald Carr (Derbyshire) and Raman Subba Row (of Northants and, later, of Surrey) had been made but proved fruitless. In 1955 Gloucestershire had appointed as assistant secretary Bill Knightley-Smith from Middlesex with similar intentions, that he should play (as an amateur) and later become captain, but he didn't play quite well enough to succeed at first-class level.

To the committee, then, the appointment in 1963 of Ken Graveney, Tom's elder brother, didn't seem strange. It certainly kept faith with their belief in the mystique of amateurs.

Arthur enjoyed a warm friendship with both Graveney brothers and their families and yet his first reaction to the appointment was guarded. 'I thought this was a bad move, not because of Ken, and not because of any doubts about him as a player, but because he'd been out of the game for a while, five years at least, and, in this sense, was past it.'

The news, when it was released, may not have come wholly as a surprise to Arthur, although it didn't alter his thoughts about its merits.

'I had been out one evening with a chap called Ted Crawford. Ted was a keen follower of Gloucestershire CCC but he had no official or direct link with the club. He had some greyhounds, as did two or three of us together, and we used to have a beer in the men's club by Eastville Stadium after a meeting, to talk about the racing. One night Ted said to me, "They're going to have a new captain next year."

'I said, "Don't be daft. Why? We've just had a very good season. We're more than happy."

'"Well," he said, "I've heard from a good source that Ken Graveney will be captain next year."

'"Don't be silly," was my reply. "He's been out of the game for five or six years."

'As it turned out that's just what happened.'

Ken Graveney was 38 when he became Gloucestershire's captain. He had last played first-class cricket in 1951, 12 years previously, when he had been plagued by a persistent back problem – not good for a fast bowler! This had brought a premature end to his first-class career, a career in which he had been good enough to have been chosen for an England Test trial.

In the interim he had continued to play club cricket, and golf, and in the summer prior to his appointment Ken had captained the county's Second XI. A strong and forthright personality with few shades of grey in his thinking and outlook, and a former Royal Marine, who had taken part in the D-day landings, it was felt he might inspire, or drive, the county's up-and-coming players to fulfil their capabilities.

One who was aware that the county was about to make a change of captain was Ken's brother Tom. He was again with the England side in Australia battling for the Ashes but, out of brotherly loyalty, Ken wanted to make sure that Tom was comfortable about his taking on the role that had once been Tom's. 'Ken rang me up – I was in Brisbane – and asked: "Do you mind if I take it, kiddie?"

'"You're very welcome," was my reply.'

In Ken's first summer at the helm, the harnessing of talents and striving for more consistent success proved effective, as Arthur recalled drolly, with a good measure of understatement: 'We weren't too bad in '63.'

Arthur again headed the batting, making two championship centuries – both against Leicestershire, first at Stroud and then at Grace Road. After a successful spell of opening he had moved down the order mostly to no. 5 under Tom Graveney and Tom Pugh and now, under Ken Graveney, he batted mostly at no. 3.

Bristol still seemed a less than fruitful hunting ground for him. In ten innings there he made a total of 133 runs, with 49 as his highest score. Those figures need to be seen against his seasonal haul of 1,301 (34.23). Looking back over his career, one notes he scored 16 of his 55 first-class centuries at Bristol (plus 43 fifties), and shared in 27 century partnerships there. He continued to protest that he found batting at Bristol difficult – at least until David Bridle's time as head groundsman. But he recognised, too, that some of his best innings were played when he was facing a challenge, either on behalf of the team or because that Bristol wicket was posing a real test and bringing out the best in him and in his boundless skills.

He made just two fewer than his seasonal tally at the county's headquarters in one innings against Leicstershire at Stroud – 131, his top score of the season; yes, on that 'Death Valley' or 'Turnip Patch' pitch. Perhaps here again he was rising to the challenge and yet, unusually, he couldn't recall much about that particular knock.

'I remember making runs at Stroud, although I don't really remember much about that innings, but I can recall making a hundred against them in the return match at Leicester. I made 102 there, and that must have been a bit of a challenge, because they were picking pebbles out of the wicket; that's what it was like …'

A challenge of yet another sort came in the championship game with Middlesex, in mid-July, at the Wagon Works Ground, a match influenced by three declarations.

The visitors had set Gloucestershire 233 to win. At 187-8 they found themselves battling to save the game. When Gloucestershire began their second innings Arthur, who had made an undefeated 30 in the first knock, was soon in the middle again after their first wicket had fallen with three runs on the board. He batted through the innings to make 96 not out and – typical team man that he was – eschewed the personal landmark of another century by blocking out the final over of the game as a maiden, to ensure they did not lose.

Although the county had battled first to win that game, then to save it, Arthur's memories of it allowed him to conclude: 'Anyway, we did manage to win a few matches with Ken.'

In that 1963 season Arthur played his first official one-day game for the county. The Gillette Cup was introduced that summer. A 65-over game, starting at the traditional time of 11.30am (and invariably finishing by 6.30pm – those were the days), it brought, as intended, vibrant new life to the county game.

The concept of sponsorship was exciting to the counties but was so novel that even Gillette did not get full credit in that first season. The new competition was initially referred to simply as the First-Class Counties' One-Day Knock-Out Competition.

Gloucestershire, like many other counties, were slow to adjust to the different tactical demands of the one-day format, and departed at the hands of Middlesex in the first round. Arthur made 12 and took a couple of catches on his first appearance.

Injuries, as has been noted, formed unfortunate marker posts at different stages of Arthur's career: 1964 was one such season and for Arthur it ended when it had barely begun.

At the end of April, as the season got under way, Arthur was at The Parks for the annual pipe-opener against Oxford University. Runs began immediately to flow sweetly from his bat, but when he had made 83 the scorebook records the ending of his innings as 'retired hurt'. He would not pick up a bat again until the home match with Middlesex in late July.

He had broken his arm or – to put it more correctly and more grammatically – his arm had been broken for him. As I was writing this, Tony Brown's words came back to me: 'The poor old bugger was always injured.'

Arthur was batting at no. 3 at The Parks and was soon into his stride. In company with Ron Nicholls and then Mike Bissex, he was delighted to find he was starting the summer in good form. The ball was coming off the right part of the bat, and his timing was well tuned.

John Mortimore, deputising as captain for Ken Graveney, had joined Arthur in the middle and was facing the leg-spin bowling of EWJ Fillary, who later played for Kent. It was a 'juicy' delivery, Arthur recalled: 'The leg-spinner bowled Morty quite a high, wide half-volley which he flat-batted, hard and straight.

'Now I'm, as usual, backing up – I always liked to get runs, so was always ready to set off – and I've got my bat in my right hand and I can't do anything to get out of the way, and the ball smashed into me and broke my forearm.'

'Stove it in' was Mortimore's own description of the injury.

'So there I was,' said Arthur, 'out of action – on 83 not out in my first knock of the season.

'One good thing came out of it. I used to smoke about 15 to 20 cigarettes a day, not heavy in those days, and, of course, when I was injured I was sitting at home smoking more, and I thought, "I don't like this."

'I was never very good at being injured and missing cricket and, even if I was frustrated at not being able to play, I was often at the ground watching the boys play. I would go down and watch for a bit and then have a drink with them in the bar afterwards just to keep in touch.'

Those who came to know Arthur only later in life, when he was still a splendid example of natural fitness, might be surprised to learn how much he smoked at this time. But so did many other sportsmen.

'Well anyway, one evening when I was having a drink with the boys, I decided this was silly, and so ordered a packet of Manikin cigars, the small, mild ones. I smoked them for a short while, but decided I didn't much like them, and so I weaned myself off Manikins – and cigarettes. The best thing I ever did.'

His arm mended, Arthur returned in the third week of July. His form didn't immediately match that he had shown against Oxford University, but two pleasing innings against Derbyshire at Lydney offered encouragement. Just a couple of weeks later, however, his season ventured into uncharted waters.

'I returned to the side in July, but I was so shocked at the way Ken led the side. It was such a mess. I gave it away until the end of the season. Looking back on that now, I know that was wrong, but I just couldn't see what he was about.

'At Cheltenham, in one game we were sitting in the dressing room, and Ken came back in and said, "We've won the toss, what should we do?" – and promptly went round the whole room asking everyone what we should do.

'I decided that was enough for me. I didn't play any more that summer after that match, I remember.'

John Mortimore offered a team-mate's view. 'We had very little batting in the side and we were struggling without him after Art was injured. We were praying for him to come back and get a few runs. He came back, and got a few, but it was in pretty difficult circumstances. We were not winning anything so, by the time we got to Cheltenham, Art had lost the enthusiasm a bit and didn't want to play – which you can understand because you come back in, and you think you're coming back into the side that you'd left.

'Now, in effect, he'd left it the previous season, because that Oxford match when he was injured was the first match of the season. He'd left when things were going OK-ish, and I think our form when he came back into the side compounded things for him.

'I always felt Art was a good opening batsman because he could influence things from there, but when he came in at no. 5 he was still a very good player but he was less able to alter the way the side was playing. And the challenge of the bowler having a bit of help early on was important to him; he needed that challenge because he was never one to get masses and masses of runs on a very flat wicket.'

Arthur's sharing of his thoughts on this episode carried a clear implication that, much against his own expectations of Ken's leadership style, the captain was doing things by consensus and was going with the majority. 'I couldn't hack this rather unstructured way of captaining, or the way the side responded to it – so I left myself out for the rest of the season.'

The season's results tended to reflect Arthur's own conclusions and, from their mid-table position of the previous summer, Gloucestershire finished the season holding the wooden spoon, something not experienced since 1914.

Seemingly there were no repercussions and, apparently, no bad feelings emanating from Arthur's action. I asked John Mortimore whether Arthur had gone off to play in the Second XI. 'Well no, because that's not Gloucestershire's way of doing things. It's that sort of county.'

Publicly it was dressed up as 'Milton missed the remainder of the season through injury' or something similar. It did test Arthur's friendship with Ken for a while, but the strength and longevity of it ensured it was a breach healed readily before too much time had passed.

Having shared this much with me, Arthur was reluctant to say more and always changed the subject, albeit gently, if I raised it again. He seemed most embarrassed that, wholly out of character, he had allowed himself to do this. Perhaps he was surprised (as well as embarrassed) because, by nature, he was not a boat-rocker, a rebel or a posture-taker. With hindsight he clearly knew he should have handled his frustration and discontent differently.

'I'd never have got away with that now – and rightly so,' he supposed. Nevertheless, underlying this episode one could see, with abundant clarity, that Arthur's stance had been coloured by his feeling for the game and how it should be played.

'Way back in our courting days Joan and I used to go and have fish and chips with Ken and "The Duchess", as she was known. They lived in Westbury-on-Trym, before they later moved to Stoke

Bishop, and we used to go and have Sunday with them. Ken used to cook the food – he went into the catering business later, and made a real success of that of course. He did incredibly well.

'Ken had two boys, David and John, who were keen cricketers, and good golfers too, of course. David was about 6 foot 6 inches and a left-arm spinner. Anyway, I got to know the two boys well. They always used to get the bat and ball out, and I had more trouble with those two on their patch of grass than ever I did with Statham and Trueman,' he recalled, smiling.

'The next time I remember playing with David was later in my career; oh, it must have been ten years later – I was probably helping out in the seconds a bit. David, who'd been at Millfield, was playing in the Second XI. He always seemed to bowl well, and I used to talk to him from slip, sometimes mid-off, encourage him and help him: "Pitch it up, pitch it up; keep it on middle-and-off; have a man on the drive, let it happen … " Anyway, he listened.

'A few weeks later I was with his father, and Ken was asking me about David and asked me what I thought about him. "Well," I said, "he's 6 foot 6 inches, left-arm, and he knows where it's going. He knows about bowling – he's got more than a chance."

'And I reckon that chat was some instigation in getting David started, and then he joined the staff.'

With those memories of Ken Graveney's family, Arthur turned his thoughts to the 1965 season.

Gloucestershire's committee had given up on their ideal of an amateur captain. John Mortimore had succeeded Ken Graveney, and would lead the county for three seasons. Graveney continued loyally to serve, firstly as a committee member and then as its energetic and pro-active chairman and, subsequently, as president.

This summer happily saw Arthur back to full fitness and form. He again headed the county's batting and in mid-summer, at the age of 37, he returned to his position as opening batsman, filling the gap created by Martin Young's retirement.

As if to make particular compensation for the events at Cheltenham the previous year, both his centuries of 1965 came at the Festival. In the three-match programme he opened with 110 against Kent and in the final match he made a first-innings 170 against Sussex. It was the highest of his first-class career.

'Some time after I'd made that score I remember talking to Jack Crapp, when he was umpiring. We were having a beer one evening and he said, a bit quizzically, "Didn't you ever score 200?"

'I replied, "No, I've only ever played three-day games – but how about you, Jack, what's your highest score?"

'"Uhmm," he said, "191 – something like that."

'"Well, you didn't get 200 either?" I responded.

'"Well, no," he said, smiling ruefully. "And how do you think I got out? We were playing at Fenners, and they were using the whole ground, the whole playing area. And I was run out going for the fifth."

'We both had quite a chuckle at the thought of Jack going for a double hundred and being run out on the fifth run.'

An innings in 1965 which perhaps reflected Arthur's love of a battle was his knock against Lancashire at Old Trafford. Gloucestershire's batsmen found Brian Statham in his pomp. His metronomic accuracy and testing pace allowed them no let-up as this superlative and undemonstrative bowler demolished the visitors in taking 8-69; Milton apart, that is.

The quality of that innings, against an attack which included Ken Higgs, Sonny Ramadhin and Tommy Greenhough alongside Statham, fixed itself firmly in the memory of David Green, Lancashire's opening bat (who, three seasons later, would join Gloucestershire and, later still, write a splendid history of his adopted county). In *The History of Gloucestershire County Cricket Club* (published in 1990 by Christopher Helm Ltd), David recalls Arthur's knock:

> *Milton came to the wicket at 20 for one and remained for four hours, making 77 and effectively winning the match for his side. First of all he took Statham, who did not seem able to get a bowl at anyone else, and when Statham rested he took Tommy Greenhough, whose leg-spinners and googlies were getting considerable purchase on the dry*

surface. Tommy bowled at close to medium pace, which did not stop Milton from chasing smoothly up the pitch to him or moving swiftly back over his stumps. Tommy, who bowled well enough to have had a hatful of wickets against less talented opposition, finished with none for 60 off 31 overs, and muttered to me at one point "I'm getting sick of the sight of Art down there, wandering around at t'back of his blade!" And "wandering about" is just what it looked like, for such was Arthur's balance and ease of movement that he performed, with the most casual air, manoeuvres that in other players would have looked desperately risky.

If Arthur's innings further heightened David Green's regard, it was a regard that grew when later they were team-mates.

In 1966 Arthur continued to occupy the opening batsman's berth, and the summer yet again saw him in his customary place at the head of Gloucestershire's batting averages. At 38 he remained fit enough, and free of injury, to play in all the county's games. His tally of 1,646 runs was his best since 1959.

One notable innings that summer was an undefeated 138 against Leicestershire – at Bristol! Not only did he carry his bat in this innings, but he also shared a 68-run last-wicket stand with Barrie Meyer, who proved yet again that he was one of the more capable no. 11s in the business.

This was one of three occasions on which Arthur carried his bat during his career, the first being his undefeated 104 on his Test debut, the other his 128 not out against Glamorgan at Lydney in 1967.

'My best season.' That was the accolade Arthur readily accorded the summer of 1967.

Wisden, reporting on Gloucestershire's summer, recorded:

Unreliable batting, unavailability of bowlers, particularly the pace men, owing to injuries, and a smaller staff of cricketers than usual, were the main factors for

And Such a Talent!

Gloucestershire finishing at the bottom of the championship table – a position they occupied in 1964. It is difficult to imagine what would have happened to the Gloucestershire batting but for the performances of Milton and Nicholls. The former in his 40th year enjoyed his best season ever, topping the 2,000 mark for the first time in his career and hitting a record number of seven centuries.

Arthur was the first of three players (Ken Barrington and John Edrich were the others) to reach the 2,000 mark that year, passing this total on 26th August against Somerset (there's a surprise) at Taunton in the course of scoring 145, the last of his summer's seven hundreds – the most by any player in the championship in 1967. In the first-class averages he appeared sixth, behind Barrington, Dennis Amiss, Geoffrey Boycott, Edrich and Roger Prideaux.

He was happy, too, to explain his resurgent form and his reasoning for declaring 1967 as his best vintage. 'David Bridle had taken over as head groundsman. I scored over 2,000 runs. It was the only time in my career I reached this landmark. And there were seven centuries included in that.'

'And I also caught 39, so it wasn't a bad season – I don't think I took any wickets, though, that year.

'In a way it was the only season that I really set out to get as many runs as I possibly could – "set out my stall", you know, to have a good summer.'

Recognising that this might be considered a strange thing for a top-class county batsman to say, on the assumption most would do this every year, Arthur went on to explain the circumstances: 'In part it was my belief that the pitches at Bristol would be better from now on, and I wanted to make the most of it. In part it was also me recognising I was now very much a senior player, and that others looked to me for a lead.'

In truth he had been the county's senior and leading batsman since Tom Graveney's departure. It was perhaps due to his natural diffidence that he had not fully recognised this for himself until then.

'David Bridle had grown up with the job; he was almost brought up to be a groundsman. His father looked after the ground at Long Ashton and was a wonderful groundsman. So we had high hopes of David, who was by then already assistant at the County Ground, assistant to Bloodworth – who, although he had played for us, was a hopeless groundsman in my view.'

It was unusual for Arthur to be so forthright or uncomplimentary in his recollections and memories of colleagues, but it was offered with feeling and accumulated frustration. Recalling similar thoughts, Tom Graveney remembered: 'Bernie? He was the scorer. They promoted him from scorer to head groundsman. We started one match at Bristol and the wickets weren't b----y straight. We had to stop, and start again. The leg stump and the off stump at the other end didn't match up.'

But back to Arthur's season of 1967. 'The club chairman – sadly I can't remember his name now – had a business making and selling kitchen equipment and appliances and he decided to give prizes to the players for scoring a hundred or for so many wickets and that sort of thing. My seven hundreds that summer won me one or two bits for the kitchen!

'I often wonder how many more runs Tom and I might have got if we'd had a decent wicket at Bristol. Cheltenham wasn't much better in those days.'

Of the county's home grounds, he most enjoyed playing at the Wagon Works ground. 'Gloucester was good, our best wicket by far in those days.'

With a professional cricketer's customary lack of hyperbole he added: 'A good cricket wicket that one.' It was a phrase which showed how appreciative Arthur was of the groundsman's efforts.

'A chap called Charlie Newman was the groundsman – he used to put red marl on it and it used to make a good cricket wicket. It'd be a good wicket for two days and then turn a bit on the last day. Yes, it was a wicket you could bat on, and bowl on as well – a good cricket wicket. And they used to use marl in a lot of places in those days, until everyone started using Surrey loam, which did absolutely nothing for most pitches, did it?'

Did he enjoy playing at Cheltenham? 'Oh yes,' he said. 'Mind you, in my earlier days we often used to finish early and have a day or afternoon off, and we'd go and play golf up on Cleeve Hill.'

Dressing room folklore, and his own interest in the performances of players of earlier seasons, had told Arthur that, in 1946, stacks of runs had been scored at Bristol, not least by Wally Hammond in his last full season.

'Do you know,' he recounted, 'during that winter they hollow-tined the square and chucked sand all over it.' Tom Goddard took 206 championship wickets the following summer, Sam Cook took 138, and the county won 18 games to finish second to Middlesex, who were spearheaded by Denis Compton and Bill Edrich – in their 'golden' year.

'These sort of things were done to the square throughout much of my time – at least until David Bridle became head groundsman. I'm amazed the senior pros didn't kick up about it more, because it seldom worked in the county's favour as it had that first year. It might have been good for the spinners – and during much of my time, of course, we had Sam [Cook], Morty and David Allen – but it didn't do much for run-scoring.'

It is said that if ever the young batsmen, Tom Graveney, Arthur, or others complained that the pitches produced by Bernie Bloodworth were too slow, too low and (when sand-doctored) too much in favour of the slow bowlers, he had a ready and seemingly incontestable riposte: 'Wally never had no problem on 'em.'

It's important to remember that Arthur played virtually all his career on uncovered pitches, which, once play had started, were left open to the elements, with only the bowlers' run-ups and footholds, and the area immediately surrounding the creases, being covered overnight or when it rained. Many rain-affected pitches proved to be very sporty and offered a critical test of even the best batsmen's skills. 'Exactly! We were brought up on all sorts. Yes, it was good for the game, and taught us something about batting.

'When I was up at Oxford coaching the university lads they didn't have too many good-quality wickets. I remember a left-hander playing for Middlesex came in. He didn't play very well and got out and said, "How can you play on there?"

'I said, "Well, in my day every county had one or two who could make hundreds on that sort of pitch."

'"I can't believe it," he said.

'"Well, it's true," I told him.'

By the time Arthur retired from the first-class game pitches were being covered when play was not in progress. As might be expected he was a supporter of uncovered pitches. He had grown up with them and, in his mind, playing on such surfaces had helped make him the player he was.

'I miss the fact that all the wickets are covered now, which makes it a bit all the same. Do you know what I mean?

'The thing is that the slow bowlers don't really bowl enough, so that when they get on a wicket that helps them they haven't got it all behind them where they can just keep going, like getting a seven-for to win a match as they did in the old days.

'Another thing was that I liked the challenge on a bad wicket, trying to get 30 or 40. You play against Locky and Bedser on a wet one and you get 30, it's like getting 200 against somebody else. And I think I was always of that nature really. I needed a kick up the backside ...'

As Arthur's thoughts returned to that summer of 1967, his memory took him back a little earlier, to near the end of the previous summer.

'Towards the end of that summer at Cheltenham I was walking round the ground with Morty, and he seemed to be under the impression I was thinking of retiring. I suppose I was 38 then and had been playing for getting on for 20 years. He said something along these lines and I said, "Good Lord, no – not now that we've got a new head groundsman in charge."'

Such a response chimed well with Mortimore: 'I was very much in favour of Art continuing to play, of course. He was a hell of a good player to lose.'

And Such a Talent!

As if to emphasise Arthur's revitalised outlook on life, each of his three seasons under John Mortimore's captaincy showed an improvement on its predecessor. And he scored runs at Bristol. The first two of seven centuries of 1967 were scored at Bristol. It was as if he was giving David Bridle a public if metaphorical pat on the back. There's little doubt that Arthur did this in person too.

In Gloucestershire's opening home championship game, against Warwickshire, he made 119, and in the next home match, against Essex, 112. He was run out, in the county's second innings, when he had made 56; as we have seen, a rare form of dismissal for Arthur.

In the field too, that same deceptively swift but silken predatory movement – and his good and accurate arm – found many batsmen stranded in no-man's land. Their brains had told them there was a run, possibly with time to spare, before Arthur's peerless fielding left them high and dry.

Cricket's records traditionally have not recorded the fielder's name when a batsman is run out, more's the pity. Thus no record exists of the batsmen Arthur dismissed in this way in his long career. Had these figures been recorded there is little doubt that these, together with his regular haul of catches, plus the odd wicket taken here or there, would have taken him well on the way to being a regular '100 wickets a year' man.

David Allen, reflecting on his team-mate's fielding skills, recalled: 'He was a brilliant and exceptional fielder, well balanced and with great speed off the mark. He often fielded backward short leg to the fast bowlers. I remember one game against Somerset at Bath, where the boundary is not very big, the batsman whipped the ball round to the leg-side. It came so quick to Arthur he could only parry it over his head. I was at fine leg, and the ball was so high in the air I thought it might reach me. It didn't. Arthur, after pushing the ball up, turned and sprinted fully 20 yards to take a diving catch at full stretch.

'He had a wonderful pair of hands, and excellent balance. As a spin bowler you did not ask him to field in an exact spot – he chose his position relating to the batsman and the pace and bounce of the pitch. He would always stand as close to the batsman as he judged right, and he had a wonderful way of giving you confidence. He would say, "Don't worry about me getting hurt – you bowl well and I will stand as close as possible." He was a great catcher.'

Allen's spin twin, John Mortimore, is highly complimentary about Arthur's sublime fielding too. 'Art was one of the very few who was good fielding in close on both sides of the wicket. I remember a game at Leicester where one of their young batters had tried to play a sort of sweep shot, and he had hit it pretty well, and the ball stuck somewhere in Art and he just said to the lad, "Son, it's not 'alf a game," and produced the ball. "It's not 'alf a game" – genuinely sympathetic to a young player who'd played an aggressive shot.

'He was a magnificent fielder, and caught some magnificent catches. In the first match I played, one went up into the covers and he and Tom Graveney collided, because no one had called for the catch. Art got knocked down but he still had the ball.

'In one game against Glamorgan we were getting through them and as Wilf Wooller came to the wicket he passed Sam Cook waiting at the start of his run. "Good afternoon Sam, I don't suppose you'd mind bowling against my clowns every day, would you?" Wilf asked, perhaps with just a hint of some wily reverse psychology.

'Sam bowled him his first ball, Wilf played forward, and Art nipped in there and caught the ball almost off the face of the bat. There was nothing Wilf could do but tuck his bat under his arm and head for the pavilion. As he went past the bowler Sam simply said, "No, I wouldn't mind at all."

'That was Sam – and that was Art, too.'

Another contemporary who rated Arthur highly as a sportsman and as an individual was Dennis Silk. Dennis, who dedicated himself so splendidly to schoolmastering, not least as Warden of Radley College, played 83 first-class matches for Somerset, Cambridge University (in that postwar decade or so when the university produced numerous outstanding batsmen, among them Doug Insole, John Dewes, Hubert Doggart, Peter May, David Sheppard, Raman Subba Row and Ted Dexter), and for MCC (captaining MCC tours to New Zealand and Canada), and went on to become an outstanding president of MCC as well as a popular and hugely respected chairman of the Test and County Cricket Board. One mention of Arthur Milton and Dennis's quicksilver mind filled spontaneously with warm memories: 'In my view Arthur was one of the greatest all-round athletes of our time. "Silk, caught Milton, bowled Wells." Oh, what memories that stirs. He was like lightning in the field.'

Arthur's continuingly brilliant fielding gave no hint that he was approaching 40; nor, of course, did his undiminished batting skills. These were enhanced by the added experience and wisdom which he tacked on to those wonderful natural gifts he had always purveyed with a bat in his hand.

Arthur had begun the season opening with Mike Bissex but, midway through the summer, the stylish and gifted Ron Nicholls rejoined Arthur at the top of the order. It was a pairing that proved almost as fruitful as his earlier partnerships with Martin Young and Tom Graveney.

Arthur clocked up home centuries against Glamorgan at Lydney and Nottinghamshire at the Wagon Works. Away from home, he passed the three-figure milestone against Warwickshire (at Coventry), Surrey (The Oval) and – yes, they couldn't be missed out in his most prolific summer – Somerset at Taunton.

I asked David Allen about Arthur's batting. 'He was a good batsman off front and back foot. He was an excellent back-foot player, and an able player on all sorts of pitches. He showed courage against fast bowlers and he enjoyed the duels with the wrist-spinnners – his excellence at playing wrist-spinners, like Bruce Dooland, George Tribe, Gammy Goonesena and Jack Walsh was something very special.

'There were many of Arthur's innings which stand out in the memory. In his younger days he was a more positive and forceful batsman and against Northants in 1953, at Rushden, he scored 85 in a partnership of 108 with TWG. There was hope this innings would help him on to the tour to West Indies that winter as it was played in front of FR Brown – but it was not to be. He was a gifted player who, with Tom Graveney, led a new generation of young players to follow the professionals of the postwar period. His class and his ability deserved better than to play a career on slow, low pitches at Bristol, which was a waste of his expertise as a back-foot player. Perhaps he should have played at Worcester with TWG.

'He scored some brilliant hundreds, of course, against Somerset but one of his most engaging innings was later in his career, in 1969, at Lydney, which I captained, on a slow, low pitch that needed patience. In that one-day match he came in after Greeny and Ron Nicholls had put on 45 for the first wicket and I told him it was very important to keep one end going so that runs could be scored at the other. We couldn't afford to lose wickets at both ends in a run chase. Arthur played his part to perfection, and worked terribly hard for the team and fully carried out captain's orders – wonderful.'

For the record Arthur made 38 not out in Gloucestershire's 130-5 (not an unusually low score in those early years of the 40-over John Player League) – enough to beat Sussex by five wickets. 'Milton played with calm assurance and dispelled some minor anxieties,' said *Wisden*.

A feature of Arthur's cricket, and of the way he played the game, is that he was admired – almost universally – by his team-mates and opponents alike.

Norman Gifford, who played for Worcestershire from 1960 to 1982, captaining them from 1971 to 1980, and who won 15 England caps, said of Arthur in more recent days: 'A great man – one of the nicest men who ever played cricket,' an instinctive recollection which genuinely placed a huge emphasis on 'nicest'.

This from a man who himself is one of cricket's widely-admired yeoman stalwarts, to whom the game means so much. Ever ready to talk about it, always keen to contribute in some way or another, and to contribute generously, 'Giff' devoted himself unreservedly to Worcestershire in his years with the county and, in his seventies and in retirement, is now devotedly coaching young Sussex cricketers. He and Arthur might have come from the same mould.

'He'd always help you, as a young player,' Norman recalled. 'At the end of the day, if you'd, say, bowled a long spell at him, he'd be more than happy to talk with you. You could learn a tremendous amount from him and from talking about the game with him – and he was always happy to talk cricket' – almost reverentially adding: 'And such a talent.'

All of this was offered spontaneously and generously – the tribute just flowed from Norman; a sign of his admiration for Arthur, and a sign too of his own great generosity of spirit. Norman's view has been echoed by many others.

If in Arthur's own words 1967 was a season in which he had 'set out his stall', it had proved richly productive. What a good summer, in his fortieth year, to fortify the long winter months.

By the time the next season opened Gloucestershire's peerless Peter Pan would have yet another string to his bow.

Chapter 14

Captain Peter Pan

GLOUCESTERSHIRE APPOINTED ARTHUR as county captain in 1968. He was happy to accept the post, recognising how previously he had enjoyed several spells as stand-in skipper. In retrospect there is little doubt it came too late for him.

Even here there's a suspicion that he might not have been at the very top of the committee's list. Gloucestershire had been making overtures to Gary Sobers. The game's greatest all-rounder opted for Nottinghamshire and Trent Bridge, and so the committee had to think again. They thought of their senior and most experienced cricketer, a loyal man of Gloucestershire.

On the field Arthur found captaincy much as he had anticipated and had previously experienced. Off it, the full-time role proved more demanding. As an out-and-out team man he found it difficult to understand that certain players were always ready to have a moan, either to the captain or at the captain, and mostly about their own role in the game rather than the overall team effort.

'Not Morty, or David Allen or Browny – but there were one or two of the bowlers who perhaps didn't cope too well when they were taking punishment. And when we were trying to save a match, they would always let you know if they felt they had been put on at the wrong time, or the wrong end. Yes, looking back I felt the pressure one or two created which, thinking about it, seems surprising now.'

David Green, who had joined Gloucestershire that summer after being let go by Lancashire, felt that as far as leadership and tactical nous on the field were concerned his new captain was fine. 'But it was the other things, the other parts of the job, that got to him. I felt that one or two tried to undermine him, too, perhaps because they fancied the job themselves, and, as in every side, there were one or two who liked to whinge. Arthur would have strong opinions about how we should play the game. He was charming – and tremendous fun – but you wouldn't call him saintly.'

Arthur's good-mannered genial nature meant that he invariably gave an impression of courteously suffering fools; if this was not always gladly, more often than not he achieved it by simply disregarding the folly and its perpetrator, and carrying on as he thought best.

Many new captains are surprised at the element of committee work, administration and public relations the role constantly imposes. Arthur was not a natural committee man (one of the very few areas where he was not a natural). He was very happy to talk about the game to anyone with genuine interest and enthusiasm, and was in his element talking with those who love the game and know its ins and outs. But his experiences suggested that many committees spend too much time talking and little enough doing, often talking about matters – especially playing matters – beyond their direct ken and expertise, albeit with good intentions and sincerity.

'In the end it all used to worry me a bit – stopped me sleeping at nights. I would have been better off in my prime. The year that Tom Pugh got his jaw broken, I was at my best then, and we played some good cricket.'

But in 1961 the committee was keeping faith in its belief in the amateur captain. Arthur was simply the acting captain. That summer was to be the midway point of Arthur's county career; not that he, of course, could possibly be aware of that at the time.

When eventually the Gloucestershire captaincy came his way, his appointment carried a certain irony. In various quarters it was thought a parting of the ways might have been on the cards, that he might have been considering retirement and looking at life beyond professional sport.

Arthur had just enjoyed his best season ever with the bat and some thought this might have been his swansong. That superlative and prolific 1967 season gave him a real sense of satisfaction that, at nearly 40, he could still play. The addition of another string to his bow, captaincy, a year later did not seem to overly faze him.

Hindsight might well say that the captaincy indeed came too late in Arthur's career, but it certainly didn't detract from his form on the field. Injury meant he missed a number of games that summer but in first-class games he scored 1,310 runs at an average of 33.58. His tally included a half-century for MCC against the champion county, Surrey. Surprisingly, considering his frequent invitations to play for MCC, it was his first appearance since 1962.

Of his year as captain he recalled: 'We had some good matches. I was always at my best when there was a bit of an extra "cause" or we were struggling. I remember batting all day to save a match at The Oval, and there was also a hundred against the Aussies at Bristol.'

That match against the tourists in July was most certainly a highlight of his summer and – one might suggest – of his career. Australia included Graham "Garth' McKenzie, as skipper, Ian Redpath, Paul Sheahan, Bob Cowper, Ian Chappell, and wicketkeeper Brian Taber from the side that had just drawn the third Test with England at Edgbaston (in which Arthur's old friend Colin Cowdrey had become the first to play in 100 Tests). To their number were added John Inverarity, Les Joslin, Ashley Mallett, Neil Hawke and Dave Renneberg.

The tourists, after making 351-5 declared, had bowled out Gloucestershire for 172 by around teatime on the second day, and then invited them to follow on.

'We had about an hour to bat that evening,' Arthur recalled. 'It wasn't a bad wicket [said with that understatement which cricketers use when they really mean it was pretty good], and Greeny and I went in.'

David Green was a seasoned professional who had played for Oxford University, where he gained Blues in 1959, 1960 and 1961, as well as for Lancashire, for whose Second XI he had played while still at Manchester Grammar School. He was also a rugby three-quarter good enough to have played for Sale RFC and for Cheshire.

'Greeny and I, we had some wonderful partnerships. We'd run for anything because for a biggish lad he was quite quick about the place. We used to run to gully!

'Anyway, against the Aussies we'd got to 60 or so for no wicket when we came in at the end of the day. Starting again the next day we eventually put on 102 for the first wicket, and time went on and we saved the match.'

'We saved the match' – that was what was important. The team had battled well, and that was the memory at the forefront of their captain's mind almost 40 years later. Gloucestershire had responded robustly and well in that second innings and had made 389-6 when time was called, with runs coming from Green, David Shepherd, the young Mike Procter (another new signing), and the captain.

I had to prompt Arthur to tell me how many he had made.

'One hundred and fifty-five. It was the only time I got runs against the Aussies – the buggers. That really did quite satisfy me.'

So it should, for it was the 50th first-class century of his career and a knock that gave cause for satisfaction all round.

Except perhaps for the 'buggers'? That was not a word that tripped with excessive frequency from Arthur's tongue. When it did, it was almost always uttered with good humour, seldom ever with vehemence. In this instance it seemed specifically to embrace that respectful love–hate for the Old Enemy along with, perhaps, a strong measure of regret that he hadn't taken the attack to them more successfully on his one trip Down Under ten years previously.

Several times in our discussions Arthur slipped into the conversation 'I always seemed to play better when the county was struggling or up against it' – and always it was said as a natural thing, not as a point emphasised for effect.

One such game in that summer of 1968 was against the might of Surrey at The Oval. Gloucestershire had been made to follow on, 192 runs behind Surrey's first-innings' 312. 'I remember batting almost all day – I was out just before the close – to save the game, and made a hundred.'

In fact he made 120, leading Gloucestershire to 293-2, and safety, at the close. Along the way he enjoyed pleasing and fruitful partnerships with David Green and with Ron Nicholls.

For one who just enjoyed playing, and felt the game should be simple and straightforward, the distractions which came with captaincy were proving a strain.

'I knew I wasn't enjoying it, so I gave it up, and only had the one year.'

David Allen concurred, feeling that Arthur would have been a more determined skipper earlier in his career. 'Arthur was a more positive player and judge of the game in the early Sixties. I believe if he had had the captaincy earlier it would have been better. When he received it, in 1968, he was a more cautious player and not such a positive thinker by then.

'The same was possibly true with his batting. If he had been picked earlier to play for England I'm sure he would have been more successful. When he did play he did well at home but then went on tour to Australia, where, of course, he broke his finger – and had to put up with the throwing controversy.'

Arthur's predecessor, John Mortimore, sympathised with Arthur. 'I strolled round the ground with him one day, and commiserated that things hadn't gone particularly well for him as captain. I think Art found it a trouble. Mind you, doing it with a bad side, or a side that's unsuccessful, is hard work.'

Again with that seemingly natural gift of understatement shared by so many cricketers, John added: 'I thought he did it not too badly – and you have to remember it was difficult because we were a bad batting side that summer. From personal experience I can tell you that with a bad batting side it's an uphill struggle.

'We had started to come back a bit, mind you – it was David Green's first year and Proccie's first season [Mike Procter] – and we had come out of three, four – possibly five? – seasons of not being a particularly good batting side. In the same way that you believe you will get runs, there are times when you tend to believe you are not going to get any runs. If you keep getting 250 in the first innings it's a very different game from getting 350. I reckoned that if you get 350 and somebody on the other side gets a hundred you can still be in front; if you get 250 and somebody on the other side gets a hundred you are likely to be seriously adrift.'

From the occasions – and there were a good few – when Arthur had been skipper when the official captain was injured or unavailable, and done so very ably, it appeared that, in carrying the office himself, he was overburdened. As John Mortimore tellingly pointed out, 'When you get the job you get all the bits that go with it, which you might happily delegate to someone else, but can't.'

One important landmark of Arthur's year as captain was Gloucestershire's appearance in the semi-final of the Gillette Cup, just one step away from a first final at Lord's. The county had never before progressed that far, never before gone beyond the third round. On the way they had beaten the holders, Kent, and Nottinghamshire, against whom Arthur made 87, his highest score in the competition. There was, however, to be no Lord's appearance for the Glosters, after their semi-final opponents, Sussex, took the honours at Hove.

Of the match at Trent Bridge, Arthur's opening partner David Green remembers, 'We put on 164 in that Gillette Cup quarter-final at Trent Bridge in one-and-three-quarter hours. Art made 87 and I got 90 in that session before lunch.' He omitted, self-effacingly, to point out that Nottinghamshire's opening attack that day was led by the one and only Gary Sobers.

Arthur had moved into the second half of his career at a time when one-day cricket became an increasingly important feature of the county game. The introduction of the Gillette Cup in 1963 was followed by the John Player Sunday League in 1969 and the Benson & Hedges Cup in 1972.

With his undoubted and undiminished cricket skills, his high-quality batsmanship and particularly his ability to work the ball into gaps, alongside his astute and instant judgement of quick singles, his razor-sharp fielding and his canny bowling, Arthur might have been expected to excel at this form of the game – and to enjoy it enormously. In truth, and perhaps surprisingly, he didn't much like one-day cricket. Perhaps it came too late for him, and he didn't play enough of it (he played only 55 one-day games for the county over 11 seasons). Perhaps it was a generational thing. He had been brought up on three-day cricket and that, for him, was the epitome of county cricket; that was 'proper' cricket.

Every captain looks to lead from the front and Arthur was no different. Frustratingly for him injury kept him out of the side for a number of games – when David Allen was an able deputy – and, although the county climbed one place in the championship table, 16th was a disappointment for the new captain.

If the year had brought its challenges – mostly off the field – there were other elements he looked back on with great affection, among them a chance to blood new players and to help the younger ones. 'I was able to help the young lads a bit – which I always enjoyed doing.'

David Shepherd, the rotund hard-hitting Devonian middle-order batsman, had made a belated but resounding start to a county career. He had joined Gloucestershire in 1965, aged 24, and scored a quick-fire century on his first-class debut. Typical of the man, he would make a considerable contribution to Gloucestershire's cricket, not least in the dressing room, before he retired in 1979. But by his third season some in the Gloucestershire committee room were having doubts and felt he might be released.

'Shep was lovely, a really good lad. He was always interested in the game, was always asking me questions about it, and that,' Arthur recalled. 'Funny thing, though, was, that year, when they wanted me to be captain, the committee were pretty much decided not to give him another contract. But as captain I wanted him, and I said, "No, I want him to play."

'I asked him about it and he said, "Yes, of course." And that kept him going with us, which was good, for him and for the county. He was a great lad. And of course he went on to be a good county umpire, a top man, and then, pretty quickly, to do really well as a Test umpire and one of the very best international umpires.

'He's a great character. A good umpire too – and he's good with the people. He loved the game, loved absolutely everything about it. I was delighted – delighted for what he did for cricket,' and as Arthur shared these reminiscences the waver in his voice said as much as his words.

When Shep heard that I was writing this book he, with typical generosity, wrote to me: 'It's important that a book should be written about Arthur so that people who are not aware of how great a sportsman he was can be made aware, and others reminded of what he achieved.

'Surely there cannot be many people who have had more sporting ability. He was simply brilliant at every game he tried whether it be cricket, football, rugby, golf, snooker, or even judging "fast" greyhounds.'

From that starting point Shep went on to say: 'We obviously had a coach at Gloucestershire [Graham Wiltshire], but the senior players also used to pass on little tips too and Milt was always helping and encouraging me with my batting.

'When I first joined Gloucestershire I was in digs in Bristol – the big, wicked city! – and found life a bit lonely. Milt used to invite me down to his second home – the dog track at Eastville. He marked the cards for visiting cricketers on Saturday nights. He would take me to the Eastville Club for a few games of snooker. Of course, he was far too good for me so used to give me three, four or even five blacks start.

'There was a time when he was invited to play Alex "Hurricane" Higgins, who was playing the best players in the area. Apparently Arthur could have beaten him but let Higgins win because he thought the professional should win.'

Shep's story tells us much about Arthur – about his ball skills and his talent with a snooker cue, a match for one of the game's top professionals; it also tells us how he rated and regarded fellow sports professionals, in this case not wishing to undermine Higgins when the latter was meant to be the centre of the action.

That particular story was one recounted for me a number of times by several others, as evidence of Arthur's inborn gifts where ball games were concerned. It had clearly become part of the Gloucestershire sporting folklore. Arthur certainly played snooker and billiards, and did so for fun and with considerable success, but not with any great regularity.

The form of the story most frequently told is of Arthur being invited as a guest opponent at the opening of a new snooker club, where Higgins was to do the official opening and play some exhibition matches. By custom the amateur, the 'local', makes the break on these occasions and then, when they've muffed an early shot, the professional comes to the table to finish the game by showing how it should be done. Arthur broke first. He was in sparkling form. He potted the reds and was working his way through the colours, his form such that some wondered if Higgins might need to leave his chair – until Arthur made way for him. Soccer, cricket, golf, rugby, tennis and table tennis, snooker and billiards came so easily to him. Even, so it seems, did croquet.

Tony Brown tells of an occasion when, at an away game, he and Arthur were strolling round the boundary, keeping an eye on the cricket and setting the world to rights. Part of their perambulation took them alongside a hedge overlooking another sports area. There a croquet tournament was in progress. As sportsmen so often do, admiring skills in others, Tony and Arthur stopped to watch. Seeing their apparent interest a very 'county' lady asked them if they played, to which both indicated they had never played and didn't really understand the game. Whereupon they were invited to try their hand. After watching Arthur play a few shots their hostess was convinced that Arthur had been pulling her leg and that he was a county-standard croquet player. He had never before picked up a croquet mallet and, in all probability, never did so again.

Admiring though he was of Arthur's amazing multi-faceted skills, Shep was keen to share more thoughts about Arthur's cricketing ability.

'When watching Milt bat it all appeared so easy for him. He seemed to have so much time to play his shots that he looked almost lazy. This, I was to learn, was the art of a class batsman. He certainly should have played more times for England.'

Shep's memories of Arthur's batting, and the immense amount of time he seemed to have to play his shots, recalls a delightful tribute to Arthur in Alan Gibson's perceptive vignette in his report for *The Times* of Gloucestershire's match against Somerset at Taunton in 1973:

> *We did, however, see one beautifully characteristic off-drive from Milton, made as usual so late that the scorers had already put down a dot.*

Although able to recall Arthur's cricketing technique from a ring-side seat, Shep – a good all-round sportsman himself, despite his Falstaffian build – always regretted not seeing Arthur in his pomp on the soccer field.

'He was naturally fit and agile. I would have loved to see him play soccer for Arsenal, especially having heard he was the quickest thing on two legs. All I saw of his soccer was at pre-season cricket training.

'At the end of my initial three-year contract with the club I was undecided whether to continue with first-class cricket. I had not been too successful although I loved the game and wanted to be retained.

'Contracts were usually decided during the Cheltenham Festival and the local press were surmising who should and who should not be retained. It was then that Arthur saved my whole career.

'One morning during the Festival he wanted me to walk round the ground with him. He asked me what I wanted to do. He then told me that the committee had asked him to become captain of the club during the following season. He said that, as captain, he wanted me to stay and play. That was enough for me.

'I stayed for another 12 seasons and then had 25 years on the umpires' list. I have everything to thank Arthur for. But for him I would probably have left the game and missed out on a wonderful experience lasting 37 years. I idolised him.'

Those who knew David Shepherd will know, if only through his umpiring, of his genuineness, easy openness, transparent honesty and undoubted integrity. A thoroughly decent man with no airs and graces who, wherever the game took him, even at the game's highest levels, had no trouble in keeping his feet firmly on the ground (except whenever the scoreboard read 111 or a multiple thereof!). He remained for ever faithful to his West Country roots and his beloved Instow.

Seen in this context his warm, heartfelt tribute to 'Milt' says an immense deal about Arthur. It says much about Shep too. It is a tribute many others have echoed with equal warmth and affection.

Shep's appreciation of Arthur's helpful insights and encouragement of his batting, and his ready sharing of his experience and expertise, is endorsed by other team-mates, including Tony Brown.

'He was always extremely helpful to people, I felt, especially about their batting. He would talk to you – to anybody who wanted help. I mean Greeny, David Green – he helped David Green enormously, especially in their partnerships. Arthur often opened with Greeny, who will tell you he learned a vast amount from playing with Arthur – although, while he was always willing to help and encourage them, the younger player had to want to be helped and encouraged. If they weren't interested then he wouldn't bother overmuch.'

Let's hear David Green happily confirm this. 'In 1965 I scored over 2,000 runs for Lancs but then suffered a steepish decline and, in a way, I was shot to pieces. But I'd always got runs against Gloucestershire and so, when Lancashire let me go, they came in for me – as did a number of counties. Gloucestershire were able to offer me winter employment too – a very important consideration for a man with a family with two young children.

'I knew Arthur, of course, before I joined the county – from playing against him, firstly at Oxford during my three seasons there, and then when playing for Lancashire. I got on with him well and we had a lot of fun. That was his way, and if occasionally he didn't really rate someone or didn't find them easy to get on with he wasn't one for being difficult or having blazing rows and suchlike, he simply worked round folk or avoided them.

'Arthur was a dual international, of course, but he was so unassuming and never ever made a great thing about it. He didn't strut about the place with his chest puffed out. That wasn't his style. Denis Compton was much the same, very easy to get along with but didn't make any great fuss about what he'd done or achieved – and another very fine player, of course.

'Art was a tremendous help and an immense influence on me when I joined the county, and helped me get my game together again. He was a great coach – teacher – about cricket.

'One of his great strengths was he told you, and spoke with you, about how you might bat, not about how he batted. So many are good at telling you how they do it, but that's not always helpful. Art clarified the art of batting for me so much – it might have taken five or six weeks for it to sink in, but once it did it was a real help and made a huge difference for me.'

To put some sort of context on Green's last remark we should note that in his first season with Gloucestershire he made 2,137 runs at 40.32 including a career-best 233, an achievement that earned him selection as one of *Wisden's* five Cricketers of the Year, a remarkable turnaround.

'I had got into the habit of moving early,' he recalled, 'and plonking my front foot down on middle-and-off. Great if you're Tom Graveney and have Tom's skills but for someone like me it meant I was often playing around my front pad, and playing across the line. Not good.

'Art said, "You've got to wait, before you move." He'd noted that I tapped my bat on the ground a couple of times when the bowler was running in, so he suggested I might tap it once more as the bowler bowled – before I moved. It took a bit of doing, but once I'd got into that routine it made such a difference.

'Because I'd been in the habit of moving early and getting on to the front foot I tended to fall over, so Art said, "Keep your weight on your heels a bit more; imagine you're sitting on a high chair." Again, it was difficult at first, because nearly everything you do in sport is about putting the weight on the balls of your feet, but it made a great difference for me.

'I was also concerned about getting right behind the ball, and Art suggested I didn't need to do this but might get just inside the line of the ball. He reckoned if I got right behind the ball I could only play it in one direction, but thought that if I got just inside the line I could then hit it either side.

'Browny came into the net to have a bat one day, and he was batting in quite a pronounced crouching position, so I asked him what that was all about. He said, "I thought I'd bat like you today!" Of course there was much less filming and virtually no videoing then so I didn't know what I looked like – but it worked. Art was a huge influence in this way.'

As Arthur remembered his year of captaincy, and the young players who were coming into the side, he began – almost on an impulse – to talk, warmly and freely, of Gloucestershire's new and highly-talented all-rounder, Mike Procter. He spoke of him in a very admiring way, as one top-class sportsman of another.

He recalled that, as young players, Barry Richards and Mike Procter had played for Gloucestershire in 1965, turning out in the Second XI and other non-first-class games. The county hoped to sign both in 1968, but the Test and County Cricket Board's registration regulations at that time precluded this. The West Countrymen opted for Procter.

Arthur began laughing affectionately as he remembered that, soon after Proccie's arrival, there was a snowfall and the young South African got his first sight of the white stuff.

And then he remembered the young player's talent – as one who had the privilege to see and admire this at first hand.

'What a player he was.' Others might have sought a quiver-full of adjectives and superlatives to describe Procter's talents but, in true Arthur style and in much the same way as he had earlier spoken of Sam Cook, those five simple words said it all.

'I used to field at first slip to him – or second. I used to love fielding at slip, because you could see everything, you know. The first three or four I had from him, I dropped. The first three or four. And it took me a while to work it out, because I was getting there but I wasn't hanging on to them. It was because I'd never fielded there to a really quick bowler before, and the pace of the ball was taking it through my hands. I was getting to the right place, so I had to learn to be more firm and then, once I had worked it out, I was OK, and I don't recall dropping one off him after that.

'Even in my last season, I caught 'em all at first slip even when I was 46 years old – I never dropped one' – this last remark made, typically, not in any trumpet-blowing sense but simply as a matter of fact, a matter of report.

David Green, as another new boy, frequently linked up with Mike Procter at the end of a day's play, and Tony Brown and Arthur Milton would often join them. 'It wasn't unknown for Mike and I to give it a thrash some evenings, but Art didn't bother about keeping up with us and would be happy to sit there with a couple of pints or so while we nattered about the day's play and about the game. Mind you, sometimes late in the evening he might go onto the Scotch, and that didn't always do him a lot of good.

'In our game at Hove that summer, he and I put on 315 for the first wicket, when we hadn't been in too good a shape the previous evening. In fact I don't think we got to bed until daylight.

'We were probably still feeling a bit off-colour before start of play and, when we talked about what we should do if we won the toss, Art and I being batters thought we should put them in. Proccie, being a bowler, was equally adamant that we should bat so he could have a sleep.

'As it happened, Mike Griffith, the Sussex captain, won the toss and what did he do? He put us in. Proccie immediately went to sleep, and Art and I had to get ourselves together and go and bat. At lunchtime we came in at 120-0. When we came in at tea it was 310-0, which is when Proccie first opened his eyes. We finished up putting on what is still a Gloucestershire championship record for the first wicket, I believe.'

For the record, that was when Green scored his career-best 233 and Milton made 122.

Such memories had David Green thinking about other innings shared with Arthur. 'He was a tremendous judge of a run, and could almost get a run anywhere. He saw a run quickly. I always felt confident running with him.

'He was very quick between wickets. I was pretty quick, mind, in a straight line, but it was always a bit more difficult, at 16 stone, turning for the second or third run. If we ran three I felt he was going to lap me on the third.

'Art taught me to block a ball with soft hands. I was inclined to block hard, with the consequence the ball would go quickly to the fielder, but Art suggested if you blocked it softly, it would get to the fielder more slowly, and if it was going to the left hand of a right-handed fielder (or vice versa) there was almost always a run to be had. And he was such a great placer of the ball. He showed me how to keep the runs ticking along. Batting with Arthur was a real education for me. I must have been 200 runs or more better off purely from running between the wickets with him,' Green recalled gratefully.

'You couldn't bat with anyone more unselfish than Arthur. If you were in the shit he would take the strike, and when you were going well he would make sure you had the strike. There was one game at Cheltenham, against Worcestershire, in the days when the wicket was nowhere near as hard and as quick as it became in later years – it was a bloody good cricket wicket; it seamed and turned but you could bat on it. Matches would quite often be over by the afternoon of the third day – and I was struggling against Giff [Norman Gifford] and the ball was continually going past the edge of the bat. After an over or two of this Art came down the wicket and enquired, "You all right down that end?" "Am I buggeree," I replied.

'"Well, push one next over," said Art, "and I'll take Giff for a while" – and that's what he did, with great aplomb.

'Nobody need ever be short of the strike when they were batting with Art, as long as they could give him the strike to get to the other end.'

When cricketers get together and reminisce, one memory so often triggers many others. David's recollections of batting with Arthur inspired other indelible and enduring memories of a greatly admired team-mate and good friend. 'Art was a beautiful on-driver. He would let the ball drift into his legs and then he would play it anywhere between wide mid-on and behind square, depending on the pace of the ball.

'His balance was a key factor in his batting, too – I don't think I saw him ever make an ugly shot; he was never incommoded.

'And he had this tremendous ability to leave balls. He was an amazing judge of where his stumps were. Batting with him sometimes, I'd watch a ball from the other end and think, "Jeez, that's going to knock his pole over" and Art would quietly let it go by.

'But it's true, he wasn't a great one for filling his boots when the bowling was easy or when the pitch was flat. It needed to be a good contest to attract his attention and get the best out of him.

'He was a great man, very intelligent, a polymath who took a real interest in all manner of things, very talented, widely read, tremendous fun.'

If Arthur's time as captain had proved more disappointing than he had anticipated and, perhaps, less fulfilling than he had hoped, with one final rumination on that summer his memory moved on: 'I knew I wasn't enjoying it so gave it up after that one year – but I wish, when I was at my best, I could have perhaps had a go then.' Nevertheless his reflections on his year at the county's helm were buoyed by many deservedly happy recollections of that summer.

His wish that he might have been given a go at the captaincy earlier in his career is one that others shared too, but time waits for no man. Arthur would be 41 as the next season opened.

Chapter 15

Time to Declare

GLOUCESTERSHIRE'S 1969 SEASON proved a good one, one of their best. Under their new captain, Tony Brown, they finished as runners-up in the championship, their highest spot for ten seasons.

'AS – Tony – was captain, and he was quite good on the field.' As the words sit on the page that 'quite good' might read as damning with faint praise, but Arthur, as we know, was not one for hyperbole or panegyric. The pared-down simplicity of his words frequently conveyed the highest regard and esteem. That was certainly so here. The inflection on the 'good' left no doubt about how highly he rated Tony or his affection for him.

'He was a really good first-class chap, really good, as well as a very good old friend of mine. We used to drive "The Bounty" about together all over the place – the van which carried all our kit, you know. It was christened that when George Emmett was captain, because we called him Captain Bligh. We knew where every fish and chip shop was on the way home.'

A simple story, recalling happy moments in a professional cricketer's life. It was very much of its time. Yet try setting it in the context of today's world. Who can imagine a top international sportsman – a double international at that – opting to travel around in the team's kit wagon today and stopping at the chippie on the way home? It would be deemed an insult. Without their minders, bodyguards and sycophantic fawning, and without predictable reservations in prestigious restaurants or clubs, some of the precious egos of modern-day sport would be severely dented.

For Arthur it was certainly not an issue, and it meant he travelled in the welcome company of a good friend, as well as using the 'company car' at a time when sponsored cars, or club cars, were unheard of.

The new captain's immense regard for Arthur was succinctly put. 'Gloucestershire was good with him in the side, and far better than without him. Generally he was quiet in the dressing room and very mild-mannered on the field. He didn't often get cross with individuals, although he could – and did – get cross with folks he considered to be "cheating".

'He once lost his temper – vividly – with John Snow and Tony Greig at Hove one day. There was a run-out incident at the bowler's end. Arthur was livid, incensed by what he saw as a distinct lack of sportsmanship. His bat certainly expressed his anger and he smote the ball everywhere – even off Snowy and Greigy.

'Art – yes, he was quite quiet most of time – he wouldn't stand up in the dressing room and address everybody. If he had any comments to make they'd usually be made to the individual or the couple of players it most concerned. He wouldn't undermine the captain. No, he would speak to one or two with comments about the game in progress and his reading of the game. He could be critical if he thought that was right and helpful, though this was directed at individuals, not into the air. As captain I never felt threatened by this sharing of views.'

The new captain did, however, have to make his mark occasionally: 'I did have to remind him once or twice about moving fielders!'

Tony Brown's memories resonated with similar recollections of John Mortimore: 'Arthur was OK, fine, in the dressing room. Now all sides are different but Arthur and Tony, and David Green and Proccie when they came into the side, tended to go off as a group at the end of the day. I used to go off in the evening with David Smith; in earlier days Sam Cook and George Lambert would go off together so there wasn't this sense of always having to be eleven together.

'Art, I suppose, could sometimes be … ' – and here John searched for the right word – '… critical of others. I didn't always agree with him but never had a problem with that, and we never had any blazing rows or anything like that. And the moving of a fielder,' as recounted amusedly by Morty in an earlier story, 'is an indication of how we would do it. Mind you, I knew when he was feeling cross when I was in charge because he would address me as "Captain" rather than the usual "Morty".'

In Brown's recollection Arthur 'was never a prima donna. If he was out in a silly way, or if he had got out when he shouldn't have done, or if he ever dropped a catch – he seldom ever missed a simple chance, so his miss would have been something exceptional; anyone else would have been glad just to get a hand on it – he would be upset about it and be a bit deflated for a while.

'Mind you, he was such a good player that often it took something special to get him out. There was the lovely incident of Colin McCool playing for Somerset at Bristol. Smudger [David Smith] was bowling from the top end and Arthur was at slip. Smudger bowled a ball which probably pitched about middle and Colin McCool got the faintest of edges, and it just hit the top of the off-stump. As he walked back past us, Colin looked at us and said, "How about that, Art? Reckon I must be in bloody good form to have got a touch on that."

'That was just the sort of thing that happened to Arthur – and he wouldn't really get upset on those occasions when he knew the bowler, or fielder, had produced something very special. He admired skills in others.

'He was never a barrack-room lawyer, in fact the opposite. I think that was what used to upset one or two people – if he was muttering quietly away. It never bothered me, because we were very good friends. If he wanted to say something to others about the cricket, that was fine, and if he wanted to say something to me, he would when the time was right. Most of the time I would get to hear about it from Arthur. We would probably have talked about it anyway at some stage, and he would then share it with the individual or those concerned or just in the general chat of the dressing room.'

This trait John Mortimore also affirmed. 'If Art rated you as a player or someone he could respect, he would make very helpful suggestions. "What about this? Have you thought about trying that?"'

Tony Brown again: 'I travelled thousands of miles in cars with Art during the cricket season and spent lots of time with him out of season, too. I learnt a lot from him about a great many things – not just cricket. What always struck me about him was that he could do most things very well if he was in the right frame of mind or if he felt something was a real challenge. I'm sure he would have loved to bat against Shane Warne or Muralitharan as he always liked the challenge of facing the leg-spin bowlers of his time, George Tribe, Jack Walsh, Roly Jenkins, Bruce Dooland, Johnny Wardle as well as the other top-class spinners like Jim Laker, Tony Lock, Don Shepherd, Derek Underwood – and lots of others then.'

In that summer of 1969 Arthur played in all but three of the county's two-dozen championship games, yet again making more than a thousand runs (1,034 in fact). While most came at no. 3, he opened against Somerset at Bristol. Again the local West Country 'derby' brought out the best in him, and he made 102. It was his tenth and last century against Somerset, a remarkable record.

Arthur recalled that during the Cheltenham Festival that year, Frank Twistleton, then the club's chairman and a senior figure in the brewers, Whitbreads, suggested that he and Ken Graveney, by then a senior member of the committee, would like to get together with Arthur.

'They wanted to take me out to lunch when we had a free day. I thought, "Hello, I wonder what's going on here?"

'Well anyway, we fixed something up. Nothing definite was said but I got the impression they felt it was getting about the time I should think about hanging up my boots. The funny thing was that I still had a year to run on my contract,' and Arthur laughed happily at the memory of that moment, 'which they'd clearly overlooked or forgotten about. That was a bit embarrassing for them.

'So I said, "I've got a contract, I may as well play," which is what happened. I still made a few runs here and there in 1970 – and some good runs. And I was still able to catch 'em.'

His second game that summer was against Derbyshire at Chesterfield – a delightful place to watch cricket but, with its juicy green, mid-May pitches, hardly a batsman's paradise – Arthur retired hurt after suffering a fractured arm.

He missed two months of the season and this largely accounted for his missing 1,000 runs, a landmark he had achieved in all but six of his 22 summers since 1949.

But he could still bat. On his return from injury, against Nottinghamshire at Trent Bridge, he made 70. Two games later, at the Wagon Works ground, against Warwickshire, he notched up yet another century.

It was an outstanding, typically Milton, innings. Gloucestershire had followed on, 177 runs behind Warwickshire. At 71-3 in their second innings, they were again struggling before Arthur went to the wicket. In an innings of six-and-a-half hours, he held Warwickshire – and defeat – at bay.

'I batted all day to save the game. Apparently, they were undecided about making us follow on or whatever. MJK was their captain and, apparently, they said, "We've only got to get one bloke out" – because we hadn't batted very well in the first innings. Anyway, they didn't get the one bloke out – and I finished on 149 not out.

'I remember feeling cross – cross with dear old Jack Crapp, who was umpiring. I hadn't made 150 for a while – and I felt sure there was time for another over, but he decided that was it, close of play, and he took us in. So I didn't make the 150.

'You always look for those moments in a match.'

If Arthur, like many other players, perhaps most, welcomed those special moments which make the game come alive, or which offered the opportunity to grasp one by the neck and turn its fortunes around, he barely did that as far as his own career was concerned. From taking the understandably inviting step from a schoolboy cricketer and footballer, his evolution into a professional of the highest class had indeed been nothing more than a steady and natural progression.

All the old skills were there: the stylish batsmanship; the fleetness of foot allied with good judgement of a run; the lightning reactions that allowed him to retain his catching ability; but his contract was coming to an end, and the chairman's words at the close of the previous summer had made him think.

'And I decided – as my contract was due to finish – I should think about giving up, retiring, which is what I did really.

'But then, the next year [1971], the county were not going very well in the early part of the season. There were a few injuries, and Browny asked me to go back.

'They were playing Somerset at Bath in mid-June and I got a few runs, and so it went on. That more or less happened again, I think, the next season.'

Following his recall, Arthur played on a match-by-match basis that summer. Such an arrangement was practical; it certainly didn't dent his enthusiasm for the game or his commitment to the county. He made 700 runs in 11 matches – a sure mark of his continuing prowess – and averaged a remarkable 41.17. Venerable golfers vie with each other to go round in under their age. Here was a cricketer almost matching average and age. His talent was undimmed.

That same form, and the valued contribution to the county's cricket, also continued into the following summer. Of this period I had remembered Arthur saying that he'd decided – once or twice – to retire but, as he explained, 'Browny kept calling me back.' And, laughing away, Arthur confirmed this: 'Yes, yes that's right. I'm sure it happened at least twice.'

Tony Brown readily verified this: 'Gloucestershire were going through a difficult spell with injuries and suchlike, and we seemed short of an experienced head, and so I was more than happy to persuade Arthur to return.'

But Tony also gave this an added dimension when he intimated: 'We felt dear old Art was finding it difficult to come to terms with not playing any more, with the thought of retirement.'

Was it possible that Tony, in league with the club, was being pastorally supportive of Arthur and concerned for him?

Whatever the circumstances and the thinking behind it by all parties, Arthur's contribution to Gloucestershire's cricket remained important. He did indeed bring not only his undimmed batting gifts but also his wise head and vast experience to their first-class cricket. There were times too when his experience and skills were as important to the up-and-coming players in the Second XI and, no prima donna, Arthur was delighted to help the youngsters when not required for First XI duty.

As we have seen, David Graveney was one of those youngsters then making his way and learning the game with Gloucestershire Seconds. 'Arthur was very good with young players, really helpful and supportive. He played with us quite a bit in the Seconds at the end of his career. He often stood at slip or mid-on to me when I started with the Second XI, and was always encouraging and helping me with my bowling. They were valuable times.

'Mind you, when I first started playing with the Seconds I didn't know what to call him – "Uncle Arthur" seemed out of place in the dressing room!'

David remembered a Sunday League game against Sussex at Arundel in 1972, towards the end of Arthur's career. Mike Procter's 5-10 in eight overs played a large part in restricting Sussex to 178-9 in their 40 overs. 'Arthur took a couple of wickets and was delighted,' David recalled. The scorecard records Arthur's successes with the ball: 'JM Parks c Procter b Milton 64', and 'PJ Graves st Swetman b Milton 28' – important wickets which broke the stand of 50 that had threatened Gloucestershire's dominance.

'We won by two wickets, and Arthur happily stayed on in the bar after the game, having the odd drink and chatting. As a young lad I was happy to be there listening in to the cricket talk and waiting – I was travelling with Arthur – like a young boy, with my packet of crisps and a Coke!

'We got home late. Arthur always drove slowly – I don't think he liked going much faster than 20mph – and there were no motorways, or there were but Arthur preferred not to use them. On the way back he chatted about his career, which was fascinating and helpful in its insights about the game. But when he talked he looked at you, not at the road. Even at 20mph that was a bit scary.

'But Arthur wasn't the slowest – that must have been John Mortimore. Greeny always reckoned that when he was due to travel with Morty he took a crate of beer and a good book as they wouldn't be going anywhere fast, and certainly not overtaking lorries.'

By now in his 45th year, Arthur resumed with ease his earlier role as an opener. In 14 championship matches in 1972 he made 637 runs, and clocked up another century, the 52nd for Gloucestershire. It was against Worcestershire, and perhaps I can declare an interest. It was my first summer with Worcestershire as secretary, and among many happy memories of that season I do recall Arthur's innings.

Our Worcestershire batsmen withstood a fiery opening spell from Mike Procter (later warned for excessive use of the bouncer) to make 302-7 declared. Weekend rain changed the character of the pitch – it was still the time of uncovered pitches – and might have encouraged Worcestershire to think in terms of bowling out Gloucestershire cheaply but, as *Wisden* recorded: 'Worcestershire lost their chance because of a masterly innings by Milton.'

The cricketers' 'bible' went on:

> *His display of defensive technique restricted Worcestershire*
> *to only one wicket in the morning and then he revealed*
> *attacking style in a stand of 146 with Knight.*

This was Roger Knight, later to become secretary and chief executive of MCC.

His hundred (his 52nd for Gloucestershire, and the 56th and last of his first-class career) took him past WG Grace in the list of Gloucestershire century-makers. Only Wally Hammond (113) and Alf Dipper (53) had scored more for the county. Of Arthur's 56 hundreds, 35 had been made, as was this last, as an opener. Sixteen had been scored at Bristol.

If his batting remained 'masterly', his catching, too, had lost nothing of its sharpness; that would remain so until his career finally rolled to a close.

In his penultimate summer he continued to open the innings, although injury regrettably restricted him to six games only. Those personal frustrations were readily forgotten in the shared delight of Gloucestershire, under Tony Brown's leadership, winning the Gillette Cup for the first time in a popular victory at Lord's.

And so to his final summer, his 26th as a professional. He was not too long in the tooth to play in the season-opener, yet again at the top of the order, against Cambridge University at Fenner's, and he also played 11 championship games that year. Along the way he made a couple of fifties, with his 76 against Worcestershire, on a fiery pitch at New Road, being his highest.

That innings was an Arthur cameo. Yet again he restored his team's fortunes, coming to Gloucestershire's rescue when they were in trouble and – as so many times in the past – relishing the challenge thrown up by the pitch and the probing contest between batsman and bowler, relishing the testing of character and skill, relishing what, for him, cricket was all about.

Batting at no. 6, Arthur joined the fray with Gloucestershire in disarray at 48-3. That was, effectively, 48-4 as opener Ron Nicholls had sustained a fractured finger in Vanburn Holder's first over. On what *Wisden* described as 'the lively New Road turf', Worcestershire's pace duo of the West Indian Holder and Brian Brain (who finished with 6-58), well supported by Jim Cumbes, gained ready advantage.

Except that Arthur, with sound support from Roger Knight, held the home team at bay. He batted resolutely for three hours, resisting all that Worcestershire could throw at him. He hit seven fours and a six, and was last man out, as Gloucestershire battled to 188.

In the next match, against Lancashire at Bristol, he made 51, top score in Gloucestershire's 143, the only innings of a rain-affected game. After a delayed start, Barry Wood's medium-paced wiles tied down all the batsmen – except Gloucestershire's Peter Pan.

Yet again rising to the challenge and confronting the testing conditions, Arthur battled away for two hours, enjoying the tussle to purposeful and rewarding effect. It was at times like this that one understood why David Shepherd – and many others too – said: 'It all appeared so easy for him.'

Then came two championship games against Hampshire, the match in Bristol following close on the heels of that at Southampton. Arthur's scores in these games were modest. Indeed at Bristol, in that corny phrase, he 'failed to trouble the scorers'.

It was perhaps not recognised as such at the time, but 'CA Milton lbw Taylor 0' would be the final entry alongside his name for a Gloucestershire home match. What a remarkable – and somewhat unjust – irony that one of the heaviest run-scorers for the county – only Wally Hammond (with 33,664) exceeded Arthur's total in all first-class matches – should 'fail to score' in his last home appearance.

The significance of this was, of course, lost on everyone. Few realised this was Arthur's last innings for Gloucestershire at the County Ground.

No sooner had rain brought that match to an early close than the team were on the road again, off to Harrogate to play Yorkshire in a match commencing the next day. There John Hampshire's 158 enabled Yorkshire to declare at 406-8 against a Gloucestershire attack in which Tony Brown and Mike Procter were unable to bowl because of injuries. The visitors responded with a dismal 71, of which Arthur – opening the innings with Ron Nicholls – made eight. Following on, Gloucestershire batted with more resolution but could not deny Yorkshire a win by an innings and 165 runs.

Arthur made six in Gloucestershire's second innings, before falling 'lbw Robinson', the same executioner and mode of dismissal as in his earlier knock.

Again, unrecognised at the time, that would prove to be his final innings for Gloucestershire, for whom he had first taken up the bat as a young amateur more than a quarter of a century before. He had scored two fewer than in his first outing for the county all those years ago.

It is fascinating to compare the Gloucestershire teams for those two matches, if only to give a scan across the generations through which Arthur Milton had played his cricket.

At Harrogate in 1974 the Glosters' line-up was: Arthur Milton, Ron Nicholls, Roger Knight, Mike Procter, David Shepherd, Andy Stovold, Tony Brown (captain), John Mortimore, Jack Davey, John Dixon and David Graveney.

Arthur was, by far, the senior of the side, with John Mortimore, Tony Brown and Ron Nicholls being his nearest contemporaries. David Shepherd, Jack Davey and Roger Knight constituted the middle generation, and the rest were the up-and-coming youngsters in whom Gloucestershire were placing their faith. Youngest of the side was Dixon, just 20 – 25 years younger than the county's senior pro.

Back in June 1948 Gloucestershire's team at Northampton looked like this: BO Allen (captain), Alfred Wilcox, Tom Graveney, Jack Crapp, Monty Cranfield, Andy Wilson, Arthur Milton, Colin Scott, George Lambert, Tom Goddard and Sam Cook. With the captain, Crapp, Cranfield and Wilson all within hailing distance of 40, and Tom Goddard as close to 50, Arthur and Tom Graveney must have felt conspicuously junior.

Had it been realised that the Yorkshire game was, in fact, Arthur's last game for Gloucestershire the team would undoubtedly have shared reminiscences, rich and happy memories over a post-match celebratory drink or two with Arthur, but the match result rather put a dampener on that. In any event this surely was not his last game for the county?

In modern sport there seems little place for sentimentality among 'focused' sportsmen and women, who see it as an overt sign of weakness. It is an attitude regrettably and typically bereft of humanity and vision. Such mean thinking, however, did not cloud Gloucestershire minds in summer's last days of 1974.

The county's season was to end with their championship match against their Celtic neighbours from across the Severn, on 4th, 5th and 6th September.

There was indeed room in their nominated squad for the man who had graced the county's cricket for so long, with a distinct prospect that his career would end with Arthur playing in front of his home crowd. What could be more fitting? His glorious ability had entertained Gloucestershire's members and supporters for 27 wonderful seasons. They had taken him to their hearts – the 'local lad made good'. He had achieved success, and done so markedly by reaching the highest level in two sports.

His team-mates, too, readily acknowledged his peerless skills. John Mortimore: 'Art was ever so gifted as a cricketer. A great placer of the ball when batting and, without being classical in quite the Colin Cowdrey mode, definitely a graceful batsman.'

Arthur's had been a career of amazing and barely fettered progress. His all-round sporting talent and his undoubted aptitude at picking the greyhounds might have seemed all part of a charmed life. Arthur, too, invariably viewed it in this light, not least in his later years as he looked back with a gratitude that was undisguised and undiluted.

And now, as he prepared to say farewell, Fate conspired against him, albeit briefly and without wicked intent. Gloucestershire's match with Glamorgan was abandoned on the second morning of the match. Not a ball was bowled. The toss was not made and, consequently, teams were not officially declared or exchanged by the opposing captains.

In Gloucestershire's dressing room they might have known which XI had been chosen from those listed in the match squad: Andy Stovold, Arthur Milton, Mike Procter, Roger Knight, David Shepherd, Tony Brown, Alastair Hignell, Jim Foat, David Graveney, John Mortimore, Jack Davey, Nicholas Cooper (for whom this might have been his debut), John Dixon and Andy Brassington.

Arthur certainly recognised this non-match as his last appearance and, recalling it in later years, was amused by the fact that not a ball was bowled. It would have been good to finish his career on the field of play doing what he had so enjoyed for the past 30-odd seasons. But the rain uncaringly denied him this. To Arthur's relief, it also precluded any emotional farewells and presentation ceremonies.

'Yes, 1974 was when I finally finished – and the next two years were two of the best summers we ever had. They were lovely for cricket. Do you remember '75 and '76?

'I was fortunate, because my very last match was at Bristol, and I didn't really want them making any song and dance about it being my last game and it didn't happen because we never bowled a ball.' And off he went again, amused at the memory of it.

Perhaps a damp end to his career should have been no surprise; 27 years earlier his first-class debut at Northampton was also hampered by rain.

Rain Stopped Play. But he had had a good innings – an exceptional and most distinguished innings, the finest of innings.

Arthur's lean, boyish appearance barely deserted him in all those seasons and, in so many ways, he remained the 'light, lean chap with buttercup hair … looking like [everyone's] kid brother …'. Remarkably, through 27 seasons he had retained his fitness and, above all, his enthusiasm for the game was undiminished. So, too, was his firm belief in the way the game should be played.

His ability to phlegmatically and meticulously pace an innings had become highly polished as the seasons advanced. His fine judgement of a run, and his ever-deceptive speed between wickets, had remained as well honed and as productive as ever.

His athleticism came not from the muscular, shirt-bulging build of the modern era's iron-pumping, circuit-training, sports-science-programmed professionals. Despite his bow legs he had the athleticism of a born games player. He did, surprisingly perhaps, admit to the benefits of pre-season training, but in his case it can only have been a case of simply topping up in April what was God-given, fine-tuning those muscles on which soccer had made fewer demands, and vice versa in September.

Team-mates believed his gifts of eyesight, coordination, reflexes and speed of hand and foot were outstanding. Few sportsmen, among them the very best, have been so wonderfully blessed.

Arthur was, principally, a back-foot player. This might be reg-arded as typical of a player of average height, but in no way should it suggest limitations. It owed much to the need to accommodate the vagaries of that slow and low Bristol wicket. As a back-foot player he excelled at the cut, especially square of the wicket, and the hook and pull-shot. But he was gifted enough to play strokes all round the wicket, and to play them with a stylish elegance and unhurried charm and, as has been seen, to play them most profitably when he sensed a challenge, when the wicket was 'doing a bit' or good spinners were working their wiles. Here his staunchness of character came into play.

He seemed always to have an inordinate degree of time to play the ball, the hallmark of a great player. From his earliest days he recognised the merits of watching the ball. Perhaps he didn't quite fulfil the adage of 'sniffing the ball' – his style was too elegant for that – but watchfulness marked his play. Vic Marks, who was coached at Oxford by Arthur before going on to play for Somerset and England, referred to him as 'Arthur Cloth Bat', and he was not alone in noting his gift at playing with soft hands. As David Green has recounted, this was one reason why he was such a great run-stealer.

In the outfield he galloped, fleet of foot, around the boundary – 'The fastest man I have ever seen on two legs on the cricket field,' Bomber Wells claimed – and picked up in one smoothly swooping swift-like movement. Amazing reflexes made him a brilliant fielder – 'He took catches with the ease of Wally Hammond' (Bomber again) – and one of the finest of all close-to-the-wicket catchers. It was here that he snaffled most of his huge haul of catches. It was the same reflexes, coordination, timing and speed that had provided the amazing acceleration down the wing for Arsenal which, when coupled with his immaculate and neat ball control and a classical body swerve, had made him such a top-class footballer.

The way he played, the way he looked, the way in which he so gracefully and stealthily prowled – almost sauntered – around the field was a model for all. It endeared him to countless fans who faithfully watched and appreciated the artistry and consistency of his performances for Gloucestershire with bat and ball, and with his stunning catching – and endeared him, as Frank Keating has so splendidly recounted in his captivating foreword, to countless youngsters who saw him only occasionally or could only read of his deeds, the young buffs who collected his autograph or his youthful image enduringly captured on cigarette cards. His boyish looks and his gentle, always approachable manner, devoid of all sporting arrogance, made them feel he might be one of them. He was an idol for so many, as Frank says, a real *Boys' Own* hero.

John Woodcock, a cricket writer for more years than he may care to remember, one of the best of any era and doyen of cricket's press corps, thought Arthur was arguably the most natural games player he had ever seen, surpassing perhaps even Denis Compton. This glowing assessment John offered from the broad prospect of his distinguished career, which stretched from covering his first Test match on Freddie Brown's 1950–51 tour of Australia through more than 400 subsequent Tests, most of them as *The Times'* cricket correspondent from 1954 to 1988. In between he edited *Wisden* for six years from 1981 and, in retirement, continues to contribute sparkling pieces to *The Times*.

His assessment was worthy of further exploration. In recent days, the Sage of Longparish (for so John was christened by his *Times* colleague, Alan Gibson) recalled his earlier view. 'He was such a lovely man with it – modest and easy-going and real. He was not as famous as Denis, or the batting genius that Denis was, but I fancy a greater or wider selection of games came more naturally to him.'

Uniting Arthur and Denis in a common tribute was praise indeed (it would have moved Arthur deeply), for the latter remains unequalled in John's affection, as this reflective piece of his so clearly confirms:

> *Oh, such a host of heavenly cricketers … My favourite? I think one's affection for the person and his innate spirit should be the yardstick, so I remain devoted to Denis [Compton], and when he walked in for the last time and raised his bat I knew for certain I could say, 'I'll never see his like again.' Similarly, of all the bowlers my fondness for*

Alec [Bedser] has never wavered. Well, I was young with Compton and Bedser, you see, I travelled with them, we were of an age. Later there was Botham; from the first I never wavered about Ian, a wonderful cricketer and wonderful for cricket.

Arthur's outstanding success in his dual sporting careers, and in those sports he regarded as his relaxation, owed so much to his natural talents, and to those skills of eye, hand and foot with which he was born. Perhaps we should acknowledge the gifts of brain too. Once, in discussion with EW 'Jim' Swanton, Arthur said of playing against spin bowling: 'It's all a matter of inches – those between your ears.'

In all of this one question is left hanging – unanswered – in the air. What more, what even greater deeds, might Arthur have achieved had his matchless skills been matched by steely ambition? Might this be one talent which just passed him by? Or was it there, perhaps, and disregarded?

Such a question might have run through the mind of team-mates from time to time. Warm-hearted, generous and yet objectively observant, Bomber Wells once described Arthur as 'a man with so much talent it was an embarrassment', but suggested that colleagues sometimes felt 'he never used half of it. Nevertheless, the half he did use was marvellous.'

Heightened ambition might well have made him a different person, perhaps one he would not wish to have been. While he recognised the limits of ambition in himself, he clearly had no desire to be other than who he was, and what he was.

Gloucestershire were in debt to Arthur and his wonderful and enduring talents to the tune of 30,128 runs (and another 1,000 runs in one-day games); 79 wickets; and a truly amazing haul of catches. Of that there was no doubt whatsoever.

In that last season he held on to 17 catches, thus taking his career tally to that outstanding 760 in all first-class games. Gloucestershire were in his debt, too, for his input as sometime captain, acting captain and notably as their long-time wise and experienced senior pro whose contribution to the county's cricket extended far beyond the runs he had scored and the wickets and catches he had taken. And then there was Arthur Milton the man: modesty and kindness personified, without ego despite his amazing achievements, his prowess and performances; universally regarded as a friend by all, even by those who spent but a short time in his company.

Little wonder he was so very popular with Gloucestershire's followers, with team-mates and opponents alike. Little wonder, too, that, as the days and months passed following his last match for Gloucestershire, he became more and more a revered cult figure in Gloucestershire's sporting world.

A quite enchanting insight into how Arthur and the joy of his cricket fixed themselves easily in the mind of young lads who admired their hero from the boundary edge, and whose admiration remained undimmed in later life, came in an interview for BBC Hereford and Worcester radio with Frank Keating when he retired from the *Guardian*.

I invited Frank to put himself on a 'desert island' of special sporting memories. 'It would be at Cheltenham,' he said, almost whispering as the idyllic memories of a Stroud boyhood bubbled to the surface. 'Arthur would be batting, with Tom Graveney – or it might possibly be at Worcester in the shadow of the cathedral with dear Dolly, Basil D'Oliveira, batting with Don Kenyon – with Arthur hitting a boundary wonderfully down to the boundary by the hospital. Yes, Cheltenham, Arthur – and Tom, a bottle of Tizer, and a pound of Pershore plums.'

Who could ask for more? What could be more delightful? Cricket is so wonderfully enriched by such magical and enduring memories, by those who weave them, of course, and by those who treasure them.

Rain had stopped play. There were to be no more instances of 'Browny calling me back' or, if there were, Arthur felt the time had come, rightly, to decline them. Amidst the soggy end of his career, without undue ceremony but with an overflowing treasure house of memories and with unlimited gratitude, he was able to steal away without being the focus of great attention and without those emotions that presentation ceremonies so often trigger, and which would have embarrassed him.

As he looked back on these things, Arthur gave himself an unexpected but gentle and, as always, unassuming pat on the back: 'And do you know, I caught everything that came to me that summer.' As was invariably the case, it was slipped into the conversation in his placid, unassuming way, with no attempt to cling on to the many glories of his past. And as he turned to look at me his face was wreathed in a smile of contentment and fulfilment, as his heart, mind and memory ranged back and forth over so many threads which made up the wonderful tapestry of his life.

Since his initial thoughts of finishing with cricket at the end of 1970, he had played another four seasons for Gloucestershire, playing in a further 42 championship games (and 31 one-dayers), but now retirement, at long last, beckoned.

Where might retirement lead him?

Chapter 16

Greyhounds and Golf

GREYHOUNDS WE KNOW had long been in his blood, ever since that day when young Arthur's three shilling investment on *Jolly Good* had proved profitable. And yet his involvement in the sport sometimes seemed unfathomably enigmatic.

A good many of his fellow county cricketers, especially his Gloucestershire team-mates, knew Arthur followed the dogs. Some knew he was extremely knowledgeable about the sport, and a dedicated expert too. Visiting players as well as county team-mates benefited frequently from his advice when he invited them for post-match visits to the Eastville track. His family, of course, knew of his abounding interest. They, too, shared the joke in later life that he was 'at the office' when he had strolled to the village branch of William Hill. But there was also a sense in which this was something private, something he shared with a few friends but otherwise kept to himself. It was not something he shouted from the rooftops. Countless fans and friends who knew Arthur through cricket probably knew little of his fascination with greyhounds and greyhound racing.

Over the years, greyhound racing as a sport has attracted some who wished to bend, or break, the rules, who wished to beat the bookies at every, and any, opportunity, fair or foul. They have given the sport a seamy reputation. But there was absolutely nothing dubious or disreputable about Arthur's interest. That was not his way. He lived his life according to standards which were always 'above board'. He was a 'good neighbour' and, frequently, a Good Samaritan who would happily help those in need, who looked for the good in people, who never looked to put anyone down or to gain an unfair or unearned advantage. Nothing diverted him from this philosophy. And yet his enduring interest in greyhounds was part of his life which he seemed happy to keep securely in its own compartment.

His enthusiasm for the dogs owed much to an interest in the animals themselves, and he often watched them in their training and early trials. This, plus a keen memory, together with his excellent mathematical knowledge aided him in deciding when to invest and when not to. He certainly didn't look to bet on every race at a meeting – only when he felt he knew and could substantiate the odds. It was again part of Arthur's character that he was able to follow the sport in this sensible and well-informed way, seldom getting carried away with any successes or becoming obsessive.

Arthur's interest in the greyhounds – almost a scientific interest in their capabilities – would likely have prevailed whether or not it was a vehicle for betting. Like all who venture in this way, he undoubtedly had losing streaks (and, equally, would have been coy about them) but, on balance, he seems to have been a reasonably consistent winner. His level-headed approach meant wagers were seldom, if ever, large, and therefore winnings were never astounding. But his long background in the sport, his good understanding and knowledge of the dogs and of the odds, his studious following of the outcome of dog trials, coupled with his ability to calculate the risk of his investments, meant that he was on the winning side more often than not.

It was only the greyhounds that attracted his real racing interest. 'I was never a horse man,' he explained. 'Horses have an added element which can make things go wrong – the jockey. I was always a greyhound man.

'Eastville Stadium has gone. It's an IKEA store now. And the greyhounds have gone to the track at Swindon, which is too far, and it has no atmosphere.

'The thing with greyhounds is that you can be your own judge. It's all there in front of you. Horses run different tracks in different ways.

'Greyhounds have to have three trials, and then they grade them. So, if you've seen them at those trial stages, you've got some idea before they come on the card.

'And they run to form. They're either dogs that need to be in front; dogs that need the inside; dogs that need the outside; all sorts. And you get to know them. And the great thing, I found, was to know which dogs couldn't win, for certain reasons. Say there would be two dogs out in front, and you know one would lead the other once they'd started because it liked to be out in front. But it almost certainly couldn't maintain that, so you could discount that one. Sometimes I was left with one dog, sometimes two; it just depends on the odds, because you always want value for money, don't you?'

Did Arthur do well following the greyhounds?

'I had a great run, after I started working for the Post Office. I was working and we had some money coming in from the shares.

'That's how it goes, isn't it. When things were the other way you couldn't pick a winner. Just occasionally I backed dogs I could have beaten myself!

'I was never a great gambler – I wouldn't want to call it gambling – I used to back my opinion. But I couldn't put money in slot machines or such-like. I certainly got to know about greyhounds though through Dad. It's always nice to back a winner.'

With this background it is understandable that Arthur definitely did not consider himself a professional gambler, though a good few of his county cricket colleagues saw him in this light. Nevertheless, an informed approach to backing the dogs meant that he came out on top often enough to be relaxed about what he was doing. Many, perhaps most, county cricketers of Arthur's generation had – and needed – a winter job to supplement their summer earnings. But

Arthur seemed to manage, and manage mostly contentedly, without a formal winter occupation once he had given up football. And during his time at Highbury there had been plenty of time to visit London's greyhound tracks.

Joan surprised me one day when she said, 'He never gambled.' There is a sense in which that was true. As he himself suggested, he was most certainly not the archetypal punter, obsessively looking for the next (alleged) 'good thing', throwing good money after bad in order to recoup losses, forever down on his luck. He was rarely tempted to risk what he couldn't afford.

Tony Brown shared Arthur's interest in the greyhounds. 'I loved watching them racing. We used to go with him, Judy and I, and I used to go to the trials with him too. At one point Judy "owned" a dog for him, *Conlusky Lady* it was called, known as *Lucy* in the kennels, and it ran in her name. She won some good class events.

'Twice a week he would go to all the trials. And he was a fantastic mathematician and his brain worked so quickly to work out the odds. He'd back three of 'em in a six-dog race, but he would back them in a way, with the forecasts and all that, so he would mathematically end up – or should do if his judgement of the form was correct – by not losing any money. He might invest £20 but if he got £21 back, he'd made a profit.'

David Milton recalls his father having some success with a dog called *String of Pearls*. He fondly remembers, too, as a very young lad, times when he and his Dad, along with a good friend of Arthur's from London, Ted Nessling, headed off to north Somerset to find a friendly farmer who allowed them to let the dogs chase after the hares – all part of their training.

Of those in the county game who knew of Arthur's interest and informed knowledge, some went happily to him for advice, even if ultimately they did not heed it.

Arthur told me of a dog briefly owned by Colin Cowdrey and friends. 'Kipper [Cowdrey], Brian Johnston, John Woodcock and Michael Melford, who wrote for the *Daily Telegraph*, owned a greyhound between them. *Kentish Kipper* it was called.

'The problem with this dog was that it could go like hell to the first bend, but it wasn't very good at turning the bends,' and Arthur laughed as he remembered the dog's quirky ability.

'So I said to Colin, "It sounds to me like he wants to run at Eastville in the winter." In the winter, down there on the grass it used to get heavy, because it was a low-lying area, better for getting the wide runners to go round the bends, you know.

'Well, I went to Eastville one night – and I'd said to them previously, "Look, send me the dog and my Dad will look after it for a month, put a bit of weight on it so when you go to run it in some trials you've got a bit of time in hand."

'Anyway, that was always a good way to get them on the card, because you don't want them in the best form when they go and have their trials, do you, that's just natural?

'I'm at Eastville this night and I see this new dog came on the card. He'd had a trial, and *Kentish Kipper* had come second to him. So I said to *Kentish Kipper*'s trainer, "What's that dog doing with you, it was supposed to come to my Dad?'

'"I was up there, in London," he said, "and they knew I was coming back, so they gave me the dog."

'So it had to stay in his kennels. And he was the bloody worst trainer on the track. I didn't feel I could tell them that.

'It was a hurdler this dog – and anyway time went on and the winter rain hadn't arrived at all, so they were getting a bit desperate about running *Kentish Kipper* – and it got beat. So I said to my mate Doug, "This dog's got some pace, it's obvious, what do you think about us having him?"

'We bought him – he cost us more than … well, never mind that! We could have almost bought him for nothing at that time, after that run. And then he won a hurdle race for us. You see, the hurdles stopped them running at a silly pace, so he could take the bends a bit better.

'Eventually the rains came, the grass track got soft – and I think Colin and them think I twisted them, you know. We won the top heat, the best race on the card, about five times on the trot. Golly, he was a consistent dog.'

John Woodcock's recollections almost harmonised with Arthur's. 'I had a quarter share, with the others, in two dogs, and they ran at Catford. They won a race or two but one of them – I think it was *Kentish Kipper*– won many more in the West Country when Arthur persuaded us that the bends at Catford were too strong for it, and bought it from us.'

Arthur was indeed a little embarrassed by the contrasting and greater successes *Kentish Kipper* achieved at Bristol. 'I'm sure they must have all thought I had conned them, you know – except they were all good blokes, great chaps. But I had said to them, "Wait until the rains come."'

If Arthur's greyhound interests were something he compartmentalised, almost all who knew him knew of his talents on the golf course.

Of course it was the Graveneys who introduced him to the sport in his early days at Gloucestershire. His appreciation to them for providing the key to this particular door was genuine and enduring.

'I've always felt so indebted to Tom and Ken for introducing me to the game of golf – they had played since they were boys. They were good – two and one handicaps,' said with the understanding and admiration of one who himself had been a single-figure handicap player throughout his playing days.

'I've always enjoyed my golf. It's been a lovely recreation. It's a great thing for getting away from it all. You play in some wonderful places, and you can have a game with anybody.

'And in the cricket season, because, when we were playing away, we'd always take our golf clubs. We didn't play cricket on a Sunday then, did we? And the thing was they'd say, "Come again next year" – and I remember playing Little Aston, Hollinwell among others I remember, lovely courses, some really nice places.

'Tom was in and out of the England side around that time and they would love to have him on their courses, so I was always indebted to him for that too. It was always my recreation, you know, golf,' and as he expressed his gratitude Arthur's emphasis was on the word 'recreation'. It was if he was saying 'golf is my game'. Cricket was 'his game', too, but it was the one by which he earned his living.

'And they, the Graveneys, could play; they knew what it was all about.' Indeed Ken was a scratch golfer at one stage, and five members of the Graveney family have played to a high standard: Tom and Ken, and Ken's sons David and John, and Tom's son, Tim.

Arthur briefly became an 'honorary Graveney' when he teamed up with Ken, Tom and David to play in the County Cricketers' Golf Society's competition.

Tom remembered: 'We represented the county cricketers at Burnham and Berrow one year, five Graveneys and Arthur.'

Tom's nephew David recalls them all playing in the Brent Knoll Bowl competition, until the organisers decided that so many Graveneys (and an honorary Graveney) was too much of a good thing. In all this reflection about the Graveneys' involvement in Arthur's golf it is worth noting that as well as captaining Gloucestershire CCC and becoming its president – itself a rare enough distinction – Ken was also captain (a role son John later also held) and president of the Gloucestershire Golf Union – a unique achievement even for one from such a sporting family.

Tom Graveney saw in Arthur 'a good chipper and fine putter. He was never off the middle of the course, and always seemed to get down in a chip and a putt. That used to frustrate me when playing against him; it was never a chip and two putts. He was a fine golfer, who made very few mistakes. He was very good, and got down to two; he might even have played off one at one stage.'

Having spoken earlier of Tom's low handicap Arthur, typically, needed prompting to disclose his own. We were talking not long after a mild stroke, in the early autumn of 2006, had left him feeling unsure about his ability to walk 18 holes (he had no intention of taking a buggy!). But the determination to resume playing was evident. Clubs were readily at hand so that he could keep his swing well oiled on the lawn whenever the winter sun spoke sufficiently warmly of summer days on fairways and greens.

As we began working together on this book he said: 'I'm hoping to hit a few balls up on the practice ground at my club at Long Ashton when the weather's a bit better as my legs are definitely better. My lads – Robert, David and Richard – they all play golf, and a couple of them, David and Richard especially, are quite useful. In recent times David and I used to play late on a Sunday afternoon. There'd be nobody on the course, you know, and then we'd come home to a nice roast, which Joanie would have done for us.

'I haven't played for a little while now but I'd be about six or seven – still in single figures, maybe eight or nine – but when I was playing regularly I got down to two. I loved it, loved anything with a ball, anything with a ball.'

After a little more prompting Arthur recalled some high spots of his golfing career.

'I had a couple of highlights in my golfing career. Denis Scanlan was the pro at Long Ashton while I was there, and Burnham and Berrow Golf Club – a super links course – staged a tournament called the West of England Open Winter Foursomes.'

For over a century Burnham and Berrow has been the venue of national and international championships, from the British Ladies in 1906 to the English Amateur in 2006. Their championship course is laid out in the traditional manner of nine holes out, skirting the sand dunes and coastline northwards, with the inward nine turning inland and southwards to follow the coast road through Berrow, past the church and back towards Burnham.

'They had 128 entries you know – it was knockout, and we actually won it twice, Denis and I, in 1971 and again in 1973. And we always played the matches on a Sunday morning.'

The Foursomes' high standard can be gauged by the fact that Arthur and Denis became only the third pairing to win the competition twice, though two other pairs achieved this subsequently. Two Ryder Cup players also appear among the winners: Peter Allis, partnering GP Hill, in 1952; and Brian Barnes, partnering DJB Jacobs, in 1964.

Arthur's affection and admiration for his golfing pal was very evident. 'Denis is a smashing chap – a lovely man. I loved playing with him, and really enjoyed his company.'

Denis can look back to a blue-chip grounding for a golfer. He was born and brought up in Birkdale, and spent many of his formative years at Royal Birkdale, initially as a schoolboy caddy. He would sometimes sneak out on to the course and play six or seven holes before the evening's darkness set in and, more above board, occasionally help out in the pro's shop.

He tells a delightful story of that time. 'One afternoon the club secretary came round to the caddy yard and asked if one of us boys would like to carry some logs down into the cellar. There weren't many takers but I thought, "It won't take long, and I might get a tip."

'Well, I carried logs into the cellar all afternoon, most of next day, and late into the next afternoon. When I'd finished the secretary came out and thanked me, and he told me that, in return, I could play a round around the full course, including the loop – after dark the next day. I took him at his word – and was hooked.'

After brief interludes at Hillside and Hesketh clubs, Denis returned to Royal Birkdale as assistant pro, but it wasn't long before he found himself as assistant to the great Henry Cotton (later Sir Henry Cotton) at Temple Golf Club, Berkshire. Seven years there opened the way to a spell in Ethiopia, at Addis Ababa as their pro, an appointment that was ended abruptly by revolution. 'Emperor Haile Selassie was secreted out of the country, but I felt it was safer to spend two or three days under the bed.'

A couple of years in America broadened his experience further, as did a spell in Dusseldorf as the pro at Mönchengladbach, before Denis took up his appointment at Long Ashton Golf Club in 1967. The club lay above the village of Long Ashton, on the edge of Leigh Woods, just across the Clifton suspension bridge from Arthur's beloved Downs.

It was a time when Denis and many fellow pros – the likes of Dai Rees, Brian Barnes, Peter Allis and others – played tournament golf in midweek, seldom with the prominence and high-profile publicity bestowed on today's golfers, and returned to their club responsibilities, teaching and coaching, at weekends. Denis was gratified to qualify, on a few occasions, for The Open. He was also a member of a team of British professionals in 1975 who played their American counterparts in the biennial PGA Cup (the Ryder Cup for club professionals) and was several times placed in major tournaments, besides winning 'all the local and county competitions at one time or another' in the west of England, where he tied the West of England Championship.

Denis retired in 2003 but he remains tall and lithe. The moment he has a club in his hand – like so many other sportsmen when given a bat, club, racket or ball – the years instantly fall away and retirement seems still far off.

Denis's delight in his chosen career mirrors that of Arthur's in his. To sit and talk with him, even for a short while, is to readily understand how well he and Arthur were matched as golf partners, not only in terms of their abilities but in their approach to, and outlook on, life. Sportsmen, in the best senses of that word, and truly delightful gentlemen.

Recalling Arthur's golfing skills, Denis suggested: 'It seemed to come easy to him. He was very clever. He knew the game. In many ways he was an "amateur professional". He seemed to have this inner knowledge, and feel and spirit for the game.

'He had these bloody old Spalding clubs, with "ptolemite" woods which were a patchy red and white. They had a plastic or synthetic material on the face of the clubs and underneath. Constant hitting of the ball, and the sole being scratched by the ground, changed the colour from red to pink and then to off-white. They looked much older than they were as a result. I always referred to them as his "bloody old clubs", but Arthur loved them and would never swap those woods. If my memory is right, they never made those "plastic" woods again.'

One clear memory Denis has of his golf partner is that 'his hands on a golf club looked beautiful, even though they were a bit big and gnarled from being broken at cricket. They fitted nicely on the grip as if they were made to be there.' This compliment, interestingly, was offered by a man who, from his time as assistant to Henry Cotton, recalled that the great man was a firm believer in the importance of a golfer's hands.

David Graveney, too, had admiringly noted Arthur's 'good hands'. 'He never looked to hit the ball hard, but somehow "finessed" it and shaped his shots. His hands, and his feel for the club, allowed him to play this way. If he was playing somewhere like

Burnham and Berrow, say, and there was a stiff breeze coming in from the sea, he would play a drive that would barely get above four or five feet, to keep it out of the wind. Amazing. He had to be really skilful to play like that. I guess of the modern tournament players Corey Pavin would be the best example in that sense of good hands and finesse.'

Denis fully recognised Arthur's all-round talents on the course. 'Arthur looked good, as if he knew what he was about, and he always had a few practice swings. And he never needed to hit the ball hard, and never seemed to want to, yet he was always on the green or round about with his second shot. If he had a weakness it was, perhaps, his chipping; and putting was certainly his strength as a golfer.

'When you looked at Arthur putting – and I can still see him now – he had a nice rhythm.' With that Denis sprang from his chair, as if waiting for this moment, and hurried off to fetch a putter to demonstrate, on the sitting room carpet.

He came back with a prized club. 'This is Arthur's old putter,' he proudly explained, 'which his son David kindly gave me after Arthur had died.'

With the lifelong skill of a pro who has watched and analysed the techniques of a great many players, able and awful, he proceeded to show how an average golfer might line up and play a putt, and how Arthur, immensely relaxed and unfussed, played it.

'He placed the putter quietly in front of the ball, and lined up his shot; then he'd put the putter behind the ball, and perhaps repeat this two or three times. His shoulders and arms were relaxed – he was never tense – and then he had this wonderful rhythm to his putting, which I wish I'd had.'

Denis started to say. 'He reminded me of Bobby Locke ...' before he got diverted. When reminded of this later he explained: 'I saw in Arthur something of Bobby Locke, as much because of his pace and his gentle manner. Bobby Locke was never hurried, walking, talking, swinging a club, even shaking hands – his hands would be brought out of his pockets almost in slow motion. Arthur was very similar.'

Denis was proud that he and Arthur had twice won a tournament with the considerable pedigree of the Burnham and Berrow Winter Foursomes, and, still demonstrating with Arthur's putter, he said: 'Sometimes in that competition I found I had left him a putt of about that length,' indicating six feet or so with a wry smile. 'What we call a character-building putt. And he would quite quietly, without any fuss, put it down.'

'Arthur always carried his own clubs. He carried them, not over one shoulder, but he had the strap across both shoulders and the bag would rest across his back, and he'd walk along, always at the same pace, his pace, sometimes with his arms on the clubs as if he was caressing them.'

Revisiting memories of those tournaments at Burnham and Berrow and others, Denis recalled, 'And, do you know, he was always chatting to the opposition. As a pro, in competition, I used to feel, "Arthur, you shouldn't be doing that" and he'd be chatting away: "That was a good shot; do you mind me asking which club you used" or "Well played" and suchlike.

'He was immensely popular. They all liked Arthur. At one stage I even wondered if he might have used this as a tactic, lulling them into a false sense of confidence, or perhaps creating a situation where they didn't like to beat this really good bloke, but then I don't think Arthur was at all like that, it wasn't his style. He was such a really nice chap. Arthur was his own man, and there were lots of things he wouldn't change even if you asked him.'

'Sometimes he would come here and have a drink with Annette and myself, and happily talk about anything. He was damned good company.'

Having heard so many friends and colleagues talk admiringly of Arthur's sporting skills and, particularly, his undeniable ball skills, I asked Denis, as an accomplished golf professional, how far he felt Arthur might have gone had he chosen golf instead of cricket.

'He would have been a first-class player, a top-class golfer, and probably a good tournament player, knowing what a wonderful temperament he had. He was so cool, and wouldn't ever get flustered.

'There were times when we might have been two down in a tournament, and I might have had a bit of a gripe about this. But Arthur would say, "If we can be two down, we can easily go two up." He used to inspire me – me, as the full pro – he inspired me,' Denis said, his eyes moistening a tad as he said it and remembered how much Arthur meant to him. 'I still miss him.'

Did Arthur's success on the golf course suggest he played or practised at every conceivable opportunity? 'Oh no, it varied. When he was playing for Gloucestershire, and, of course, when he was playing away from home, golf had to fit around his cricket. In later years it could be intermittent. He might suddenly get a love for it and come to the club for two or three days running, then we might miss him for a fortnight.

'When he was away with the county they would often play on Sundays, when there was no cricket, or perhaps he might have been playing with the County Cricketers' Golf Society, and he would come back and say he had played at Sunningdale or at The Berkshire or it would be "Oh Den, that course at Rye, or Sandwich ..."'

'And it was always with his old bag of clubs. Sometimes – knowing the new clubs that were available, and the advances there had been in technology and club development – I would say to him, "Arthur, why don't you try this new driver?" and he would almost always say, "I don't like it, Den, it hasn't got the feel."'

And, after a moment or two's further rumination, Denis added: 'He didn't take it seriously.' From many people's lips that might have sounded heretical. Denis said it without reservation; it was offered as a genuine compliment. For Arthur, golf wasn't meant to be taken too seriously. It was not something to get het up about or flustered by, not something to get angry about or fall out with friends over (or even opponents). It was, above all, to be enjoyed. Little wonder he said: 'It was always my recreation, you know, golf.'

Recreation is how he might have viewed it but in Arthur's way it still had to be played well. With his gifts that meant being played and enjoyed at a high standard. Arthur and Joan's youngest son Richard happily remembered playing with his Dad. 'I did get to play golf with Dad quite a bit later on. He was brilliant with the putter and around the greens. I used to think he was lucky because he seemed to hole from off the green two or three times a round. Then I realised that, since this happened almost every time we played, he *was* lucky – lucky to be that gifted.'

Told in other company, that tale might bring out a recycling of Gary Player's oft-quoted adage. When someone once referred to the great golf champion's good luck, Player is said to have commented: 'Funny that – the more I practise, the luckier I get.' Even in his admiration of a fine sportsman and golf professional, the merits of Player's adage were probably lost on Arthur, who was never an ardent practiser. In fact he was known to say of practising, 'It makes you worse – you have to look forward to playing.' As Richard said, 'He was lucky – lucky to be that gifted,' immensely fortunate that his gifts allowed him to just go out and play.

'Dad must have thought at some stage that I "had some idea", as he used to say' – that was a typical Arthur compliment – 'because he started trying to straighten things out in my swing. He could never have taught anyone anything much from scratch, simply because he had no concept of trying a ball game out and struggling with the basic concepts.

'I do remember once we played foursomes: Dad, Dave, Dympna my wife, and me. I can't recall who won, but on the 14th at Long Ashton, a long four, he hit a terrible drive leaving the green seemingly unreachable. I nailed my driver off the fairway and it finished eight to ten feet from the hole. Dad holed the putt – he said to me, "I wasn't going to miss it. I had to do justice to such a good shot." That was him all over. Once he made up his mind, there was never any doubt.'

As well as golfing partners, Arthur and Denis were also great friends who enjoyed each other's company on the course and off it. My short interlude with Denis, inviting him to reminisce about Arthur and his golf, made abundantly clear why that was. It had been a magical hour.

As I was leaving, Denis shared a story which brought together his old pal's love of golf and the greyhounds. It gave, too, an insight into their friendship.

'We had been playing in a Pro-Am at the West Wilts Club near Warminster,' Denis explained, 'and when you leave the course there's a long straight road up towards the M4, where, of course, we would turn left for home. I should say that Arthur always gave me some petrol money, he wanted to share the cost.

'Well, this day we left the course, came up the straight towards the motorway, and just before we reached it Arthur said, "Den, turn right." After I'd pointed out that we'd normally go left he said, "No, do you mind going right," which we did – and ended up at the dog track at Reading.

'We watched one race, and we came away. I asked him if he'd had a bet, and he said, "Oh yes," and when I asked him how he'd done he said, "I did all right," and that was it – and off we went home.' Denis chortled at the memory of it, and at the memory of a much-cherished friend. 'He was a lovely man, very agreeable. A great chap.'

Denis also recalled another occasion when Arthur's sporting talents were again to the fore: 'One day we were due to play and it rained so we played snooker instead, and Arthur made an opening break of 72!'

His three boys welcomed the chance to play with Arthur but it was his middle son, David, who probably played most often with him. David recalls the fun they had playing on those Sunday afternoons 'when the course was quiet. We often played the last three holes for a side-stake of a beer, but no matter how well I was playing I never seemed to get that beer. It didn't stop me enjoying playing with him.

'When we'd finished out on the course we might have a beer or two, and then head for home. Golf like that was great fun for Dad. That's how he liked it.'

Arthur continued to enjoy his golf until the last eight or nine months of his life, until that mini-stroke made him less confident in the ability of his legs to get him around the course. But his clubs were not put away. He had not yet retired.

Chapter 17

A Golden Oxford Sunset, Evening Shadows and a Bright New Dawn

RETIREMENT. WHERE WOULD this thing called retirement take him now that his cricketing days were behind him?

His whole life, up to then, had seemed one long natural progression. Indeed there was a sense of destiny about it. It had been hugely enjoyable and Arthur never tired of recognising and expressing his gratitude for his sporting life, never tired of acknowledging how generous sport had been to him.

But what now, now the time had come to put away the bat and the pads, the flannels and sweaters? In many senses he was wholly unprepared for retirement. No firm plans had been made (no vague plans even!). No training had been undertaken, no retirement courses attended. Life to this moment had led him along an obvious and gentle path. Might it not continue that way?

It was now, and in his remaining years, that he expressed regret that, after leaving school, he had not continued his studies, either at university or college or by hands-on learning in a profession. But such regret was rational; it carried no rancour and seldom, if ever, overrode his gratitude for what destiny had generously shared with him.

One great advantage of professional cricket is that it is a vast world-wide freemasonry. Some illustrious colleagues are well known; many others are known of; but all are esteemed for who they are, for what they do, or for what they have achieved. Within this network some are recognised universally as really good fellows, good human beings, reliable, knowledgeable, talented and sound colleagues who might confidently be recommended to anyone, colleagues in whom one can place immense trust.

Such thoughts undoubtedly floated through Colin Cowdrey's mind when endorsing Oxford University's decision to appoint Arthur as their coach. Cowdrey, of Kent and England, and a former Oxford Blue, would later become president of MCC, chairman of the International Cricket Council, be knighted for his services to cricket and, subsequently become a peer of the realm. He was a man of real stature in the game. In the mid-Seventies he was also president of the university cricket club.

Cowdrey recognised the benefits a coach would bring to the university's cricketers. He understood, too, the merits of a coach who was knowledgeable, whose talent and playing record spoke for itself, someone with an awareness of the ambitions and needs of young men seeking to make their ways in the game and in the world, and with the capacity benevolently to help them along these ways. A coach offering maturity, breadth of vision and understanding of life could enable young cricketers to make the best of their sporting talents at the same time as fulfilling academic ambitions and expectations.

In Bristol's very own gifted protégé he recognised one of nature's philosophers, as well as a fine cricketer and a model sportsman who, through his sporting reputation and achievements and his distinctive personal qualities, had much to offer Oxford's cricketing men.

Arthur was never easily swayed by flattery, but a suggestion from someone like Colin Cowdrey that he might have much to offer the university's young cricketers certainly made him think, and think seriously.

It was time for earnest thought. He had considered retirement in each of the previous three or four years, but each time he had come to a mind on this the county again called him to the colours. Each time he responded loyally. Retirement was put on hold.

It might be argued that this extended lead-in towards retirement should have offered Arthur adequate time to prepare. On the other hand it was difficult to prepare for something that remained 'in the future', that never quite became a reality.

The way his life had unfolded meant that he seldom, if ever, needed to grab hold of it, to structure it or make it change direction. He had happily gone with the flow.

Unknown to Arthur the seed of his coaching association with OUCC had been sown by the university's captain, Tim Glover, and by Bob Reeves. Glover, formerly of Lancaster Royal Grammar School, was the captain for the 1975 season. An early and, for the time, innovative decision to upgrade the university side's pre-season preparation led him to invite Bob Reeves to assist them.

Reeves, a member of the teaching staff at Lancaster RGS during Glover's time there, had been an influential mentor to Glover, but had gone on to join the academic staff of Bristol University's Centre for Sport, Exercise and Health (where he is now its Special Projects Manager). With his university's permission, Reeves was happy to put OUCC through their pre-season paces. Much as he enjoyed this, he recognised his Bristol commitments would not allow him to help throughout the summer, though he and Glover appreciated the benefits of having an experienced cricketer as coach throughout the university's season.

So the seed was allowed to flourish. Colin Cowdrey's customary perception and rounded understanding were to the fore when giving his seal of approval to the initiative. He was more than happy to recommend and approve Arthur's appointment as the man to mentor and coach Oxford's cricketers.

Who, in Arthur's time, were those young men?

With ease and obvious affection he began a mental roll call. 'Wingers Diggers – Andrew Wingfield Digby – was up at Oxford when I was there. He was a good man. I liked Wingers. And he got some good wickets. And there was Vic, of course, Vic Marks and Tim Glover. Imran Khan was another, though I didn't find him too easy. He always seemed a bit aloof and reserved. But he was mostly committed to exams in that first season, so we didn't see a lot of him until later in the term.'

As a result, Imran (Worcestershire, Sussex and Pakistan) didn't know Arthur well, and didn't really appreciate how much he was admired and respected both as a man and for his achievements in a long and distinguished career. In any event, Imran's youthful but burgeoning anti-colonialism constrained his respect for many, if not all, of the hierarchies and traditions within the English game. A contemporary fellow Blue commented: 'Imran's academic work kept him from The Parks for much of that summer, so he and Arthur had little time to get to know each other. Consequently Arthur wouldn't have known Imran well enough to recognise the benefits of saying, "Imran, you're wonderful."'

As Arthur reflected on his Oxford days – he was coach for the 1975 to 1978 seasons – contented memories of cricket in The Parks reminded him of the privilege of working with young men who possessed the gifts of rich academic potential and considerable sporting ability. Being true to himself and to them, he encouraged them as best he could to succeed in both spheres. If their cricket flowered even more abundantly it was a bonus.

'Vic Marks was captain when I was there. Chris Tavaré – he's a nice lad – was also in the side. It's nice to think that you worked with players who went on to be Test players.

'John Claughton [captain in 1978] and Paul Fisher [secretary in 1975 and again in 1978] were in the side, too. I had a lot of time for them.

' Vic is a delightful lad, a country boy, and he had some talent,' Arthur reminisced, his natural gift of understatement again tuned to concert pitch. 'A good cricketer, not the worst. He's a good bowler too, and knows the game. We got on well. When he was picking the side and that, he'd say, "What do you think about so-and-so?" We spent a lot of time talking about the game.'

After finishing with Somerset and England, Marks became a valued member of BBC's *Test Match Special* team, as well as a, perceptive, and occasionally idiosyncratic, cricket correspondent for the *Observer* and the *Guardian*.

'Tim Glover was captain in my first year there, and Vic was captain the next two years. Yes, we had quite a bit of talent, and it was nice. Because of what had happened to me – without any qualifications – it rather encouraged me to encourage them in their academic side as well, because I realised how important it was – and would be – to them. You don't realise it at the time, do you, when you're young? And we had some bright boys. John Claughton got a double first in Classics. Vic Marks did Classics as well.'

Arthur's regard and affection for Vic, whose time at Oxford largely coincided with Arthur's, was very evident and warmly reciprocated. 'I first came across Arthur in a Somerset Second team game at Bath in 1974,' Vic recalled. 'Somehow he was playing for Glos Seconds. It puzzled me why he was known as "Arthur Cloth Bat", until he batted. The ball seemed to make the softest of sounds on his bat, almost a muffled "plop" as it hit his bat. He scored runs effortlessly even then, gliding between wickets.

'Then, later, he was an inspired choice as coach of OUCC – not least because he could finish the *Daily Telegraph* crossword far quicker than any one of us, as well as pluck out a few fast greyhounds from *Sporting Life*.

'Mind you, he was hardly a tracksuit coach. Arthur would rarely offer advice unless asked; he certainly did not want to pressurise students who, in his mind, were playing for fun and should be playing for fun. But when asked, he would share his knowledge generously in the nets or over a beer in Vincent's. Tavaré and Claughton picked his brain the most, I guess – as well as the Cambridge men.'

Bob Reeves had noted elsewhere that 'Arthur only spoke if it was worth saying'.

'Apart from knowing the game inside out,' Marks recalled, 'his greatest gift was that he cared about us as young people. I suspect he regretted not going to university himself, and he wasn't going to let us miss this opportunity. And we soon thought the world of him.

Vic's memories of Arthur at Oxford resonated happily with those of Andrew Wingfield Digby. Back in the Seventies, Andrew was almost a perpetual student, initially reading history at Keble College and later training for ordination at Wycliffe Hall. He gained four cricket Blues – the first in 1971, with three more following in 1975, 1976 and 1977 – and might well have been elected captain, but for an orchestrated coup by overseas members of OUCC determined to shoe-in one of their number, Peter Jones. Andrew subsequently played for Dorset and the Minor Counties, and was the founding director of Christians in Sport.

Ted Dexter, chairman of England's selectors, later appointed him as chaplain to the England team. With typical pastoral sensitivity and encouraging enthusiasm he fulfilled the role to widespread approval (and with very senior ecclesiastical favour and backing) until Ray Illingworth succeeded Dexter. Illingworth, eschewing the patient preliminary reconnaissance he would expect of his best batsmen, decided England players didn't need 'a shoulder to cry on' and peremptorily dispensed with Andrew's services. This hasty decision overlooked Andrew's wide-ranging pastoral gifts, and showed no awareness of why other Test-playing countries and many major sports clubs understood the merits of chaplaincy. Andrew learned of his demise via an early-morning phone call from Radio 4's *Today* progamme.

His dismissal gave the newspaper sub-editors yet another opportunity for never knowingly undersold headlines: *Knickers to the Vicar* was one, rivalled by another red top's *Illy sacks God*. Andrew, of course, would readily and joyfully claim to be one of God's representatives but not the deity himself. Despite the headlines, Andrew continued his chaplaincy role for another four years, albeit less formally, still welcomed by the players.

Known affectionately throughout the cricket world as Wingers Diggers, Andrew nowadays is the popular and respected vicar of a thriving and lively north Oxford parish, whose church on most Sundays is bursting at the seams. Looking back fondly to his university days he recalls, 'I loved Arthur, and thought he was perfect as coach for Oxford.

'He was a gentle, decent, modest and encouraging man. He didn't feel the need to justify his existence like some coaches with endless interfering, but he was there when you needed him. He was, I think, professionally most help to our captains as they tried to hold their own with county sides. Don't forget it was a very different world to today, with often two first-class games each week against the counties, a visit from the touring team, and Benson & Hedges Cup games as well. I loved it, and Arthur was a key part of it.'

Two endearing recollections of Arthur stood out for Wingers.

'After he had watched us for a few days in the nets in his first year with us, I asked him if he had tips for me as a bowler. I shall not forget the gist of his answer. "I have watched you closely. Do people really get out to your bowling? If they do I dare not say a thing. It's a mystery to me, but if it works I wouldn't care to interfere!"

'So I just kept running in and we never mentioned my bowling again as far as I recall. And that was fine with me.'

Wingers would take 96 first-class wickets in his colourful university career, including some very notable scalps, so Arthur's perceptive advice worked.

'One evening, in 1976 I think, we were sitting in Vincent's Club,' Wingers continued, 'talking with Dennis Amiss, Warwickshire's opening bat, about how to play the Windies' quicks. "Back and across," Dennis said. "Get right behind the ball." He'd begun to wear a helmet by then, I think.

'We asked Arthur how he played Meckiff and Rorke in Australia in '58–59.

'"You don't want to get in line to them buggers ... step away and flick 'em over the slips." Amiss was very nonplussed, I recall.'

Many moons later I asked Tom Graveney about his fellow tourist's approach to Meckiff and Rorke. Tom chuckled, saying: 'When you were batting against Meckiff and Rorke you had no chance to make a plan about playing them as you had no idea where the ball was going to be. They hit second slip or short leg quite often – and the batsman – so you never knew where the ball was going.

'We were playing in Sydney, against New South Wales I think, and Rorke started an over at three minutes to six, and didn't complete it until well gone six minutes past six. He broke a stump, bowled no-balls and wides ... everything.

'Because he was a big dragger, probably one of the biggest draggers in the game, and a big lad, when he pulled himself up to his full height and then threw it at you from far less than 22 yards it was interesting.

'There was no comparison between Meckiff and Rorke and the other chuckers of that era and the great West Indies bowlers of the Sixties; they bowled a lot straighter.

'Arthur was a bloody good player, especially off the back foot too, and I don't recall him stepping away to play Meckiff and Rorke and co. In later years he might have felt that would have been a more sensible option but I'm sure his suggestion was made with his tongue firmly in his cheek.'

Arthur's suggested approach, ironic or not, might not have been an orthodox coach's view, but then Arthur was not a conventional coach and, as a gifted back-foot player, he had the skills to play that way if he so chose. An average in the thirties for that challenging tour suggested he had found ways to play the "chuckers" that worked for him.

The archetypal pattern of a coach of Arthur's Oxford era – tracksuited, anxious to take players' games apart and remodel them, placing great emphasis on fitness drills and running laps (sometimes in preference to developing cricket skills in the nets), and overflowing with sports science theories – was not his way. Far from it.

Andrew Wingfield Digby's thoughts about Arthur were endorsed by two fellow Blues, John Claughton and Paul Fisher. Today both are respected and successful headmasters, Claughton at King Edward's School, Birmingham (where he holds the grand title of Chief Master) and Fisher at Loughborough Grammar School. We had met, at John's invitation, at KES Birmingham and over lunch they painted a delightful, but objective, picture of Arthur's time with OUCC.

Talking of coach and captain, John told me, 'Arthur and Victor [Marks] were very similar, intelligent, self-effacing, West Country, quite humble folk, and it wasn't at all surprising therefore that Vic and Arthur always got on.'

Paul Fisher added, 'That was a key relationship. You tend to think of Victor as this inevitable Test player coming through, but he wasn't at all. When he came up to Oxford he was simply a lad from Blundell's who'd scored some runs. He hadn't bowled seriously at that stage, perhaps only occasionally. Arguably if he hadn't come to Oxford he probably wouldn't have bowled for England. A county team probably wouldn't have brought him on.'

John Claughton expressed a frustration that Marks' gifts of captaincy, honed at Oxford and encouraged by their new coach, were not later and better used by his county. 'One of the sadnesses, and maybe one of the minor tragedies of Somerset history, is that Victor was an absolutely wonderful captain – especially with Arthur there to back him and talk to him. Victor should have been a great captain of Somerset.'

The memories of the two headmasters made it abundantly clear that their admiration for their fellow undergraduate matched their mutual regard for their coach.

Claughton recalled, 'You always wanted to play for Victor. He didn't have to demand anything, he never got histrionic in team talks ... you did your bloody best for Victor or you felt you'd let him down. Victor learned a vast amount from Arthur, just sitting there with him, sitting watching the game, talking things through. I always felt that, although we might have been pretty inexperienced, as regards the first-class game that is, we were pretty well captained as a University side. We weren't just cannon fodder, guarding all 360 degrees of the compass.'

Paul Fisher added his own postscript to this memory. 'Arthur and Vic are similar in that neither of them has done – in the way the world understands it – a day's work. In the most delightful way they've just stumbled into things ...'

As to Arthur's coaching style and philosophy they were very clear. 'He was not a tracksuit coach,' they insisted.

'Arthur did not take off his Gloucestershire blazer, he did not do throw-downs in the nets ...' said Claughton, laughing uproariously, as he added, 'Well, he might have hung his blazer on a stump occasionally.'

'Arthur, even in 1976, was not doing what you might have expected a coach of that time to do,' Claughton recalled, with no hint of criticism or exasperation but with real awareness that this is what worked for Arthur and what had worked for them too.

As befits a dedicated Classicist, Claughton's regard for Arthur, as a person and as coach, found voice in his paraphrasing of Ovid: *'Ars Arthur est celare artem'* – 'Art's art is to conceal his art'. It wasn't clear whether the scholar had ever shared this thought with the old pro but, had he done so, the old pro would have been delighted and very touched, at the same time humbly recognising that the Merton man had been pretty perceptive.

Against good county bowlers university cricketers were often inclined to freeze, especially against good spinners. Arthur advised, 'There's no point dying in the block-hole.' Claughton recalls a game against Gloucestershire: 'I was caught, as was frequently the case, at forward short leg, pushing too hard at their off-spinner. Arthur said, "You might as well have been caught at deep mid-wicket giving it the full face of the bat."

'I remember asking David Graveney in that match how Arthur had played. He laughed and said: "He played everything off the back foot except half-volleys, which he played delicately forward to."

'I often wondered whether that was in Vic Marks' mind, Arthur's tip about "You might as well bloody get on with it", when he got all those runs – three fifties, I think – against Pakistan and Abdul Qadir [in 1984] when, by his own account, he claimed not to have a clue, and made his runs by playing back to almost everything and only played forward at half-volleys.'

One thing readily apparent to the students was the universal admiration and respect in which Arthur was held by former colleagues. Paul Fisher: 'Another thing about Arthur is that, although he was self-effacing, everybody who came to The Parks – everybody, but everybody – the umpires and the players, they were always pleased to see him. You couldn't conceive of anyone having a bad word to say about him. As a player he must have had the unspoken respect of everyone. And what's more, Arthur probably never realised it, never thought about how much people cared for him.

'Players like Boycs [Geoffrey Boycott] would come down with their counties to play against us and we students would be in awe of them. But having Arthur around was important for us. Even Boycs was nice to him, and it was evident that there was this immense – and appropriate – respect for Arthur, for someone of his standing. It made it immeasurably easier for us.

'Arthur, in their minds – in everyone's minds – was a legend,' Claughton affirmed, 'the absolutely consummate professional. He was the embodiment of what everyone in those generations and in those decades saw as making a profession out of your art, which is what Arthur did year in, year out – much as Tom Graveney did in Arthur's eyes.

'One of the first things that almost all the county players and the umpires said about Arthur was what a fantastic catcher he was, about how ridiculously close he would field – without any protection, of course. And he was still a brilliant catcher when he was with us, in our fielding practices.'

Those who knew Arthur would not be at all surprised by this, or to learn that as a coach he was happy to help anyone who sought help. Paul Fisher noted, 'There was a real sense in which Arthur wasn't "party". Sitting in The Parks in the morning he would talk to the oppos as easily as to us. That meant we might find ourselves in conversation with Arthur and a Test player. That was a real bonus for us, and it made it that bit easier for us at 11.30am to play against them. It made them that degree more human, and not so much a name.'

That applied also to Oxford's rivals, Cambridge. 'In a sense he didn't understand our rivalry, or didn't let it get in the way of his way of doing things,' Fisher, laughing, admitted. 'Yes, he talked to the Cambridge men. He certainly didn't mind helping them at all. You could almost have expected to see him sitting on their balcony. Of course he got on well with Alastair [Hignell] anyway, as they were both Gloucestershire. He would talk cricket with any of the opposition, help anyone.'

Stephen Coverdale, Cambridge University's wicketkeeper, spoke warmly of Arthur's involvement with the Combined Universities' side when they found themselves playing against the might of the first-class counties in the Benson & Hedges Cup. 'Arthur was inspirational, and was very perceptive and wise in the advice and guidance he gave us. And of course we beat one or two counties along the way when he was coaching us. Our victory over Yorkshire is still talked about up there.'

Arthur's input was greatly valued by Chris Tavaré (Kent and England). 'Tavs was a great respecter of Arthur,' Claughton explained. 'He would sit and talk to Arthur for long periods of time. What was probably true is that Arthur found it easier with guys of the calibre of Tavs than with a lot of the other guys. In a funny way you could ask some of those who played at Oxford about Arthur and they might say he didn't impinge on their consciousness. If you didn't go out of your way to seek his help … and yet for some of us he was the most amazing man and coach.'

Similar thoughts might have occurred to some of Arthur's Gloucestershire colleagues over the years. Those who took the opportunity to draw on his knowledge and experience – and there were plenty – found him a willing source of advice and expertise, ever ready to share the insights he had gained along the way. If there were some who felt Arthur had not been as helpful as he might, this was entirely because that help and support had not been sought.

Arthur's innate modesty determined that he was not one to push in, or to impose his views onto others, unless invited. On the other hand, towards the end of his career when he played a bit in Gloucestershire's Second XI, many of those young players thought the world of him, in much the same way as his Oxford protégés, for the way he helped them, sharing his cricketing expertise and wisdom.

'Art was certainly very, very useful,' Claughton continued, 'when Tavs was feeling his way as to how he was going to become a good player, a very good no. 3 – which is what he was in 1976. Arthur undoubtedly was of great value.'

John Claughton often found himself batting with Tavaré in that 1976 season. 'Batting with Tavs at the other end that summer was absolutely bloody awesome. It's difficult to believe that later, in his England period, he became something of an icon of circumspection. But that summer he just stood there with his great metronomic blade and smashed it. I can see it now – fantastic. Tavs was getting stacks of runs, and you would have said that at that stage he was as good a player as Gatting or Gower. It would be worth getting *Wisden* out and looking at the scores of our Sussex game at Pagham. We were on tour, just prior to Lord's and the Varsity Match. The wicket, on the club ground, was exploding. It was impossible. And Tavs got 120 not out or something. I'll never forget, the Sussex lads came into our dressing room afterwards to congratulate him, because what Tavs did was absolutely un-do-able.

'Tavs waiting to bat was an incredibly dull bloke, absolutely fascinating. Sitting there behind the glass in The Parks, sitting there absolutely focused on what he had to do, you know. I can picture Arthur sitting there, just passing the time with Tavs, talking with him. Arthur, in his own inimitable and very, very gentle way, was a very good guru. Arthur would have known what it was like to bat with the score at 0-1 or 150-1 and Tavs was as constant, consistent as the Northern Star in that way. I'm sure he would say how very valuable that was to him at that time, and in his subsequent career.

'Arthur liked Tavs' sense of purpose. Tavs wanted to be the best cricketer he really could be and, to some degree, in the end, that's what he achieved.'

But let's hear Chris Tavaré's own thoughts of those golden years: 'One of Arthur's greatest gifts was in helping us keep things in perspective, especially on the bad days when we were being bowled out cheaply or chasing the ball around the outfield all day. He was always respectful, and wanted us to do well. Thus we enjoyed our cricket and looked to learn as much as we could from the experience.

'From my point of view, being a fairly intense young man at the time, he always stressed the importance of enjoying the game. Technically he emphasised the need for soft hands. My Kent colleagues told me that he had been an outstanding player of spin, using soft hands, and was a very good judge of line too.

'My recollection of Arthur is of a wonderfully kind, cheerful and decent man who was ideally suited to coaching young, sometimes overawed, students at Oxford. We had huge respect for him, as a top footballer and cricketer, and a "gentle man".'

If Chris Tavaré had found Arthur's guru-like gifts empowering then Vic Marks, too, responded to those same qualities. He recalled how Arthur's great calming influence had been valuable to him as captain. 'At the toss I would badger him, "Bat or bowl, Art?" He would pause and say, "I don't think it'll make much difference."'

When I later recalled this story for Claughton and Fisher, both laughed rumbustiously. Their coach's laid-back response was something they had come to expect. 'That was Arthur, "No worries,"' Fisher noted. 'In a way both Arthur and Vic were down to earth and straightforward like that.'

Yet Arthur was committed all right. Vic remembered: 'He could lose his temper occasionally, not with us, but with any of the first-class umpires who he felt were giving "university decisions" so they could get the game over quickly and have a day off.'

Marks' recognition of Arthur's infinite support for his young protégés was endorsed by Paul Fisher: 'His greatest gift was that he was on our side. He bridged the gap for us with visiting sides, and this made us feel we could cope. It made some of them – especially those who had gained a reputation or mystique – more human and again this helped make us feel we could better compete.'

But let's turn back to Vic Marks for a moment, and his assessment of Arthur's contribution. 'Arthur was extremely gifted, there can be no doubt about that, and yet he was one of the least ambitious sportsmen I've ever come across. He was generous, gentle, wise. We were so fortunate to have him as a guide and mentor, and a good friend. Many others could capably have filled the technical coaching role, but Arthur's broader vision and his boundless encouragement for us to fulfil our full potential – as cricketers and as students – was something from which we all benefited, at the time and certainly as we look back on those years.'

One of the joys of talking of Arthur with Andrew Wingfield Digby, John Claughton, Paul Fisher and Vic Marks was to be aware of the boundless, almost unqualified affection they all had for him. Their memories seemed endless and ever-flowing: 'Whatever he did, he made look simple and easy – so the catches he caught, he wouldn't have made any fuss about – and you feel that he never ever made his runs flamboyantly,' from Claughton; and from his fellow headmaster: 'Arthur was a great observer of human nature – and that helped make him a good coach for us.'

The ever convivial Wingers Diggers recalled: 'He would go to Vincent's or to the pub with us. We loved his company and yet Arthur never had that sense of ever wanting to be centre of the stage. He wouldn't be the person around whom everyone was huddled, telling his stories like Fred Trueman or Dickie Bird – he wouldn't hold court in that way.'

Claughton again: 'Arthur's anecdotes were always kind of just slipped in almost, so you had to listen quite carefully. And then you'd realise he'd said something quite important or interesting because he would chuckle at his own jokes, wouldn't he? And all the subtle asides, like his comment on Roy Swetman, when he said he didn't realise how good he was until Swettie dropped one. He was just like that, he'd look at you, his eyebrows would go up ... and then he'd start chuckling ...'

John Claughton shared a story of a day when the weather had beaten them all. Cricket at The Parks was rained off at an early stage. If rain had stymied the cricket it, apparently, did not preclude a visit to the golf course.

'We went off to play golf, including Arthur.' As Claughton told the story he broke into a Milton-like chuckle as he pictured Arthur still in his county blazer. 'Art was using his Gloucestershire blazer as a raincoat. He never ever removed it all day, yet he never played a bad shot – he was always down the middle,' and, again, his face lit up at the memory.

Arthur based himself in Oxford during the week and travelled home at weekends or when the university had no match. 'I used to stay with Roy Surman, who was a bank manager in Oxford,' he explained. 'We had met in the Services, playing against one another, and we had kept in touch. He was a very useful bowler, if I remember rightly. Anyway, when I went up there to coach the boys, he and his wife invited me to stay with them. I used to go up on a Monday and come back on a Friday. He loved a beer and loved to talk cricket.'

When I reminded Paul Fisher and John Claughton of this they smiled. 'That was another thing which we always used to laugh about,' the former explained, 'as being in Oxford made it convenient for going to the dogs. When he wasn't with us at the end of a day's play Arthur used to go up to the White City or Reading in the evenings – sometimes even back to Bristol – to follow the greyhounds. He would just slip off quietly at the end of the day. He called it a sensible man's form of betting and it was his way of earning some additional income.'

Not everyone was fascinated by Arthur's love of the dogs. Claughton recalled: 'One of the things that used to annoy Dick Stone [senior treasurer of OUCC who, as a senior administrator in the university, oversaw arrangements in The Parks and kept a benevolent eye on things] is that around a quarter-to-eleven Arthur always used to be on the phone, down the stairs in the pavilion, on the phone – about the dogs.'

Maybe it was this that led to a comment, recalled by Claughton, made at a meeting held at one season's end to plan arrangements for the following summer: 'We sat down and on the agenda was "coaching". I can't remember exactly whether it was me, or Paul Fisher, who said, "Well, we're all agreed about Arthur, aren't we?" and Dick Stone said, "Well yes, of course, he has got to go, hasn't he?"'

It was a suggestion so far removed from the views of everyone else around the table that, some 30 years after the event, John and Paul chortled at the outrageousness of the idea.

Wingers Diggers also remembered Arthur's great interest in the greyhounds. 'Yes, of course there were the dogs too. He had great charts laid out on the pavilion table, and had to endure gentle ribbing from me about the evils of gambling. He was fascinated that

I was training for the ministry and quizzed me – and teased me – endlessly. Great fun.'

Other members of the wider Wingfield Digby clan were noted and enthusiastic admirers of racehorses, and their investments in racing form certainly would not have been unknown to Andrew, even if he himself declined to condone it. Reflecting many years later on Arthur's interest in the dogs, and recalling those pavilion table charts, Andrew noted, 'I'm sure he did not really see it as gambling. He approached it very scientifically and meticulously as a way of bolstering income … and saw it much as others might move money around on the Stock Exchange. I suspect he was never reckless, though.'

All the university cricketers with whom I spoke saw this as a golden time. For those young men privileged to play first-class cricket and to study at the same time, it was indeed idyllic. All recognised their good fortune, not least at being around when Arthur was coach. As Andrew Wingfield Digby put it, 'I loved it, and Arthur was a key part of it.'

Without exception, Andrew's contemporaries echoed this.

John Claughton again: 'One of the nice things about Oxford when Arthur was with us was that we were … we were not an archetypal jazz hat, cravat-wearing, public school Oxford team. Actually, if anyone was flash and fancy then perhaps [Alastair] Hignell and [Paul] Parker and the Cambridge lads, they were the beautiful people at that time. We – Tavs, myself, Paul from Enfield and the others – were, in the nicest possible way, a funny mixture, with Diggers in his middle-20s training to be a vicar, and David Gurr, Aylesbury Grammar School, and Ken Siviter, Liverpool College – with perhaps Richard [Savage, from Marlborough] the only one who was near a "jazz hat".'

Paul Fisher offered his own affirmation. 'That's right, Richard was the only one who might be considered a classical jazz hat; Marlborough and Pembroke College, Oxford. Wingers was from Sherborne, but he was that much older and therefore much more rooted and sensible, and played cricket not remotely extravagantly.

He played cricket like a northern league player, grinding batsmen down.'

The Oxford sides of Arthur's era had an attractive and appealing character, as Fisher noted, 'And not least because of Alan Gibson's reporting at the time. There was this wonderful hilarity about Gibson's reporting in *The Times*. Coming to The Parks became a great theme of his.

'At one point, in one of his pieces, he bet that Wingfield Digby would get a 50 at Lord's – and whole hosts of Wingfield Digby relations had written to him taking up the bet,' Claughton recalled, chortling away.

And Claughton recalled: 'Arthur's first year was '75, when Dave Fursdon got a hundred at Lord's. We were immensely lucky to be at Oxford when Arthur was coach. And '75, '76 and '77 especially, those three years. You'd be jolly lucky in the last 50 years if there was a time which could better this. We were reasonably competitive, and with a really interesting bunch of people – and Arthur was a great part of it.'

Not everyone necessarily recognised this, as Paul Fisher noted. 'At the time it was pretty much unnoticed. The local crowd would say, "Ah well, shame the cricket isn't as good as it used to be in olden days" – the olden days of Cowdrey and so on. And when you look at the results, our results were much better than those allegedly golden times. We were even more successful.' To which Claughton added: 'At the time, of course, you don't know who are going to turn out to be your great players but when you look at the boards around the Pavilion and you can see Tavaré, Marks, Imran and Pathmanathan all played Test cricket, and six or seven of us went on to play county cricket, that was quite a good turnout. We had a lot of fun, we worked hard, and yet we were quite ordinary. It was an exhilarating time, but the fact was that we were an ordinary – and an extraordinary – bunch, and day by day in our dressing room it was pretty interesting. To that extent we were a motley crew and that variety appealed to Arthur.'

If Oxford's young cricketers of Arthur's era saw it as a golden time, that too was how Arthur unreservedly viewed it, especially as the years elapsed. Beguilingly, in later times he couldn't recall, with certainty, whether he'd actually had three or four seasons at The Parks. Only by collating Arthur's own happy recollections, with John Claughton's confidence that Arthur was coach in 1978, his year as university captain, did it seem right to suppose that Arthur coached the Oxford lads in the four seasons from 1975 to 1978.

Just as Arthur's own career had been a natural progress, in which he hadn't spent overmuch time forensically dissecting or re-modelling his talents – of course he had worked to develop them to the full, and he had constantly and quietly built on the experiences gained – so his coaching was built on an easy approach and light touch.

His reputation as an international cricketer and international footballer would have helped, too, not that it would have influenced Arthur's own approach to his young charges.

Arthur's mature and broader view of life – certainly maturer and broader than many who had spent their life in professional sport – benefited the young men with whom he worked. Without it being acknowledged by either party, he was a coach in the philosophy of life too, and they valued this and respected him for it.

This can be seen in that Arthur didn't feel the need to be at their shoulder all the time, playing every shot, bowling every ball, thinking every thought, as his memory of his first Varsity Match unveiled.

'They beat Cambridge at Lord's the first year I was there, in what was said to be the best Varsity Match for years. In fact, I left them on the Saturday morning, the first day, in a good position. I'd previously promised to play in a charity game – at Clifton College I think – so I couldn't let them down and so had to get back. I think you'll find that we, the Oxford lads, were struggling a bit and getting a bit anxious, but I said, "There's a long way to go yet. Keep at it." And one of the bowlers, David Fursdon, got a hundred and Andrew WD stayed in with him, and they put on a good score together.'

Of that partnership *Wisden* reported: 'Fursdon displayed forthright power ... [and] found another ally in the assured

Wingfield Digby and he swept on with increasingly audacious strokes.'

If Arthur's Oxford years provided a warm and glowing sunset to his cricket career, it provided him too with lifelong friendships which he greatly cherished. 'I often think about those days,' he said.

'Some years after I had finished playing, and after my time at Oxford, I used to be asked by the TCCB to go down and watch some county games as well as do some man-of-the match awards – quite often down at Taunton. One time I presented Vic with a man-of-the-match award, which was rather nice.

'And during his benefit year he asked me to go down and say a few words on his behalf at a function. I remember starting out by saying we first met up at Oxford, and we both had hair in those days. And I said, well, we were both reading Classics. His was Latin and Greek, and mine was the Derby, Oaks and the St Leger.'

Such was the depth of the friendships that, some 30 years on, he was still keeping them in good shape. 'I went, with Joan, to see John Claughton at King Edward's, Birmingham. He'd had 17 years teaching at Eton before that. And he invited Paul Fisher and his wife, too. John was a bright lad – he got honours with everything. He was a good cricketer but I remember talking to him about it – and I think he must have asked me about it, about playing cricket – and I said to him, "You're better suited temperamentally to passing on your academic abilities in that way." He had a dodgy knee anyway, but I didn't think he had the right temperament to play regularly, day in day out, at first-class level.'

As Arthur recalled this memory of lunch with two of his former charges, his eyes again welled up.

The two headmasters also remember that occasion with great affection, as John Claughton explained. 'Arthur and I were very close – and I was honoured that day Arthur came back and spent a day with me and my family. I remember, in a funny way, I wasn't Victor or Tavs, neither on my ability nor on my becoming a professional cricketer [though he did play briefly and successfully for Warwickshire before determining that academia was for him].

I wasn't an obvious first-class cricketer. I was deeply committed to my work and even when I was captain I was trying to put in a lot of time in the library – if you were trying to find me in the summer term outside cricket the best place to find me would be in the Merton library.

'I really loved Arthur and I've always treasured the fact that he wanted to come back and see Paul and me, and I'm really proud that my children met him.'

In the light of what Arthur had achieved at The Parks, and the profound impression he created there among his charges, he might well have forged a lengthy career as coach to OUCC. But it was not to be.

John Claughton cannot remember a huge debate about Arthur continuing. 'I just can't remember a conversation where Oxford University Cricket Club decided ... or what was decided ... or whether we thought he no longer wanted to do it, which is the more probable explanation.'

Why did he finish after just four seasons?

Unsurprisingly with Arthur, there was both a practical and a philosophical aspect. 'Well it wasn't enough financially, you see, for me to exist on. And I was not too great a believer in coaching. I've seen too many people not helped ... they tend to make them think a bit too much, rather than being natural with it.

'My theory about it is you're born to play, and the coaches are there to ... not to talk to you too much, not to spoil it, but to encourage you to play. I remember at Arsenal, Alex James, of the famous side they had during the Thirties, was coach. All he used to say to you was, "Go out and show 'em you can play."'

That approach, of course, may have suited a hugely and naturally talented sportsman like Arthur but others, without those special gifts, valued the input of coaches.

It is true that Arthur did not, as he explained, set too much store on the style of coaching then in vogue (or on coaching in general), and so it may be that he began also to question what he was doing. Was he being true to himself? As with other sportsmen of supreme natural ability, Arthur was happiest as a mentor or guru.

On the other hand, Tom Pugh's recollection of how Arthur had perceptively suggested a small adjustment of his top hand, before Pugh went on to make his career-best score, points to his skills in this sphere.

Claughton reflected: 'I wondered also whether watching us play and develop was a bit like watching his own children who he'd never been able to watch [because of his own playing commitments].' Paul Fisher suggested in a similar vein, 'It was as if his generation of boys – Victor, Wingers, Tavs, John and myself – had gone and, to that extent, the joy had gone out of it.'

Claughton and Fisher both reminded me that the university's season finished early. 'By mid-July, and you could almost imagine it, at the end of the university season, it was like Arthur being Charlie Chaplin, going off into the sunset. What did he do, what did he go back to, in that kind of way?'

Together they agreed: 'He'd done so much and achieved so much in his own playing careers and, probably, there was (on the wider canvas) more for him to touch and take – and he didn't, so maybe there is just this small cloud of sadness, of unachieved greatness in a way.

'Looking back to those years and Arthur's time with us, for us they were golden moments, and Arthur was such an important part of those,' a vision that carried their strong, if implied, belief that these had been cherished times for Arthur too.

But before we leave the cloudless glow of Arthur's Oxford years, let us conjure up one more recollection which crystallises beautifully in the gentle, warm regard Oxford's cricketers felt for Arthur Milton.

It's a story told by Andrew Wingfield Digby. 'Perhaps the greatest compliment to Arthur was paid by David Fursdon, who named his car Ken, after Ken Barrington – it was a very slow Morris 1000 – and his bat Arthur. When he asked Catriona to marry him they were sitting in Ken with Arthur, the bat, on the back seat.

Then according to 'Wingers', 'Dave solemnly turned to Catriona, I'm told, and said: "Arthur and I have something to ask you."'

David Fursdon happily confirmed for me that, in essence, the story was true. 'Yes, I had a Morris Traveller named after Ken Barrington – a slow, steady accumulator, with a bit of a "two-eyed" stance, nothing flashy.

'Yes, I had a bat, a Stuart Surridge, called Arthur, named after Arthur M. To be honest, because I was a bit erratic with my batting, to say the least, I needed a name that was dependable and gave the impression that I knew what I was doing with it ... need I say more. I hoped the name would bring me more runs than I thought I was capable of making on my own. The name Arthur written on the back did draw comments from wicketkeepers and, yes, it was with Arthur that I made my ton in the Varsity Match in 1975.

'As to the story of our engagement – I'm afraid it was slightly elaborated by my effervescent vicar friend AWD. We were sitting in Ken, that's true. Arthur was in the car, that's true too, as, bizarrely, I was going to a fancy dress party the next day as Sir Gary Sobers and the bat was part of the costume. My wife-to-be Catriona had to accept me as I was, with cricket fixtures, Ken and Arthur, but I didn't actually utter the line as quoted by Andrew.'

Countless coaches in other sports and other places have established special relationships with their protégés but few will have tied such treasured bonds as did Arthur in his Oxford years. This story of 'Ken' and 'Arthur', typical of many others, tells us much about the good-humoured and unqualified regard in which Arthur Milton was held by the cricketers of Oxford University.

Could this regard and affection, and his reputation, now support him as he set off to make a new life outside cricket? Would it sustain him as he headed off 'into the sunset'?

His Oxford years undoubtedly had provided a glorious gilding to his own distinguished cricket career. But with the setting sun come evening shadows before – one hopes – a bright new dawn.

Chapter 18

Master of the Arts – There'll Never Be Another

ARTHUR WAS NOW 50. What might he do? A generous-hearted good friend and keen Gloucestershire supporter promptly offered a helping hand. Les Hodge recruited Arthur to his carpet-fitting business. Grateful though he was for this practical benevolence – and he was grateful – Arthur managed at the same time to feel somehow uncomfortable and unfulfilled.

Les, an easy-going chap, was inclined to be relaxed as to when work started and cricket chat ceased (if he'd had his way cricket talk could happily have filled all their working hours), but Arthur, having retired from cricket and made the mental gear change, felt he should be working in a more organised and purposeful way. He wanted to be gainfully occupied. In truth, he wasn't at ease feeling beholden. Perhaps this was not surprising for a man of independent spirit, who was well content to be self-reliant and self-sufficient, even though he greatly loved his fellow men.

His career had unfolded without any plan. He had barely sought it; it had come to him. But now he discovered an Anglo-Saxon Protestant work ethic. An additional source of income would be helpful, it was true, and while, in his rather vague way, he backed

316

himself to keep things ticking over, he needed to be active and to contribute. What was he to do?

This was a testing time. 'I had a difficult period around that time when I finished playing, and after my time at Oxford.'

Joan helpfully confirmed this: 'Artie got into a big depression when he finished playing and, yes, he found life very difficult for a while. He hadn't got anything set up. He was never very good at approaching people' (i.e. about possible work).

'I think perhaps because he'd been too long in sport and been cushioned by sport, he had never needed to do this on his own behalf. Also, because he was in sport and kept himself fit there was a sense of it going on for ever, and not knowing when to end. He never took a long-term view in that sense. When he finished playing he didn't know what he wanted to do. It was a tricky – and frustrating – time. The help of friends and family was very important to him, and to both of us, then.'

As we talked in this vein Arthur spoke of an article by our mutual friend Frank Keating. 'Frank once wrote a piece on suicides of sportsmen. Do you know – cricketers were almost top of the list. After they've finished their cricket they've nothing to do, don't know anything else and a lot of them found it difficult, and took their own lives.

'And I got myself into a situation where I could realise why they did it, because they knew nothing else.'

One moment he had been talking brightly and animatedly of his playing career and of his Oxford days and then – in a quiet, understated way, seemingly without change of tempo or modulation of speech – with the swift, hinting brush marks of an impressionist painter he had sketched in these unexpected shadows.

His thoughts, some implied, some spoken, seemed to suggest a man walking past the end of a road, a cul-de-sac of houses cast in sombre shadow in an otherwise sunlit scene.

Some, forlornly, had ventured into the cul-de-sac. For many it proved a one-way street. Arthur could understand why they had been pulled that way, but he had no desire to follow. Yet, as the man crossed the top of the road, his pace had slackened, slackened sufficiently to allow the briefest of glimpses into the shadows. Perplexed, he fleetingly took it all in and then, without a backward glance, resolutely, determinedly he had walked on.

As he shared these thoughts, a sympathetic understanding, coupled with a clear sense of liberation, became recognisable in Arthur's voice. There had been no suggestion of taking a step in that direction, difficult though that time had been.

And whatever it was in his voice that spelled this out, it also indicated that the image had swiftly been wiped away. He had moved on, with a spring metaphorically back in his step again.

'Looking back to that time, I realised it was sad I wasn't qualified in any way. When I look back on it now, that was stupid. I wasn't born without a brain. I'd taken Higher School Cert, but the thing that happened was that I had to do my National Service, and I'd started into the football world by then. By the time I'd finished my National Service, I was 20 I suppose, and I was playing both games.'

Those who knew Arthur in those early days have suggested – sometimes as much by implication as by assurance – that he had the ability, and perhaps the opportunity, to go to Oxford or Cambridge. But it was the doors of Highbury which had swung open first.

'In the normal course of events, without any National Service, I'd have gone to university if I'd been good enough,' he continued, 'or qualified in some way, probably as a quantity surveyor – because that's all mathematics.

'It's something I regret now. But you take life as it comes, don't you? Lee Trevino said – I was always a great admirer of him – "In life you don't get to play the course again, you only get to play it once," which is very true, not like golf, of course, where you can go back again and again. Everything is very easy in hindsight, isn't it?'

Then, to follow the joy of his Oxford years, and the fleeting dusk and evening shadows as he searched for a new direction, happily and fortuitously came that unexpected meeting with Cyril Wood from Westbury-on-Trym Post Office. For Arthur it was to prove life-changing and life-enhancing. A new dawn was lighting the horizon.

'I was walking … I'd had a car accident and bumped my head, and was left in a bigger state of confusion than usual,' he recalled, smiling away, 'and I was struggling for a time. I was walking down the hill in Westbury village one morning, and coming up the pavement was the postmaster, Cyril Wood, who looked after the sorting office and that. He was a good local cricketer. And that's how it all began. I never looked back.

'Of course one thing, when I became a postman, was the fact that I always had to perform, as it were. On the county scene and what-have-you, this made you rather inward-looking, I think, in some way more introverted, looking to your own performance. Of course, it's a team game, and that's important, but when you think about it, it's made up of individual performances. When you have to go and serve the public, that's another education in itself. You have to serve them, and it really turned my whole life around – and made me a much better person,' Arthur recalled, his voice again cracking a little with emotion, in gratitude for the opportunities that had unexpectedly come his way.

How long had he served as a postman?

'Ten years or so, until 1988, I think. It was ten years I really enjoyed, because we used to go up to the Downs every morning, through all the seasons of the year. And through all winds and weathers,' he added. 'And I got to know a lot of people.

'But it was lovely for me – I could ride up there and round, back across the Downs, and home. Yes, I loved it all, especially in the early morning when it was still and quiet, and the stars were still out or the sun had started to come up. The Downs – do you know our Downs at all? – it's a fabulous area, and my round started right on the edge, and then I used to ride up and do a few until "lunchtime" [the postman's mid-morning break], and then on home across the Downs, home at 12 o'clock or something like that – and, in a way, home all the time compared to when I was playing. It's a very difficult life for a woman with a cricketer for a husband,' he reflected, his voice betraying hidden sensibilities.

'You're away for half the season, and even when you're playing at home they're long days – you don't get home till 7 or 8 o'clock.

So it was nice. We grew together a lot more then,' his voice again providing ready evidence of their shared fulfilment and pleasure. 'You know, seeing more of one another.

'I really enjoyed the job. Well, I used to get the first delivery done and home for breakfast, and then back to do the second delivery – but second deliveries and all that, they've all gone by the board now.

'So, as a postman, I saw my boys all the time. You know, I'd missed some of their growing up, which I regret now, their schooling and what-have-you.'

Typically, once into his new role he was fully committed and was more than happy to go the extra mile. Instead of having their mail pushed unthinkingly through the letter box, certain elderly or infirm clients would receive a knock at the door, so their postman could ascertain for himself that they were up and about and well.

On another occasion – a wet slushy winter's morning, grim after snow – he was to be found lying in the road, endeavouring to reclaim from a roadside drain all the mail snatched by a swirling winter wind.

John Mortimore adds to the picture: 'There's a story that someone tried to knock him down on his rounds and Art threw the Post Office bike at him.'

Arthur Milton was not going to let ne'er-do-wells deter him from his routine and his responsibilities. Clearly it had its testing moments, and I well remember Arthur arriving at Worcester on another occasion with his arm in plaster. A jogger had come round the corner without care, collided with him and knocked him off his bike, but Arthur was still determined to fulfil his match adjudicator duties with us that day.

Becky Graveney, daughter of old pal Tom, lived on Arthur's post round at one time. Before popping her mail through the letter box 'Uncle Arthur' would sometimes scribble a message on the envelope, seeking to soften the imagined blow of any mail which looked 'official', especially any bearing the legend HM Revenue: 'Hope this isn't bad news.'

Most who have played professional sport or been in the limelight in other ways might well feel a marked loss of status in becoming a postman. Many would not countenance such a step.

It was not a move Arthur had planned; it had fallen into his lap like much of his earlier career. Yet Arthur's gratitude for his postie's role was genuine. This was no token indebtedness, and his gratitude and sense of fulfilment was readily apparent from the animated and quite passionate way he spoke of this unexpected part of his life.

'I felt like a millionaire. I found it very good for me really, because it got me out of myself more, you know, and of course in the end, when it was time to retire we had a lovely send-off from them all, those at the Post Office and those I had delivered mail to. They arranged a party for me and I was given two excellent prints of local scenes, by Frank Shipsides, one of our well-known local artists' (which were proudly displayed ever after in the Milton's sitting room). 'I'd made a lot of friends, you know – and that was very special.'

But when he retired from the Royal Mail he couldn't countenance leaving his round completely, which was why he became a paperboy. 'I used to get over that far delivering the papers, you see, and so could see them regularly, which was rather nice.

'Well, you should have seen it! On Sundays I had a job to look over the top of the papers. And the weight … Jeez!

'On Saturdays especially, I used to use the car a bit, too. I had a lovely old Carlton at the time, and I used to split the round into two halves and take the second half with my bicycle up to the Grange, halfway over, and then deliver the first half. When I'd finished that, I'd go over from the Grange, get my bicycle from the car, put the papers on, and finish off the rest.

'When I first started, I used to do the paper rounds for the Post Office at Rockleaze, just alongside the Downs. They were always struggling for paperboys over there, so I used to finish up sometimes doing four or five rounds some Sundays.'

There came a time when the local store stopped paper deliveries and, when their successors failed to keep the suppliers happy, Arthur discovered an entrepreneurial streak. He took over the organisation himself. 'I thought, "What shall I do?" because I had quite a nice round going over there - so I found another supplier, paid for the papers, and then delivered them. I saw a lot of old friends. My lad David helped me for a while latterly, too. I used to collect the money on a Monday morning, which saved a lot of the old people having to go out to the newsagents to pay for their papers themselves, which they liked really. It meant Mondays took a good bit longer to get round, but I enjoyed it and the older customers enjoyed having someone to chat to.'

At one time a murder in nearby woods had, understandably, caused local anxiety, especially among the elderly and housebound. Arthur was at hand. 'Some of them in those parts don't see many people, you know, so I give them some time. Some of them are really interesting to talk to; they've travelled a lot in days gone by and done quite a bit in their lives and now they don't see so many people, so I'm happy to give them some time.'

Joan recognised how grateful Arthur had been about his postman's and paperboy's roles, and had loved being out and about in the great outdoors. 'Artie once had a job, during one of the winters when he was with Gloucestershire, with the Inland Revenue at the Tax Office. But he didn't much enjoy being in an office all the time. It was hot and stuffy, and they weren't keen about his opening the windows. Anyway, he got flu very badly, and that was the end of his office work!'

If his new life gave him more time at home with Joan – when he wasn't at the Eastville greyhound track, Long Ashton golf club or 'the office' – he felt no compelling need to watch a lot of cricket, or any sport, on TV. He was still involved enough himself. It was a time, too, when he and Joan could pursue their joint interest in the arts. 'Joan was always into the arts, and she and I have always been pleased that when we were first going out together, up in town, in London, we used to go to the theatre and classical music concerts as well, in Hornsey Town Hall and the like. There was always plenty going on up there.'

Joan added: 'We often went to the Proms in the Albert Hall then we supported the Bristol Old Vic here and went to the Hippodrome too, and sometimes to concerts at Colston Hall. I even introduced Artie to ballet. He didn't have much of an opinion of ballet before that, and thought it was "poncy", but the London Contemporary Ballet Company were performing in Bristol, and I persuaded him that the modern dance would be very athletic. That appealed to him, and he came with me – and loved it. He became quite a fan after that. But I could never really get him interested in opera.'

During those fulfilling years delivering mail and newspapers, Arthur also found himself playing a part in first-class cricket again. He was delighted to be able to put something back into the game which had given him so much. After he became a paperboy, he found his early morning rounds gave him greater freedom of time. The Test and County Cricket Board felt they could use this, as well as his knowledge, experience and expertise.

The Board appointed him as an observer. The team of observers was a far-sighted idea of Ted Dexter, then chairman of England's selectors. Experienced and shrewd former players were invited to watch up-and-coming players in county matches and to brief the selectors on the talents they saw. Arthur was an ideal choice.

How long was he an observer? 'About three years. I covered mostly the West Country, Somerset, Gloucestershire, Hampshire sometimes, Glamorgan, up to Worcestershire. And I got to see quite a lot of players in that time, yes.'

A real bonus for Arthur was meeting up with old colleagues on his travels. Of course, such meetings often awoke hosts of memories. On a visit to Northlands Road, Hampshire's old ground in Southampton, he met Don Roper. 'Don scored about four goals in that game Arsenal played against Hibs for the National Playing Fields Association. I remember I was right through, with only the goalkeeper to beat, and I thought, "I've got one here," but then saw Don just outside me, so I slipped it to him and he belted it in the net.

'Many years after our Arsenal days I was down at Southampton, looking at players for the TCCB, walking round the ground and I looked up on the terraces and there was Don, up the top. He hadn't been well so it was nice to see him. That took us back, and of course we talked about our Arsenal days.

'He played a bit of cricket down there. Quite a few of the Hampshire lads played soccer: Ted Drake, Henry Horton – he used to get some runs. Our boys thought that they'd got him sorted out. It didn't matter how wide they would bowl it, he would go fishing for it. But he certainly used to score some runs. Butch White – he was a good bowler. He wasn't the worst. He did for me two or three times, especially with a yorker early doors.'

After three summers, and before the TCCB reviewed the system of observers – on the face of it a valuable tool in the selection process – Arthur had begun to have his doubts about the system and his own role in it. 'I used to go down to Taunton. And Roy Marshall [a former exhilarating opening batsman for Hampshire, Somerset and the West Indies] was almost always there, especially if Somerset were batting.

'Over the months I'd seen this lad, Mark Lathwell, play and next time I was down there and saw Roy I said, "Why have you come in today?"

'"I've come to see young Lathwell bat," he said. "He's a good player."

'The selectors had asked me about him. Goochy [Graham Gooch] was England captain, and Micky [Stewart] was in charge of those of us looking around. He would ring me sometimes and say, "You know, we'll have to have a look at young Lathwell, won't we; what do you think?"

'"Well," I said, "I think it's too early to play him in the five-day game yet, but you might give him a couple of games in the one-day stuff, because he can get on with it, he's a nice timer of the ball, and he's got plenty of ability."

'And what did they do? They picked him for a five-day Test match. It ruined his bloody life, you know.' Arthur's anger – and his empathy – on behalf of a similarly minded player, in whom he must have seen himself as a younger man, could be heard in his voice as he re-told the story several years later. 'Sad. Very sad.'

'He was a quiet, introverted lad. I knew what he was like. It all came too quickly for him. He had lovely timing …' and his voice trailed off as he recalled an exciting talent frustratingly lost to the game.

'That was one of the reasons why I gave it up. There was another lad, at Glamorgan, who I rated, Matthew Maynard, but I didn't think he was handled well by England. He was a real good athlete, and a magnificent fielder as well. He had so much talent. He only played a few times for England in Tests [Maynard played four Tests and 14 ODIs]. They didn't give him many opportunities, did they?

'Another one I rated was Paul Parker,' and as the picture of Paul formed in Arthur's mind it was accompanied by that familiar and friendly laugh. 'I met him when I was with Oxford, at the Varsity matches when he was a member of the Cambridge team, and also through the Combined University side. Gosh, he was another athlete-and-a-half. He was so quick about the field; he could let the ball get right to him before he needed to do anything about it.

'These days when batsmen are looking to run for anything, they [the coaches] still want the players walking in towards the ball. That's no good; you're accelerating the pace of the ball by doing that. I used to talk with Jim Foat, one of our young Gloucestershire players, about it. I used to say, "You don't want to move too soon; wait until you see it."'

Listening to Arthur was to sense a man who, in principle, saw the merits of the observer's role but, as someone who lived life being true to himself and to his beliefs, became frustrated when his advice and guidance, apparently, was not heeded. Had he enjoyed it?

'Looking back, not really. In truth I've never been a great watcher of the game. If I've got something to do, though – watching players for the board or doing man-of-the-match awards – I could watch readily enough and tell whether people were good enough.

'Another player I was asked to watch was the fellow we had here at Bristol, Syd Lawrence.

'Now, you know, I saw him, and Micky asked me about him. And he was ready. He went in and showed he was ready, and played at The Oval, and had quite a good match. Then he went on the tour and he did his knee in that horrific incident in New Zealand. That was sad, very sad.

'He was quick too. I used to like to see him bowl. And he meant it.

'Actually he lived up in Sneyd Park where I delivered the papers. I was out one morning and this fellow came pounding down the pavement and said "Morning, Arthur" and it was him, determined to return to playing at the top level.'

Those county visits allowed Arthur to burnish old friendships with cherished opponents. 'I used to meet old friends and I could pick their brains too. At Glamorgan I would see Wilf – Wilf Wooller. I loved him, and of course when I was looking on for TCCB, I used to go down to Sophia Gardens and Wilf would give me all the gen, and we used to chat away. We had some great days together in those later years, just as we had when we were playing.

'Micky let you know the players they were interested in and I would go and look at them. I used to go down to Hampshire too, Somerset of course; I used to love to come up to Worcester and see all the boys – Don [Kenyon] was alive then – but that was probably when I was adjudicating and doing NatWest Trophy Man of the Match awards for NatWest Bank.

'They were very nice days out for us, you know, those NatWest adjudication days. But one or two took advantage and overdid the hospitality bit.

'Joan and I used to go up, often stay overnight, usually in a B&B. Gordon Ross – who I knew quite well from my football days – and then Barbara Quinn looked after their arrangements for years, including looking after us adjudicators. I liked them.'

Serendipity, providence, coincidence, good fortune – call it what you will – had opened the door to what Arthur, in hindsight, saw as fulfilling later chapters of his life.

His time as a postman, and then with his paper rounds, had offered him so much and given him a contented and broader outlook on life. It brought satisfaction and a sense of being useful, of contributing to the general good, in a way that was almost certainly there in his earlier sporting career but which he had somehow failed fully to recognise.

' It was the making of me; it made me a better person, and I never looked back.'

Not the expected reaction from a double cricket and soccer international reflecting on a career change to become a postman, but the accompanying smile and gentle laugh emphasised that Arthur knew it to be true. 'I loved my years of cricket, they were wonderful days in the sun, but I'd like to have worked and played. I think that's what sport is for – recreation and exercise, something away from what we do most of the week. In a way I'm not sure I really agree with professionalism.'

The deeds of his best-ever season, 1967, were faithfully recorded in the following year's *Wisden Almanack*. In that same edition the editor gave space to the views of Leslie Deakins, the respected and far-seeing secretary of Warwickshire CCC and driving force in the rise of Edgbaston as a top-class venue. Speaking at the Forty Club dinner in the autumn of 1967, Leslie advocated a restructuring of the county game. He proposed a championship of 16 games, eight at home and eight away, with all games being played Saturday, Sunday, Monday when the bulk of county members and paying spectators were free to attend.

He also suggested, with supporting arguments, that 'county staffs be done away with, and players be invited from the clubs within the county to play at a fee of, say, £50 per man, per match'. Novel though it was, and counter to the long traditions and history of the county game, there can be little doubt that such a programme would have appealed to Arthur, especially if it had been established back when he joined Gloucestershire. Like so many good ideas worthy at least of further consideration little was ever heard of it again.

How much were Arthur's later thoughts about marrying a career outside the game with his professional cricket career the retrospective view of a talented sportsman pondering in the maturity and wisdom of his dotage? How much was this a rational rethinking of how he might have lived his life again, given that chance? It is not an easy question to answer.

My guess (and it can only be a personal view) is that, given his time again, he would still have entered the doors of Highbury and the dressing room at Nevil Road to play as a professional footballer and cricketer. That was his calling. It is what he was born to do. But almost certainly alongside his sporting vocation he would have sought a university degree or other professional training that would have enabled him to build a career around his sport. Ideally that career would prepare him for (and might have flowed naturally into) his life after sport. Even more idealistically, it might also have allowed him to forego his professional status and play as an amateur. That he might have welcomed – but whether the clubs concerned, and the FA's selection committee and England's Test selectors, would then have been as far-sighted and as willing to embrace such thinking is a moot, and wholly academic, point.

To hear the soft Gloucestershire voice recalling his distinguished and successful sporting career was to hear a man full of gratitude that he had been able to play sport and to make the most of his God-given gifts: 'I always felt privileged to have been born with a talent to take my place in the games that I loved. It enabled me to fulfil myself in a way not given to many in this life.'

His years coaching in The Parks with Oxford University had added a burnished glow to his sporting career. Then, chasing away the evening of shadows and heralding a sun-lit new dawn of unexpected prospect, came his time delivering mail and popping newspapers through letterboxes – and, most importantly, new friendships with acquaintances and customers across Bristol's picturesque downland in his own backyard.

Yes, serendipity, providence, coincidence and good fortune had made this possible. The unexpected opportunities had fallen into his lap, and he had taken them. But the memory of this providence reminded him, on the other hand, that when his Gloucestershire career had finally closed, and when the Oxford encore had been played, he had felt a need to do something – and had recognised that he was not explicitly qualified for life beyond sport.

Today a double international whose achievements matched Arthur's would be accorded, and might expect, superstar status. The acquisition of an agent would be a given. A media role as a newspaper columnist or TV pundit might be created alongside an overstated lifestyle that most sports fans wisely would not envy. But this was not for Arthur. It was not his way nor, in truth, was it the style of his times.

Postman Milt had no regrets, no ego, no overweening desire for a high-profile. He knew genuinely his proper worth, in the sporting world and in the wider context, and was a man at peace with that, with himself and with the world at large. Totally without vanity or any desire for self-promotion, more so than almost any other soccer or cricket international you care to name, his innate humility – and his warmth and regard for his fellow man – was entirely genuine.

Looking back over Arthur's life, with two professional sports being all-consuming into his mid-twenties, and with cricket offering him a comfortable life and a focus into his mid-forties, would a combination of sport and academic studies ever have been seriously considered at that time or been a realistic proposition for him? I wonder.

For a man whose nature was to take life in his stride, he might well have opted for the academic route had it presented itself, but in the 1940s and 1950s few academic institutions accommodated part-time students or offered distance learning for high-level courses. A professional sportsman, particularly one engaged in two sports, might not have been considered a serious student. Time to study might have been a problem too.

'But it needn't have been if I got my head down to it.'

So life as a professional footballer and cricketer unfolded easily for Arthur. Academia did not leap in its way.

His regrets were undoubtedly real. Perhaps, they were, too, the wistful and retrospective thoughts of a man who had needed to think seriously about a new career and direction to his life when he had passed the age of 50. At this point many others were viewing retirement looming into view, with plans and preparations already laid.

If earlier opportunities for serious academic study had floated by unnoticed, Arthur was thrilled, in his mid-seventies, to find himself again engaged with students and caught up, to a degree, in university life.

Wills Hall is one of the University of Bristol's halls of residence, and its warden, from 1997 to 2009, was Donald Shell. To add to the customs and culture of the hall, Donald introduced occasional Friday evening dinners, black tie affairs, for staff and students. The appeal of these evenings was widened by introducing different themes. Donald decided one should be a sporting dinner and he invited Arthur, as one of Bristol's sporting heroes, along with Joan. Bob Reeves, Arthur's colleague from his days with Oxford University CC, was a fellow guest. Bob, by now director of the university's Centre for Sport, Exercise and Health, was encouraged by Donald to invite the university's own sporting stars.

An enjoyable evening was shared by all. For Arthur it was the start of an ongoing connection with Wills Hall and its students, most of whom, initially, would be unaware that Arthur already had some contact with the place.

Talking of his introduction to Donald Shell, Arthur recalled, 'I first met him, of course, because I delivered the papers there, to the hall,' and yet again he was amused by the memory.

'With Donald there was always something going on in the hall. It's been very enjoyable having this link with them because any functions they have we get invited and we usually end the evening eating with the whole hall.'

But let Donald Shell recall his own memories of Arthur and his links with Wills Hall.

'My recollection is that he delivered his papers most frequently on Saturdays, or at least that was when I met him. I chatted to him several times, before asking him one day what he had been up to earlier in life. I vividly remember him leaning on his bicycle and saying that he used to play cricket.

'When I pressed him further, he let slip that he'd played for Gloucestershire and for England and then, with the same diffidence, I recall him telling me that in the winter months he had played football for Arsenal and that he had also been capped for England.

'I was amazed and expressed some astonishment, even incredulity. He was such a modest man, and the realisation that I was actually speaking to such a sporting star was almost unbelievable.

'Following that we spoke together frequently; I remember saying I didn't think David Beckham would be delivering newspapers on a pedal bike when he had retired. Arthur's response was that he absolutely loved what he did, and also felt that when he played football – probably for a paltry match fee – he and his contemporaries actually had far more fun out of the game than current players.'

Donald went on to speak of instituting the formal Friday evening dinners held in hall during term-time.

'I was trying to theme some of these occasions. So I asked Arthur if he would be guest of honour at a "Sports Formal". The dinner was preceded by a reception, to which I invited student members of hall, saying they would have the opportunity to meet someone who had played both cricket and football for England. Among other guests that evening was the newly appointed vice-chancellor of the university, Eric Thomas.

'Arthur spoke with such ease and such obvious sincerity. One student asked him rather bluntly how it was that, if he had played football and cricket for England, he was delivering newspapers because surely he must be a millionaire. Arthur answered memorably that his generation had tremendous fun playing sport; that it was a very big mistake for people to equate money with happiness; and that just watching the beauty of the sun rise over the Bristol Downs as he went about his newspaper rounds was now a source of great joy to him. He added that he would have loved to go to university but never had the opportunity and that they, the students present, should all value the privileges they had.

'That was one of the best moments in my 11 years' wardenship of the hall. Around a hundred or so of the brightest, most talented and most privileged students were hearing a piece of true wisdom delivered by someone possessed of immense natural authority.

'Arthur later lingered in the bar, utterly at ease with the 18- and 19-year-old students, having his photo taken with them, and chatting away about his sporting accomplishments: his maiden Test century; hitting the winning runs for Gloucestershire against Kent following a sporting declaration by Colin Cowdrey; and so on. The students were enthralled.

'Thereafter he and Joan became regular guests and welcome visitors to hall. We had a "Sports Formal" every year, always with a capacity 200 in the dining room, with Arthur and Joan as chief guests. We invited them to hall plays, musicals and our end-of-year barbecue. We even held a fun internal hall cricket match, Old Quad versus New Quad, which he umpired; that was a big draw.

'Both Arthur and Joan were so friendly to the hall, and I always felt the encouragement of their friendship to me personally too. Just as he must have had an utterly natural talent with ball games, so he seemed always to be utterly natural in his conversation, with whoever he was talking to. He loved the young, and they loved his sincerity, his modesty and, dare I say it, his charm.

'The vice-chancellor was very impressed with him on his first visit. As you know, the university later conferred a well-deserved honorary degree on Arthur and, when Bob Reeves put his name forward for this award it was certainly popularly supported, and I'm sure the vice-chancellor must have thought back to that first meeting with Arthur and readily recognised in him an obvious – and ideal – candidate.'

Bob Reeves vividly recollects one of those hall dinner evenings. 'I think it may have been one of the last evenings Arthur attended when, after they had eaten, he was invited to join a group of students who went to the bar and were wanting to talk with him. There they happily put the world to rights – and Arthur was in his element in wide-ranging discussions with a lively bunch of students. With his customary diffidence and geniality he responded to the questions they all seemed to want to put to him. The evening was advancing, discussion was bubbling along, when a brief gap appeared in the conversation. One of the girls asked Arthur if he would dance with her. He happily joined her on the floor, and was merrily bopping away. The whole thing was just such a delight for Arthur – and the students were equally delighted at this 70-plus-year-old local celebrity enjoying their company. He loved young people, and loved being with them.'

As Bob recounted this story I wondered aloud whether part of his joy of being with young people – the students at Wills Hall and, earlier, with the Oxford boys in The Parks and, above all, with his much-loved grandchildren – might have compensated Arthur for missing so much of his own boys' growing up when he was playing cricket for his living. Was he making up for lost time and sadly missed opportunities? 'You may be right, you may well be right,' thought Bob.

As to those young people, and advising those who sought his guidance on a sporting career, Arthur was quite clear. 'My advice to any youngster, and to anybody who comes to talk to me about their youngsters … when fathers talk to me about their sons, I say: "You know, if they want to do it to, and if it's born in them that's all very well, but the main thing is to make sure they've got something behind them before they go into their sport, because life can be a bit unkind sometimes, with illness and injury or loss of form. As long as they are qualified that will help them with their play."'

Bob Reeves added, 'Donald continued to invite Arthur for a number of years, not only to hall dinners but at other times too, when he was asked to talk with the students about his career. Unfailingly he would emphasise the importance of getting qualified.'

When, in 2002, the University of Bristol invited Arthur to accept an honorary degree he was completely bowled over. It is difficult to put into words just how much the award meant to him. He was immensely proud, and proud too that it was by his home city's major university that he was being honoured.

He was honoured not only for his sporting prowess but also for his remarkable and unique contribution to the life of his home city. The closing words of Bob Reeves oration, as he presented Arthur before the university's vice-chancellor, summed this up:

'Mr vice-chancellor, I present to you Clement Arthur Milton, sportsman, gentleman, and true Bristolian, as eminently worthy of the degree of Master of Arts *honoris causa*.'

Of such an accolade anyone could justifiably be proud. And yet for Arthur acceptance of this honour wasn't a given. It wasn't something to be automatically accepted. He thought it over for several days, feeling he did not deserve such recognition and then, with a little prompting from Joan, he accepted.

'I was quite surprised when the letter came, and I dilly-dallied a little bit,' he recalled. 'I would have liked to accept but wasn't sure if I should. Why me? Joan encouraged me, however, and after talking some more we decided that I might go ahead and accept the honour.'

To have reached the heights in two sports and to have been wholly fulfilled in his unexpected post-cricket career; to have earned and retained the esteem, the ready friendship and warmest regard of former playing colleagues, and of countless Gloucestershire members and legions upon legions of other sports lovers; to have won and retained the same respect from his Royal Mail colleagues, and the many friends seen on his daily paper rounds, were indeed riches galore for Arthur – providing him with a lifetime's treasure-house overflowing with wonderful memories. But then came Bristol University's invitation.

For Arthur it was the icing on the cake.

His recollections of the awards ceremony, with wave upon wave of seemingly endless applause affirming Bristol's unqualified regard for this favourite son, and of the dinner held later in his honour in the university's Great Hall, bubbled from Arthur.

'After the presentations and the graduation ceremony,' he remembered, recalling the moment when he was awarded his degree and shook hands with the vice-chancellor, 'the vice-chancellor said to me: "I've never heard any noise – applause – like that at a graduation," which was very nice. I had the old gown on and the hood, and the mortar board too – and I took it off and waved to them all,' he explained, laughing.

A few days after the degree ceremony Arthur was back at the university, this time as guest of honour at a dinner which Bob

Reeves had organised to mark Arthur's degree and his contribution to sport.

A good many people, from the university, the city and every aspect of Arthur's cricketing and soccer life, were delighted to be there to honour him. Bob was thrilled that a group of ten of those who had played for Oxford University during Arthur's time there as coach were present, some making a considerable effort to attend. 'They were a particularly interesting group,' Bob recalled. 'Arthur was there just at the right time for them, and it was just the right time for him to be coach. And they all loved him.

'That they wanted to be there, to take a table at the dinner for Arthur, was a real measure of the esteem they held him in.'

A number of Cambridge University players made a point of being there, too, alongside their Oxford contemporaries.

'Ken Friar, from Arsenal – he's a top man – came down to that dinner also, and agreed to speak. Although he was in his seventies he drove himself down, and asked if he might speak first as he had to get back for an Arsenal directors' meeting next day. He spoke brilliantly, and movingly, about Arthur, for about 15 minutes – just right – and that, and his determination to be there, was a testimony to his own and Arsenal's affection for Arthur, and testimony to the general affection in which Arthur is held by those with whom he's worked and played.'

Ken Friar's attendance had taken his own thoughts back to those days immediately after the Second World War. 'I first met Arthur in 1946, I think, when as a 12-year-old I was running messages between the main entrance and the ticket office at Highbury. I used to meet all of the players and in fact collected autographs at the time.

'My early recollections of Arthur were that he was always a gentleman, even then, and always prepared to speak, even with a lowly lad who was completely at the bottom of the lowest rung, if not underneath it.

'Mind you, he was one of those people you could happily "hate" in a way, because he excelled at everything. He was truly a gentleman and one who, as a young man, I respected, and continued to do so ever after. If he was still playing today there's no doubt he would be a household name but he was, as ever, modest and never one to let people know just how great a sportsman he was. He was a golden man in so many ways.'

It was a tribute from a man who remarkably worked his way up from being a messenger boy to become company secretary, managing director and a director of the club, and a legendary and widely respected figure in the club's chronicles, whose name will for ever be linked indelibly with 'the Arsenal'.

In recalling this occasion, which meant almost as much to Arthur as the degree ceremony (in fact, Arthur tended to couple them together when talking about them), Bob Reeves mentioned Mike L'Estrange several times. Mike, an Australian and an Oxford cricketing Blue from Arthur's time in The Parks, had gone on to be Australia's High Commissioner in London. Shortly before he left that post, he invited Arthur and Joan, along with a number of contemporaries from OUCC days, to a splendid private dinner in the High Commissioner's personal residence on the edge of Hyde Park. Vic Marks, Tim Glover, John Claughton, Paul Fisher and Rod Eddington (a recent chief executive of British Airways) were among those present. 'And they all wanted to be there for Arthur.'

While still enjoying the uplifting embrace of that prestigious dinner, Arthur, feet firmly on the ground as always, was nevertheless soon back on his paper round. 'One of my neighbours came in the shop when I was getting my papers ready. He's walking, and I'm riding my bicycle down with him back home, when he said, "I thought you might like to know that in 1946 I worked for a firm who did all the refurbishment on the Great Hall [it had been gutted by incendiaries during the Second World War]. It's a wonderful place, isn't it? There's lots of wood – fantastic. My firm were given the job of restoring and conserving it."'

Intrigued by this, Arthur asked his neighbour about his role in the restoration. '"I was the quantity surveyor," he told me, and I thought: "That could have been me."'

To a young man beginning to follow the path that unfolded before him all of this would have seemed the stuff of dreams.

Indeed, it might have seemed so far-fetched as to never register in dreams. But his honorary MA, and all that surrounded it, all that had led to it, was no dream, though Milt sometimes spoke as though it might have been. He long continued amusedly to mull it over as, now an honorary graduate of the university, he continued delivering daily papers to the student halls of residence.

'I got a degree in the end, but it took me a long time to get a qualification,' he quipped. 'Fifty-four years. Fancy, my home-town university honouring someone like me. It's amazing, beyond belief. That was the proudest time of my life, I think.'

What Arthur would never know is that, after his death, Bristol City Council decided his memory and his supreme sporting skills were worthy of permanent commemoration and, fittingly, a street near the County Ground was named after him. Arthur's outstanding sporting deeds provide their own enduring memorial, but now, in Arthur Milton Street, Bristol BS7, the last-ever double international is honoured in perpetuity.

His mortar board, his academic 'cap' – immensely deserved, like the other caps he had won, for Gloucestershire and England, for Arsenal and England – crowned a distinguished sporting career, and crowned, too, that part of his life he regarded as most fulfilling.

'We've all got different talents, haven't we, and I think most people look on theirs as I look on mine. You know, it's just part of them and that's it. I don't think I'm anything special in any way, really.

'I'd much rather be remembered as somebody who acted as a good neighbour and did things for the neighbourhood, and what have you. I hope people would say there's a side to me that is a decent human being really. I hope that's the first thing. It's nice to have done what I have done, in sport, but I don't see it as the be all and end all.

'Mind you, I had lots of letters in my time about how much pleasure I have given people, so there is that side to it, and I can take that on board and appreciate what they mean.'

Friends and family readily recognised how, for Arthur, his later careers had turned his whole life around. In his words this had 'made me a more rounded person and a better human being', and given him a sense of real satisfaction and an inner peace, perhaps the peace for which he had searched when his playing career had come to an end. None but the most mean-spirited could doubt that Arthur Milton, the most naturally talented of all-round sportsmen, double international, and a man who enjoyed serving his fellow men and women was, in so many ways, in so many spheres, truly and deservedly Master of Arts *honoris causa*.

All those who knew him, from sport or from other spheres of his life, not least Joan and their three sons, are of one mind: 'There'll never be another.'

'There'll never be another.' That favourite saying of Arthur's was conferred with his customary economy of words on those whose deeds he admired or appreciated.

Arthur, surely, was the last of those sporting heroes inhabiting that era whose passing many deeply regret, of fresh-faced, clean-cut sporting idols often depicted on treasured cigarette cards. In the delightful imagining of their legions of fans, they could be weaving light-footed down the wing to score a breathtaking goal one afternoon and crafting an exquisite century the next. Arthur was, undeniably, a star of that age when players like him, modestly paid and not seeking or expecting privilege, could travel to Highbury by bus or tube amidst the fans, or jump on the train to Gloucester and the Wagon Works ground alongside dedicated supporters looking forward to a good day's cricket.

There will, indeed, never be another Arthur Milton, a truly gifted sportsman, the last of the double internationals, a genuine sporting star and yet so modest and unassuming a human being that he could become a postman and paperboy and sense the importance and value of this part of his life, as important as had been the days of his sporting glories. For many who played alongside him, for those who watched and admired him from the touchline, terraces or boundary edge, or on the fairways and greens, there will long be special and treasured memories, enduring memories. How very fortunate are they, and how truly blessed have we been, to know him.

There'll never be another.

Acknowledgments

'MIKE, I'M THINKING of doing a book,' Arthur had said. That phone call, surprising and improbable though it seemed at the time, heralded the way to what has been an amazing journey as together we decided to 'see how things go'.

It began in Arthur's company and, later, of course, it continued without him. That said, the tapes and the notes – his voice – have continued to guide and encourage me. I hope, therefore, that this book is somewhere close to what he anticipated. I hope it tells *his* story.

It has been great fun and an immense privilege to 'see how things go', so my first thanks are to Arthur for his 'invitation' and for the faith he placed in me, however unwisely. It was an invitation for which I never really thanked him, partly because he threw himself enthusiastically into the project, from its infancy, and we never really had time to stand back and contemplate. Belatedly and posthumously, certainly no less sincerely, I record here profound gratitude to Arthur for the marvellous and unexpected chapter he has written in my life, and for generously allowing me to write about his, without qualification or stipulation.

Thanks go to Joan similarly. She has continued to welcome my visits (often ending with yet another splendid lunch – and I never did learn to keep the recorder running). Joan and her sons, Robert, David and Richard, were all anxious – and insistent – that the work should be completed, and Arthur's story shared. To them all I offer warmest thanks, for their help and encouragement generously offered – and for their patience at the work's slow gestation.

339

Robert, David and Richard deserve particular thanks for being a key reason why, at last, Arthur decided he was 'doing a book'. He had recently overcome prostate cancer and was making a good and steady recovery from the mild stroke he had suffered at the end of the summer of 2006. Nevertheless, it had given him a hint of his mortality. That, and the gentle prodding of his boys, prompted him to tell his story. He had recognised that his three lads knew little of his dual sporting lives. When he ended his soccer career they had not been born, and they were only in their teens when he finished playing cricket. Richard, the youngest, was just 12. Arthur's book was, and is, very much for them, that they might know something of his halcyon days and of the regard in which he was, and is, held.

Initial drafts of this book relied heavily on recorded discussions with Arthur, but there came a point when I wanted to check facts with him, to ask further questions. Alas he was no longer with us. Those questions therefore have necessarily been asked of Arthur's friends and team-mates. To all of them – and certainly all quoted, directly or indirectly, in this book – I offer warmest thanks. With barely an exception those approached readily came to my aid and were more than happy to play their part in commemorating Arthur.

Tony Brown has been kindness personified and an unquenchably enthusiastic source of information and insight, as well as a valued checker of Gloucestershire facts and figures (though if any remain incorrect the fault is entirely mine). In so many of Arthur's stories Tony was there alongside him. A valued and long-time mutual friend, he has gone beyond the confines of friendship to ensure Arthur's story is properly told and I am truly grateful. On Gloucestershire facts the county's First XI scorer, Keith Gerrish, readily came to my aid; even, sometimes, in the height of the season. Arthur's team-mates David Allen, David Graveney, David Green, John Mortimore, Tom Pugh (with whom several mid-evening phone calls generated many happy memories and much laughter) and the late David Shepherd readily shared their memories and anecdotes. Roger Gibbon kindly researched and located some of the Gloucestershire photographs. To all the members of this Gloucestershire 'team' I offer boundless thanks, included in which is the county's chief executive, Tom Richardson, for his ever-ready help and encouragement.

The telling of Arthur's story would have been more difficult without Tom Graveney's help. As great friends from their earliest playing days, good team-mates and supremely gifted cricketers their careers progressed side by side, and Tom's perceptive recollections and cricketing wisdom have helped me enormously. In many instances Tom, like Tony Brown, was there and his first-hand account has been so valuable – and appreciated. Talking cricket with Tom, even now he is in his eighties, one can confidently rely on his amazing encyclopaedic recall of every game in which he played, often remembering others' performances as clearly as his own.

Arthur Shaw, Arthur's Arsenal team-mate, provided important and amusing insights into his namesake's Highbury years. So too did Jimmy Gray, Arsenal colleague and fellow county cricketer. Jimmy, with his late wife Betty, were great friends of Arthur and Joan long after their soccer days finished, so his memories were especially valuable and he was happy to share them for Arthur. Ken Friar, of Arsenal, also offered his delightful recollections of Arthur's time at Highbury, for which I was most grateful. Johan Karlsson, and his 'Gunnermania' website, kindly provided some of the statistics and answered other queries of Arthur's Arsenal career. Of his Ashton Gate days, Graham 'Dougie' Douglas of Bristol City was similarly helpful, and I am grateful for the aid offered by such reliable and informed sources. It goes without saying that the contributions from Sir Tom Finney and Arthur's England team-mate Ivor Broadis were warmly appreciated.

If anyone – unwisely – was to doubt the reputation and high regard Arthur established when coaching Oxford University CC then the contributions offered by Andrew Wingfield Digby, Vic Marks, John Claughton, Paul Fisher, Chris Tavaré and David Fursdon will immediately disenchant them. They were generous champions of a man they all deeply admire and whose regard and friendship they continue to value. It was a privilege and an inspiration to hear their memories. That they were willing to share such reminiscences of Arthur, and have gone on from Oxford to do great things in cricket or in life (both, in some cases), would have thrilled him enormously. My gratitude, as Arthur's assuredly would have been, is immense.

Other county cricketers, unstinting in their affection for Arthur, proved ready narrators of stories about him. Special thanks therefore go to Brian Close, Norman Gifford, Doug Insole, Peter Richardson, Dennis Silk and Micky Stewart. Bryan Richardson, Peter's younger brother, and himself a former Warwickshire player, pointed me towards Tom Whittaker's *Arsenal Story*, which offered insights I would never otherwise have discovered and for which I was particularly grateful.

As a long-time admirer of John Woodcock and his cricket writing, and of Frank Keating and his writing on many sports, I am immensely grateful to them both: to John for his kindness in allowing me to quote him (even from those days when *The Times* gave him no byline other than 'Our Cricket Correspondent'), and to Frank, firstly, for showing, in an earlier interview, just how greatly Arthur was admired and loved by young schoolboys ('us urchins') as much as by top-flight, worldly-wise sports journalists. As a young Stroud boy (after he had migrated with his parents from Herefordshire), Frank saw Arthur play at Stroud, Gloucester and Cheltenham and was one of those youngsters entranced by him. Those indelible memories were diminished not one jot during his later illustrious career covering many of the world's biggest sporting events, and writing so vividly and perceptively about the very best sportsmen and women of our age. There is, of course, a second reason why Frank deserves our boundless thanks. That is for his marvellous foreword, in which he paints such an evocative picture of Arthur and the era in which he graced the game.

Stephen Chalke, of Fairfield Books, another mutual friend, kindly offered wise advice and encouragement. Neil Robinson of MCC's library at Lord's; Michael Blight, managing secretary of the Burnham and Berrow Golf Club; and Chris Wilmore, secretary, South Gloucestershire Mining Research Group, offered specialist assistance which was most welcome. At one point transcription of recorded tapes became pressing, and I valued Joy Martin's efficient help.

Acknowledgments

Denis Scanlan's charming memories of his revered golfing partner were particularly special, and gratefully welcomed; it was a joy to visit Denis to record these.

Of Arthur's links with Bristol University, and of his elevation to an academic 'peerage', Donald Shell and Bob Reeves were ready advocates. I am grateful to both for their accounts of this part of Arthur's life, which meant so much to him and truly 'capped' his later years.

With Arthur, and especially without him, it was necessary to draw on other sources to check facts or to quote them in helping tell his story. I am therefore grateful to the Association of Cricket Statisticians (particularly for their 'Famous Cricketers' series No. 55 – Arthur Milton, which Gerald Hudd produced for them); *Wisden*; *The Times*; the *Daily Telegraph*; *The Cricketer* magazine; *Playfair Cricket Annual*; *Bristol Evening Post* (and their forerunners), and the *Western Daily Press*.

It is good to include, and to gratefully acknowledge here, some marvellous photographs. Every effort has been made to give the correct attribution to those whose pictures appear here (and apologies are offered for omissions or for any work unattributed).

Without the well-disposed support and assistance of all the above, and of many others, Arthur's story could not have been told, or told so fully, and so to them all, to others who feature in the text and many more, I offer here my boundless thanks.

It is near impossible for me to pay sufficient thanks to Eileen, my wife, for her encouragement and support, even at those times when, though firmly rooted in my study, I was decades, or runs, wickets and catches far away, and when she might have had other (equally appealing) plans for us and for my time. At other times she has gladly, and helpfully, checked the manuscript alongside me. On occasions without number I have recognised my immense good fortune in being married to a keen cricket lover – not least to one who numbered herself among Arthur's countless (if more distant) fans. Our two wonderful daughters, Helen and Morag, with their husbands and families, were kindly tolerant when visiting and discovering that Dad was keen to hold on to a productive line of thought before it slipped away; and the 'under fives', our grandchildren Zac and Albie, Tom and Hope generously were not excessive with their interruptions.

The wise head of the team captain, Randall Northam, of publishers SportsBooks Ltd of Cheltenham, has been of the greatest possible benefit. His ideas and suggestions have helped make this the work it is, and have extended beyond mere professional or commercial interest. As one who watched and admired Arthur's play, he had his own reasons to ensure this book provides what we sincerely hope is a fitting tribute to Arthur Milton.

At the beginning Arthur agreed that there would be no over-reliance on statistics. I trust I have kept faith with this, and that such stats as appear are sufficient to tell the story or provide context. It was our hope that those who would like more facts and figures would gain much enjoyment in searching them out in *Wisden Cricketers' Alamanack*, Gloucestershire Year Books and the like and on the internet (where Cricinfo has proved an amazing source).

'There'll never be another' – Arthur Milton enriched the lives of many, through his personal friendship, by his sporting deeds, and by the way he wore his sporting prowess and successes so lightly; in fact by being Arthur Milton. It all came naturally, as if his life had been simply a matter of natural progress. For all of this, in fact for simply being Arthur, Artie, Dad, Grandad, Art, Milt (even Clement and Archie in times past), and for much more, it is good to acknowledge our gratitude for all he shared generously with us, and to say 'thank you' that, at last, he felt he would share his story by 'thinking of doing a book'.

And what an amazing and delightful story was his to tell.

Mike Vockins
Birchwood
Herefordfshire
Easter 2011

Appendix 1

ARTHUR MILTON
Gloucestershire and England, Arsenal and England

A brief summary and overview of statistics

Although Arthur had little interest in personal statistics and averages, he did enjoy comparing players of different eras, even though he recognised such comparisons were difficult because of contrasting playing conditions, opponents, etc. It would appeal to his cricketing and mathematical nous to compare, say, Wally Hammond's performances with those of Herbert Sutcliffe or Colin Cowdrey, and Hedley Verity's with, say, Sam Cook.

To keep faith with these thoughts, no attempt is made here to set out an all-embracing survey of his career, but merely to place him in context, to give a flavour of his phenomenal record and also, perhaps, to encourage the reader, seeking greater detail, to turn to *Wisden* and enjoy the scholarship of searching this and other sources.

It is also important to remember that all of Arthur's career was played in the period of uncovered pitches.

CRICKET
GLOUCESTERSHIRE
Matches and Innings

Two games for Gloucestershire, as an amateur, in 1948.

Joined professional staff in 1949, and played until the 1974 season, when he retired from first-class cricket.

Played 585 first-class matches for Gloucestershire (a number exceeded only by Charlie Parker, 602, and John Mortimore, 594).

In all first-class cricket (including Test appearances and games for other teams) he made 620 first-class appearances in total.

1,017 innings for Gloucestershire, more than any other Gloucestershire player, scoring 30,218 runs for the county (average 33.65), with 52 centuries and 152 half-centuries. In all first-class cricket he made 32,150 runs, scoring 56 centuries and 160 half-centuries.

As a comparison the records for the county of three other Gloucestershire 'greats' are:

	matches	innings	runs	average	centuries
WR Hammond	405	664	33,664	57.05	113
WG Grace	360	612	22,808	40.51	50
AE Dipper	478	860	27,948	35.28	53

Scored his maiden first-class century (125) in 1951, against Somerset at Bristol, and the last of his 52 for the county was that against Worcestershire (117) at Worcester in 1972.

Highest score 170, versus Sussex at Cheltenham in 1965.

Of his centuries 35 were made as an opener, seven when batting at no. 3, eight at no. 4, five at no. 5, and one (his first) at no. 6. He shared 108 century partnerships.

Arthur scored more runs (2,753 at average 39.32) against Somerset than against any other county, perhaps unsurprisingly, as he scored 10 hundreds against them in 43 innings.

Nottinghamshire suffered most consistently from his bat; against them his batting average was 49.30.

Bowling and Fielding

His aggregate bowling analysis for the county was:
1,383 overs, 343 maidens, 79 wickets, 3,534 runs, at average 44.73. Best bowling, 5-64, versus Glamorgan at the Wagon Works ground in 1950.

Arthur, one of the best fielders of any era, held on to 760 catches in all first-class games. Of these 719 were for Gloucestershire, five in Test cricket, 28 for MCC (including games in Australia), and eight in other first-class games. By comparison Wally Hammond took 551 for the county, Tony Brown 489, and WG Grace 373.

His haul of catches places him seventh in the all-time list of catchers (excluding wicketkeepers), behind Frank Woolley, Tony Lock, Wally Hammond, Brian Close, John Langridge and Wilfred Rhodes. Of the recent generation of cricketers only Graeme Hick, with 719, comes close.

Of the great many run outs he made for the county, some of them truly brilliant, there is no record, but it is not idle to speculate that if his wickets, catches and run outs were added together he may well have captured 1,000 victims for Gloucestershire.

ONE-DAY CRICKET

First one-day game for the county was in the Gillette Cup competition, against Middlesex at Bristol in 1963, the year in which the competition was launched. His last was against Hampshire at Lydney, in the John Player Sunday League on 14th July 1974.

He played in 55 games for the county in all one-day competitions: 12 in the Gillette Cup; 9 in the Benson & Hedges Cup; and 34 in the John Player Sunday League.

In those 55 games he batted on 52 occasions, was not out five times and scored 1,095 runs, his tally including five half-centuries. It was against Notts, in the Gillette Cup match at Trent Bridge, in 1968, when Glos won by 25 runs, that he made his highest one-day score (87) for the county. Took 22 catches in one-day games and, again, his splendid athletic fielding was a vital and prowling deterrent to opposition run-pinching.

TEST CRICKET AND OTHER FIRST-CLASS MATCHES

Arthur won six Test caps for England, the first against New Zealand, at Headingley in 1958, the third of that series. He opened the innings with MJK Smith, another double international (he had also won a rugby cap for England), and scored 104 not out. Was on the field throughout the game (the first England player ever to achieve this) although rain, and the early demise of the opposition, reduced play to three days.

Won his second England cap at The Oval in the fifth Test of that New Zealand series (an injury sustained in the Players v Gentlemen match kept him out of the fourth Test).

In Australia, on the 1958–59 tour, he won two more Test caps, in the first at Brisbane and the third at Sydney. He had suffered a fracture of the middle finger of his right hand, when batting against South Australia, and missed the second Test as a result. In the match at Victoria which followed the third Test he was again struck on the same finger, re-opening the fracture, and his tour was prematurely over.

In the home series against India in 1959, he played in the first and second Tests, but was omitted for the third Test and was not again selected to play for England.

In his four home Tests he made 166 runs, averaging 41.50. In Australia his Test average was 9.50, although he made 658 runs on the tour, at an average of 33.85.

In addition to his appearances for Gloucestershire and England, Arthur also played 21 times for MCC (ten as a member of the 1958-59 touring team, and the remainder at home), and in eight other first-class games including one appearance for the Players v Gentlemen; three appearances for an England XI – against the Australians, a Commonwealth XI and the South Africans; one for AER Gilligan's XI against a Pakistan XI, and one match for the Rest of England against Surrey.

FOOTBALL
ARSENAL AND ENGLAND

Played for Arsenal in wartime friendly games in 1945 (his first against Maidenhead on 12th May), and joined them on professional terms in 1946–47. At that time soccer clubs had special contractual arrangements with players still serving in the Forces or about to undertake National Service (as was the case with Arthur, until he was demobbed in January 1949).

His early seasons with Arsenal were played in the third team (principally in the Eastern Counties League) and, occasionally, in the youth side. With Arsenal reserves he played in the Combination League, the Combination Cup (where he scored 10 goals in 25 outings), the London Challenge Cup and the London Mid-Week League.

Made his Arsenal First Division (now the Premier League) debut on his birthday, 10th March 1951, against Aston Villa at Highbury. Arsenal won 2-1.

After just 11 further First Division games at the start of the following season he had impressed enough to win his England cap.

In 1952–53 Arthur helped Arsenal win the League Championship, when he played 25 games, scoring seven goals.

Arthur's playing record for Arsenal in the First Division can be summarised as follows:

Season	Appearances	Goals
1950–51	1	–
1951–52	20	5
1952–53	25	7
1953–54	21	3
1954–55	8	3

Additionally he made nine FA Cup appearances for the club, scoring three times.

In total Arthur appeared in Arsenal colours in 202 games between 1945 and 1955, scoring 65 goals and, in the manner of the brilliant right-wing that he was, making a great many more for others.

Won his England cap in the match against Austria on 28th November 1951.

The match was drawn 2-2.

BRISTOL CITY

Having told Arsenal he intended to retire at the end of the 1954–55 season, Arthur agreed to a transfer to Bristol City, who were striving to win the Third Division (South) title. He joined them on 16th February 1955 and played 14 games, scoring three goals, and won a Championship Winners' medal as Bristol City secured their title and won promotion. Although a gifted all-round sportsman Arthur was not a showman, but he managed to finish his soccer career with a flourish, scoring the only goal in City's vital away win against Bournemouth and Boscombe Athletic.

Appendix 2

THE TWELVE DOUBLE INTERNATIONALS

The twelve players designated as double internationals, who have been capped by England at both cricket and soccer, in chronological order are as follows:

ALFRED LYTTELTON
born: 7th February 1857
died: 5th July 1913
England soccer caps: 1 – March 1878, v Scotland, as full-back
Soccer clubs: Eton College and Cambridge University
England Test caps: 4 (between 1880 and 1884)
First cap: September 1880 v Australia (The Oval)
Cricket clubs: Cambridge University and Middlesex

The Hon. Alfred Lyttelton was also a fine rackets and real tennis player. As a cricketer he played 101 first-class matches. Of his four Tests, two were particularly notable: England's defeat by Australia in 1882 gave rise to the Ashes; and the third Test against Australia in 1884 provided the only instance in England Test cricket when all 11 players were called upon to bowl. Alfred Lyttelton, the wicketkeeper, took off his pads, and with WG Grace deputising behind the stumps took 4-19 with slow lobs, as Australia made 551. Was a member of MCC committee from 1881 to 1885, and president in 1898. He had been called to the Bar in 1881, was made a QC in 1900, and served as MP for Leamington, from 1895 to 1906, and for St George's, Hanover Square, from 1906 to 1913. Secretary of State for the Colonies 1903 to 1905.

Appendix 2

WILLIAM GUNN
born: 4th December 1858
died: 29th March 1921
England soccer caps: 2; v Scotland, and v Wales (March 1884,
scored in 90th minute of England's 4-0 win)
First cap: 15th March 1884 v Scotland
Soccer clubs: Nottingham Forest, Notts County (he was later a
director of the club)
England Test caps: 11 between 1886–87 and 1889
First cap: January 1887, v Australia (Sydney)
Cricket clubs: Nottinghamshire and MCC

Billy Gunn was a right-hand batsman who played 521 first-class
matches, 363 of which were for Notts. Highest score in tests 102
not out, in first-class cricket 273. Helped found Gunn and Moore,
the cricket bat manufacturers and sports goods firm.

LH GAY
born: 24th March 1871
died: 1st November 1949
England soccer caps: 3 between 1893 and 1894 (twice v
Scotland, and v Wales)
First cap: v Scotland April 1893, as goalkeeper
Soccer clubs: Old Brightonians, Cambridge University,
Corinthians
England Test caps: 1, v Australia in December 1894 (first Test to
last six days)
Cricket clubs: Cambridge University, Somerset, Hampshire, MCC

Leslie Gay was a wicketkeeper and right-hand batsman who
played 46 first-class matches. Highest score in first-class cricket
60 not out, and behind the stumps he took 70 catches and made
20 stumpings. His highest score for England was 33, and he took
three catches and made one stumping. His sole Test was the first
of the five-match series in Australia in 1894–95; it is the only Test
in which a side made to follow on has gone on to win the game
(England won by 10 runs).

RE FOSTER
born: 16th April 1878
died: 13th May 1914
England soccer caps: 5 between 1900 and 1902 (three caps
versus Wales, 1 v Scotland, 1 v Ireland)
First cap: March 1900 v Wales, inside-forward
Soccer clubs: Malvern College, Oxford University and Corinthians
England Test caps: 8 between 1903–04 and 1907
First cap: v Australia December 1903 (Sydney)
Cricket clubs: Worcestershire, Oxford University and MCC

'Tip' Foster was one of seven brothers, sons of a Malvern College
house-master, who all played for Worcestershire; Tip, arguably,
was the most talented. A right-hand batsman in the classical style,
he won cricket Blues at Oxford in the seasons from 1897 to 1900
and captained the university in his final summer. In first-class
cricket his highest score was 246 not out and he scored hundreds
in both innings of Worcestershire's match with Hampshire in 1899
(as did his brother WL); scored 22 centuries in all first-class cricket,
four of them before lunch. For England his highest score was 287
on his debut against Australia (still the highest for a debutant in
any Test, and highest for England in Australia). Captained England
in the series v South Africa in 1907 but declined the captaincy for
the winter tour, for business reasons. Foster is the only one of the
twelve double internationals to have captained England at both
sports. Died relatively young as a result of complications from
diabetes.

CB FRY
born: 25th April 1872
died: 7th September 1956
England soccer caps: 1, versus Ireland, March 1901 (as right-
back); RE Foster also played in this game
Soccer clubs: Corinthians, Southampton (with whom he
appeared in an FA Cup final), Portsmouth
England Test caps: 26, between 1895–96 and 1912, captaining
England in his last six Tests in 1912
First cap: February 1896 (Port Elizabeth)
Cricket clubs: Oxford University, Sussex, Hampshire, MCC,
London County

Charles Fry was an imperious right-hand bat, and right-arm fast bowler (though with a questionable bowling action). Captained Sussex from 1904 to 1908. Highest score in first-class cricket 258 not out; in all he scored 30,886 runs at an average above 50 (when such averages were uncommon). His tally of first-class runs included 94 centuries, of which six were scored in consecutive innings in 1901. For England he scored 1,223 runs in his 26 Tests, and his highest Test score was 144. Won Blues for cricket, soccer and athletics and almost certainly would have won one for rugby also had he not been injured just before the Varsity Match. A man for whom the description 'polymath' might have been invented he was, in addition to being an outstanding sportsman, a politician, academic and teacher, diplomat, writer, editor, publisher and speech-writer; stood for parliament as a Liberal candidate, and served on the League of Nations. He was once described as arguably the most variously gifted Englishman of any age. For 40 years was director of the Training Ship *Mercury*, which prepared countless boys for service in the Royal Navy. Was, reputedly, offered the throne of Albania.

J ARNOLD
born: 30th November 1907
died: 4th April 1984
England soccer caps: 1, v Scotland, April 1933, at outside-left
Soccer clubs: Oxford City, Southampton, Fulham
England Test caps: 1, v New Zealand, June 1931 (Lord's) in only his second season with Hampshire
Cricket clubs: Hampshire (1929 to 1950)

John Arnold was a Hampshire stalwart for 17 seasons (like many of his generation the Second World War meant he missed six seasons when he would have been in his pomp). An outstanding right-hand batsman for Hampshire, with his brilliant stroke-play he delighted in taking the attack to the bowlers. Scored more than 21,000 runs for his county, which included 37 centuries. His soccer career took him to Southampton (from 1928, when he moved from his native Oxfordshire in order to qualify for Hampshire CCC) and for Fulham (from 1933 to 1939). When he retired as a county cricketer he served as a respected first-class umpire (until 1972).

J SHARP
born: 15th February 1878
died: 28th January 1938
England soccer caps: 2, v Ireland and v Scotland, as outside-right
First cap v Ireland, February 1903
Soccer clubs: Hereford Thistle, Aston Villa, Everton (later director)
England Test caps: 3 (third, fourth and fifth Tests against Australia in 1909)
First Test cap v Australia, July 1909 (Headingley)
Cricket club: Lancashire

A right-hand batsman and left-arm fast-medium bowler, in first-class cricket Jack Sharp scored almost 23,000 runs, with 38 centuries, and a highest score of 211. He was a superb all-rounder who took five wickets in an innings on 18 occasions; his best bowling figures at first-class level were 9-77. Highest score for England was 105 in the fifth Test against Australia, batting at no. 5, at The Oval in 1909, for which he was picked principally as a bowler. It was his last England appearance. He was the first Test cricketer to come from Hereford (Peter Richardson would later follow in his footsteps). Jack played as a professional for Lancashire before the First World War, and continued his career with them when hostilities had ceased, but now playing as an amateur. Captained Lancashire from 1923 until 1925, and was an England selector in 1924.

JWH MAKEPEACE
born: 22nd August 1881
died: 19th December 1952
England soccer caps: 4, 3 games v Scotland and 1 v Wales between 1906 and 1912
First cap v Scotland, April 1906, as right-half
Soccer clubs: Everton (later coached Everton and Holland)
England Test caps: 4 (second, third, fourth and fifth Tests against Australia in 1920–21)
Cricket clubs: Lancashire and MCC

Harry Makepeace was a right-hand bat, occasional leg-spin bowler and excellent fielder particularly at cover point. In a first-class cricket career spanning the years 1906 to 1930 he scored 25,799 runs, which included 43 centuries. His highest score at this level was 203, and his best bowling figures 4-33. His best Test was the fourth against Australia in 1921, at Melbourne, when he scored 117 (out of England's first-innings score of 284), and followed this with 54 in the second innings (becoming, at 38 years and 173 days, England's oldest player to score a maiden century). Coached Lancashire from 1931 to 1951. With Everton won an FA Cup winners medal in 1906, though was on the losing side the following year.

HTW HARDINGE
born: 25th February 1886
died: 8th May 1965
England soccer caps: 1, versus Scotland, April 1910, at centre-forward
Soccer clubs: Maidstone United, Newcastle United, Sheffield United, Woolwich Arsenal
England Test caps: 1, against Australia, July 1921, at Headingley
Cricket club: Kent (1902 to 1933)

Wally Hardinge made his debut for Kent as a 16-year-old. He was a reliable, stylish opening batsman and occasional slow left-arm bowler who, like others, found his way to the England team blocked by the success of Jack Hobbs and Herbert Sutcliffe. Hardinge played his only Test when Jack Hobbs was taken ill shortly before the game. Scored 33,519 runs at first-class level and made 75 centuries, with a highest score of 263 not out, and took 371 wickets, with best bowling figures of 7-34. When his playing days were over he briefly coached Leicestershire and, retaining his links with soccer, was coach to Tottenham reserves in the mid-1930s and caretaker manager for a brief spell in 1935..

A DUCAT
born: 16th February 1886
died: 23rd July 1942 at Lord's
England soccer caps: 6, at right wing-half
First cap: February 1910, v Ireland
Soccer clubs: Southend, Woolwich Arsenal, Aston Villa, Fulham (whom he later managed)
England Test caps: 1, versus Australia, July 1921, at Headingley
Cricket clubs: Surrey, MCC

Andy Ducat, popularly known as 'Mac', was a right-handed batsman for Surrey who scored his runs in attractive fashion and, frequently, at a good pace. In first-class cricket he scored 23,373 runs, with 52 centuries, and a highest score of 306 not out. His Test selection owed much to his courage and resolution, as England sought batsmen to combat Australia's Gregory and McDonald. On receiving a telegram inviting him to play for England he needed to be convinced it wasn't a prank set up by his Surrey team-mates. Ducat's only Test was also that in which Wally Hardinge (above) made his sole England appearance. Of his six soccer internationals three were played in 1910 (when with Woolwich Arsenal), and the final three were played ten years later in 1920 (by which time he was playing for Aston Villa). As captain of Villa he led the team to its FA Cup final win against Huddersfield Town in 1920. When his county cricket career ended Ducat coached at Eton College for several years. His death was one of which many cricket-lovers might dream – he died at the crease while batting at Lord's, playing for Surrey Home Guard in a wartime match against Sussex Home Guard.

W WATSON
born: 7th March 1920
died: 23rd April 2004
England soccer caps: 4, as right wing-half
First England cap: November 1949 v Northern Ireland
Soccer clubs: Huddersfield Town, Sunderland, Halifax Town (player-manager and manager, manager of Bradford City)
England Test caps: 23 between 1951 and 1958–59
First Test cap: v South Africa, June 1951 (Trent Bridge)
Cricket clubs: Yorkshire (1939 to 1957); Leicestershire (1958 to 1964, captain 1958 to 1961)

Always known as Willie (rather than William), Watson was a left-hand bat who, in his prime years, often opened the innings but for England batted in the middle order more often than not. In all first-class cricket he scored 25,670 runs, with 55 centuries and a career-best score of 257. He made two centuries in Test cricket, his highest score being 116. Like Arthur Milton he made batting look graceful and easy, and he made many more runs by the speed and judgement of his running between wickets. As might be expected of one who was naturally athletic he was a fine fielder, especially as an outfielder. He is fixed in cricket's enduring psyche as a result of his five-hour partnership with Trevor Bailey at Lord's in 1953 when, on a worn pitch, they withstood the Australian bowling attack to earn England a draw. It was Watson's first Test against Australia; he made 109 (in 346 minutes) and Bailey 71 (in 257 minutes) in one of the classic and most remarkable rearguard partnerships of Test cricket. Coming together at 73-4, with England needing 340 to win, they added 163 for the fifth wicket and ensured England drew the game. With the first four Tests of the series drawn, England regained the Ashes in the final Test at The Oval.

Watson moved to Leicestershire in 1958 as assistant secretary and captain and enjoyed considerable success in the Indian summer of his career. Served as a Test selector from 1962 to 1964. His cricket and soccer careers overlapped more than most. In the mid-Fifties he was with Halifax Town as player-manager, and in 1964 rejoined them as manager. For two seasons from 1966 he was manager of Bradford City and took them to the top of Football League's Divison Four. During his soccer career he was a member of England's World Cup squad in Brazil in 1950. Walter Winterbottom, the manager, preferred his wing-halves to be strong, defensive players whereas Watson was more of an attacking player and, as a result, he did not play a match. He later emigrated to South Africa where he successfully took up the post of administrator and coach at the Wanderers Club in Johannesburg.

CA MILTON
born: 10th March 1928
died: 25th April 2007
England soccer caps: 1, v Austria, November 1951, as outside-right
Soccer clubs: Arsenal (1946 to 1954–55) and Bristol City (for end of 1954–55 season)
England Test caps: 6, in 1958 and 1959
First Test cap: v New Zealand, July 1958 (Headingley)
Cricket clubs: Gloucestershire and MCC

Arthur Milton, surely the last-ever double international, was a right-hand batsman and a right-arm medium-pace bowler. Those are the bare bones. As one of the most naturally talented sportsmen of all time he was a fine batsman, who batted with graceful ease; one of the quickest runners between wickets; and a splendid, high-class fielder either out (where he would get to the ball with deceptive speed and throw it in with a good unerring arm) or close to the wicket. In his career he held on to 760 catches, putting him seventh in the all-time list of fielders. His remarkable record as a cricketer for Gloucestershire is summarised in Appendix 1. In his first Test for England he made a century, 104 not out, and became the first Gloucestershire player since WG Grace to score a hundred on his England debut. Prior to winning his England Test cap he had been called to England's colours in previous seasons as their nominated twelfth man on the strength of his superlative and nigh-infallible fielding.

For Arsenal he first appeared as a schoolboy in a wartime friendly match. He made his Football League Division One debut on his birthday in 1951. Injury brought that season to an early close but after just 11 further Division One games at the start of the following season he was selected by England to play against Austria in place of the injured Tom Finney and ahead of Stanley Matthews. Has there ever been a more meteoric rise by an England player? Arthur won a Football League winners' medal in 1952–53, and closed his soccer career by playing 14 games for Bristol City to help them win the Third Division South title.

Whenever the subject of the 12 double internationals arises it is seldom long before Denis Compton's name is mentioned. Denis was both an Arsenal colleague of Arthur's and a fellow county cricketer, who played in England colours at cricket and soccer. However, his name is not included in the official list of double internationals, principally because his soccer appearances for England were in wartime internationals. In this period Service commitments often seriously limited the availability for selection of England's first-choice players; opposing teams also were seldom at full strength. Despite not being included in the official list Denis's record is remarkable, and is included here for comparison.

DCS COMPTON
born: 23rd May 1918
died: 23rd April 1997
Played 12 wartime soccer internationals for England, but never played in a full official international match
Soccer clubs: Arsenal, 1932 to 1950
England Test caps: 78, between 1937 and 1956

First Test cap: v New Zealand, August 1937 (The Oval)
Cricket clubs: Middlesex, MCC

Denis Compton was a flamboyant (though sound) right-hand batsman and a richly talented cricketer whose cavalier approach brought great enjoyment, especially to postwar crowds, and won him boundless affection. He was a sporting icon of his generation, and yet a man of immense good-natured charm and modesty. Neville Cardus, writing in 1947, after the dark days of war, with many restrictions and little or no first-class cricket, said of Compton: 'The strain of the long years of anxiety and affliction passed from all our hearts and shoulders at the sight of him. There were no rations in an innings by Compton.'

He played for Middlesex from 1936 to 1958, and in all first-class cricket scored 38,942 runs at 51.85, scoring 123 centuries; he also took 622 wickets and held 416 catches. In his 78 Tests for England, between 1938 and 1956, he was almost a permanent fixture in the side. Scored 5,807 runs for England at 50.06, making 17 centuries and capturing 25 wickets and 49 catches. With Arsenal he won a League Championship medal (1948) and an FA Cup winners' medal (1950). Scored 90 goals for Arsenal (some in wartime fixtures). His soccer career was brought to an end by problems with his kneecap, which also blighted the latter years of his cricket career (it was later removed). The Compton knee almost became an item of major national news; although it restricted his mobility it did little to limit the joy and charm of his batting.

Index

Index

Index